Praise for Home Winemaking For Dummies

"A thorough, practical, and entertaining guide, this text takes tips from the pros and brings common sense and approachability to the art of winemaking. Mr. Patterson's vast experience and contagious passion for the subject make Home Winemaking For Dummies an enjoyable read while the format makes it an excellent reference and allows the reader to delve as deep into the subject matter as he or she wishes. Whether problem-solving or pursuing stylistic ideals, Mr. Patterson holds the reader's hand when needed but still encourages creativity within safe boundaries. From sourcing fruit to healthy fermentation habits straight through aging, bottling, and even enjoying home-made wine, this guide has you covered at every step — I even learned a few things myself! This book would be a welcome addition to any wine enthusiast's library and is equally accessible to novice and connoisseur.

— **Ondine Chattan,** Winemaker, Geyser Peak Winery

"As a 20-year amateur winemaker with an addiction to winemaking books, I now have a new 'go-to' book for my first reference! After the excellently accurate coverage of basic winemaking, Tim's tome takes the wonderful turn of emphasizing the subtle, and not-so subtle, differences that make the distinctions between the popular varietals — all in one place! Home Winemaking For Dummies is now prominently on my shelf in front of all the textbooks!"

— **Dave Lustig,** President, Cellarmasters Home Wine Club Los Angeles

"Tim Patterson is able to express his knowledge and passion of winemaking in a very understandable, humorous, and practical way. If you follow the advice in this book, you will be able to produce wine that will likely be better than inexpensive commercial wine, and could be as good as any wine ever made. I applaud Tim's effort and wish this book was around when I started making wine."

— **Kent Rosenblum,** Consultant Winemaker, Rosenblum Cellars, and former home winemaker

by Tim Patterson

John Wiley & Sons Canada, Ltd.

Home Winemaking For Dummies®

Published by
John Wiley & Sons Canada, Ltd.
6045 Freemont Boulevard
Mississauga, Ontario, L5R 4J3
www.wiley.com

A number of the quotations from winemakers in this book originally appeared in articles by the author for *Wines & Vines* and *WineMaker* magazines, and are reprinted here by permission.

For details on how to create a custom book for your company or organization, or for more information on John Wiley & Sons Canada custom publishing programs, please call 416-646-7992 or e-mail publishingbyobjectives@wiley.com.

For general information on John Wiley & Sons Canada, Ltd., including all books published by Wiley Publishing, Inc., please call our warehouse, Tel 1-800-567-4797. For reseller information, including discounts and premium sales, please call our sales department, Tel 416-646-7992. For press review copies, author interviews, or other publicity information, please contact our marketing department, Tel 416-646-4584, Fax 416-236-4448.

Library and Archives Canada Cataloguing in Publication

Patterson, Tim, 1946–

   Home winemaking for dummies / Tim Patterson.

Includes index.

Issued also in electronic formats.

ISBN 978-0-470-67895-4

   1. Wine and wine making—Amateurs' manuals. I. Title.

TP548.2.P38 2010   641.8'72   C2010-906320-1

ISBN: 9780470681121 (ebk); 9780470681138 (ebk); 9780470681145 (ebk)

Printed in Canada

1 2 3 4 5 RRD 15 14 13 12 11

WILEY

Publisher's Acknowledgments

We're proud of this book; please send us your comments at http://dummies.custhelp.com.

Some of the people who helped bring this book to market include the following:

Acquisitions and Editorial

Acquiring Editor: Robert Hickey

Project Editor: Kathleen A. Dobie

Production Editor: Pauline Ricablanca

Copy Editor: Laura Miller

Cartoons: Rich Tennant (www.the5thwave.com)

Composition Services

Project Coordinator: Lynsey Stanford

Layout: Samantha Cherolis, Tim Detrick, Cheryl Grubbs, Christin Swinford

Proofreaders: Leeann Harney, Jessica Kramer

Indexer: Sharon Shock

John Wiley & Sons Canada, Ltd.

Deborah Barton, Vice President and Director of Operations

Karen Bryan, Vice-President, Publishing Services

Jennifer Smith, Publisher, Professional and Trade Division

Alison Maclean, Managing Editor

Publishing and Editorial for Consumer Dummies

Diane Graves Steele, Vice President and Publisher, Consumer Dummies

Kristin Ferguson-Wagstaffe, Product Development Director, Consumer Dummies

Ensley Eikenburg, Associate Publisher, Travel

Kelly Regan, Editorial Director, Travel

Composition Services

Debbie Stailey, Director of Composition Services

About the Author

Tim Patterson writes about adult beverages and makes some of his own in Berkeley, California. In previous lives, he wrote about national politics, television, techie stuff, and hillbilly music. He roots for glamour-free wine regions and low-profile grapes; wants to know how wine is really made; and bottles his own in his garage, just to keep himself honest.

He does the monthly "Inquiring Winemaker" column for the industry trade magazine *Wines & Vines,* digging into winemaking theories and techniques, and writes frequently for consumers in the *Wine Enthusiast.* More to the immediate point, he has expounded regularly about home winemaking for several years in the pages of *WineMaker.* Past prose has also surfaced in *Diablo,* the *Livermore Independent, Central Coast Adventures, Vineyard & Winery Management, Sommelier Journal,* and *The Vine,* and on various now-defunct Web sites.

He coauthored (with Jim Concannon) *Concannon: The First One Hundred and Twenty-Five Years,* a history of that venerable Livermore Valley winery; contributed an introduction on the history of world dessert wine styles to Mary Cech and Jennie Schacht's *The Wine Lover's Dessert Cookbook* and a true-life tale to Thom Elkjer's *Adventures In Wine.* He contributed to *Opus Vino,* a global wine encyclopedia. With veteran California winemaker and wine educator John Buechsenstein, he's working on a book about the science — and often the lack of it — behind the wine world's most fascinating concept, *terroir.* And of course, there's a blog: Blind Muscat's Cellarbook (`http://blindmuscat.typepad.com`).

His made his first home wine in 1997 — a small batch of Carignane, hardly the noblest of grapes — and when it turned out to bear a striking resemblance to real wine, he was hooked. Since then he has collected a small wall full of ribbons from amateur wine competitions and recruited a circle of friends to do most of the hard work. He leans toward Rhône reds and aromatic whites, but he's willing to try anything that grows on a vine.

Dedication

For my brother Byron, who taught me that normal humans could make good wine at home — and that he could, too — as well as so many other things.

Author's Acknowledgments

When the opportunity to write this book materialized, I was one happy winemaker. For that I have a string of folks at John Wiley & Sons to thank. First and foremost, Acquisitions Editor Robert Hickey made the early stages close to painless. From start to finish, he was enthusiastic, supportive, helpful, and prompt, all at a distance of several thousand miles. Likewise, working with my Project Editor, Kathleen Dobie, was a delight: just enough guidance to keep me on track, just enough humor to make hearing from her a pleasure. Despite all the warnings that print is dead, the entire crew at Wiley makes me believe the medium is very much alive.

Thanks to my tag-team of Technical Editors, Tom Leaf and Thomas Pellechia, both crackerjack winemakers, for helping me get the details right.

This book draws on interviews and conversations about winemaking for articles I've written, so thanks to my editors and publishers at *Wines & Vines* (Chet Klingensmith, Tina Caputo, and now Jim Gordon) and at *WineMaker* (Kathleen Ring, Brad Ring, Chris Colby) for paying me to learn how to be a better winemaker. For the details on doing this in your garage, the crew at the Oak Barrel in Berkeley — Bernie Rooney, Homer Smith, Kel Owen-Alcala, and Bob Lower — have been invaluable and generous beyond belief. Thanks to Peter Brehm for educating me about grapes.

Finally, thanks to the many people who read parts of this book, offering numerous helpful suggestions. The list, composed of professional winemakers, homies, and at least one published poet, includes John Buechsenstein, Roger Campbell, Pat Darr, Ken English, Tricia Goldberg, Nato Green, Marcia Henry, Gil Kulers, Don Link, Mark Magers, Bill Mayer, Michael Michaud, Ray Paetzold, Byron Patterson, Gene Patterson, Susan Patton-Fox, Ivan Pelcyger, Eileen Raphael, Bill Rohwer, Jennie Schacht, Joel Sommer, Pete Stauffer, Ron Story, Thy Tran, and Linda Yoshino. Thanks to Lisa Van de Water for a short course in remedial microbiology, and to Wanda Hennig and Eileen Raphael for the photos that got worked up into this book's illustrations.

The book is dedicated to my brother Byron, who showed me the ropes of home winemaking. But heartfelt thanks also go to my wife, Nancy Freeman, who graciously allowed this runaway hobby to take over our house and a good deal of our social life, resulting in this book.

Contents at a Glance

Table of Contents

Introduction

*U*ntil you've done it, making your own wine at home seems like an impossible challenge. Don't you need endless rolling hills covered with vineyards; hundreds of thousands of dollars worth of stainless steel tanks; row upon row of French oak barrels; a huge, temperature- and humidity-controlled facility; and a Ph.D. in enology from the University of Somewhere Famous?

Nope.

One day, when my stepson Diego was about eight years old, my wife, Nancy, announced she was going to make jam from the plums hanging off the tree in our backyard. "Mom," he said, "you can't make jam; you have to buy it at the store!" Nancy smiled, shook her head, and went to work with some pots and a strainer and a big kettle for sterilizing the lids and jars. And sure enough, in a couple of hours, we had jars of jam cooling on the counter and one awestruck kid. (For the record, the kid has gone on to do things that seem hopelessly impossible to me, like building entire hospitals from scratch.)

Home winemaking works the same way as jam — except that it takes longer. Like baking bread or knitting a sweater, making wine takes simple materials and produces amazing results. If millions of people — that's a conservative estimate — all over the world have made good, drinkable wine for nearly 8,000 years, you can do it, too.

My older brother Byron was the first in our family to try his hand at the ancient craft of winemaking. He liked to drink wine, and he thought he could save some money and maybe even get a tax break by planting a few rows of vines on a piece of scraggly land he owned up in the foothills of California's Sierra Nevada mountains. I tried his wine and, by golly, it tasted like wine! I figured that if my brother could do this, so could I, and when I made my first tiny little batch of Carignane, I had my own plum jam experience: It tasted like wine!

Since then, I've gotten in way over my head trying one grape after another, and I've made a few bucks writing about winemaking. I'm lucky to live in Northern California, near hundreds of thousands of acres of prime grapes and a vast storehouse of winemaking knowledge. But in the 21st century, with the advantage of the Internet and modern transportation — and, of course, this book — you can make great wine anywhere and everywhere.

About This Book

Whether you're just dipping your toe into the world of winemaking or you've made many batches already, this book has something for you. First of all, it's a basic how-to and reference guide for first-time home winemakers. I cover all the necessary steps and procedures in detail. With this book, some grapes, and minimal equipment, you can make good wine — a few gallons or an entire barrel — in a spacious dedicated garage winery or in the corner of an apartment kitchen.

Other home winemaking books on the market cover the same ground and are chock full of good advice. But what's different about this book is that it goes on to offer information and opinions about different grape varieties — which need very different treatment — and advanced winemaking techniques. No one, professional or amateur, simply makes generic red wine; people make Cabernet or Pinot Noir or Tempranillo or Chambourcin, and they don't all do things the same way.

In a dozen years of garage winemaking, I've worked with a lot of grapes, made some nifty wines, won a bunch of medals, and made my share of mistakes. Along with my firsthand experience, my day job is writing about commercial winemaking trends and topics. I spend hours every week talking to winemakers about how they handle different grapes, how they choose yeast strains, whether temperature matters, what they think of filtration, how they fix problems, and on and on. So this book passes on that expert information so you can use it in your home winery. Sure, home winemaking is a hobby, but why not pursue it like a pro?

I hope that these various tricks, tips, and insights from the world of commercial winemaking make this book useful for experienced home winemakers as well as beginners. And if you simply want to understand how wine is made — whether you intend to get your hands dirty or not — this book answers your questions. Where do all the unpronounceable grapes come from? What the heck is *malolactic fermentation*? Why does Chardonnay taste so different from Riesling?

Conventions Used in This Book

The *For Dummies* series uses the following conventions to make information easy to understand:

- ✔ All Web addresses appear in `monofont`.

- ✔ New terms appear in *italics* and are followed closely by an easy-to-understand definition or explanation.

- ✔ **Bold** text highlights the action parts of numbered steps.

In addition, this particular book follows a few of its own conventions:

- All temperatures, weights, areas, and volumes are first given in standard U.S. measurements (Fahrenheit, pounds, acres, gallons), followed by the (rough) metric equivalents (Celsius, kilograms, hectares, and liters) in parentheses. However, some measurements are always done in metric (such as grams per liter of acid), and these appear in metric only. I use the abbreviations F, C (Fahrenheit, Celsius) throughout, as well as ° — the degrees symbol.

- The U.S. dollar (USD) may not be the strongest currency in the world, but it's the currency I use when estimating costs.

- For simplicity and clarity, all grape variety names and wine varietal names are capitalized: Pinot Noir grapes make Pinot Noir wine.

And, lest you think I'm trying to be too cool for school, I use the term *homies* to mean you, me, and everyone else who ferments wine at home.

What You're Not to Read

This book aims to be a comprehensive reference, which is no doubt more than you need to make your first batch of wine or to explore a specific grape or technique. If you're of a mind to prioritize, you can skip the following without damaging your wine:

- **Text in sidebars:** The sidebars throughout the book offer background information, forays into related topics, and tips from winemakers who have a handle on whatever topic the chapter addresses. Depending on how you're using the book, they may be entertaining, enlightening, or both, but they aren't essential.

- **Technical Stuff icons:** In a few places, the text contains detailed technical or scientific background and explanations. This information helps with the *why* of certain points, but isn't part of the *how to*.

Foolish Assumptions

Here's what I assume about you, dear reader, including some things you should assume about yourself going into this winemaking business:

- You like to drink wine.

- You're considering making some of your own, or at least want to know how — the same way you picked up a copy of *Home Brain Surgery For Dummies* — just to check it out.

✔ If the potential payoff is good enough — great, inexpensive wine — you're willing to do some manual labor, work through numerous third-grade math problems, and learn a teensy bit of chemistry (yikes!).

✔ You have more patience than the folks who brew beer at home. No offense, beer people, but wine does take a lot longer from start to finish.

✔ You have a number of friends who like to drink wine — because you will surely end up with more wine than you can reasonably drink on your own.

How This Book Is Organized

The book comes in seven parts, with 23 chapters and 4 appendixes tucked into those parts. Many topics show up more than once — a first time to explain a particular procedure or describe a certain winemaking direction, and a second time with more detail, multiple variations, or a caveat about the exception that proves the rule. If you're looking for a specific topic, the Table of Contents and the Index are the best ways to find everything relevant.

Part I: Motivation, Materials, and Methods

In which Your Author dissects the various reasons why people take up home winemaking; lays out the basic steps; surveys the range of available equipment; counsels on the importance of starting with good grapes; and emphasizes the essential trio of sanitation, temperature control, and oxygen management.

Part II: Phases and Stages

In which Your Author takes you and your grapes on the journey from harvest to bottle, pausing for consideration of destemming, crushing, adjusting wine chemistry, fermenting, pressing, racking, aging, fining, filtering, blending, bottling, and troubleshooting, not to mention the mysterious malolactic. I finish off with a chapter on storing, aging, and tasting your wines. This part more or less corresponds to standard books on home winemaking.

Part III: Deeper Into Reds

In which Your Author surveys a number of techniques commercial wineries use in fine red wine production, most of which can be adapted for home winemaking, and then mixes and matches these techniques with information about noteworthy red grape varieties. Suggestions are included for what might work where and what the impact on your wine might be — with a lot of commentary by professional winemakers.

Part IV: Deeper Into Whites

In which Your Author follows the same approach as Part III on reds. This part includes a survey of advanced, optional white winemaking techniques, and a closer look at a broad range of popular white grape varieties, the wine styles they work best in, and how to get your grapes from here to there.

Part V: Beyond Red and White

In which Your Author explains the whys, wherefores, and special joys of pink wine, takes a look at dessert wine styles — late harvest and fortified — and sketches out ways to put a little sparkle into your wine.

Part VI: The Part of Tens

A *For Dummies* standard, this part contains helpful lists: home winemaking mistakes to avoid, ways to save money, and the eternal tension between wine people and beer people — in society at large as well as in your garage.

Part VII: Appendixes

A set of appendixes follows the main parts: a glossary of winemaking terms; a listing of resources for obtaining grapes, equipment, supplies, and information; conversion tables; and detailed information and formulas for using sulfur dioxide and calibrating usage with wine pH.

Icons Used in This Book

In the *For Dummies* tradition, some sections are highlighted with *icons* — amusing (I hope) little images in the margin — to draw your attention to certain kinds of information.

This icon flags the most important points in a particular section, information that has a big bearing on the topic.

I use this icon to point out "insider" information, such as things I learned the hard way, or neat little tricks that aren't obvious, or pointers from the world of commercial winemaking.

A paragraph or section tagged with this icon delves deeper into more geeky, scientific detail or background that isn't necessary for immediate winemaking tasks.

Watch out for the warning icon, which I use to indicate places where following (or not following) a certain procedure could be hazardous to your wine, or even your health.

When you see this icon, you know you're getting advice and insights — some technical, some philosophical — from commercial winemakers across North America.

Where to Go from Here

Where to start and how to use this book depend on what you're after:

- ✔ If you're a first-timer wanting to get The Big Picture — or trying to decide whether to do this at all — head for Chapter 1 to get the lay of the land.
- ✔ When you're ready to take the leap and make some wine, skim through the phases and stages of Part II to find out what you'll be doing in the next few months, and then come back to specific chapters as your crush progresses.
- ✔ If you have a pressing winemaking problem to solve right now, check the Table of Contents and the Index.
- ✔ If you already know home winemaking basics and want to try a new grape variety or explore a technique, Parts III and IV offer some inspiration.

I figure that if you've gotten this far, you're hooked, so turn the page and read on!

Part I
Motivations, Materials, and Methods

The 5th Wave
By Rich Tennant

"Look kids, Mommy and Daddy need a thermostatically controlled environment for their wine until the cellar is finished."

In this part . . .

Before I have you start making wine at home, I give you a preview of what you're getting into. Anybody with a nose, a mouth, and a decent attention span can make very good wine.

These first chapters give an overview of the whole shebang, rhapsodize about the wonders of good grapes, survey equipment you will need, speculate about the home winemaker mindset, and preach the gospel of safe home winemaking.

Chapter 1

Making Great Wine at Home

These are the greatest days for wine consumers in the 8,000 years of wine drinking. Wine quality around the globe has increased exponentially in the past three decades. Good-to-great wine at affordable prices fills the shelves at supermarkets and wine shops, and if you can't find the wine you want down the street, chances are you can find it on the Internet. Today's wine fans have access to a vast range of vintages, regions, and price points — lucky us!

So why go to the trouble of making your own? Back in the day — oh, let's say Crete in 3,000 BCE — if you wanted wine, you made your own. And for much of Western Europe, that was the norm well into the 19th century. But that was when people also chopped their own wood, milked their own cows, grew their own string beans, stitched their own clothes, and built their own huts — things most of us no longer do for ourselves, but pay someone else to do for us. Wine has gone off the chore list and onto the shopping list.

Because we're surrounded by good wine, you need to be motivated to get your hands — and arms and legs and clothes and everything else — dirty to produce your own. You also need a serious passion for wine, an intense curiosity about the miraculous chemical reactions, an urge to get closer to nature and away from the pre-packaged life, or some other motivation of your very own. Full disclosure: Making wine takes a fair amount of work, requires considerable patience, generates amazing messes, and involves endless cleaning — so your motivation matters.

I got interested in drinking wine — or in paying attention to what I was drinking — in order to impress my father-in-law, who knew his way around a bottle of wine. When I started writing about wine, I realized that if I was going to criticize other people's wines, I had to make some myself (which not enough wine writers do). A couple harvests into it, I noticed how much satisfaction I was getting from working with my hands, back, and senses — a whole different life-discipline from the desk work I'd always done. A dozen years later, my little home winery, known as subterranean cellars, is the center of its own social scene, halfway between a community and a flash mob, where people get together to crush grapes, bottle wine, and eat, and drink . . . in moderation, of course.

Did I mention that making your own wine is a ton of fun?

Choosing to Make Cheap Wine or Really Good Wine

When you decide to take the plunge, a defining question quickly arises: What kind of wine are you going to make? I don't mean deciding between grape varieties; I mean, are you doing this to save money on wine, or are you shooting for home wine good enough to compete with the pros?

Saving money on your adult beverage expenditures and making premium quality wine aren't mutually exclusive; many home winemakers do both. But these two divergent paths present themselves again and again, in the many small decisions you make — by the end of a vintage, they add up. Some home winemakers want to economize; some want to prove they can keep up with the big players. Your humble author is squarely in the second camp.

Making wine to save money

Making your own beer can be a bargain, because the principal ingredient is water. But for wine, it's grape juice, which costs a lot more than water. The big money-saver, of course, is labor — yours — which presumably comes free. Plus, your home winery has little need for advertising and marketing, because you can't sell your wine. Nor will you be sending many samples to wine writers. (Though if you do, please include me on your list.)

Cheap-track homies can try to cut costs and corners in several ways:

- Look for bargains on grapes or get free grapes through friends.
- Follow a standard routine from harvest to bottle, and don't bother testing or tweaking each batch along the way.
- Soak and scrape labels off every wine bottle you empty.
- Bottle the stuff as soon as it's drinkable, or sometimes just draw it out glass by glass straight from the barrel.

These points describe how several generations of Italian, German, Iberian, and Central European families made their own wine in their basement or garage in the New World for decades. You can use this approach, too, and end up with drinkable wine — most of the time — but not much more.

If you're thinking of following any of these methods to save costs, keep these points in mind:

- ✔ Getting free grapes often indicates the fruit is of poor quality.
- ✔ Skipping the testing substitutes guesswork for control, often leading to unpleasant surprises.
- ✔ Scraping labels off old bottles can work, as long as you get them really, really clean before you re-use them; new bottles are a huge work-saver.
- ✔ Bottling too soon, before your wine has stabilized, can mean unpleasant surprises in the bottle.
- ✔ Keeping wine in tapped barrels, full of air, is a recipe for vinegar production.

So yes, you can — and will — save money by making your own wine. But if saving money is your only motivation, your wine will show it.

Making really good wine

There is no reason whatsoever why you can't make one stellar wine after another in your humble home winery.

The wine doesn't care where it's made; it just cares how good the grapes are and whether the winemaker is paying attention. True, making wine on a very small scale presents its challenges, and making great white wines in particular without refrigeration and strict oxygen control takes some doing. But you can easily make wines that hold their own with wines that cost $15 or $20 in the marketplace. You just have to think like a pro.

Making great wine isn't mainly a matter of spending money or buying fancy equipment. The key is attention to detail, constant tasting, and asking yourself at a hundred different choice points, *What can I do to improve this wine?*

Just as in cooking, or most anything else, if you start to think like a professional, the quality of your handiwork improves. Okay, positive thinking alone won't make you a major-league shortstop or the next Meryl Streep, but it absolutely will make you a better winemaker.

Commercial winemakers have great economic motivation to get the details right. If they cut too many corners, the wines suck, the owners get mad, and the winemakers become unemployed. If you mess up in your garage, you feel bad, and you lose a few bucks, but your world isn't in flames.

Which means you have to pay attention to your wine out of love, not out of fear. Is that so hard? With this book as a guide, of course not!

Getting into the Home Winemaking Mindset

Successful home winemakers are as diverse as the wine they make. They work with different grapes in all manner of facilities, from impressive to laughable. And they're happy to quarrel with each other about the value of this or that technique. But they all share a few common mental traits, some of which come easily, some of which may take a little adjustment in thinking.

Surrendering to the grapes

Most home winemakers are city folk, oblivious to the rhythms and hazards and realities of agriculture. Home winemaking provides an education in a hurry. Grapes rule, and you had better get used to it.

And because grapes are the heart and soul of your undertaking, they may cause you to adjust how you think about a lot of things:

- **The weather:** You don't worry about whether you need a raincoat, but about whether your future grapes are getting rained on, or suffering a heat spike, or are about to be wiped out by frost.

- **Vacations:** You no longer go away in the Fall; sorry, you have grapes coming in.

- **Your schedule:** Grapes ripen when they're good and ready, not when you schedule them. I virtually guarantee that when you arrange for a day off from work to pick up your prize fruit, the grower will call the night before and change the date, and then change it again. Get used to it.

- **Disappointment:** When you get the grapes, they may be full of mold, too ripe or not ripe enough, or have spent eight hours cooking in the blazing sun before you get them. These are winemaking challenges, remedies for which I cover throughout this book.

- **Your vision:** That is, your hopes and dreams for the wine you're about to make. Your grapes will have the characteristics they have, not necessarily those you envisioned. You may have to scale back your plans for a fat, jammy Zinfandel because the barely-ripe fruit won't support that style. Your goal of a lean, mean Sauvignon Blanc may have to be scrapped for plan B because of the high-sugar grapes. The Merlot you got to fill your new oak barrel turns out to be 2 gallons short of capacity.

Trust me, you're going to love it.

Good news: Nine times out of ten your harvest will go just fine. But winemaking is unpredictable, and you have to listen to your grapes. With beer, you can just decide to make a nice Pilsner, get the supplies, follow a recipe, and schedule the bottling in a couple weeks. You can't do that with Chardonnay — exactly why winemaking is so compelling. (Chapter 23 highlights other differences between making wine and brewing beer.)

Developing patience, precision, and a little chemistry

The chief difference between home winemaking and home brewing is the turnaround time: Beer takes a couple weeks; wine, even in small batches, takes months — three or six or twelve or eighteen! For most of that time, your winemaking tasks consist of . . . waiting. The biological and chemical processes that make wine wine take a while, and you can only speed them up so much. Winemaking is like baseball: slow and drawn out, with lots of spaces between spurts of action. You get time for reflection and the opportunity for tactical adjustments.

You also need patience because the harvest comes only once a year, so you only get that one annual shot. If you decide to try a different approach and the wine doesn't work out, you have to wait a year for the next crop of grapes — you may be looking at five years of trying to get a particular wine absolutely right. Winemaking is not a craft you pick up over a long weekend.

Winemaking, even with the most modern equipment, lives by ancient rhythms. For some people, the slow-motion pace is intolerable; for some of us, it's mighty relaxing. The stretched-out timeline has the advantage of leaving plenty of opportunity to think before you leap. You have time to work through the zillion little details that can affect your wine for good or ill. Your fruit is your fruit; in the cellar, you're in charge, and little things count.

For thousands of years, people made drinkable wine without having a clue about the underlying biochemistry. (They were also short on running water and indoor plumbing.) Learning a tiny bit of chemistry — the basics of the solids and liquids you're working with, how they interrelate, and how oxygen and temperature affect things — gets you on top of what's going on, gives you more control, and helps you predict the results of a particular operation.

Remember that details matter in winemaking. Find out your juice and wine's makeup: How much sugar do the grapes have, how much acidity, what's the pH? (I tell you how to measure these things in Chapter 3.) When fermenting, find out the temperature of the juice/wine, and if it's too high or too low, fix it. If the yeast manufacturer says to rehydrate the yeast before using it, rehydrate it. When you add sulfur dioxide as a preservative, don't just add "some," add an amount correlated with the pH of the wine. Weigh, measure, and do the math two or three times (and do it on paper!).

As the winemaker, you can only do so much to influence your wine; why not do it right? If you take care of your wine as you make it, your wine will pay you back when you drink it.

Tasting and talking about wine

The most important equipment you can apply to winemaking is your senses — smell, taste, and sight. Just as winemaking is in service to the grapes at hand, all the scientific biochemistry stuff is in the service of the senses — how the wine smells and tastes as it develops.

You don't master the art of winemaking out of a book, not even the fine one you have in your hands. You develop your skills with your nose, your mouth, and your memory of sniffs and sips.

As you seek out good deals on equipment (see Chapter 3 for more about equipment), you may want to upgrade your own sensory equipment — not by organ transplants, but by practice. One of the most useful things a winemaker can do is taste other wines, and try other grapes, styles, regions, and vintages.

I think taking a wine appreciation class should be mandatory for home winemakers. Classes in wine styles, wine regions, and how to taste wine are readily available from community colleges, wine shops, and wine education centers; seek one out. Training in how to sniff out common wine faults — what oxidized wine or hydrogen sulfide smell like — is also valuable. Most wine appreciation classes cover these things, and kits of reference samples of good and bad odors are also available (see Appendix C).

Most everyone can smell and taste, but few of us are born with the vocabulary to describe what's in a glass. Putting words to wine is one of those activities that resembles dancing about architecture — it's another world and, at best, indirect. The more you do it and the more you say out loud what you're tasting, the easier it gets. Plus, to make wine you really like, you have to learn how to describe it. Appendix A can help you find the right words.

Learning the lingo is important because your most important task as a home winemaker is to taste, taste, taste as your wine moves from grapes to bottle. Testing is useful to know what's going on in your fermenter or barrel, but the only way you really "know" your wine's mood and plans is through your nose and your mouth. This is, by the way, one of the great joys of home winemaking: Tasting your wine all along the way, not just starting with the finished, bottled product, nice as that is.

Aiming high

The final aspect of the home winemaking mindset is aiming high. Set out to make something that is more than just technically wine. Set out to make good wine you can be proud of. Because you can.

The first time people make their own wine, they tend to worry that something will go haywire. But when they're done and the finished product actually tastes like wine, it's a revelation! (Not quite up there with giving birth, but at least as big a deal as learning to ride a bicycle.) The next year, with more confidence and tricks up your sleeve, you're going to make even tastier wine. By your third harvest, if not sooner, you'll be making wines that are varietally correct — your Merlot really tastes like Merlot, your Pinot Grigio like Pinot Grigio — and hold their own with the offerings at the local wine shop.

You're gonna love this hobby.

Going from Vine to Glass

Figure 1-1 gives you a short overview of what you'll need to do in your home harvest, start to finish. The sections that follow flesh out the basic steps.

Practicing "safe" winemaking

Winemakers endlessly debate the merits of *reductive* winemaking — where oxygen is kept as far out of the picture as possible — and *oxidative* winemaking — where the useful role oxygen can play is maximized. Wine philosophers go round and round about *natural* winemaking — with little or no intervention — and *manipulative* or *industrial* winemaking — where technology is brought to bear at every point.

This book promotes *safe* winemaking. I want to maximize the chances that you'll produce a clean, stable, expressive wine and minimize the chances that you'll produce a microbial playground. Consequently, I advocate that you use commercial yeast strains, not whatever yeast happens to live in your garage. I want you to go out of your way to worry about oxygen exposure and temperature control, and use sulfur dioxide to safeguard your wine against alien microbes. Equally important is that you do a lot of testing to supplement what your nose and palate tell you, and, above all, remember that you can never do enough cleaning. You can make wine at home in many ways — I discuss alternatives throughout this book — but safe winemaking is absolutely the way to start.

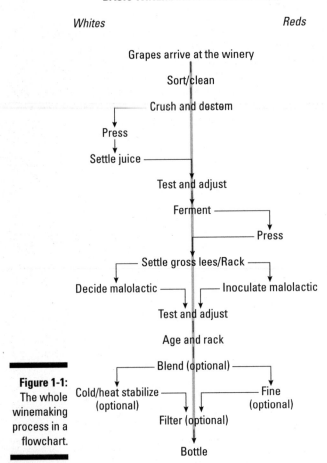

BASIC WINEMAKING DECISION TREE

Whites   *Reds*

Grapes arrive at the winery

Sort/clean

Crush and destem

Press

Settle juice

Test and adjust

Ferment ———— Press

Settle gross lees/Rack

Decide malolactic ———— Inoculate malolactic

Test and adjust

Age and rack

Blend (optional)

Cold/heat stabilize (optional) ———— Fine (optional)

Filter (optional)

Bottle

Figure 1-1:
The whole winemaking process in a flowchart.

Getting grapes

No grapes, no wine. (I reveal the few exceptions in Chapter 2.) Purchasing grapes doesn't take a lot of time, but deciding about them should. What kind of wine do you like to drink? What are your options for fruit sources? Can you find a wine someone else made from that vineyard and test it out? What other grapes might be good to have around as potential blenders?

Put some time into researching your grapes. Even though this book is all about what to do after you have the grapes, I can't stress enough how much the quality of your wine depends on the quality of the fruit.

Getting outfitted

Before your grapes arrive, you need to think through all the equipment and supplies you will need and plan on whether to beg, borrow, rent, buy, or steal it — no, forget that last option. You can acquire some equipment as you go — renting a press at the time of fermentation, or picking up some fix-it agent only when a problem arises. But you can stockpile supplies that you know you will need: a container to ferment the fruit or juice in, a vessel to age the wine in, tubes and hoses for moving liquid around, basic chemicals, a scale, and buckets (lots of buckets). That way you're ready ahead of time. Chapter 3 runs through lots of options.

Measuring grape chemistry

When the grapes are harvested, or at the latest, once you have them home and crushed and can measure the juice, you need to test for the basic parameters:

- ✔ **Level of ripeness,** measured in *degrees of Brix*, essentially the percentage of sugar by weight.

- ✔ **Total acidity (TA),** normally measured in grams of acid per liter.

- ✔ **pH,** a measure of the electrical ionization of the juice, which you can think of (roughly) as the inverse of the total acidity. (That is, the higher the TA, the lower the pH, and vice versa.)

These three parameters have normal ranges and problem ranges, and the only way to find them out is to do simple testing. You may need to make adjustments to the grapes and juice before you do anything else: Add water if the sugar is ridiculously high, add acid if the pH is too high, and so on. Chapter 5 walks you through these adjustments.

Destemming, crushing, and pressing

Home winemaking takes physical work. The three stages where grapes could not become wine without forceful human intervention are during the destemming, crushing, and pressing.

You want to use the grapes, not the stems, so step one is *destemming*, stripping off the berries and separating them from the stems. Most often, the same continuous process also *crushes* the grape berries, which isn't nearly as violent as it sounds. What really happens is that the skins get cracked and the juice starts oozing out, which is a good thing because the liquid is what ferments. Gentler crushing is generally better; you're not making a smoothie.

After destemming is where white wines and reds part company. Whites generally go immediately to *pressing*, squeezing out the juice, which is clarified by gravity settling, then fermented on its own. Red wines ferment with their skins, allowing for extraction of color, tannin, and other goodies that won't come out on their own, no matter how nicely you ask. Reds go to press after fermentation, not before.

Juice ready for fermentation is known as *must*. White must is simply juice, red must is juice with a slurry of skins and pulp and seeds floating around in it. To go from must to wine, the juice goes through fermentation.

Witnessing the miracle of fermentation

The period of *fermentation* — during which yeast cells transform sugar into alcohol, among other things — is brief, intense, and absolutely critical to the final wine. Technically speaking, this is the *primary* or *alcoholic fermentation*, to distinguish it from the optional secondary, malolactic fermentation. Your job is to set it on a good course and then watch it happen.

Grape juice exposed to air will start fermenting on its own, because yeast cells and other critters that love a sugar high are everywhere. For controlled winemaking, standardized, commercial yeast strains do a much more predictable job. Look for suggestions for good yeasts to use with specific wines in the chapters where I discuss those wines.

Dried yeast works best when briefly rehydrated before it goes into the must. And most winemakers also add some packaged yeast nutrient to keep the little workhorses happy. The yeast cells multiply quickly, and within a day or two, their activity will be evident: You'll hear and see it bubbling — releasing carbon dioxide — and smell wondrous fermentation aromas.

Done on a home scale — fermentations of a few hundred pounds or less — red wines take roughly a week to ferment, white wines two or three weeks. During that time, winemakers have to pay attention to temperature — which generally means ensuring red fermentation temperatures get up into the 80s Fahrenheit (around 30° Celsius) and whites stay down under 60°F (16°C). Because the yeast and must may not produce the desired temperatures on their own, you may need to be creative with heating and cooling — electric blankets, tubs of ice water, swamp coolers, and so on. Monitor progress in the fermentation twice a day for temperature and for the drop in Brix, as more and more sugar turns to alcohol. (If the fermentation stops, or slows to a crawl, head for Chapter 6 where I give tips on troubleshooting.)

When white wines have fermented to *dryness* (all the fermentable sugars have gone to ethanol), the yeast slowly dies off from the lack of sugar and the toxicity of the alcohol. The yeast then slowly falls to the bottom of the fermentation vessel, partially clarifying the new wine. When reds are dry, the wine gets pressed off the skins and put into containers for aging.

Performing a post-fermentation tune-up

After the wine is dry, another round of decisions comes onto your agenda. You measure basic wine chemistry again, with emphasis on the post-fermentation pH and total acidity. You may need to make further adjustments.

This is also the time to take action on the mysterious matter of *malolactic fermentation* (the transformation of malic acid from the grapes into softer lactic acid, by way of certain bacteria — Chapter 7 takes you through malo). Nearly all reds go through malolactic, and so do some whites including most California Chardonnay. Your choice is stylistic, but either way, you need to promote malo or stop it in its tracks; leaving it to chance means unstable wine which can explode in the bottle later on. Don't go there.

Once the malolactic issue is resolved, give your wine a stiff dose of sulfur dioxide (SO_2), the amount based on the wine's pH, to shut down further microbial activity. Sulfur dioxide math is the subject of Appendix D.

Also, at this point you implement your strategy for aging your wine — in carboys, stainless tanks, beer kegs, or barrels. All containers have their pros and cons, which I weigh in Chapter 8. Before heading to the chosen aging vessel, whites and reds both generally get a *racking* (siphoning the cleaner wine off of the sludgy mess at the bottom of a container) to get rid of the *gross lees*, which are the thickest, funkiest remains of the expired yeast.

Aging and blending

Now your wine sits for a good long spell. Your main job during aging is to sniff the wine and taste it periodically and to think about whether it might need some minor tweaking. Also, make sure whatever containers you're using are topped up so that very little air is between the wine and the top of the container. Your sniffing sessions may also identify some things you'd just as soon not have in your wine, so you may need to take remedial action (details on that in Chapter 8).

Dead yeast and other stray stuff in the wine continue to fall to the bottom (thanks to gravity) so periodically, your wine gets racked, keeping the wine and losing the sludge. Depending on the wine, you'll do two or three or four rackings over the course of three to twelve months. Time and rackings won't get your wine crystal clear, but they'll get it most of the way there.

As your wine ages and its true character emerges and stabilizes, you may want to consider *blending* — adding a bit or even a lot of some other wine or wines to your pride and joy to make it even better. Blending is a great resource for home winemakers who don't have hundreds of barrels or thousands of gallons of wine to pick from. (Chapter 8 has plenty of suggestions about blending options and procedures.)

Finishing and bottling

When your wine is ready for prime time — normally three to six months for whites, six to twelve months for reds — some final prep steps may be in order. Several substances are available for *fining* (cleansing the wine of one or more compounds), which can help get the wine clear, stabilize it against heat and cold, and remove excess tannin and other unwanted elements.

Another option is *filtration*, mechanically removing particulate matter from your wine by running it through a filter under pressure. Filtration isn't absolutely necessary, but helps with wine appearance and stability, and gives the whole project a more upscale gloss.

Bottling is another exercise in good sanitation, and a fine opportunity to recruit some friends into an assembly line.

Thinking beyond bottling

Bottling your wine is by no means the end of the process — it's just the start of a new one. Sure, you drink some of it immediately. But you also need to figure out how to store it, how long to age it (if at all), and whether to enter some into competitions. You need to get samples of your handiwork to your grape growers and wine equipment suppliers, who made it all possible. You can have great fun comparing your wine with the commercial competition and pick up some new ideas in the process.

And, of course, you need to start planning your next harvest.

Chapter 2

Finding Good Grapes

In This Chapter

▶ Sorting through grape varieties and sources

▶ Picking great reds and whites to start with

▶ Making wine without getting your own grapes

"**G**reat wines are made in the vineyard" is the constant refrain coming from wine writers, winemakers, and certainly from winery PR departments. Technically speaking, of course, this proposition is false: No wine in history was ever made in a vineyard; every single one was made in a winery. Wine, alas, does not make itself; humans do. Nonetheless, allowing for some romantic exaggeration, the "vineyard" mantra captures an important idea: The quality of a wine depends fundamentally on the quality of the grapes that go into it. Winemaking wizardry can salvage inferior grapes and make a drinkable wine, but no technology or chemical hocus-pocus can morph mediocre grapes into stunning wine.

Selecting the grapes you work with on your home project is the single most important decision you make as a home winemaker. After you settle on the source of your fruit and the grapes arrive, much of what you do as a winemaker is try to avoid screwing up the grapes. Your job is to capture all the grapes' potential and make sure stray microbes and other unforeseen factors don't spoil them.

This chapter helps you pick your way through choosing grapes, which I guarantee is time well spent.

Grape Expectations

Some of the criteria for choosing grapes are fairly obvious: the variety, the price, and the availability. Some grapes require a little more digging and fact-finding.

In sorting through the maze of grape options, you can get help and advice from many sources:

- ✔ Other home winemakers, including members of home winemaking clubs and associations
- ✔ Your local winemaking supply shop
- ✔ Home winemaking publications — print and online
- ✔ Anyone you happen to know connected to the wine industry

People who make wine talk to each other incessantly about where to find good grapes; why shouldn't you join in?

Getting grapes you like to drink

Start by aiming for grape varieties you know you will want to drink after you've made the fruit into wine. Why spend a lot of time and money and take up all the space in your garage to make ten cases of something that doesn't grab you?

This first step requires you to really reflect on your own taste. Do you like Big Reds, or drink a lot of whites, or have a particular fondness for Italian grapes? Have you had bad luck with commercial Merlot, finding too many of them boring, flabby, and simple? Or do you find that when Merlot is good — with some muscle and backbone to it — it's very good indeed, and maybe you can get it right? Maybe oaky Chardonnay drives you nuts; but why not make one without any oak? (I describe the terms used to describe the taste of wine in Chapter 10.)

Once you become the winemaker, you gain some control over your wine supply. So think carefully about what kind of wine you like and — even more important — what you like about it. Do you tend to like wines with lots of bright acidity, or not so much? Are you in love with the exotic, floral aromas of some white wines, or does that turn you off? The more you know about your taste in wine, the more motivated you will be to do the grunt work, and the better you will be at making all the little winemaking decisions that affect the final outcome.

The best preparation for winemaking is wine drinking — and paying attention to what you drink.

Checking out your sources

Even though the quality of the grapes is the key to winemaking, most home winemakers have little or no control of how their grapes are grown, when they are harvested, and so on. A tiny minority grow their own, but most homies never even see the vineyards their grapes come from. You may meet your grapes when they arrive at a local winemaking shop or when the grapes come to your door frozen by way of a shipping company. Consequently, knowing as much as possible about the sources of your grapes is essential.

When it comes to wine grapes, *source* has two meanings: The place the grapes are grown, and the people who grow or supply the fruit.

The natural conditions under which wine grapes are grown — soil, climate, elevation, and so on — have a profound effect on how the grapes and the eventual wines smell and taste. Much of this relationship is captured in the French concept of *terroir* — the notion that the place grapes are from, especially the soil, leaves a distinctive signature on the wine those grapes make. Millions of words, some fanciful, some scientific, have been written about terroir. But the implication of *terroir* for your home winemaking project is fairly simple: Think twice about where your grapes come from.

In deciding between multiple sources of the same grape, the prestige of the growing region isn't automatically the best indicator. I usually go with climate as the deciding factor. Some varieties need relatively cool climates to flourish: Pinot Noir, for example, does best in cooler areas in which Cabernet Sauvignon would never get ripe; good, warmer Cabernet-growing areas can cook away all the charms of Pinot Noir. Riesling likes it cool, and Muscat is another highly aromatic white grape that can take the heat.

The chapters in Parts III and IV focus on specific grape varieties and make suggestions about climate preferences. But you can also mine your consumer knowledge for clues. Take note of the regions that produce the wines you enjoy. The Finger Lakes in upstate New York and the Niagara Peninsula in Ontario, Canada, produce plenty of excellent Riesling; but you never see a Finger Lakes Zinfandel. If your favorite Chardonnays all seem to come from the Carneros region of southern Napa and Sonoma counties in California, try to find grapes from there.

Besides evaluating the growing region, find out about the people who grow and supply your grapes. If you work with a wine shop that has brought in grapes for 15 years, chances are they know what they're doing. Ask them for references to put you in touch with customers who have worked with whatever grape you're interested in. Ask your supplier where the grapes come from; not just what county, but who farms them, how long they've been at it, what commercial labels they sell to, and so on.

One important way commercial wineries evaluate potential fruit sources is to taste wines made from those same grapes. As a home vintner, you should try to do the same, either by finding other homies who have bottled the results or locating commercial wines based on the same fruit. Your own taste buds are a great way to identify promising grape sources.

Calculating quantity

You can make great home wine in very small quantities, such as one 5-gallon (19-liter) *carboy* — the standard glass or plastic home winemaking container — of fresh, zingy Sauvignon Blanc. Or you can make wine on a near-commercial scale and produce several barrels of heavyweight reds. Your budget, the space available for your winery, and the time you have to put into the project are all limiting factors. Another factor is that certain wine styles (like most serious reds) work best with a little more volume, maybe 15 to 30 gallons (about 55 to 115 liters) — enough to make use of barrel aging.

Table 2-1 gives a few very rough translations of grape volume to wine volume.

Table 2-1	From Grape Weight to Cases of Wine		
Grape Weight	*Liquid Yield*	*Bottles of Wine*	*Cases of Wine*
100 pounds (45 kilos) white	6 gallons (23 liters)	30	2½
100 pounds (45 kilos) red	7 gallons (26 liters)	35	almost 3
250 pounds (113 kilos) white	15 gallons (57 liters)	75	6 plus
250 pounds (113 kilos) red	17 gallons (64 liters)	105	almost 9
500 pounds (227 kilos) white (quarter ton)	30 gallons (114 liters)	150	12½
500 pounds (227 kilos) red (quarter ton)	35 gallons (132 liters)	175	14½

Notice that red grapes yield, on average, a little more juice/wine than white grapes. The reason isn't that reds are inherently juicier, but that the liquid (wine) is extracted from red grapes after fermentation, which helps decompose the grape pulp. White juice gets extracted before fermentation. (Chapter 6 explains the different steps in detail.) Also remember that the yield in juice and wine can vary from grape variety to grape variety and from year to year. Commercial-scale wineries get slightly higher yields for both red and white grapes because they use more sophisticated technology.

Get a few more grapes than your wine volume target might suggest, because some wine will go astray along the way. You lose wine to evaporation, testing, tasting and sampling; you lose some when you move wine between containers, filter it, and okay, spill it here and there. Figure that 5 to 10 percent of your theoretical wine will disappear, so buy accordingly.

If you plan on barrel aging, calculate backwards from the size of the barrel to the quantity of grapes. Then bump up your order a bit to leave yourself some wiggle room in case the grapes are a little stingy in their yield. For a half-sized barrel, 29 to 31 gallons (110 to 120 liters) (common for home winemaking), aim for 500 pounds (about 225 kilograms) of grapes, leaving you a 10 percent cushion of extra wine for contingencies.

Choosing fresh, frozen, crushed, or juice

Grapes can appear at your winery in many forms. You might go off and pick them yourself, or collect them from a supplier as whole grape clusters. In either case, your first job is to crush them and let the juices start flowing. Your grape supplier might crush them for you — for a small fee, most likely — to spare you that step. For white grapes, your supplier might both crush them and press the juice out, letting you take home nothing but liquid — saving you even more muss and fuss. On the other hand, you may want to do the whole business yourself, complete with a stomp-the-grapes festival in your driveway.

The form in which fresh grapes arrive at your winery — clusters, crushed, juice — doesn't make much difference for wine quality. What does matter is temperature: The cooler the grapes are from the minute they leave the vine, the better.

If you are your own harvest crew, pick early in the morning. If you have your choice of pickup times at your winemaking shop, choose an early one. Grapes that cross the country in train cars spend long periods at warm temperatures, and can even start fermenting on board. When you have the grapes at home, get them out of the sun as soon as possible.

Another option is frozen grapes or juice. Some suppliers specialize in providing frozen fodder for home winemakers. These suppliers ship plastic buckets of crushed red grapes or white grape juice all over North America, and many winemaking shops can arrange to freeze a lot for a good customer. Because of the extra processing and shipping, frozen grapes cost a little more. But their quality isn't compromised; freezing actually seems to preserve some aromatic compounds and often gives a slightly higher yield of juice. Most important, this somewhat unorthodox approach allows home winemakers who don't live in major grape-growing regions to get their hands on terrific fruit. Plus, frozen grapes are a way to decide in, say, the middle of March, smack between harvests, that you really need to make a little Cabernet Franc.

Find more information on grape sources in Appendix C.

Maximizing quality or minimizing price?

Grapes are the single biggest cost in home winemaking, so weighing price and quality is an important judgment. Grape prices are all over the map — both for commercial wineries and for home winemakers. Some sought-after varieties (like Pinot Noir these days) can cost four or five times as much per pound or per ton as low-glamour varieties. Growers in prime growing regions (such as the Napa Valley) can charge much more for the same variety than growers in less-prestigious areas — even though some grapes with the lesser pedigree may be just as tasty.

Winemaking philosophy plays a definite role here. For home winemakers whose goal is saving money on their wine budget, keeping grape prices down and avoiding the fancy lots can be very attractive. For other home winemakers who are aiming high and determined to outdo the commercial outfits, price may be no object, and quality may be all.

Most of us fall somewhere in between saving money and producing outstanding quality wine. A balancing act goes on every harvest. The math is different for every winemaker, depending on the grape varieties, the amount of wine being made, the number of available choices, and the size of the budget. I have three general pieces of advice to help you choose your grapes:

- ✔ **Be willing to spend a few extra dollars for quality grapes.** Grapes are the main ingredient in your wine and the main determinant of how good it is in the end.

- ✔ **Look for value.** Seek out prime grapes from less-than-prime regions, and think about blending pricey grapes with less expensive supporting players.

- ✔ **Keep the economics in perspective.** Remember that even when you splurge on grapes, the total cost of producing your wine is still much less than buying a comparable bottle from your local wine shop.

Prices for grapes vary widely — by variety, by where they're grown, by what quantity they come in. The more hands they pass through between the grower and you, the more surcharges get added. Your supplier will also charge extra for processing (crushing, pressing, and so on).

As a very, very general rule, expect to pay something around (USD)$1 a pound ($2.20 a kilo) for good grapes. In my past three harvests, working with several grapes every year, I've paid as little as $0.53 a pound, as much as $2.10, and gotten some absolutely free.

A final note about bargains. Home winemakers living in grape-growing regions often trip across offers or rumors of free grapes — perhaps from someone's backyard mini-vineyard, or maybe a commercial winery is letting people pick the *second crop* (clusters of grapes that grow on secondary shoots and ripen later than the main crop). For the record, free is good — as long as the grapes are good. Some amateur growers know what they're doing, and some don't. How clean and how evenly ripe those second-crop grapes are varies wildly. Even if the grapes are yours for the picking, check them out before pinning your hopes on them.

Winemaking takes a lot of your time and resources, and if "free" turns out to be worthless, then you've just invested a lot of effort that could have been spent with better grapes.

Picking First-Time Winners

If you already know what grapes are in your future, skip this section. If you're taking your first crack (or crush!) at winemaking, and you're scratching your head about which grapes to choose, this section helps you get started. The grapes I tell you about here are likely to help you succeed from your very first batch. They're tasty, aren't too cranky or finicky in the winery, work in a number of different styles, and are relatively easy to get. Naturally, your own taste and preferences in wine should trump anybody else's advice — even mine! More detail about the characteristics of specific grapes and the winemaking to go with them appear in Parts III and IV.

All of these suggestions are wine grapes of the species *Vitis vinifera*, vines that originated in Europe and remain the dominant players in fine wine worldwide. They also dominate the West Coast and warmer parts of Canada, and since California is where I live, my knowledge and experience is certainly *vinifera*-centric. But I know from tasting wine, in competitions and elsewhere, that you can also make excellent wine from certain indigenous North American grape varieties and the large number of French/American hybrid vines (which I talk more about in Chapters 15 and 18). For now, I'm sticking with *vinifera*.

Sure-fire reds

This handful of varieties includes the most common homie starter grapes, certainly on the West Coast, and frequently shipped and imported East and North. Chances of success with your first batch are very good.

Wine grape families

Every grape variety has its own individual characteristics. But certain combinations of varieties, particularly reds, are traditionally grown together (at least in the same region, benefiting from the same climate) and often blended together, making them into grape families — whether they share any DNA or not. So when a writer or winemaker or grower talks about *Rhône varieties* or *Iberian grapes*, here's what they're talking about:

- ✔ **Alsatian varieties:** Although other grapes are grown in the French region of Alsace, including some reds, the term generally refers to aromatic whites: Pinot Gris, Riesling, Gewürztraminer, and Pinot Blanc.

- ✔ **Bordeaux varieties:** For reds, this includes Cabernet Sauvignon, Cabernet Franc, Merlot, Malbec, and Petit Verdot; Carménière, which used to be grown in the Bordeaux region of France, now flourishes mainly in Chile. For whites, we have Sauvignon Blanc and Semillon. Wines labeled Meritage, mainly from California, are made from these same grape varieties.

- ✔ **Burgundian varieties:** Pinot Noir and Chardonnay just about cover it, though another white, Aligoté, is allowed there, too.

- ✔ **California field blend varieties:** From the late nineteenth century on, northern California growers often mixed several red vines in their vineyards and mingled them in their wines, a practice some still follow today — particularly with the trio of Zinfandel, Petite Sirah, and Carignane.

- ✔ **Champagne varieties:** The official varieties for the Champagne region are Chardonnay, Pinot Noir, and Pinot Meunier, though sparkling wine can be made from just about any grape.

- ✔ **German varieties:** White grapes, Riesling above all, but also Sylvaner, Müller-Thurgau, and Scheurebe.

- ✔ **Iberian varieties:** Despite their proximity, Spain and Portugal share just a few grape varieties: Spain's Tempranillo is Portugal's Tinta Roriz, Spain's Albariño is Portugal's Alvarinho. Spain is also home to red Garnacha, Monastrell, and Cariñena, and white Verdejo and Godello. Portugal excels with red Touriga Nacional, Touriga Franca, and Trincadeira, as well as white Verdelho, Malvasia, and Moscatel.

- ✔ **International varieties:** Grapes that dominate the international marketplace, such as Cabernet Sauvignon, Merlot, Syrah, Chardonnay, and Sauvignon Blanc, often grow in places with inhospitable climates and much more interesting indigenous grapes.

- ✔ **Italian varieties:** Way too many grapes are included here to be a tight family, because each region of Italy has its own star varieties. Many of the reds share generally high acidity, strong tannin content, and the need for a longer growing season to ripen.

- ✔ **Rhône varieties:** Reds include Syrah, Grenache, Mourvèdre, Cinsault, Carignane, and Counoise, plus several bit players. Petite Sirah, a California specialty, was created in a nursery in France from Rhone-region parents. Whites include Marsanne, Roussanne, Viognier, Grenache Blanc, and a large supporting cast.

- ✔ **Merlot:** Probably the best bet for your first try with Bordeaux red grapes, Merlot is widely available and generally costs less than Cabernet Sauvignon fruit. It's not temperamental, nor prone to excessive, astringent tannins, which Cabernet can sometimes be. If you find a Merlot source from a not-too-warm climate, you should end up with a very versatile wine ready for drinking soon after bottling. Merlot is also a good blender.

- ✔ **Petite Sirah:** This relative of Syrah (see Chapter 12 for the full story) is guaranteed to make you a big, dark, mouth-filling red wine. Still considered a little rude and unmannered by much of the wine establishment, Petite delivers a lot of bang (fruit, color, tannin structure) for the buck and makes a fine blend partner with both Zinfandel and Syrah.

- ✔ **Syrah:** Plantings of Syrah enjoyed a huge growth spurt in North America in the 1990s, partly as a response to the amazing popularity of imported Australian Shiraz (same grape), partly because Syrah grows well in a broad range of climates. It also makes good wine in a number of different styles, from lean and taut to fat and juicy. Syrah is a master blender as well.

- ✔ **Zinfandel:** Ever since trainloads of Zinfandel crossed the country destined for home winemakers during Prohibition, Zinfandel has been the default first-time red in the nation's garages. Zinfandel is fairly plentiful, not terribly expensive, and though it can have a lot of sugar and alcohol to manage, it's not very troublesome in the winery. Making truly great Zinfandel at home is a challenge; making pretty darn good Zinfandel is a good bet.

Winning whites

Whites are less expensive to make, work just fine in small quantities, and are ready to drink while reds are still getting their acts together. Here are four good bets.

- ✔ **Chardonnay:** Chardonnay is the most widely planted, made, and consumed white. It is easily available to home winemakers. The flavor from the grape itself is often rather generic — simply fruity, sort of apple-ish — which makes Chardonnay an excellent canvas for the winemaker to color in, with oak, malolactic fermentation, or other techniques in the cellar. Chardonnay works in many styles.

- ✔ **Riesling:** If you are among the small but growing band of Riesling lovers, feel free to start there. Riesling is one of those varieties that comes out best when fussed with least. You can find good Riesling grapes in eastern and western Canada, upstate New York, Michigan, Washington, Oregon, and California.

✔ **Sauvignon Blanc:** Sauvignon Blanc goes high on the list because, among widely available white grapes, Sauvignon Blanc is your best bet to make a wine with real character the first time you try. Sauvignon Blanc has an assertive aromatic and flavor profile, is not likely to come out neutral or diluted, pairs well with a range of foods, and is straightforward to make — no tricks.

✔ **Viognier:** Viognier was an obscure grape from the south of France 30 years ago. Today it is thoroughly mainstream among North American wine drinkers and planted everywhere from California to Virginia. Viognier combines the body and heft of Chardonnay with the delicate, exotic aromas of grapes like Riesling or Gewürztraminer. Just far enough out of the ordinary to make your first white a crowd-pleaser.

Looking Beyond the Usual Suspects

Half a dozen grape varieties dominate the consumer wine marketplace in North America. Cabernet Sauvignon, Merlot, and Zinfandel among reds, Chardonnay and Sauvignon Blanc among whites. Yet good wine, sometimes great wine, is made around the world from several hundred different grape varieties. Lesser-known grapes — like Albariño from Spain and Malbec from Argentina — are leading the growth of wine sales. Home winemakers, too, are expanding their horizons.

Some of the "newly discovered" (they were around all along) grape varieties can be hard to find, both for commercial wineries and homies. But if you hunt around a bit, your options are almost unlimited. The following sections talk about some lesser-known grapes to watch for. (Find more detail about these varieties in Parts III and IV.)

Here I suggest a few grapes that make tasty wine, aren't generally too expensive, and are grown in enough quantity that homies can probably get them with some effort. Remember, wine drinking helps winemaking: The more different wines from different grapes and places you try, the more likely you are to discover how much you like grapes beyond the usual suspects.

Reds

Eight more red grapes to consider, all with excellent credentials on multiple continents:

- **Cabernet Franc:** This relative of Cabernet Sauvignon (genetically, Cabernet Franc is the father grape) has a similar flavor profile, but is less likely to contain too much tannin or too much alcohol. Drinks well young and ages well, too.

- **Cabernet Sauvignon:** King Cabernet is a staple among home winemakers, not just drinkers, and fairly easy to locate. Fancy Cab grapes command fancy prices, but good ones are out there within reason. A gentle warning: Cab requires a bit of restraint (see Chapter 12).

- **Grenache:** One of the most cheerful, inviting reds around, Grenache can make terrific rosé, light and lively picnic-style wine, and even deep, dark, age-worthy stuff. Worth twice its price as a blender.

- **Malbec:** Originally from the Bordeaux region of France, Malbec has gotten everyone's attention in its Argentine incarnation. Good color and plumy flavors make Malbec a very solid red wine.

- **Mourvèdre:** Also known in Spain as Monastrell or Mataró, Mourvèdre makes substantial red wine. This grape shows not only fruit but earthiness, and it has an interesting little wild streak.

- **Pinot Noir:** Pinot has developed a huge buzz in the last few years, but retains the mythology of being impossibly hard to make well. The fact is, Pinot is one of the simplest wines to handle in the cellar, but cheap the grapes are not.

- **Sangiovese:** Tuscany's pride, the heart of Chianti, Sangiovese makes delicious, food-friendly wines without being huge and heavy.

- **Tempranillo:** The signature grape of Spain is finally catching on in the New World. Tempranillo takes a little work but produces medium-bodied wines of great depth and complexity.

Whites

The more whites you try drinking and making, the more you realize how much variety is in the varieties.

- **Chenin Blanc:** Somewhat out of fashion in the United States, but the pride of France's Loire Valley and popular in South Africa (where it is known as Steen), Chenin Blanc is another aromatic, honey-tinged white that can go dry or sweet, blended or straight up.

- **Gewürztraminer:** Made famous in Alsace, now grown well in British Columbia, upstate New York, Washington state, and other places. This white grape is known for heady aromatics, spicy flavors, good body, and can be dry or off-dry.

- **Marsanne, Roussanne,** and **Grenache Blanc:** These mainstays of white winemaking in the south of France are all full of flavor. They take some work to find, but if you locate some, go for it!

- **Muscat:** The mother of all aromatic whites with exotic aromas to burn, Muscat makes head-turning dry-style wines as well as sweet dessert and fortified styles. Muscat comes in half a dozen variants; Muscat Canelli (or White Muscat) is the most elegant, but others are worth a shot, too.

- **Pinot Gris** or **Pinot Grigio:** Two names for the same grape that are gaining popularity in the United States and are now being grown in several states. Can be made light, bone dry, and zingy, or round and full, always with engaging aromatics.

Versatile blenders

As I explain in Chapter 8, blending is the best friend a home winemaker has and a great way to overcome the limitations of small-scale winemaking. Here I talk about grapes to consider having around in small quantities, even if they're not the main event in your harvest.

Some grapes are fine for particular blending combinations. The grapes I talk about in the following list are, in my experience, the most versatile and most likely to come in handy. I start my planning for every harvest thinking, "I know I want a little Syrah and a little Viognier, but what am I really going to make this year?"

- **Grenache:** Great for livening and lightening up wines that seem a little flat, Grenache adds red fruit and sparkling personality. Plus, you have the basis for a nice little rosé to drink while your reds mature.

- **Merlot:** Of all the Bordeaux varieties, Merlot is the most congenial in mixed company. Merlot is not likely to take over a blend and is good for filling out wines with a little too much edge.

- **Syrah:** Harmonizes with most other red grapes, fills in the holes to complete one-dimensional wines, bumps up fruit and color with everything from Cabernet to Rhône varieties to Spanish grapes. No wonder Syrah is known in France as "the improving variety."

- **Viognier:** Excellent for discreetly adding body and aromatic intrigue to many whites, from Chardonnay to Pinot Gris to Chenin Blanc. Viognier can also give a nifty aromatic dimension to Rhône reds and blends.

Growing your own

The great advantage of growing your own grapes is that you have complete control over what you grow, how you farm the vineyard, and when you pick the grapes. And, after the initial investment in vines and site preparation, your grape costs go down substantially. Grape growing, however, can be challenging, involves a good deal of manual labor, and puts you and your crop at the mercy of nature — the weather, insect pests, and gophers, for example.

This book isn't the place to find out about grape growing. But keep these ideas in mind if you're interested in growing your own:

✔ You need at least 50 vines to bear enough grapes to make a reasonable amount (a few gallons or couple dozen liters) of wine; anything less than that is landscaping.

✔ Be prepared to wait three years from the time you plant to the first harvest that produces a reasonably sized crop.

✔ The climate at your vineyard site determines what you can grow and not grow; ripening Cabernet in Minnesota would be tough, for example. If nobody grows grapes where you plan to plant, find out why before you dig in.

✔ Make use of your state/province/county's agricultural extension services to find out what grapes do well, what issues are likely to arise in the vineyard, and what kinds of education or assistance are available.

✔ Besides consulting books and pamphlets on grape growing, check out the regular home vineyard coverage in *WineMaker* magazine.

I don't mean to discourage you from trying to grow your own. The satisfaction of doing everything from digging the first holes to opening the first bottle could be worth all the work!

No Grapes? No Problem

Can you make wine at home without grapes? Sure. Sometimes, grapes just aren't available where you live, or you don't have the space for much grape processing, or maybe you waited too long to order any grapes, and you're stuck. Several alternatives exist to produce good wine, and with each choice you will gain more winemaking experience.

Making wine from kits

Home winemakers in North America and the United Kingdom have been making wine from kits for decades. A *wine kit* comes with wine grape juice *concentrate* — all the color, flavor, and texture elements of the grapes, minus the water — yeast, various chemicals and additives needed for the winemaking, and full instructions. Almost literally, you take a kit, add water, and you end up with wine.

Wine kits naturally vary tremendously in price and in the quality of the grapes that go into them (even with the water removed, grape quality is still important to the quality of the final wine). Some of the fancier kits allow home winemakers to use fruit they would never be able to obtain as fresh grapes, such as grapes from famous regions in northern Italy or southern France.

Most kit wines come in 5- or 6-gallon sizes (20 to 25 liters) and are designed for making wine in carboys. And most kit wines can be finished and bottled quickly (usually in under two months) simply by following the instructions. But if the winemaker wants to, kit wines can be barrel aged and get the same deluxe treatment of any other wine.

Kit wines are very popular, especially in places with climates that make grape growing difficult or impossible. In some quarters, they have a somewhat tarnished reputation — as a second-rate backup plan when you can't get real grapes. Some kits do indeed make simple, generic wine, but then, so do some standard winemakers, amateur and commercial. Kit wines have often been known to win competitions against fresh-made wines.

Kits are an excellent alternative in the right situations, and not a bad way to get started in home winemaking. The major downside is missing the fun, the grunt work, and the wonder of starting with the fruit itself and seeing it through the transformation — which involves more than just adding water.

Employing a winemaking service to do it for you

In the past few years, winemaking shops that let you participate in making your wine while the shop handles most of the work have sprung up all over the United States and Canada. In many cases, these shops sell wine kits, and the shops have branched out into making kit wines on-site for and with their customers.

Typically, the customer picks a wine to make, initiates the process by tossing in the yeast, checks in periodically, and comes back to work at bottling time. Sure, this isn't how Robert Mondavi did it, but you get more involved in the wine than you would pulling bottles off the store shelf.

On a more upscale track, winemaking facilities have popped up in several cities that make small custom lots of premium wine from grape to bottle for their customers. Such operations have commercial-grade, commercial-sized equipment, trained winemakers on staff, and access to ultra-premium lots of fruit. Customers can decide how involved they want to be, everything from simply writing a check to getting down and dirty during crushing, pressing, and barrel-washing. Some facilities even offer the possibility of selling a customer's wine, under the servicer's legal bond, sparing the customer the rigmarole and expense of all the permits and licenses required to produce and sell wine commercially. By and large, these places turn out excellent wine, and charge a hefty premium for doing it.

Winemaking beyond grapes

Grapes aren't the only fruit you can use to make wine: Anything with sugar in it that can be fermented into alcohol is a candidate. And somewhere in the world, at one time or another, everything with sugar in it has in fact been made into wine, including most vegetables and many flowers. Beetroot wine, anyone? It's been done.

With some care, fruit wines can be terrific, both as sweet dessert wines and dry table wines. Most of the winemaking steps and stages are similar to those in grape winemaking, and the methods that are different are covered in a number of excellent books and multiple websites.

Making mead

And finally, there's mead — an alcoholic beverage made from honey — occupying the vague borderline between beer and wine. Mead can be made at relatively low, beer-like alcohol levels, or as strong as any wine. It can be made sparkling or still, sweet or dry. Mead books and resources abound.

Chapter 3

Provisioning Your Home Winery

*T*his chapter lists all the equipment you may ever need to make wine at home. It doesn't read like a good suspense novel, if I say so myself, but you can skim it to get a sense of what to expect, then come back to sections as needed.

A complete roster of all the store-bought and jerry-built contraptions for home winemaking in North American would easily fill another *For Dummies* book. And since winemakers are a tinkering lot, new workarounds crop up every day — and will in your winery, too. To sort through the labyrinth of equipment choices, you need to prioritize according to your winemaking philosophy, and here's mine:

✔ Grapes — how they look, smell, and taste — are far more important than the equipment you process them with.

✔ Your initial investment should be as small as possible. Buy your way up only as you get more and more hooked on winemaking (which you will!).

✔ Every process described in this book requires only a small outlay for anything besides grapes, and with little purchased equipment.

Minimalist home winemaking requires buying only a vessel to ferment juice and grapes, a vessel (could be the same one) to age wine, a few dollars' worth of yeast and chemicals, and some corks and bottles. You can rent or buy other equipment or services for a small fee.

Weighing the Heavy Equipment

Four stages in the life of a wine — crushing, pressing, filtration, and bottling — require using large amounts of physical force, or at least moving large amounts of grapes, juice, or wine. Two more stages — fermentation and aging — require a place to hold the stuff. Those stages need the heavy equipment.

Crushing and destemming

Many home winemakers receive their grapes already destemmed and crushed, either by a winemaking shop that supplies them or by the grower. Having somebody else crush and destem saves time, work, and a lot of mess. However, letting a third party come between you and your grapes cedes a bit of control and costs money. For your first couple of wines, farming out the work may be easier. But the fees mount with larger quantities of fruit, and investing in a new or used crusher-destemmer starts to make economic sense.

Home-scale crusher-destemmers have a metal hopper on top, with sloped sides that encourage grapes to move towards the rollers that crack the skins; larger crushers have a rotating auger to push the grapes along. Clusters of grapes get squished between the rollers, then drop down to the lower level, where a rotating bar studded with spokes knocks the grapes from the stems, sending the stems out one end. The bruised but liberated berries fall through a perforated bottom, down a chute, and into a collection bin. (Figure 3-1 shows what a crusher-destemmer looks like.)

Crusher-destemmers come in two basic models:

- ✔ **Hand-crank manual models** work perfectly well, and, in fact, allow you a little more control of the process. For example, you can stop quickly to remove a jam of stems or stray leaves or to avoid crushing someone's hand. However, when you begin crushing a ton of grapes at a time, your arm may suggest gently that you look into a motorized model. A manual model costs in the range of (USD)$200 to $300.

- ✔ **Electric crushers** cost roughly twice as much as manual ones — in the (USD)$500–$600 range — but you can eventually make that up in savings on sore-muscle salve and massage treatments.

Some models come with stainless steel hoppers, which are better, but more expensive than painted ones. Some crusher-destemmers have removable or adjustable rollers, better for gentle crushing.

Both types of crusher-destemmers are a pain to clean after use, since sticky grape slop sticks to everything and works its way into all the hidden places. But clean you must, because grape gunk is an invitation to infection.

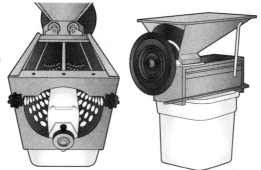

Figure 3-1:
A crusher's
innards and
that crusher
in working
position.

Full disclosure requires mentioning a third alternative: the *I Love Lucy* method of grape crushing. Most humans on the planet have seen the famous 1958 episode of this TV sitcom in which Lucille Ball and company stomp around in a vat of grapes (a method I discuss in more detail in Chapter 5) — no special equipment needed. And indeed, you can stomp your own in your driveway if you like. But then you have to figure out how to get rid of the stems and get the mush into a fermenter — topics I don't cover in this book.

Fermenting vessels

Your wine has to ferment somewhere, and not in the vineyard. Five basic options are available, although the plastic "trash can" and the glass carboy, both shown in Figure 3-2, along with wooden barrels, are the most popular.

Trash can fermenters

The staple for home red wine fermentations is food-grade plastic vats that come in various sizes, from 20 gallons (75 liters), good for 100 to150 pounds of grapes (50 to 75 kilograms), up to three times that size.

The plastic material imparts no flavors to the juice or wine and is easy to clean and sanitize. After multiple uses, however, these trash can fermenters get scratched, their laminated linings can crack, and they need to be replaced. The cost range is (USD)$20 to $50, including lid.

An older variation that is still available is using food-grade liners. These liners are made of heavy, flexible plastic sheeting and go inside non-food-grade containers — such as real, active-duty trash cans. Stainless-steel or food-grade plastic drums originally used for something else can also be cleaned and re-purposed.

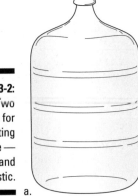
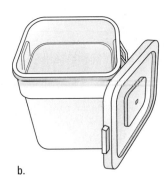

Figure 3-2:
Two choices for fermenting your wine — glass and plastic.

a.   b.

Carboys

A *carboy* — a small-mouthed, clear-glass jug — is probably the iconic symbol of home wine (and beer) production. The 5-gallon (19-liter) size is the most common, but other capacities are available.

One advantage of a glass carboy over a plastic container is that the surface is non-porous, which means you can clean it repeatedly to a very high standard.

Carboys last forever — until you drop them, and then they break, and then you buy new ones. An alternative has emerged in the form of PET plastic carboys, which are lighter, non-breakable, and less expensive: standard-size glass carboys run over (USD)$50 each these days, with plastic versions more like $30. The suppliers certify that the plastic carboys neither add not subtract flavor. Many people use plastic carboys, although many old-school home winemakers have their doubts. For quick turnaround whites and other short-term uses, or to save on shipping costs, plastic carboys are an option.

Stainless steel tanks

While beginners tend to start with plastic "trash cans" and carboys, small stainless steel tanks are an alternative, both for fermentation and for white wine aging. Home-scale tanks resemble their bigger commercial brothers in many respects: legs to hold them off the floor; movable tops fitted with silicon gaskets that can be raised and lowered to put an airtight lid on any volume of wine; and the superior sanitation potential of stainless steel.

Stainless steel tanks have their drawbacks:

- Home-scale tanks don't include provision for temperature control.
- The fittings — for draining wine, racking, and so on — on home-size models are not as sophisticated as the commercial ones.

> ✔ The relatively thin stainless steel walls — compared to large professional tanks — are easily dented.
>
> ✔ Gallon for gallon, stainless tanks cost at least twice as much as carboys.

Although stainless steel tanks look much snazzier than glass or plastic, they don't add much functionality, unless you're making wine on a large scale.

Barrels

Oak barrels are used for some white wine fermentations, especially for Chardonnay. As with carboys and tanks, the fermentation barrels usually go on to be storage vessels for aging, too. Barrel fermentation can impart both flavors (from new oak) and mouthfeel texture to wines, and allows for more oxygen access than carboys or tanks.

On the other hand, barrels are harder to keep squeaky clean, especially between uses, and malolactic fermentation is likely to kick off with barrels, whether you planned it or not.

Beer kegs

In recent years, beer kegs have invaded the world of home winemaking, as brewers who try their hand at wine see no reason to buy new equipment when the old stuff will do.

Kegs comes in sizes comparable to carboys; their insides are stainless steel, great for sanitation and entirely inert; they generally cost a little less than carboys, at least without the fancy fittings; and they don't break when you drop them. You can't see your wine through a keg wall, but then, you can't see your wine inside a barrel, either.

Equipped with the right fittings and pressurized gas, you can also use kegs for making sparkling wine — beer has bubbles, too, after all.

Pressing matters

White wines get pressed right after crushing, then fermented; red wines get fermented with their grape skins, then pressed. Either way, sooner or later, you have to separate the liquids from the solids.

The standard home squeezer is a _basket press_ — one's shown in Figure 3-3. You put the grapes, fermented or otherwise, within a circular cage of vertical wooden slats on top of a metal base, the slats spaced so that juice can come out but not grapes.

The grapes are pushed down from the top with wooden semi-circles, with more force applied by a ratchet mechanism that steadily ups the ante until the cake of smashed skins and seeds yields no more juice or wine.

Basket presses come in sizes to accommodate various quantities of grapes. The most common size, called a 35, holds about 200 pounds (91 kilograms) of grapes. Basket presses cost from about (USD)$400 up and last forever.

Figure 3-3: The grapes aren't there (they go under the wood blocks), but otherwise, this press is ready to go.

Renting a basket press for the first couple of harvests is a great idea, and, for that matter, so is having your local wine shop press your white grapes at the same time they get crushed.

If you press both white and red grapes, keeping the slats clean enough after red pressings so as not to turn your whites pink is a challenge — you may need a second set of slats. Metal mesh cages are also available; they're lighter than the wooden originals and easier to sanitize, but in my experience are harder to clean, because bits of grape matter get stuck in the tiny holes.

The upscale alternative is a *home-scale bladder press*. Grapes are loaded into a horizontal cylinder with an inflatable bladder inside; you pump up the bladder by air or water pressure, squishing the grapes against the sides of the container and forcing the juice out through a drain hole. Bladder presses make the technique of whole-cluster pressing, favored for some white wines, much more possible than basket presses do. On the downside, bladder presses cost at least twice as much as comparably sized basket presses.

Storing and aging

With the exception of the plastic bins used in red fermentations, all the other fermentation vessels can do double duty and store wine during aging.

Winemakers looking for an extra dash of complexity often mix and match: They ferment white wine in barrels, then age it in glass or stainless; or they let a red fermented in a "trash can" age for a few months in oak, and then transfer it back to carboys for a few months so as not to overdo the oak.

Carboys are fine for small batches; barrel aging imparts characteristics carboys can't. Barrels cost a good chunk of change, around (USD)$400 for a half-size, 30-gallon (115-liter) barrel. The choice is yours.

No matter what your protocol, you'll use carboys at some point. Red wine fermented in a plastic bin, for example, will go into carboys when it's pressed — the mechanics of getting it directly into a barrel are daunting in your garage. After settling, the wine gets siphoned into the barrel. A few months later, unless you're equipped with spare barrels and an electric pump, you'll need those carboys again: Wine will come out of the barrel into the carboys, the barrel will get rinsed and cleaned, and then the wine will go back in. Racking a 30-gallon (115-liter) barrel, half the standard commercial winery size, requires six 5-gallon (19-liter) carboys. It may seem nuts to own carboys to use for an hour at a time, but most home winemakers do exactly that.

Over time, you'll figure out your own routines and your own storage-vessel math. If you do nothing but red wines, aged in barrels, you don't need many carboys; if you do a lot of whites, you may need a small carboy farm. Start slow and build up your inventory.

Filtering wine

Filtering your homemade wine is an optional step. I'm a fan, because it makes my white wines sparkle with clarity, and makes the reds seem much more finished and less rustic. (More on filtration in Chapter 9.)

Filtration involves forcing wine (or juice) through a barrier that traps solid particles and lets the cleaner liquid move on. Some setups use vacuum pressure to pull wine through a filter medium, some use pumps to push the wine through, but either way you need force — coffee-style drip filtration won't work for your wine. Figure 3-4 shows a standard pad-type filter rig.

The two common filter options are

- ✔ **Canister:** In a canister setup, a small pump draws wine from a source container, pushes it into and through a cylindrical canister with a cellulose filter medium inside, and then into a target container. This equipment is relatively inexpensive — around (USD)$100 — and works fine for small batches of wine.

- ✔ **Pad:** Up a notch are the Buon Vino filter rigs, in the (USD)$400 range, that pump wine under pressure through a series of three filter pads held together with plates and a hand-crank pressure screw. This is a home-scale version of commercial plate filtration, and better equipped for handling larger volumes — 30 gallons (115 liters) or more at a time. A smaller version of the Buon Vino is designed for carboy-sized lots.

Both types of filters can handle cartridges or pads of varying *tightness* — the size of particles they trap — which I discuss in detail in Chapter 9. Winemaking shops often rent Buon Vino systems. For winemakers who use kegs, another option is to move wine from one keg to another, through a filter, using pressurized gas to push it, not a pump.

Bottling

The final act of brute force in winemaking is bottling: stuffing a large volume of wine — even just one carboy — into a bunch of much smaller bottles. Although possible, bottling wine by filling the bottles a measuring cup at a time through a small funnel gets old fast.

Figure 3-4:
Filtering your wine isn't mandatory but does make it shine.

Two basic approaches dominate the home winemaking scene: *single-bottle wands* and *multi-spout bottling rigs* — Figure 3-5 shows both. Both are great examples of the design ingenuity of small-scale winemaking equipment:

✔ A **bottling wand** is a clear, plastic tube that tucks into a bit of plastic hose, attached to a simple fitting at the bottom of a plastic bottling vat — such as a small, food-grade fermenter modified for this purpose. The wand has a spring-loaded tip. Press the tip against the bottom of a bottle, and wine flows through by gravity; lift the tip up, and the spring closes off the flow so that you can remove the wand without any leaks. Remove the wand from the now-filled bottle, and you have just enough room for the cork and a tiny bit of headspace. They cost (USD)$10, tops.

The wand assembly can also work by inserting the hose into a carboy and creating a siphon flow.

✔ A **multi-spout bottling rig** is larger, better suited to large-scale production, and more expensive — (USD)$200 to $300 — to purchase than a wand, but you can often rent one. In this setup, wine flows from the source vessel — a bottling vat, a barrel, a carboy — into an aluminum or stainless steel basin. The winemaking equivalent of a toilet float controls the flow. Wine flows out by siphon action into bottles hung on spouts, and the spouts displace just enough wine to allow for corking.

Figure 3-5:
A bottling rig and a bottling wand in action.

a.   b.

Which gets us to corking. Small, inexpensive, hand-held plunger corkers insert natural or synthetic corks — just whack the plunger with the heel of your hand. As your bruise fades, a stand-up manual corker, which uses the power of leverage to do the job, starts looking attractive: They're under (USD)$100 to buy and usually rentable.

Final finishing touches like labels and capsules get their due in Chapter 9.

Going gaseous

Once wine is wine, it needs to be protected against oxygen, which can dull flavors and encourage spoilage. The best way to prevent excessive oxygen exposure during many winemaking operations is to blanket the movement of wine with an inert gas.

Pressurized carbon dioxide is the popular home choice; nitrogen is more expensive but has less of a potential impact on wine. Gas comes in canisters with hoses so you can squirt the gas into carboys, fermenters, barrels, or bottles. The canisters cost around (USD)$50 and are refillable.

Scanning the Smaller Stuff

Like a well-stocked kitchen, your winery makes use of a zillion little items during the course of the annual cycle. No matter how long I make this list, I don't have the space to include everything, but I cover most of the normal needs. Figure 3-6 shows many of the smaller tools you'll use. Over time, you'll come up with your own variations and adaptations.

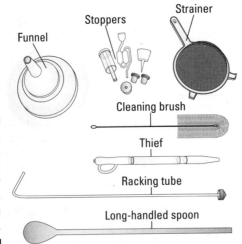

Figure 3-6:
A collection
of the
smaller
tools you
use in
winemaking.

Funnel

Stoppers

Strainer

Cleaning brush

Thief

Racking tube

Long-handled spoon

Collecting containers

A truism of home winemaking: *You can't possibly have too many buckets.* Just when you think you have every size and shape of container on earth, and backups for each, you'll have leftover wine or an emergency drip or whatever.

Large plastic buckets — 3 to 5 gallons, 12 to 20 liters — are good for capturing wine coming out of a press and for major cleaning operations. One-gallon pails, preferably with wire handles, are useful for nearly everything. Besides major storage vessels like carboys and barrels, you need some place to put dribs and drabs of wine and juice — gallon jugs, liter bottles, standard 750-milliliter wine bottles, double-size 1,500-milliliter magnums, half-size 375-milliliter splits, and so on.

Somehow, wine moved from place to place never comes out even: 15-gallon barrels really hold 14.5 gallons, or 15.3 gallons; "standard" glass carboys can differ by as much as two cups/half a liter in their true capacity. After racking, your 5 gallons of wine will be more like 4.8 gallons, now that the sludge is gone. As a result, you need lots of sizes of containers that can be sealed and extra wine to make sure they're all nice and full.

Closing closures

Carboys have narrow mouths to minimize the volume of air intake, and what plugs that small opening is an *airlock* — a small plastic fitting you fill with water and insert into the carboy mouth with a rubber stopper, putting a liquid barrier between your wine and the atmosphere. During fermentation, carbon dioxide can bubble out, but nothing gets in.

One style, the three-piece airlock, comes apart for more thorough cleaning. The traditional S-shaped version — think of the shape of the trap under your kitchen sink — uses less water and is less prone to losing its barrier due to evaporation. Cost for either is about a buck. Different containers have different mouth sizes, so you may need multiple stopper options.

Barrels can be fitted with airlocks and larger-diameter stoppers for use during alcoholic or malolactic fermentation, to allow for carbon dioxide release. Silicon *bungs* — solid stoppers with no airlocks — are the norm for barrel aging because they provide a fairly secure oxygen barrier and are easily cleanable every time you open the barrel for sampling, topping up, or racking. Figure 3-7 shows an airlock and barrel stoppers.

The best way to seal all those little wine bottles that end up holding a bit of wine is with *bar-tops* (or *T-tops*), short mini-corks (natural or synthetic) with horizontal disk tops — common in things like olive oil — which are much easier to pop in and out than actual corks. Bar-tops work best for short-term storage, because their air seals are less than perfect.

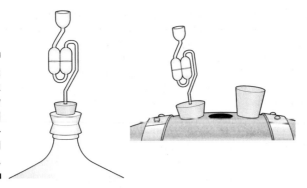

Figure 3-7:
An airlock
on a carboy
and barrel
options —
airlock and
bung.

Stirring and punching

From time to time, you need to stir your wine to mix in a chemical addition, circulate the *lees* (the spent yeast) during aging, and so on. Because the bottom of a carboy or a barrel is quite a ways from the opening, you need something longer than a normal spoon — 30 inches (75 centimeters) is about right. Get a long-handled plastic spoon; the spoon end won't fit into a carboy, but the other end is fine for stirring — see the spoon in Figure 3-6.

During red wine fermentation, the floating cap of skins and seeds needs to be *punched down* into the liquid juice/wine once or more a day. You can buy punchdown tools or construct them at home. The tool is simply a length of metal or plastic or wood — smooth and easy to clean — with a horizontal foot attached for pushing clumps of grapes gently down under the surface of the liquid. Imagine an old-style potato masher; in fact, you can make your own out of a potato masher and a length of plastic pipe (I did). (Chapter 6 gives you the details and the images to go with punchdowns.)

Racking and transfer

As your wine clarifies and the dead yeast and other solids settle, you need to move the wine and lose the sludge, preferably with as little exposure to oxygen as possible, a process known as *racking*.

When you need to rack your wine, picking up container A and just dumping it into container B is not the best plan. The simplest and most flexible option is transfer by *siphoning* — sucking on a length of tubing inserted into a liquid to start a flow, then putting the end of the tube into an empty container and letting gravity complete the job.

Clear plastic racking tubes come fitted with a cap on one end, so that the flow of liquid into the tube comes not from the very end, but from half an inch (about 15 millimeters) higher; that way, the clean(er) wine gets siphoned and the mire gets left behind. Racking tubes and the plastic hoses that attach to them come in various diameters; make sure to match the outside diameter of the tube to the inside diameter of the hose. Four or five feet of hose (1.5 meters) should be enough. Figure 3-6 has a view of some racking tools.

For the siphoning-impaired — getting a siphon to work every time is an art — auto-siphon racking tubes with plungers to start the flow are available.

Having a backup racking tube is a good idea just in case you step on it in the middle of a racking — or one of your helpers does.

For people who move a lot of wine around, particularly on the multi-barrel scale, siphoning has its limits — including the need to have the source container higher than the target so that gravity can work, which is not always easy with heavy barrels. Enter the *pump*. Small ones suited to home-scale use come in the (USD)$100-to-$150 range; you can hook up the pump to a filtration system or a bottling line, as well as use it for racking.

For some operations, wine gets poured from place to place, and for this you need *funnels* — a large one (6 inches or 15 centimeters) and a smaller, kitchen-sized one (2 inches or 5 centimeters).

Straining and sieving

Before, during, and for a while after fermentation, grape juice and wine contain lots of particulate matter — stray seeds and stem fragments, the occasional dead fruit fly, and other debris. To get rid of such flotsam, you need at least two sizes of sieves or strainers:

- A large-diameter version (perhaps 6 inches or 15 centimeters) for handling larger volumes of liquid, like the wine coming out of a basket press (as in Figure 3-6).
- A smaller size (2 inches or 5 centimeters) for straining small amounts of wine or juice headed into a narrow-necked container.

The finer the mesh, the better the straining job.

For moving wet grapes around — right after crushing, during fermentation — another useful variation is the perforated, conical device known in the restaurant trade as a *China cap*. The holes are larger than sieve mesh, but smaller than a grape, so the tool is great for moving grapes from one fermenter to another, or for draining juice from crushed red grapes for a rosé.

Cleaning equipment

Even after my repeated warnings, you'll be amazed at how much winemaking time you spend cleaning equipment before and after using it. That means lots of scrubbing tools, sponges, clean rags, and brushes of various shapes and sizes. Among the brushes should be one with a flexible wire handle long enough to get to the bottom of a carboy, but bendable so it can curl up under the mouth at the top. You'll also need one small-diameter bottle brush, not only for cleaning bottles, but for sticking into plastic hoses, tubes, and fittings. A toothbrush comes in handy, too. Nooks and crannies are fine things on English muffins, but not in your winery.

Glassware

Since repeated tasting is the key to good winemaking, you need glassware with two qualities: They should match, and they should be cheap. The matching part is not because your winery needs to look elegant, but rather for comparative tasting — for example, a blending trial with four options and three tasters. The glassware shape shouldn't be a variable. The cheap part comes up both because you'll need a fair number and because you're going to break some. Save the fancy crystal for serving your wine, not making it.

Winemaking log book

One of the most important pieces of equipment in your winery is a *log book*, a place to keep records of everything you do and everything you observe in the life of each particular wine. Every year I get a fresh three-ring binder, separate the whites, reds, and blends with divider tabs, and insert a page for each grape. The harvest information — volume, price, harvest date, growing region, basic juice chemistry numbers — goes at the top, followed by lines for dating and describing everything that happens from crushing to bottling. If I add some acid, I write it down; test results, I write them down; if the wine starts smelling weird, I make a note; when it gets un-weird, another note.

Because the grapes only come in once a year, you don't get very many shots at winemaking. The more information you can mine from each try, the better. Do it on paper; do it in spreadsheets; just do it.

Equipping Your Home Wine Lab

Most of your winemaking decisions will be based on how your grapes and wine smell and taste, but having objective numbers available is essential. The more you know about your wine's biochemical innards, the more control you have of its future. Some advanced forms of testing are best left to the commercial wineries and professional labs, but you can handle the basics with minimal equipment, some of which is shown in Figure 3-8.

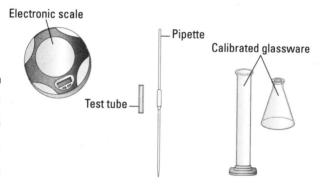

Electronic scale

Pipette

Calibrated glassware

Test tube

Figure 3-8: An assortment of testing equipment.

Pulling samples

The wine world's signature device for collecting samples of wine for tasting or testing is the *thief*, a long glass, metal, or plastic tube you dip into the wine until it fills up — Figure 3-8 shows a thief. You remove the thief (and the wine) without leaks by putting your thumb over the hole at the top end.

Glass thieves are breakable; metal versions don't show wine color; plastic thieves can get scratched up and are hard to clean — pick your preference.

Making calculations and conversions

For chemical additions and adjustments, for blending and fortifying, and even for deciding how many bottles you need, you need some elementary math.

Having a pocket calculator is a no-brainer but may cause a problem: Doing calculations with a digital assistant (or a spreadsheet) can sometimes disengage your brain a little too far. I suggest, whenever possible, doing important calculations by hand, or checking your calculator's work with pencil and paper. Manual calculations keep you more involved with the subject matter, and more likely to keep the decimal points in the right place. Doing math by hand is a useful reality check.

You will also need ways to convert one type of unit into another: U.S. measures to metric equivalents (if you use U.S. measures at all), parts per million of sulfur dioxide to grams of the stuff, and so on. Tables for just this purpose are in Appendix B.

Measuring with calibrated glassware

For measuring liquid volume, kitchen measuring cups and tablespoons won't do the job. Small calibrated beakers — marked in milliliters, not ounces, for greater precision — are essential for working out dosages and scale-model blends — 150 and 250 millimeters are handy sizes, shown in Figure 3-8.

Plastic versions are cheaper and less breakable, but get scarred and roughed up much easier than the sturdier glass ones.

A supply of disposable plastic *pipettes* for measuring liquids down to a single milliliter, which some forms of testing require, is also well worth having.

Weighing in with a winery scale

For measuring dry chemicals and other additives, a scale accurate to one-tenth of a gram is invaluable. Until a very few years ago, you could get this level of precision only with a balance beam-style scale with sliding weights, which cost about (USD)$200. These days, reliable electronic versions are available for about (USD)$30. I'm still using my expensive balance beam, only because I'm determined to get my money's worth; the electronic one is in the kitchen.

Testing equipment

At points too numerous to count, this book advises you to check on fundamental juice and wine chemistry parameters: sugar, pH, and acidity. Your grapes or juice will usually arrive with that information, which is a good start. Your local winemaking shop will be happy to do simple tests along the way, for a fee. The deeper you get into winemaking, the more you will want to handle basic testing yourself.

In the following sections, I try to describe the kinds of test kits available for home winemakers, but I don't go into all the exact steps involved. For that, follow the supplier's directions, which may differ from product to product or change over time; I don't want to give you a bum steer.

Home-grade tests are never quite as reliable as the ones done in well-equipped commercial wine labs, but they are way better than your own hunches. Some home tests depend on visually identifying a color change, usually some shade of pink or red; color-blind folks (like me) may need to recruit a full-spectrum friend.

Two things you will likely need at many points along the line are a good liquid thermometer, suitable for immersing in juice, wine, and chemical stews — mercury thermometers can break and spoil your wine — and a small supply (half a gallon/two liters) of distilled water.

Surveying sugar

Test number one is for sugar, starting with the *Brix* level — the percentage of sugar by weight in the unfermented grape juice. Brix gets estimated in the vineyard with a *refractometer*, a hand-held device that displays a sugar reading as a visual scale. In your home winery, the device of choice is a *hydrometer* — a slender glass float that shows the Brix through markings at the surface level of the liquid juice or wine inside a glass or plastic cylinder. During fermentation, hydrometer readings track the drop in sugar and the rise in alcohol, until your wine reads as dry.

When a wine is apparently dry, a good precaution is to run a simple test for any *residual sugar* (often abbreviated as *rs*) which may still be around, using Clinitest tablets dissolved in a tiny bit of wine. A final pinch of unfermented sugar can find the last surviving yeast cells weeks down the road and cause a mess; better to be sure the wine is dry, or to do something to make it dry.

Parsing pH

Of all the chemical markers for wine, pH rules. In the scientific world, *pH* is defined as the negative of the decimal logarithm of the hydrogen ion activity in a solution. (No, that won't be on the quiz.) Those with a less technical bent might think of pH as the "power of hydrogen" — a scale for rating the strength of hydrogen ions in a liquid. The higher the strength, the more acidic or base the solution is, and the lower the pH value; the weaker the hydrogen ions, the more alkaline the solution, and the higher the pH. The scale ranges from 0 to 14, with water, perfectly balanced, smack in the middle at 7.0, and wine generally in the 3.0 to 4.0 range.

The logarithm part of the technical definition is relevant in one sense: As you move up the scale, small differences have bigger and bigger consequences. The difference between a pH of 3.6 and 3.7 is a much bigger deal than the difference between 3.1 and 3.2. You don't smell or taste pH, but it has everything to do with key chemical reactions, the preservative power of a dose of sulfur dioxide, and the chances of unfriendly microbes surviving.

Knowing the pH of your juice or wine, and knowing it accurately, is the difference between guesswork and informed winemaking.

Inexpensive paper strips that change colors with pH levels to match a reference chart are readily available at winemaking shops and web suppliers. For higher precision, testing pH with a hand-held pH meter, accurate to a tenth of a point or better, is as simple as sticking the end of the meter into a beaker of liquid, which you may want to do half a dozen times in the life of your wine. You can find good-quality hand-held pH meters for around (USD)$100. A pH meter is a great investment if you make multiple batches of wine over several years. Follow the care instructions that come with the pH meter; otherwise, the electrodes that do the work will become useless.

Assaying acidity

The third variable you want to know about your juice or wine is the acidity. Acidity and pH are intimately related; in general, the higher the acidity, the lower the pH. Alas, the relationship is complicated and can't be reduced to a simple formula. So you need to measure acidity independently of pH.

The standard measure is *total acidity* (or titratable acidity, or just TA) — the sum of the multiple forms of organic acid found in grapes and wine. Tartaric acid is the primary acid, but malic, citric, and other acids play bit parts.

Test kits with all the chemicals and containers necessary for measuring juice/wine acidity are available for a few dollars, and most rely on reading some form of color shift. A more sophisticated variant uses a stirring plate to agitate and mix wine with chemical additives and relies on a pH meter to determine results: No color vision required.

Malic acid needs its own testing to determine if a wine has or has not gone through a malolactic fermentation (which I talk about in Chapter 7). It also helps to know how much malic acid is in your must to start with, which might determine how you handle the malolactic option.

You can measure both the amount of malic and the progress of malolactic fermentation with Acuvin test strips, which change color in juice or wine and get matched to a reference chart. A more advanced malo test involves *paper chromatography,* where wine drips on specially treated paper change color.

Scrutinizing sulfur dioxide

Sulfur dioxide (SO_2) is a critical winery chemical, for both sanitation and protecting the wine against spoilage. Tables in Appendix D of this book tell you how much SO_2 to add to your wine at different points (usually in the form of powdered, dissolved potassium metabisulfite).

Trouble is, after you make the addition, some of that SO_2 gets bound up with other compounds and goes out of service, and you need to know how much *free* or active SO_2 is still on the job.

Inexpensive test kits are available, based on the so-called "Ripper" method of sulfite analysis. (Where this test got its name remains a mystery to me.) The troubles with the Ripper are many: It depends on seeing a red color shift, which makes it much more useful for whites than reds; and even if you can read it correctly, other extraneous factors can produce unreliably high numbers for free SO_2 in reds. Unfortunately, a more accurate test, the aeration/oxidation method, requires much more extensive and expensive equipment, or paying a winemaking shop or testing service to run the test. Still, using a Ripper-style test, plus keeping careful track of your SO_2 additions, is far better than just guessing.

Analyzing alcohol

You went to a lot of trouble to convert that sugar to alcohol, right? And when you want to measure the alcohol at the end, you're stuck — there's no great method for doing this at home. Gizmos called *vinometers* do exist, and they don't cost much, but they're not worth very much, either (vinometers are not very accurate and are unable to deal with any sugar). You're better off simply taking the Brix you started with (and measured accurately!) and multiplying by 0.55 to derive the alcohol. That calculation will be close, if not precise, and doesn't cost a penny.

Shopping for Perishable Supplies

The following sections list winemaking supplies you definitely need to have around, and some you may want for particular situations.

Finding good microbes

To conduct a fermentation and turn those grapes into wine, you need yeast. As Chapter 6 explains, you can take your chances with whatever yeasts are on your grapes or living in your garage or left on your equipment from last year. Better, you can make a conscious choice and buy a commercial strain.

Dried, active yeast comes in an astonishing number of strains, optimized for various purposes. At least a couple dozen yeast strains are readily available to home winemakers in small, 5-to-8 gram packets, enough for 5 or 10 gallons

(15 or 20 liters) of wine. The yeasts do all the work, or at least all the interesting work, in your winery, and cost about (USD)$1.50 a shot — the best deal in winemaking. Liquid options are also available.

For larger quantities of grapes — several hundred pounds — splitting the fermentation into two or three batches and using multiple yeasts is an inexpensive ticket to complexity.

You may or may not also want to invest in *malolactic bacteria* (see Chapter 7 for an explanation of malolactic fermentation) to transform the character of the acid in your grapes. Again, a host of bugs in nature will be happy to dine on your juice's malic acid; the ones you want come in freeze-dried pouches or in liquid form, at about ten times the price of yeast. Still a bargain.

Feeding the good microbes

Most of the nutrients your yeast and malolactic bacteria need are already in your grapes, but for stressed, deprived fruit, or for a little insurance, you can try a packaged nutrient product. The baseline yeast food is *diammonium phosphate* (DAP), a form of nitrogen-rich ammonia; most winemakers, myself included, prefer to use "cocktails" that include not only DAP but several other vitamins and goodies. (Did you know yeast really like thiamin?) Separate nutrient products help malolactic bacteria whistle while they work.

Killing the bad microbes

Beyond the beneficial microbes, plenty of rogue yeasts and malevolent bacteria exist that you want to keep away or get rid of. Sanitation gets a good treatment in Chapter 4, but the basic goals are cleaning and sanitizing your winery and equipment, and protecting the wine itself.

A number of good cleaning and sanitizing agents are on the market. My favorite is generic sodium percarbonate, which is cheaper than brand name cleaners, works on just about everything, and is not highly toxic to the environment. Sulfur dioxide (SO_2), which I talk about in Appendix D, also serves as a sanitizing agent, normally as a rinse after a serious scrubbing. SO_2 is also used as a wine preservative, fighting off critters and excess oxygen.

Also of interest in the battle against bugs is *lysozyme*, an extract from egg whites that snuffs out lactic acid bacteria. Lysozyme at the crusher helps prevent early spoilage, especially during stuck or sluggish fermentation; it also plays a role, along with SO_2, in suppressing malolactic fermentation later on if that is not part of the program.

If you're flush with cash, consider buying a steam generator; the hotter the water, the better the cleaning.

Aiding fermentation

Besides yeast and nutrients, a large array of enzymes, tannins, and other preparations are on the market, claiming to do wonderful things. I have been blessed in California with high quality fruit and have never had much need for these products, but they can clearly play a useful role:

- ✔ **Pectic enzyme** helps break down the cellular structure of grape pulp, potentially yielding higher volumes of liquid juice and wine.
- ✔ **Color enzymes** (sometimes under the name ColorPro), also in the pectin family, help extract more pigment from red wine skins.
- ✔ **Grape tannin,** usually in powdered form, can supplement natural tannin, aid in clarification of whites and reds, and help stabilize red wine color.

The better your fruit is, the less of these products you will need.

Fixing wine issues

Two categories of additives share the spotlight in this section. Some may be useful for improving wine balance and chemistry; others can eliminate imperfections, imbalances, and instabilities.

Getting the acidity right

Acidity is essential to the wine package, but only within a certain range, and winemakers not lucky enough to have perfect grapes — that would be most of us — routinely fiddle with acidity, often as a way of fiddling with pH.

When acidity is too low — as in most of California most years — you need to add acid. The main form of organic acid in grapes is tartaric acid, which is the most common addition. Some winemakers prefer an *acid blend* — a mixture of tartaric, malic, and citric acids in about the proportions grapes normally contain — because it is a little softer to the taste. Tartaric by itself is the most effective way to reduce pH, which is often the reason for adding acid.

When acidity is too high (as is often the case in cooler climates like the northeastern United States and parts of Canada, or with hybrid grape varieties), acid either has to be masked — usually by retaining some residual sugar or by blending with a lower-acid wine — or taken out. To remove acid, the chemicals of choice are *calcium carbonate* or *potassium bicarbonate*. In extreme situations where both pH and acidity are too high, the "double salts" method is used: A portion of the wine is treated with calcium carbonate to induce a large rise in pH, which produces acid crystals that fall out, and then the two components get blended back together. Try not to go there.

Citric acid is primarily used for adjusting pH after water-based cleaning, which raises pH well above normal wine levels. For example, you may use citric acid after the final rinsing of a barrel, or for nudging the pH of water-rinsed filter pads into line. Citric is generally not used to raise wine acidity, because it can impart a distinctly citrusy flavor.

Fining and fiddling

Here I give you another long list of preparations designed to help in the later stages of wine production to fix or prevent problems Most of these are *fining agents*, substances that remove unwanted compounds (more about each of these as they come up throughout the book):

- **Ascorbic acid:** Used at bottling to preserve freshness

- **Bentonite:** Used to remove protein in wine that can form haze with temperature changes

- **Casein:** Milk-based product that removes excess tannin from red wines

- **Gelatin:** In liquid form, used for removing tannin and clarifying wine

- **Isinglass:** Processed from sturgeon swim bladder (seriously), another tannin remover

- **Polyclar:** Fining agent for removing oxidized compounds and unwanted pigments

- **Potassium sorbate:** Used to kill off yeast in wines that will receive additions of sugar

- **Sparkalloid:** All-purpose fining and clarification agent

Designing Your Winery

This section starts with the most important point: it's your *winery*. It could be a corner of your garage, one side of your laundry room, or maybe a carboy or two tucked into a tool shed, but it's still your winery. The most atmospheric home winemaking space I ever saw was a small living room in a friend's modest house, his barrels lined up along one side, and his partner's harps — she being a professional harpist — lined up on the other side. No coffee table, no lounge chairs: barrels and harps. Great wine.

The points to ponder as you design your space include:

- **Small is fine:** Winemaking takes up very little room. You can ferment several hundred pounds of grapes in the space an oven or dishwasher takes up; carboys occupy the same footprint as a bathroom scale; one side of your two-car garage could be home to several hundred gallons of barrel capacity. The operations that take larger space and create bigger messes are crushing and pressing at the start, and bottling at the end. Otherwise, your wine makes modest demands on space.

- **Think about your movement to and fro:** You need to get carboys and barrels and other supplies in and out of the space, so lots of stairs are not your friend. And you need to clean all the surfaces in the area thoroughly and repeatedly — carpeted floors, for example, are not the best idea.

- **Access to water:** Wineries, including yours, go through a lot of water — cleaning, rinsing, diluting, dissolving, cleaning again. The farther your water source is from your winery, the more exercise you'll get. A sink with real faucets makes life good.

- **Temperature control:** Chapter 4 goes on and on about the importance of temperature control, and if I could have said even more, I would have. Wine simmering over the summer in an uninsulated, 90°F (32°C) garage isn't going to turn out well, and red grapes relying on ambient temperature in the 50°F-range (low teens in °C) in a late fall fermentation may simply not ferment. You need a way to keep the either room or the fermentation and storage vessels within a reasonable temperature range, which may mean buying electric blankets or dry ice or something.

- **Ventilation:** Fermenting wines, both whites and reds, throw off about 55 times their volume in carbon dioxide while they do the sugar/alcohol dance. The aromas of fermentation are enough to bring pleasure to your entire neighborhood; but you don't need these aromas in an unventilated space. If you are fermenting indoors — a closet, a basement, a laundry room — make sure those lovely fumes can escape through windows or doors, and keep a fan handy.

- **Anticipate height, weight, and gravity:** This design feature may not be so obvious. Containers full of wine are heavy: A full five-gallon (19-liter) glass carboy weighs about 50 pounds (23 kilograms); a filled 30-gallon (115-liter) oak barrel tips the scales at about 280 pounds (127 kilograms). You don't want to pick up a full carboy any more often than you have to; you can't pick up a full barrel, period, even with help.

Consequently, in designing your winery, think about height, not just floor space. For racking carboy A to carboy B with gravity and a siphon tube, the bottom of carboy A has to be just a bit higher than the top of carboy B — up on a table, a stand, some kind of riser. Filled barrels have to be high enough off the ground that they can be drained out into carboys whose tops are beneath the barrel bottoms. Emptying a barrel sitting on the ground requires a pump.

Since I have never joined the pumping world, I have my own homemade solution, which is only one of many ways to handle the height problem. My barrels sit on top of wooden frames, which sit on boards with casters. That way, the barrels are high enough to rack into carboys, and moveable enough to get close to a counter for refilling before they get rolled back into place. Not elegant, but — like many of the workarounds home winemakers dream up — it works.

Chapter 4

Obsessing over Temperature, Oxygen, and Sanitation

*W*inemaking involves lots of small steps, lots of decisions, and a fair amount of work. But above all else, in making wine, you need to pay careful attention to three things: temperature, oxygen, and sanitation. If you get this trio right, you're most of the way toward making really good wine. These three variables come up again and again throughout this book — often enough that they qualify as useful obsessions, and deserve their very own chapter.

What's more, these concerns lie at the heart of an essential rule of home winemaking: You cannot possibly worry too much about temperature, oxygen, and sanitation.

Controlling Temperature

Temperature affects every aspect of grape growing and winemaking, and all along the winemaking way, some temperatures are better than others. Grapevines can't flourish — or even survive — in the extreme temperatures at the South Pole or in the Sahara. Different varieties do better in different climates. Red wines demand different fermentation temperatures than whites. Winery barrel rooms are cool for a reason, and the temperature at which bottled wine is stored has a major effect on how well it ages.

Commercial wineries invest massive sums in equipment for heating and cooling their wines; home winemakers have to be a little more creative.

Understanding why temperature matters

Raising or lowering temperature can encourage or discourage several important processes in the biochemical stew that makes up your wine — or your potential wine. Even small differences in temperature — a few degrees here, a few degrees there — can have an impact over time.

In general, higher temperatures make things happen faster; cooler temperatures slow things down. Warm fermentations go lickety-split; cool fermentation may go on for weeks. (Fermentation details are in Chapter 6.)

Warm temperatures tend to encourage the growth and activity of the various microbial critters that live in your wine — both the good, useful ones (like yeast) and the bad ones (like bacteria that turn your wine into vinegar). Bottled wine ages more rapidly at warmer temperatures: One afternoon on the hot back seat of your car is worth a year in a cool cellar. On the other hand, truly hot temperatures — like boiling water — are great for killing microbes.

Heat encourages evaporation, which may or may not be a good thing. In making white wines, cool temperatures help retain all those delicate, aromatic elements that make the wines so charming. High temperatures can leave a white wine smelling as flat as a glass of water. With red wines, especially high-alcohol reds, warm temperatures during fermentation can burn off a small percentage of the alcohol and result in a more balanced final wine. For wine stored in barrels for aging, warmer ambient temperatures mean more wine lost to evaporation — what winemakers call the *angels' share.*

Finally, temperature can affect the appearance of your wine in unexpected ways. Certain chemical compounds that stay happily dissolved in wine at 60°F (16°C) may solidify and drop out at 40°F (4°C) (the temperature in your refrigerator), leaving a tiny sediment of harmless but uninvited crystals in the bottom of the bottle. Similarly, some proteins in wine are fully dissolved at certain temperatures, but may show up as a slight haze at other temperatures. (Chapter 9 offers some suggestions about how to prevent sediment and haze.)

Grapes and wine are resilient, and being off a couple degrees from the "perfect" temperature won't spoil your party. But going out of your way to make sure temperatures are in range, especially during the critical fermentation period, is well worth the effort.

Measuring temperature

With wine as with head colds, you measure temperature with a thermometer — though not quite the same type of thermometer. Since wine is mostly liquid — even red wines, full of skins and seeds during fermentation, are mostly liquid —

the job calls for a waterproof thermometer large enough (with sufficient space inside the glass or plastic shell) to float. Numbers that are large enough to read through a coating of red wine are helpful, too.

Different thermometers handle different temperature ranges; as long as yours handles everything from 40° to 100°F (4° to 38°C), you're covered. Most thermometers give readings in both Fahrenheit and Centigrade, so the conversion — if you need it — is done for you. (If you end up with a one-scale-only thermometer, conversion help is in Appendix B.)

Tying a piece of string around your thermometer gives you more options for using it. Dangling the thermometer from the string lets you measure temperature inside a small-mouthed jug or other container, and also lets you submerge the thermometer inside a fermenter full of red wine and skins, to make sure the temperature in the middle matches the temperature on top. Either way, you get your thermometer back.

Warming up reds

During the period of fermentation — about a week or ten days — red wines need to feel some heat. The fermenting mass of grape skins, seeds, juice, and yeast needs to spend at least a day or two around 80° to 85°F (27° to 30°C), sometimes a bit higher, to extract all the goodies from the skins. Heat is the primary factor for extraction early in a fermentation; later on, more and more sugar is converted to ethyl alcohol, and alcohol serves as a solvent to pull out more good stuff. Getting a red fermentation warm in the first few days is a key ingredient — er, gradient? — in making good red wine.

In large commercial wineries, the fermentation tanks hold several tons of grapes or thousands of gallons of wine and the heat problem almost solves itself. As the fermentation gets going, the yeast activity, which automatically generates some heat, may produce more than enough. In fact, the issue may be cooling the temperature back down into the 80s Fahrenheit (or low 30s Celsius), not ramping it up. But in a drafty garage, 200 or 300 pounds of grapes in a small fermenter can't get themselves up to where they need to be.

The time-honored solution for warming up your fermentations is an old household favorite: the electric blanket. Take a trip to your local department store, not your winemaking shop, and invest a few bucks. If you end up making several batches of different grapes at the same time, you may need to invest in more than one blanket. The warm embrace of the blanket gets your fermentation off to a good, quick start.

I fold my blankets lengthwise until I have something roughly 8-feet-long and 2-feet-across, and then wrap the blanket in plastic sheeting to keep stray blobs of grapes and wine from soaking into the fabric. I take wire coat hangers and bend them into long loops; the blanket gets threaded through three or four hangers, and the hooks fit nicely over the rim of the fermenter (or maybe two smaller ones), holding everything in place. A little duct tape secures the ends. For the aquarium-minded, submerging fish-tank heaters could do the trick.

Cooling down whites

With white wines, the issue is keeping the temperatures cool enough. Because your home winery is probably not furnished with refrigerated fermentation vessels, you may need to intervene in other ways.

White (and pink) wines like it cool. Holding down the temperature during fermentation allows the yeast more time to do its work. Cooler temperatures also increase the chances of holding on to those elusive, intriguing, hard-to-describe aromatic qualities that make some white wines great.

White fermentations in carboys or small, home-scale stainless steel tanks generally do best at temperatures in the 50s Fahrenheit (low teens in Celsius), or just a bit higher, a good 30° lower than red wine fermentations. Even when whites are fermented in barrels (as Chardonnay sometimes is), the temperature rarely gets much over 70°F (21°C), still quite low by red standards. Too cool is also a possibility: Down around 40°F (4°C), the yeasts behave like zombies and lack the energy to do their fermentation thing.

Home winemakers generally do their whites in small, 5-gallon carboys, and a fermentation of that volume won't generate much heat on its own. What matters most is the ambient air temperature. If you're making wine in a cool climate in late fall in an unheated garage, the available temperature may be just what your wine needs. But if the ambient temperature for most of the day is in the 80s Fahrenheit (or high 20s Celsius), you need to think cool.

One classic method for chilling out your whites is to put the container in a larger tub filled with cold water, periodically refreshed with ice. Another is to cool the room the wine is fermenting in.

I have found two other cooling methods quite successful, and neither of them requires having a ready supply of oversized tubs:

 ✔ If you have room in a refrigerator, and the rest of your household approves, take out the bottom shelves and shuffle the carboy(s) in and out for a few hours at a time. This alternates the ambient temperature between the 40°F (4°C) or so of the refrigerator and room temperature.

 ✔ If nighttime temperatures in your area drop below 60°F (16°C), let the carboys spend the night outside, and bring them in only when the outdoor temperature gets higher than indoors.

You can, of course, combine the two methods. Neither guarantees a steady, cool fermentation temperature, but either or both can keep the average temperature of your fermenting white wine somewhere in the range it needs.

Adjusting the temperature for aging

Temperature control for all kinds of wine is most critical during fermentation. When the juice has become wine, you have more leeway, within limits.

In a perfect world — or a well-designed commercial winery facility — 60°F (16°C) is just the ticket for aging reds in barrels, maybe a few degrees lower for whites in tanks. Underground wine storage caves usually register a steady 60°. Temperatures up to 70°F (21°C) are probably okay for most home purposes, but prolonged periods — days and weeks — in the 80s Fahrenheit (high 20s Celsius) and above can "cook" your wine and flatten out its flavors and aromas. If your storage temperature is above 70°F (21°C), fix it.

As with cooling and heating during fermentation, look for creative ways to avoid extreme temperatures and fluctuations in your wine as it ages:

✔ Invest in or build your own *swamp cooler* — a fan blowing across a container of cold water — to fight off the heat.

✔ Move your wine from place to place in your house, garage, basement, and outdoors as the seasons change.

✔ Put those carboys in tubs of ice water.

✔ Rig up a fan to draw cool night air into your garage.

Don't drive yourself nuts fretting about Fahrenheit or sweating over Celsius. Just be aware that even when your wine is resting, it deserves the right environment.

Identifying Oxygen as Friend or Foe

Winemakers quickly develop a love-hate relationship with oxygen. Oxygen in the wrong place at the wrong time can ruin a good wine, and yet no wine gets made without it. Entire conferences are held on the intricacies of oxygen's role in wine, at every step from harvesting techniques to bottle aging.

Oxygen is a Big Deal because it's such a gregarious, outgoing chemical element, always ready to combine, recombine, and otherwise fool around with neighboring molecules. Oxygen can unleash the power of aromatic compounds or wipe them out forever. It's an essential part of the diet for the yeast that turns juice into wine, and small amounts of oxygen allow wines to age gracefully in the bottle. *Oxidation*, on the other hand, is the umbrella term for what happens when oxygen runs amok, making wines of any color — white, red, or pink — turn an unappetizing brown, covering up good aromas and producing bad ones, and finally finishing off old wines entirely.

The overall rule is that oxygen generally is your friend early on, through the end of fermentation, and your foe — or at least something to be wary of — after that. And of course, exceptions to that rule abound.

Encouraging happy fermentations

The zillions of little yeasty beasties in a fermentation crave sugar, but they also need oxygen (dissolved in the juice) to do their thing. Fortunately, enough oxygen is almost always present. Oxygen comes aboard when grapes get crushed and have their insides exposed to air, and when grapes and juice get dumped into fermenting vessels. Fermenting red wines also get additional oxygen through punchdowns (see Chapter 6) and racking (see Chapter 7).

In overly squeaky-clean wineries, fermenting wines can become starved for oxygen, but in the home winemaking context, the problem is more likely too much oxygen exposure than too little.

Oxygen dissolved in juice or wine is one thing; oxygen on the outside, bumping up against the surface, is quite another. Oxygen on the surface of grapes and juice is the best friend stray bacteria ever had. Leave grape juice exposed to air for long enough and it develops regular conventions of bacteria, not all of them helpful.

After a fermentation gets going, the chemical mash-up releases a constant stream of carbon dioxide, which provides a kind of oxygen-free blanket on top. But before the fermentation develops that security blanket, the grape juice is unprotected. (Handling that pre-fermentation vulnerability is something I discuss in Chapter 5.)

Keeping oxygen spoilage at bay

Once a wine has finished fermenting, it stops generating carbon dioxide, leaving it open to the air. Now you have to take over oxygen management.

For the most part, oxygen exposure after fermentation is a no-no for both whites and reds. Excessive oxygen during aging can

- Degrade wine color, pushing both whites and reds toward brown
- Neutralize the effectiveness of sulfur dioxide (which I discuss in the following section)

> ✔ Dampen or obliterate fruit flavors and aromas
>
> ✔ Combine with the alcohol in wine to produce aromas that belong in sherry
>
> ✔ Put out the welcome mat for uninvited microbes

The first line of defense is making sure your wine is stored in containers with airtight seals and as little oxygen as possible inside. For carboys, this means airlocks; for barrels, tight-fitting bungs (find out about equipment in Chapter 3). And for both kinds of vessels, make sure to minimize the *headspace* — the area between the top of the wine and the top of the container.

The possibility of excess oxygen exposure increases during certain winemaking operations: transferring wine from one container to another (known as *racking*), filtering, and bottling. The discussions of those steps in Chapters 7 and 9 include detailed procedures for keeping the lid on oxygen.

Keeping a little oxygen around because it (almost) never hurts

If the general rule is to keep wine away from oxygen after fermentation, the exception is . . . a little bit actually helps. The prime example is barrel aging, in which the water-tight but air-permeable wood allows a tiny trickle of oxygen to penetrate slowly over time, encouraging the development and maturation of the wine.

White wines, mainly aged in glass or stainless steel, don't get this oxygen boost, and most don't seem to need it. After a wine is bottled, tiny amounts of oxygen, either in the bottle's headspace or that come in through the closure, can contribute to continued development.

Airing out problems

In some situations, oxygen, normally the enemy of wine while it ages, can help a problem wine out of a jam. *Aerating* a wine — purposely flooding it with air or oxygen — can clean up a stinky wine.

One of the most common forms of wine stink comes from hydrogen sulfide, the by-product of unhappy yeast struggling in a stuck fermentation (see Chapter 6 for more on the causes of and cures for stuck fermentations). Hydrogen sulfide smells like rotten eggs. (The compound is added to natural gas to make sure you can smell a leaky stove burner — probably not a scent you want in your wine.)

If you sniff out a hydrogen sulfide problem early — emphasis on early, during or right after fermentation — a good blast of oxygen may fix it. You add oxygen by simply moving the wine from one container to another with a siphon tube and intentionally splashing the wine around so it gulps in some air. Because oxygen loves to interact (chemically) with sulfur-based compounds, and vice versa, the offending stink often just gets neutralized.

Aeration is a fix-it used when something has gone wrong, and not the normal routine to follow. It only works early — during or just after fermentation — not later on. The technique provides further proof of the only hard-and-fast rule about oxygen in winemaking: Oxygen is very, very important.

Sanitation, Sanitation, Sanitation

Everyone knows that the three key elements in real estate are location, location, and location. In winemaking, that could be rephrased as sanitation, sanitation, and sanitation. Wine is a living product: It only gets good — for that matter, it only becomes wine — through the hard work of various microbes. But wine can also go bad, very bad, through the nefarious sabotage of other microbes. All the equipment used in winemaking has to be clean — and so does the wine itself.

All the scrubbing and rinsing and flushing in winemaking help stack the odds in favor of the good guys and against the bad guys. The time spent on winemaking operations often breaks down as something like 40 percent devoted to cleaning equipment beforehand, 20 percent doing whatever it is with the wine, and then another 40 percent cleaning up afterwards. Glamorous? No. Essential? Yup.

Cleaning, sanitizing, and sterilizing

In a winemaking context, not all cleaning is created equal. The basic hierarchy of hygiene has three tiers:

- ✓ **Cleaning:** Simply applying physical pressure and water, diligently done, can get rid of up to 99 percent of unwanted microscopic critters.
- ✓ **Sanitizing:** Using very hot, boiling water or steam, as well as a chemical sanitizing agent, can accomplish a 99.9 percent bug removal.
- ✓ **Sterilizing:** All the tools of sanitizing, plus complete control of the air supply (perhaps a vacuum) to prevent a microbial comeback; close to impossible in a home winery environment.

Cleaning makes up an amazing amount of winemaking. All the surfaces that grapes or juice or wine touch or pass through or otherwise encounter need at least to be cleaned before use, and preferably sanitized. Microscopic life forms may not be all that visible. Don't let the sparkle of a glass jug or the shine on a piece of metal equipment fool you: Clean it anyway.

Sanitizing — bringing in heat and the chemical troops — is especially important for all those little corners and crevices and bug hideouts, the places it's hard to scrub. When wine gets filtered, for example, the only way to make sure the innards of the pump and tubes are wine-bug-free is to run a sanitizing solution through the filter rig. (I flag steps where extra attention to sanitizing is important throughout this book and cover cleaning agents in Chapter 3.)

You can't really sterilize at home, or at least not keep anything sterile for long in your garage. Not to worry. Cleaning and sanitizing will do just fine.

However you handle the sanitation chores, please, please do not use chlorine bleach anywhere near your winery. Bleach seems like a great cleanup candidate: It removes stubborn stains and you can find bleach at your local grocery store. But when it comes in contact with anything that contains phenols, especially from wood — barrels, boxes, wooden racks, shelves, cardboard, even some hoses and pumps — chlorine becomes the anti-cleaner, laying the groundwork for a most unpleasant chemical compound known as TCA (2,4,6-trichloroanisole) that results from the interaction of chlorine and common molds. Because TCA can taint your entire winery and be difficult to get rid of, avoid bleach (and other chlorine-containing cleaners) entirely. Plenty of good alternatives exist (see Chapter 3).

Explaining the myths and uses of sulfur dioxide

The sometimes-complicated relationship between sulfur dioxide (SO_2) and wine could be the subject of a book unto itself. (This is not that book — you're grateful.) *Sulfur dioxide* — one atom of sulfur bonded with two of oxygen — is one of the compounds yeast activity produces during fermentation, and also the winemaker's friend in many situations.

Until you get your hands on a copy of *SO_2 For Dummies* (and don't hold your breath waiting for publication of *that* title), here are some quick facts about this compound as they relate to winemaking:

- SO_2 gets added to wine as a preservative.
- The presence of SO_2 shows up as the "contains sulfites" notice on wines that have been treated with SO_2.
- It serves as a sanitizing agent in some winery situations.
- SO_2 can be poisonous at high enough concentrations, though the levels used in wine are far, far below that.
- At the modest levels used in home winemaking, SO_2 may or may not cause adverse reactions in some people who drink wine.

How clean is "clean enough"?

Clean winemaking produces clean wine — a good thing. But winemakers are human and have lives, and somewhere you have to draw the line between cleanliness and madness. Specific suggestions about cleaning and sanitizing procedures are included with the specific winemaking steps in various chapters. But here are some more general rules:

✔ Be especially careful about cleaning and sanitizing procedures at bottling time (see Chapter 9) to prevent unpleasant surprises in the bottle after all your hard work.

✔ Clean anything and everything used in winemaking at least once before use.

✔ Clean equipment, containers, tools, and surfaces right after using them; the longer you wait, the harder you'll have to scrub (and you give bugs a chance to set up shop).

✔ Periodically sanitize surfaces that can't be scrubbed — the inside of plastic tubing, the insides of equipment for filtering and bottling. They should also be rinsed with a sanitizing agent and then with clean water before each use.

✔ Whenever you move from one batch of wine to another — drawing off samples, stirring, taking temperatures — make sure to rinse whatever implements you use between containers, preferably with a sanitizing solution, to avoid transplanting microbes.

✔ Worry more about cleaning the insides of containers and equipment — the parts that come in contact with grapes or wine — than the outsides.

SO$_2$ is a constant topic of debate in organic and biodynamic farming circles; and it is the subject of all manner of scary urban legends.

Because SO$_2$ in various forms has been used in both home and commercial winemaking on several continents for hundreds of years, I'm willing to conclude that it is both safe and extremely useful. On the safety front, a small number of people, primarily people with asthma, react very badly to SO$_2$, and it makes sense for them to avoid drinking wines containing sulfites.

On the usefulness front, SO$_2$ plays two different and important roles. It is a sanitizing agent for equipment, bottles, and so on; and it is an anti-microbial and anti-oxidative preservative in the wine itself. Winemaking without the use of sulfur dioxide is possible, and even fashionable in some circles, but that represents a minority viewpoint in the world wine industry. In a home winemaking context, where would-be winemakers lack all the fancy equipment and controls commercial wineries enjoy, leaving SO$_2$ out of the mix means taking a big risk. So in the spirit of "safe home winemaking," sulfur dioxide shows up throughout this book — in several chapters where its use is appropriate, and in Appendix D.

Part II
Phases and Stages

The 5th Wave   By Rich Tennant

"Oh, no – Phillip crushes all his winemaking grapes in a machine, but he does eat jelly sandwiches with his feet."

In this part . . .

Winemaking comes in endless variations; options for grapes, techniques, blending, and stylistic tweaks abound. But an inexorable logic remains: Grapes get ripe once a year, and certain steps, phases, and stages come before others.

Cooks can make it up as they go. But you cannot crush grapes before you harvest them, nor age a wine before you ferment it. The next several chapters detail the universal rhythms of red and white winemaking.

Chapter 5

Sorting, Crushing, and Pressing

· ·

In This Chapter

▶ Thinking before you crush

▶ Considering crushing options and approaches

▶ Pressing white grapes

▶ Tweaking for pre-fermentation balance

· ·

After your grapes arrive, and before the serious business of fermentation starts, some important preliminaries are in order. You need to clean the grapes up a bit; measure the basic wine chemistry — juice chemistry at this stage; perhaps make some adjustments to guide the fermentation onto the right track; entice the juice out of the grapes; and most importantly, you have to pause and take a deep breath before you dive into the pool.

What to Do Before You Do Anything

You are about to put your innocent grapes through the wringer — almost literally. Their time in the crusher is doubtless the most traumatic few minutes of their lives. Okay, you're not exactly being cruel, but respect for your fruit obliges you to get to know it a bit before you rip it apart.

Chill out

The grapes are perfectly happy on the vine in hot weather and full sunshine, but the moment after harvest, the rules change: They need to chill. No matter how gentle the harvest, grapes chopped off from their vines and piled on top of each other start oozing juice, and that juice comes in contact with oxygen and whatever airborne microbes happen to be in the neighborhood. A whole string of unscripted biochemical escapades start immediately, and only accelerate through crushing, destemming, and, in the case of whites, pressing, all well before fermentation actually starts.

You can't keep your grapes from coming into contact with unknown elements, but you can slow the fraternization down. Your best tool is cool temperature' make sure the grapes are down at 60°F (16°C) or even a bit cooler. If your grapes have been sitting in the sun, get them in the shade. If the only cool spot is indoors, get 'em indoors. If you get them late in the day when it's hot, do something to cool them down before doing anything else.

Think first, crush later

Good winemaking depends on moments of reflection as well as many hours of physical work, and your first job is to stop and think: What am I trying to do with these grapes? Is this my shot at a true blockbuster wine, or is this just destined to be a background blender? Am I really happy with the yeast strain I've selected? Should I split this into two batches and use two yeast strains? Can I find a way to get these grapes a few degrees cooler before crushing them? Do I really trust the numbers I got from the grower about sugar and acid and pH, or should I retest? (Check out Chapter 3 and see "Get your numbers straight" later in this chapter for more about testing levels of pH, sugar, and acidity.)

The grapes and the yeast do all the heavy lifting in making wine, but their human assistants can steer things in the right direction and help avoid certain problems. Knowing your grapes — where they come from, what they look like, what they taste like, how their numbers stack up — is the key to nudging them toward their fullest potential.

If you were planning a turkey dinner, and someone gave you half a dozen really nice Cornish game hens instead, you'd make the most of what you had. The same goes for grapes. If your plan was to make some Cabernet Sauvignon grapes into a huge, Napa-style fruit bomb, and the grapes come in useable but barely ripe and tartly acidic, you need a new plan. No amount of manipulation can force those grapes to yield a wine foreign to their nature; you need to think about making a smaller wine, or maybe finding something riper to blend with. Or if your Cab comes in at a terrifyingly high Brix, posing the risk of a stuck fermentation and a super-high-alcohol level, you may need to do some quick math on how much water to add to bring this concoction down to earth.

Get to know your grapes. They can't talk to you in words, but they're happy to reveal themselves to your senses — smell, sight, taste — and to a bit of lab work. Listen to them.

Sort out the MOG

The goal of every conscientious grower is harvesting grapes of *uniform ripeness* — all the bunches at the same point of development and all the berries in each bunch at the same stage. The dream of every winemaker is having fruit arrive not only uniformly ripe, but nice and clean. Harvest after harvest, Mother Nature's peculiar sense of humor thwarts these fantasies.

Even if your grapes look good overall, sort through them for the outliers. Discard bunches that are moldy, or look like they're been eaten by insects, or contain nothing but hard, shriveled raisins. If only half a bunch is afflicted, snip it in half and toss the junk. Don't be surprised to find a suspiciously green-looking bunch amidst deeply red grapes; the poor dear probably got too much shade and is likely to taste like a bell pepper. Sunburn on white grapes looks just the way you think it would — toss 'em.

Careful sorting should only expel a small fraction of the fruit, a sacrifice well worth it for wine quality and avoiding weird flavors down the line.

Sorting through your fruit also gives you a chance to practice using one of those cool, inside-the-wine-world terms: *MOG* (pronounced *mawg*) for *Material Other than Grapes*. You planned to make your wine from grapes, right? So why would you make it from grape leaves, or stray chewing gum wrappers, or insects? This MOG and more may show up with your grapes. Get rid of it. Grape leaves are pretty obvious to spot; insects can be tougher. (At least bugs are a healthy sign that the vineyard wasn't cluster-deep in pesticide sprays.) Truth be told, very, very few wines, commercial or otherwise, are fully vegetarian; bugs come with the category. Do your best.

If your grapes have a lot of MOG in them, spread them out on a table and separate the good stuff from the bad stuff. If your grapes are clean and just have an occasional stray grape leaf, you can clean them up at the crusher.

Get your numbers straight

Making good wine doesn't require a PhD in analytical chemistry; it doesn't even require knowing how to read those chicken-wire diagrams chemists use to describe their sub-microscopic world. But it does require knowing a few basic pieces of information about how your juice or wine is put together — a teensy bit of wine chemistry. Blowing that part off because it's too much trouble is like baking in an oven without a temperature dial: Things might come out just dandy, or your pound cake could be toast.

Three basic numbers — sugar/alcohol percentages, pH, and total acidity — come up again and again in this book, starting from when your grapes show up. These numbers may come from your supplier, or you may need to test for them yourself as soon as you have some juice to work with.

Sugar and alcohol

The first number you need, the one your grape source will undoubtedly supply, is the sugar level, expressed in *degrees Brix* — essentially the percentage of sugar by weight in the grape juice. (Technically, the Brix scale measures *specific gravity* — the density of a liquid relative to the density of water, which has a value of 1 — and then turns that value into a sugar percentage.)

The Brix level of a batch of grapes is a very rough measure of how ripe they are; the roughness comes because sugar development in grapes is not always on track with flavor development. A heat spike near harvest time, for example, can make the Brix shoot up without changing the flavor profile one whit; or, a long, cool end to the growing season can produce grapes with full flavor maturity and much less sugar.

Brix is measured in two ways:

- ✔ **In the vineyard,** growers use an instrument called a *refractometer;* juice from berries gets squeezed into one end, the tester looks through the other end, and the refractive effects of sugar on light produce a reading on a visual Brix scale.

- ✔ **In your home wine lab,** you measure juice Brix with a *hydrometer.* A floating bulb calibrated with Brix and potential alcohol scales goes into a cylinder of juice, and the numbers at the surface level are the readings for that particular juice. (Chapter 6 has an image of a hydrometer if you're interested.)

Neither method is hyper-accurate; both test results are well worth having.

You can't just assume your fruit has the right amount if sugar: you have to measure, and you may rethink your winemaking as a result. For the newer, high-octane grapes, measurement can be complicated; sampling from healthy berries gives one reading, but including the raisined grapes, which might be 40° Brix, would give a much higher true number.

If the numbers for your grapes are outside the traditional ranges (as explained in the next section), check the "Adding, Subtracting, and Tweaking" section later in this chapter.

Measuring Brix in white grapes

The rough rule for converting sugar to alcohol is that 1° Brix of sugar produces 0.55 percent ethanol in a completely dry wine; and so the 20° to 24° Brix range yields wines between 11 and 13.2 percent alcohol. All rules have exceptions, but that's the white grape/wine ballpark.

The normal range for white grapes grown in North America is somewhere between 20° and 24° Brix, though ripe-tasting grapes can come in lower than that in chilly climates and many high-end warm-weather grapes come in higher. White grapes destined for sparkling wine are generally harvested in the high teens, and grapes for sweet dessert wines might be pushing 40°.

Going higher in reds

Red grapes run a little higher than whites. The customary Brix range goes from about 22° to 25°; the alcohol content from just over 12 percent to almost 14 percent. Red grapes for sparkling wine, like the whites, are picked at much lower sugar levels.

Saying that these used to be the ranges may be more accurate. In the last decade, particularly in California, the trend in sugar and alcohol has been up, up, up. Most California Chardonnay is harvested at sugar levels that make wine over 14 percent alcohol; high-end Cabernet Sauvignons, Syrahs, and Zinfandels routinely show up over 15 percent. Explanations for this trend range from the power of certain critics who love huge wines to the early effects of global warming. Some people love these high-alcohol wines, some people have sworn off them in favor of more modest, Old World styles. I'll stay out of this whole debate (for the moment). Be aware that high sugar can be too much of a good thing.

The indispensable pH

The single most important number you need is the pH of your juice. I don't want to sound all geeky, but your wine's life could depend on this number, because an overly high pH can make your wine vulnerable to all manners of less than appetizing microbial marauders — and make it taste lousy.

In your winery, pH testing is important enough and you should do it frequently enough — several times in the life of a wine — to make investing in a hand-held pH meter — under (USD)$100 — a wise decision.

The *pH value* measures where a particular solution lies on a scale that stretches from extreme acidity (a value of 0) to extreme base (14). Water, considered neither acidic nor base, comes in at 7. Underneath the hood, what's being measured is the strength of hydrogen ions; think of it as an inverse measurement of acidity — the lower the pH, the more acidic the juice/wine; the higher the pH, the less acidic.

Normal wine pH runs somewhere from 3.0 to 4.0, and those tenths of a pH point matter a lot. Tart, high-acid whites may have a pH of 3.1 or 3.2, sometimes even a squeaky 2.9. Big Reds score something like 3.5 or 3.6, and these days, with super-ripe, high-alcohol grapes, red pHs may get to 3.8 or higher. Levels in this elevated range are warning flags, not badges of honor.

For two reasons, pH is critical — and critical to know:

✔ The higher the pH, the happier the organisms that can spoil your wine. Your pH 3.9 wine is a Petri dish growing tiny microbes you don't want in your wine.

The standard way to control these critters is by adding sulfur dioxide (SO_2); but as the pH rises, the amount of SO_2 required to do the job rises, too, and not in a linear way. The amount of SO_2 needed for microbial control of a wine at pH 3.7 is nearly three times the amount needed at pH 3.3; at 3.8, it's nearly four times higher. And still not as likely to be effective. Up in this range, in fact, adding large doses of SO_2 is more a sign of desperation than a strategy for microbial management. Getting the pH down is far better than treating its effects.

✔ High pH undercuts both flavor and color. Flavors become dull and flat, making the wine seem thin; color, especially for red wines, is reduced and the wine loses its sparkling appearance.

The tipping point for pH is somewhere around 3.5 to 3.6. Above that, the chemistry starts changing, affecting everything from the rate of certain reactions to the populations of microbes. If your juice is over pH 3.5, check the "Adding, Subtracting, and Tweaking" section later on in this chapter.

Total acidity (and its parts)

Wine grapes contain numerous acid compounds, some easily measured and some of which are acidic only in ways a chemist can understand.

The two most common acids are *tartaric*, the largest component and the signature acid of grapes, and *malic*, also commonly found in apples. Along with some minor partners, these elements add up to *TA — titratable* (measurable) or *total acidity*.

When your grapes arrive, you should get a TA reading from the grower or supplier. You can also test for TA at home either with test kits or by using calibrated additions of sodium hydroxide and a pH meter and doing a little math (I tell you more in Chapter 3). One way or another, get that number. If the TA is out of range, check out the "Adding, Subtracting, and Tweaking" section a bit further on in this chapter.

Although the most important aspect of acidity in wine is how it tastes and how it contributes (or not) to the balance in the mouth, the numbers are also essential information for the winemaker.

The logic of acidity seems simple enough: more acid, more tartness, less acid, less tartness. Oh, if only it were that simple. Acidity by the numbers may or may not square with perceived acidity. A wine I think is nicely balanced may make you scream from pain at the acid level; a wine with numerically high acidity, combined with some residual sugar, may not taste acidic at all. Winemakers have to deal with acidity in both its measures: grams per liter and tartness per swallow.

Ballpark TA numbers for whites — both grapes and finished wine — are in the range of 6 to 8 grams per liter; for reds, 5 to 7 grams per liter. Below those levels, wines may taste flat and flabby and are also likely to have high pH; above those ranges, wines may seem too tart and hard and need a bit of blending or even de-acidification.

Beyond total acidity, a breakdown of how much of the acidity is tartaric and how much is malic is useful information. Malic acid is the active ingredient — along with some bacteria — in the process of malolactic fermentation, which can significantly change the perceived acidity of a wine. The more malic in your juice, the bigger the potential effect of a malolactic will be, and the sooner you know that, the better. (More on all this in Chapter 7.) Inexpensive malic test kits are available from wine shops and web suppliers.

Crushing, Delicately and Otherwise

No matter how gorgeous your grapes are, no matter how exemplary their basic wine chemistry numbers, your responsibility is to smash them. What growers call the harvest, winemakers call the *crush,* and without crushing, there is no wine.

Crushing does not mean obliterating or shredding; you're not making sausage. The trend in commercial winemaking, for both whites and reds, is toward ever more delicate handling of fruit as it comes in, barely cracking the skins during crushing, keeping individual grape berries as intact as possible. Crush them, you must; but be gentle.

Standard crushing

In the standard scenario, grape crushing involves two distinct processes — crushing and destemming — done in one continuous motion:

- ✓ Whole clusters of grapes go into a hopper/feeder, as shown in Figure 5-1.
- ✓ A rotating augur pushes the grapes toward an opening above a pair of rollers.

✔ Paddles push the clusters down through an opening between the rollers, cracking most of the grape skins.

✔ The oozing clusters fall onto another rotating rod studded with paddles or spokes.

✔ The rotating spokes knock the individual grapes off of the stems, and they fall through holes in a grate at the bottom into a container.

✔ The stems from the now berry-less cluster catch on the spokes and work their way out one end of the crusher.

Figure 5-1:
Whole bunches of grapes go through the crusher.

The design of these machines, home-style or industrial-grade, is quite ingenious. Home crushers come in both manual and motorized versions. Hand-crank models are cheaper and more fun, allowing a very direct connection between your biceps and your fruit. If you crush a lot of grapes, however, turning the crank for hours may be more "natural" than you need.

Even though the operation is called crushing, the destemming is usually the heart of the matter. After the grapes are stripped off the stems and piled on top of each other, they start to ooze juice themselves because of the weight. Many winemakers adjust the rollers on their crushers (if they can) to spread them as far apart as possible, widening the opening and handling the grapes more gently. Some fancy commercial equipment dispenses with crushing entirely, simply removing jewel-like berries from their stems.

One person can run a crusher, but two people are much better: one to load in grapes, one to crank and control the machinery. I offer a few crushing tips:

- ✔ Give the crusher a good cleaning beforehand; this equipment is full of hiding places for mold and microbes your wine doesn't need. (I talk about sanitation in Chapter 4.)

- ✔ Place the crusher on top of a large plastic *fermenter* (essentially a large bucket), so that the berries fall down into a convenient container, which can also be home for their fermentation. If the crusher is too long, use two fermenters side by side and cover any crack between them with plastic sheeting.

- ✔ Place a container at the end of the crusher where the stems exit for easy collection and disposal.

- ✔ As each container of grapes is lifted up and poised to be dumped into the hopper, take a moment to pull out any remaining MOG (material other than grapes) or funky clusters before they get engaged with equipment.

- ✔ Do *not* stick your hands anywhere near the rollers while the crusher is turning. If you have to dig for something, turn the machinery off and save your fingers for hoisting wine glasses.

- ✔ If the accumulation of stems starts clogging up the mechanism, stop, take off the cover, and pull the stems out by hand.

- ✔ When you're done, clean the crusher immediately, inside and out, between the rollers, and under the cover; don't let sticky grape juice turn to vinegar, which you definitely don't want in your next batch of wine.

Keep crushed white grapes cool and preferably covered until they go to press. Crushed red grapes go into whatever vessel they'll be fermenting in, which should have a lid (to keep out fruit flies and wandering microbes) and a layer of carbon dioxide to minimize spoilage.

Stems from red grapes are good for composting; but save the stems from white grapes; you'll need them shortly to aid in pressing.

Non-crush options

Now and then, winemakers let part of a batch of grapes escape the crusher and proceed to the next step intact. These options are a bit risky for your first wine, but they're worth a quick review.

Please tread on me

I guarantee that as soon as you start telling people that you're making your own wine, they will ask, "Oh, so you're stomping grapes in your driveway?" Even in this highly mechanized age, people seem to be born with an association between winemaking and foot power.

The kernel of truth in this connection is that foot treading was in fact standard technique for hundreds, perhaps thousands of years. And it turns out that the human foot is a terrific instrument for crushing and massaging grapes; it comes down with enough force to do the job, and flesh is much softer and gentler than industrial stainless steel. Assuming someone is

paying attention to sanitation issues, foot power is an excellent alternative to machine crushing.

The only significant remnant of this practice in commercial winemaking is in Portugal, especially the Douro Valley, home to classic port wines and delicious dry reds. There, foot treading is still the norm, practiced by the most prestigious producers both for the initial crushing of grapes and for the equivalent of punchdown or pump-over during fermentation. Keeping up with the times, the latest wrinkle in this time-honored tradition is the robo-treader, a mechanized stomper that mimics the original human extremities with plastic "feet" — and never asks for a break.

Some red wine styles and winemakers make use of whole berries, uncrushed but taken off the stems; others rely on whole grape clusters — no crushing, no destemming — placed at the bottom of the fermenter under the crushed grapes and juice. In either case, the intact berries at the bottom ferment in a different way, called *carbonic maceration*; the fermentation takes place inside the berry, without yeast, and not out in the juice/grape slush, and the result is a rounder, softer wine. The presence of the stems can add structure and tannin. (More on carbonic maceration in Chapter 10.)

For white grapes, many winemakers skip the crushing-destemming stage and proceed directly to press. This not only saves a step but reduces the time juice spends in contact with split skins and in the presence of oxygen, a strategy some claim produces purer, cleaner wines. Whole-cluster pressing requires a bladder press, a step up from the standard home basket press. (Flip to Chapter 16 to find out more about white grapes.)

Pressing Whites

White grapes usually go directly from destemming and crushing to *pressing*, the process of forcing the juice out and making it ready for fermentation as soon as possible. Crushed reds ferment with their skins, seeds, and pulp and only get pressed after the fermentation is (at least nearly) complete.

Pressing procedures for both are similar, with one key difference: White grapes fresh from the crusher, still mostly solid and pulpy, need to be mixed with their stems for a good press; fermented reds need no help.

The standard home squeeze uses a *basket press*. Oozing grapes get scooped by the pail full and dumped into the press; the wooden or metal slats or screen keep the skins and seeds inside the press, while the juice flows through the openings and into a bucket to catch it. Eventually, pressure is exerted by a ratchet gear and wooden plates, squeezing more juice from the grapes.

One great thing about manual basket presses is that you probably can't press hard enough that you extract the harsh compounds and flavors you don't want in your wine.

The basic steps in pressing crushed white grapes go like this:

1. **Check that all the parts of the press that come in contact with the grapes and juice are as clean as possible.**

   Rinse and scrub the metal base, the wooden slats, the wooden half-moons that go on top of the grapes, and the central pole on which the ratchet sits, as needed.

2. **Place the metal base on flat ground or on the floor and assemble the press:**

   Figure 5-2 shows a dissembled press and its parts.

   • Secure the ratchet pole with a large nut underneath the base.

   • Center the slats around the ratchet pole.

   • Insert the short metal pins into the brackets on the outside of the slats.

   Make sure that the juice can flow to the lip of the base and drain off into a collection bucket.

3. **Place a bucket under the lip of the press base, and put a fine-mesh strainer over the bucket to strain seeds and skins out of the juice.**

4. **Scoop grapes and any juice into the press, alternating layers of grapes and layers of the stems removed at the crusher; this is important for white grapes.**

   The stems leaven the mass of grapes and you recover more juice as a result.

5. **Assemble the parts that exert the pressure:**

   • Place the two wooden half-moons on top of the wet grapes so that they fit side by side, and give a little push by hand to seat them firmly.

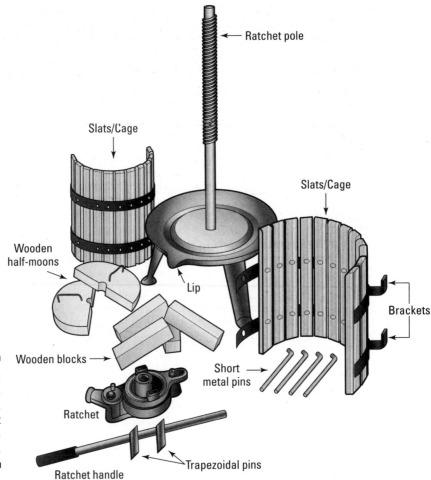

Ratchet pole

Slats/Cage

Slats/Cage

Wooden
half-moons

Lip

Brackets

Wooden blocks

Short
metal pins

Ratchet

Figure 5-2:
A press,
undressed,
or at least
unassem-
bled.

Trapezoidal pins

Ratchet handle

- Place one or more layers of wooden blocks on top of the half-moons, raising the height of the stack at least 5 inches (13 centimeters) over the rim of the slats.

- Thread the ratchet onto the top of the pole, and screw it down until it rests on the wood blocks.

- Insert the two trapezoidal metal pins into the ratchet, pointing in the direction for ratcheting downwards (see Figure 5-2), and insert the ratchet handle.

6. **Making slow, steady, back-and-forth motions, work the ratchet downwards, increasing the pressure on the grapes and squeezing more juice out and into the bucket.**

Figure 5-3 shows a ratchet in operation.

Figure 5-3:
Many hands
make for
a (slightly)
easier
pressing.

Eileen Raphael

7. **Pay attention to the flow of juice; when the bucket is more than half full, stop the pressure, wait until the flow slows down, then swap out the bucket and sieve and swap in another.**

   Empty the bucket of juice into a storage container — most likely an empty, clean carboy.

8. **Repeat Steps 6 and 7 until the flow of juice has reduced to a bare trickle and it becomes quite difficult to keep working the ratchet.**

9. **Turn the two ratchet pins in the opposite direction and use the handle motion to move the ratchet upwards.**

10. **Take out the blocks and half-moons, remove the pins from the slats, remove the slats, and dispose of the solid cake of grapes left behind.**

11. **Take everything apart and clean it before storing it.**

Exactly how this works depends on the size of your press and the volume of your grapes. You may need several layers of wooden blocks to get the right pressing leverage; you may have such a small batch of grapes that you can simply dump them in the press, stick in the half-moons, and stand on them, exerting pressure the old-fashioned way. Or, you may have a larger volume of grapes than your press can accommodate, so you may need to stop when one round of pressing is done, take the slats of the press apart, remove the spent grapes, and start over.

Put the juice from a pressing immediately into clean containers — most likely one or more carboys or a small stainless steel tank. Even white juice destined for barrel fermentation should be settled overnight in glass or stainless containers. Protect the juice against oxygen exposure with carbon dioxide and airlocks.

Your white grape juice will not be a pleasant sight. Freshly pressed juice doesn't look like clean, clear wine, or like apple juice from the store; it looks more like pea soup, a vaguely greenish-brownish, sticky-sweet, opaque smoothie. Don't worry; once it starts fermenting, it will look even worse.

Adding, Subtracting, and Tweaking

After you reduce your white grapes to juice, or your red grapes to *must* — a slurry of punctured grape berries and pinkish juice — you need to prepare these raw materials for fermentation. If you haven't already gotten the basic juice chemistry numbers, do the testing now. (See "Get your numbers straight" earlier in this chapter for info on which measurements to take.)

Your juice may be just fine. Chances are good, though, that your juice and/or grapes need some small tweaking before fermentation starts, and the earlier, the better. If a juice/wine is out of balance — too much or too little acid, a scary-high or -low Brix level — fixing it pronto is simpler and less invasive than waiting. The longer you wait, the more stubborn the problem will become and the more firepower you will need.

All the suggested additions and treatments in this section require thinking about your grapes in their liquid form, in gallons or liters, not pounds or kilograms. After white grapes are crushed and pressed, this is obvious. But for reds, dosages are based on the potential volume of wine that will come out at the end of fermentation, even if the juice is mostly still hiding in the grapes.

Rule of thumb: 100 pounds (45 kilograms) of white grapes should yield about 6 gallons (23 liters) of juice/wine; the same amount of red grapes should yield about 7 gallons (26 liters). These ratios are not as high as commercial winery yields — but you don't have their equipment.

The various substances you use to add, subtract, and tweak are readily available either from the local grocery store or from winemaking and brewing shops — Appendix C lists some cyber-suppliers if your local shop . . . isn't.

Pass the sugar, please

The most elementary issue in juice composition is the sugar level, ideally somewhere in the low 20s Brix for whites, the mid 20s for reds. If your juice tests far outside that range, and the grapes still seem otherwise sound and flavorful, a little sugar or a little water can put things right. Grapes with unusually low Brix are also likely to be quite acidic, and the result can be thin, puckery wine. Grapes with excessively high sugars are increasingly common these days in warmer climates; they can be hard to ferment successfully and may give rise to hot, alcoholic wines. Fix these problems on day one.

Sweetening things up

In the wine world, adding sugar is known as *chaptalization,* after the French minister who first allowed it as a practice in the wines of that country.

Granulated white cane sugar is recommended. Dissolve the sugar in just enough warm/hot water (90°F/32°C) to make a solution or just enough warm/hot wine. A two-to-one ratio of liquid to sugar should work. Neither of these methods is fault free: In one case, you're watering down your wine, in the other case, cooking your juice. But these small adulterations ultimately improve the balance of the finished wine. Table 5-1 shows the amount of sugar needed to raise the percentage in various increments.

Table 5-1	Regulating Sugar	
Desired Sugar % Rise	*Grams to Add per Liter*	*Ounces to Add per Gallon*
.25	2.5	0.33
.50	5.0	0.66
.75	7.5	0.99
1.00	10.0	1.33
2.00	20.0	2.65
3.00	30.0	3.97

After adding the sugar solution to the juice or crushed grapes, stir to mix thoroughly. Let the juice rest an hour to make sure all the sugar is in solution, and then retest the Brix with a hydrometer to make sure you achieved the sugar level you were aiming for.

Lowering the sugar by adding some water

When the sugar level is crazy high — Brix over 26° or so — the solution is to add water. Adding water was once illegal, at least in the United States, for commercial winemaking, but wineries often resorted to "rinsing their bins" anyway; now watering down fruit is a common practice for high-Brix grapes.

Extreme sugar levels are often the result of water evaporating from the grapes near harvest time, so you can think of diluting your juice as restoring the water that should have been there anyway. Or think of it as joining a proud tradition of turning water into wine — sort of.

One good way to minimize the diluting effect of water on red grapes is to calculate how much water you will need, draw off that amount of juice and put it to work making rosé, and then add the water to the grapes. The result is that the red skins will be swimming in the same volume of liquid they arrived with, not more, just at a lower sugar level. If you draw off the juice shortly after crushing, color loss is minimal.

Use these steps to calculate the amount of water to add:

1. **Divide the current Brix (CB) by the desired or target Brix (TB) to get a rehydration ratio (RR) number greater than 1.** (CB ÷ TB = RR)

2. **Multiply the current volume (CV) of juice (or projected liquid volume from crushed grapes) by the rehydration ratio to get the target volume (TV).** (CV × RR = TV)

3. **Subtract the current volume from the target volume to get the necessary water addition (WAD).** (TV – CV = WAD)

Use clean, clear water, not water that smells like the inside of your garden hose or is heavily chlorinated; distilled water from the grocery store is best. The water should also be *acidulated*, so you need to add enough tartaric acid to bring the pH — which for water is about 7.0 — down to the wine range — 3.0 to 4.0. Acid additions should be about 7 grams per liter of water (or 0.9 ounces per gallon); dissolve the acid thoroughly in the water before adding to the juice. Mix the water well into the juice/grapes, then re-test with a hydrometer to verify the new Brix.

Adjusting acidity

Most grapes from sunny California, white or red, arrive with insufficient acidity to make balanced wine, and so acid additions are a routine part of the crush. In cooler parts of North America, the acid may be right on target, and some grapes may be harvested with too much acid. In all cases, look at acid levels (and their counterparts in pH) closely and adjust as needed before fermentation.

Ideally, total acidity (TA) for white juice should be in the range of 6 to 8 grams per liter, and the pH should be between 3.1 and 3.4. For reds, TA should normally be between 5 and 7 grams per liter and the pH 3.6 or under. A little bit off either way, no big deal. But if you have a TA of 4 grams per liter and a pH at 3.9, get to work.

For increasing acidity, the math is straightforward: Subtract where you are from where you want to be, multiply by the volume of juice, and add acid. If your 10 gallons of juice (38 liters) tests at 4.5 grams per liter, and you want to bump it up to 5.5 grams per liter, add 38 grams of tartaric acid.

Adding acid for the purpose of lowering pH isn't quite so simple. As a theoretical rule, adding 1 gram of acid to 1 liter of grape juice (or .13 ounces to one gallon) should lower the pH by 0.15. By that formula, dropping the pH of 10 gallons (38 liters) of juice from pH 3.8 to pH 3.5 would require 2.7 ounces (76 grams) of tartaric acid. In reality, the result of the addition can vary, because other elements affect pH besides measurable acidity. Start with a theoretical dosage; a few hours later, test for the real results.

You can add acid with an acid blend, containing a combination of tartaric, malic, and citric acid, or with pure tartaric acid. Blends are somewhat softer to the taste buds; tartaric is the most effective in lowering pH.

Dry acids dissolve best in warm to hot (90°F/32°C) water or wine, about three parts liquid to one part acid crystals. Mix your juice thoroughly after the addition, and re-test both the pH and the TA after an hour to verify the changes.

Slightly high acidity before fermentation may not be a problem. The TA generally drops a bit during the primary fermentation; a bit further through malolactic fermentation, and a final bit if the wine goes through cold stabilization (explained in Chapter 9). Slightly tart wines can be blended to take off the sharp edges; some grape varieties (including many French-American hybrids) get their balance from retaining sugar, not dropping the acidity. Excess acidity that doesn't take care of itself is best handled when the wine has finished fermentation and reached its new level of acidity. Extremely high acidity, like high sugar, can be ameliorated by water additions, but the resulting wine is likely to be quite thin. De-acidification after fermentation is covered in Chapter 7.

Managing microbes with SO_2

Besides balancing your juice/grapes, I strongly recommend an initial small addition of sulfur dioxide (SO_2) as an all-purpose preventive measure. Sulfur dioxide in modest quantities does not interfere with yeast activity — not even with most of the "wild" yeast strains that may hang around your garage.

But it does markedly lower the bacterial population in your juice, and at this stage of winemaking, bacteria are not helpful and can lead to spoilage. This initial SO_2 addition will disappear or be neutralized during fermentation.

The standard precautionary dosage of SO_2 is 25 to 50 parts per million (ppm). Using dry potassium metabisulfite, the weights involved are so small that the only sensible way to talk about them is in grams, not ounces. For 1 gallon of juice (3.8 liters) 25 to 50 ppm translates to 0.16 to 0.33 grams. (For more on SO_2 additions and measurements, see Appendix D.). For 10 gallons (38 liters), 2 grams would be about right. Dissolve the potassium metabisulfite in a little cool water, add, and mix thoroughly.

Including endless enzymes

In the perpetual quest for wine perfection, winemakers, enological researchers, and product suppliers have created a huge array of additives. These products are designed to fix this or that alleged shortcoming in grapes or heighten this or that desirable characteristic. The most common pre-fermentation additives are *pectic enzymes*, which can help break down grape pulp and increase the yield of juice; *color stabilizers*, which can help bind pigments from the skins to other compounds and prevent them from precipitating out of wine; and *tannins*, derived either from grapes or from oak, which can add to the final wine's structure and counteract potential oxidation during fermentation.

My strong recommendation for your first few batches of wine is don't bother with additives; use them when you have a real-world problem to solve, not because of a supplier's hypothetical scenario.

One pre-fermentation additive I do suggest using in *lysozyme,* an enzymatic product derived from egg whites that helps to suppress *lactic acid bacteria* — critters that feed on grape juice or wine and produce, among other things, lactic acid. Most of these bacteria are not your friend. Before and during the primary fermentation, you don't need these bugs even if you may want them for a successful malolactic fermentation later. Adding about 100 ppm of lysozyme (1 gram for every 10 liters or 2.5 gallons), dissolved in cool water, is a good precaution.

Chapter 6

Letting Yeast Do Its Thing: Fermentation

*M*aking a bottle of wine from start to finish may take six months or a year, but everything hinges on what happens in the week or two of *fermentation* — the period in which yeast activity extracts all the flavor, aroma, and texture goodies from the grapes and skins and converts the sugar to alcohol.

Fermentation can be fast and furious; the snap, crackle, and pop of gases escaping from the fruit or juice can be downright noisy; the aroma can carry a block away. Fermenting white wines turn strange, greenish colors and grow a head of foam on top; They look like a pot of pea soup gone bad. But not to worry — that's just yeast at work. The spectacle of those tiny microbes making such a huge commotion is truly awesome.

Winemaking's Secret: Yeast, the Fortunate Fungus

This idea may be humbling, but get used to it: The success or failure of your home winemaking project depends much more on a single-celled fungus than it does on you. That's what *yeast* is — the one and only single-celled fungus in the universe, and without its miraculous properties, wine would not exist.

Grapes turned into wine for thousands of years, thanks to whatever yeasts happened to be floating around in the neighborhood, well before Louis Pasteur identified the little critters as the active agents in the early nineteenth century.

These days, a whole industry works at identifying, selecting, isolating, breeding, packaging, and marketing hundreds of specialized yeast strains with different characteristics and winemaking potential. Wine quality may be made in the vineyard, but every wine ever produced was made by a swarm of single-celled fungi.

Yeast loves to do two things that are essential for turning grape juice into wine: eating sugar and reproducing. The diagram in Figure 6-1 shows the yeast-sugar relationship. Drop a few thousand dried cells from a standard home winemaking yeast packet into a jug of sugar-laden grape juice, and they're in hog heaven within minutes, noshing on sugar molecules, breaking them apart, and turning each one into two molecules of alcohol (ethanol), two molecules of carbon dioxide, and a tiny amount of other stuff. Figure 6-1 captures the essential dynamic of winemaking.

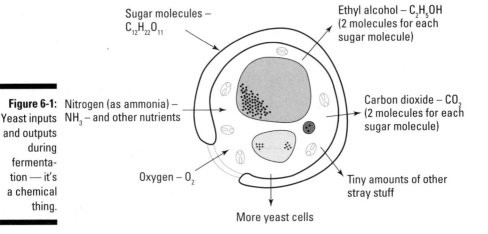

Sugar molecules – $C_{12}H_{22}O_{11}$

Ethyl alcohol – C_2H_5OH (2 molecules for each sugar molecule)

Figure 6-1: Yeast inputs and outputs during fermentation — it's a chemical thing.

Nitrogen (as ammonia) – NH_3 – and other nutrients

Carbon dioxide – CO_2 (2 molecules for each sugar molecule)

Oxygen – O_2

Tiny amounts of other stray stuff

More yeast cells

The first time the first yeast cell does this, you're on your way to wine. Since sugar is so abundant at the start of the process, the yeasties breed way faster than rabbits, soon numbering in the millions and tens of millions, all pigging out on the sugar and turning it into alcohol. But after a while, they eat themselves out of sugar, or get pickled by the rising alcohol level, or both, and expire. Zillions (roughly) of yeast cells die for your wine.

Because yeast is at the heart of winemaking, you should survey the range of available strains and know how to take care of them. Doing so increases the chances that yeast achieves its destiny — making your wine come out really tasty.

Selecting a strain

You could spend a lifetime — and dozens of PhD researchers have — worrying about the fine points of yeast strains. Sometimes these distinctions matter a lot, and I get into that more in later chapters on specific grapes and particular wine styles. But only a few basic considerations go into picking your first yeast strain.

Most wine-friendly yeasts are members of the species *Saccharomyces cerevisiae*, and a number of these have been used successfully in home winemaking long enough to become standard offerings at home winemaking shops and through mail-order and web-based suppliers.

Yeast for home-scale production generally comes in small, airtight, plastic or foil packages containing from 5 to 8 grams of dried, but still viable, yeast — known as *active dry yeast*. Yeast in this powdery form and these tiny packages is pretty uninspiring stuff — slightly dingy, off-white, dusty little granules. One good sneeze and your yeast will scatter to the four winds. But a teaspoonful of this remarkable stuff can make cases and cases of wine.

The various strains of yeast on the market differ in two important ways:

- ✔ **Performance characteristics:** How fast they do their work, how rapidly they multiply, what temperatures they prefer, how much alcohol they tolerate, and what nutrients they need.

- ✔ **Sensory characteristics:** The various kinds of aromatic, flavor, color, and texture compounds different strains tend to extract or create as they do their work (also known as *organoleptic properties*).

For making your first bottle of wine, one indispensable performance characteristic towers above all others: Use a yeast strain that can get your wine dry — that has the ability to plow through all the available sugar without stumbling, stopping, or, as we say in winespeak, sticking. You do not want a *stuck fermentation* — when the yeast activity shuts down before the fermentation is complete. I tell you more about measuring and achieving dryness in the upcoming section on "Monitoring fermentation," and more about dealing with stuck fermentations in the upcoming "Troubleshooting a Stuck Fermentation: When the Fermentation Won't Ferment" section. But try to get a yeast strain that avoids the problem.

Performance is the place where "wild" (or spontaneous, or indigenous) yeast fermentations easily go awry. Chances are good that some yeast or other in your garage will set your wine a-bubbling; the stray species might even add some interesting aromatics. But non-*Saccharomyces* species (those are the commercial ones) don't tolerate much alcohol, and unless you've been making wine in your facility for a few decades and have a terrific resident *Saccharomyces* population, you have no guarantee that the wild ones will get the job done and finish the fermentation.

Good yeast choices for red wines need to tolerate slightly higher fermentation temperatures and alcohol levels, while white wine yeasts have to handle cooler temperatures (see "Checking temperature" later on). Table 6-1 lists some widely available options for putting your first wine through its paces.

Table 6-1	Good Yeast Strains to Start With		
Yeast Strain	*Wine Color*	*Performance*	*Sensory*
Pasteur Red, Fermirouge	Red	Proven performers, unlikely to stick	Bring out varietal character
RC212	Red	Gentle extraction	Excellent for lighter reds
D21	Red	Steady performer, tolerates high alcohol	Makes for big, structured wines
Pasteur White, Fermiblanc	White	Old reliables, never miss a beat	Bring out varietal character
D47	White	Steady performer, tolerates high alcohol	Brings out varietal character
QA23	White	Gentle action, good at cool temperatures	Enhances fruity/floral aromatics
EC1118, Uvaferm 43	Either	Powerful, tolerate high alcohol, good for re-starting stuck/sluggish fermentations	Relatively neutral, don't contribute aromas and flavors of their own

You can find information on where to obtain these and other yeast strains, and a range of other microbes, chemicals, and additives in Appendix C.

Re-hydrating and adding yeast

If you simply sprinkle some yeast on grapes or juice in a fermenter, it will probably work. But all the yeast suppliers recommend — and I strongly endorse this — *rehydrating* the dried yeast first in a little warm water. Rehydration is a critical step when you're adding pounds and pounds of yeast to a huge commercial winery tank, and it's just as important in your garage.

The extra step of rehydrating eases the yeast's transition from chilled and inert to warm and active by providing an intermediate way station — a little warmth, water, and oxygen — before full immersion in the juice or grapes.

Instructions for different yeast strains from different producers may vary slightly. The typical steps go like this:

1. **Warm half a cup (120 milliliters) of water (preferably distilled water, if you have it) to about 90° to 95°F (32° to 35°C), either from the hot water tap or by briefly warming it in the microwave.**

   Measure the water temperature with a thermometer the first few times to learn the feel of this temperature range. It should be warm to the touch, but not so hot you yank your finger out (remember, your own temperature is 98.6°F or 37°C).

2. **Open the yeast package and sprinkle the contents on top of the water, without stirring.**

3. **Let the mixture sit for 15 minutes to rehydrate the yeast.**

4. **Stir the mixture gently to distribute the yeast, and pour onto the crushed grapes or into the juice in your fermenter.**

That's it. Rehydration takes a little more work than just dumping yeast in, but it's well worth the trouble. Getting your yeast going reliably and quickly gets you past the preliminaries and into the fun part of fermentation. Letting your grapes or juice just sit there a couple days because your yeast died of shock is a ticket to spoilage.

The small home-winemaking yeast packages are designed to *inoculate* — populate with a particular microbe — 5 to 10 gallons (20 to 40 liters) of potential wine. In my experience, a packet can often stretch further than that; you just need a little more time to build up a sufficient population to do the job. If you're fermenting, say, two 5-gallon carboys of Chardonnay, one small packet split among them should be fine. Similarly, a single 5-gram dose of yeast can handle 200 to 300 pounds (about 90 to 135 kilograms) of crushed red grapes, which might yield 15 to 20 gallons (60 to 75 liters) of wine. To get your fermentation going a few hours faster, add a little more — two packets instead of one. In other words, don't get tied up in knots about the precise dosage.

Although most home winemakers work with packets of active dry yeast, some yeast producers also sell home-scale batches of liquid yeast in small foil pouches or bottles. Yeast, in whatever form, is pretty much yeast. The liquid preparations let you can skip the rehydration step, but offer a much narrower range of yeast strain choices. Information on obtaining liquid wine yeast appears in Appendix C.

While you're waiting to use your yeast, treat it right. To keep the yeast immobilized until its time has come, keep it refrigerated, not frozen. A couple of days of shipping or a couple of days at room temperature won't spoil it, but longer-term refrigeration is best. After a package is open, humidity can creep in, so saving half a packet of yeast for later may not work. Properly stored yeast, still in the original, unopened package, can potentially stay active for months.

Feeding your yeast, but not too much

Yeast needs more than sugar to stay happy; the grape juice needs to provide several vitamins and other nutrients, the main dish being a sufficient supply of nitrogen. Many grapes contain enough nutrients for fermentation, and most yeast strains can tolerate a little shortage here and there. But some soils are particularly nutrient poor and some harvests are especially problematic, and even otherwise healthy grapes can be nutrient-deficient, with the potential for a stuck fermentation that shuts down the action.

To remedy the problem of nutrient deficiency, several products on the market provide either simple nitrogen — in the form of DAP, *diammonium phosphate* — or a cocktail of useful boosters. They work well, don't cost much, and come with instructions about how many grams or teaspoons to add for a certain volume of juice.

But the problem is, how do you know exactly what your juice needs and how much? The answer is, unfortunately, you usually don't. Commercial winery labs can measure nutrient levels and treat their wines accordingly, but home winemakers generally have to guess. If you guess too low on nutrition requirements, or simply hope for the best and add nothing, you raise the chances of a sluggish or stuck fermentation. If you guess too high — adding much more than your juice needs — you may put your yeast in overdrive, so that it finishes the fermentation without pulling out all the interesting aromatic goodies. (One winemaker I know describes this as "feeding your children only on bon-bons.") Worse yet, overfeeding, especially through excessive amounts of straight, nitrogen-rich DAP, leaves a bountiful supply of nutrients behind, after fermentation, which is a dinner invitation for a host of spoilage microbes.

When I don't know my grape source well and have no clue about the grapes' nutritional status, I split the difference in the spirit of safe winemaking. Just for insurance:

- ✔ At the beginning of fermentation, when you add the yeast, also add one-quarter of the vendor's suggested dosage of a broad-based, multi-nutrient additive, such as Fermaid-K or Superfood (the instructions usually call for dissolving the nutrient in water first, so be sure to follow those directions).

- ✔ Once the fermentation gets going, add another one-quarter dose of nutrient to keep the yeast happy.

- ✔ If the fermentation is steadily moving along, add another quarter does a day or two later. But if it's burning sugar at warp speed, stop; that's enough.

- ✔ In any case, once the fermentation is halfway done — half the sugar has gone to alcohol — stop adding more nutrient; all it can do is backfire by feeding things other than your yeast.

If the fermentation stalls out entirely, nitrogen nutrients probably won't help. Stir the wine, and perhaps add some yeast hulls. If you end up with a thoroughly stuck fermentation (unlikely but certainly possible), you'll need more than nutrients; see the final section of this chapter, "Troubleshooting a Stuck Fermentation: When the Fermentation Won't Ferment."

If you work with the same fruit from the same vineyard for several years, you'll get to know the nutritional needs of the grapes from experience and can handle the feeding chores accordingly.

Monitoring and Massaging Fermentation

When the yeast starts doing what yeast does, 99 percent of the fermentation will take care of itself. Your job as winemaker — actually, I think of myself as the winemaker's assistant, and the yeast as the winemaker — is to keep track of how things are going, fiddle with some environmental variables such as oxygen and temperature, and sniff out any problems that arise. Incredibly, when the winemaking is all done, you get the credit anyway.

Punching down reds

Red wine fermentations require you to exert yourself a bit. As the fermentation proceeds and the yeast population multiplies exponentially, greater and greater amounts of carbon dioxide gas (CO_2) are given off. From start to finish, a wine fermentation creates over 50 times its volume in CO_2. The escaping CO_2 provides a kind of protective blanket covering the wine, pushing the oxygen in the air away from the scene. This constant carbonation pushes the crushed grapes and skins ever upward, creating a floating mass on top known as the *cap*. Seeing a cap form on your red fermentation is good news, proof that things are in full swing, and a sign that you need to swing into action, too.

If all the grape skins are floating on top, the liquid below can't extract color compounds, tannins, or flavors, which remain trapped in the drying cap. As the fermentation warms up, the cap becomes the hottest part, potentially overheating and killing off some of the yeast. Pushed to the top, the cap is exposed to the surrounding air, with its stray microbes, possibly fruit flies, and other intruders.

The solution is a procedure called *punchdown* — using a flat-ended tool to push the grapes in the cap back down into the liquid juice/wine. The goal is keeping the cap wet, so do the punchdown with gentle, steady pressure, not rapid, hard strokes. Don't treat your grapes like mashed potatoes even though the punchdown tool, as shown in Figure 6-2, could be made from a potato masher.

Figure 6-2:
Punching
the cap
back into
the pool.

For best results, do a thorough punchdown of the entire cap two or three times a day, perhaps more often for more extraction, through to the end of fermentation — a week to ten days from the start. This irrigates the grapes and skins, keeps the goodies flowing into the solution, and evens out the temperature in the fermenter.

Checking temperature

When the yeast gets down to business, the onset of fermentation is obvious: The red grapes in your fermenter start hissing at you, the white juice in carboys develops a head of foam, and the airlocks on the carboys start gurgling audibly.

As a rule, white wines ferment best at cool temperatures, in the 50° to 60°F (10° to 16°C) range; barrel-fermented whites go a few degrees higher. Depending on the temperature your white juice started at, it may take a day or two to get up or down to that range.

Making sure the temperature is right, or as close to right as you can make it, is worthwhile (a point I emphasize in more detail in Chapter 4). Generally with whites, the issue is getting the temperatures cool enough, which may mean putting carboys in tubs with ice, moving them outside in the cool night air, swapping them in and out of a spare refrigerator, or rigging up air conditioning.

When a white fermentation is nearly complete, allowing the temperature to rise a bit — into the 60s Fahrenheit/high teens Celsius — can help finish off the last little bit of sugar.

Reds as a rule need to spend a day or two at 80° to 85°F (26° to 29°C) to get complete extraction from the skins. The grapes will likely start the fermentation at a lower temperature, and they may take two or even three days to get into this range. In general, the earlier a red fermentation hits its temperature stride, the better. Since most home fermentations are done on a small scale — a few hundred pounds of grapes — yeast activity alone may not get the temperature high enough. The classic helper is an electric blanket, wrapped around the outside of the fermenter and cranked up as high as needed. (I offer my tried-and-true blanket tips in Chapter 4.)

If you use an electric blanket, make sure to monitor the fermentation temperature carefully and often — at least twice a day. The temperature can rise rapidly and spike past where you want it, up above 90°F (32°C), which can eventually kill off your yeast. A short time in that range, fine; a long time way over that range, trouble.

When a red fermentation is in its warmest phase, the conversion of sugar to alcohol happens rapidly. After a peak day or two, the yeast activity starts to slow down — the yeast's reaction to less sugar and more alcohol — and generate less heat. Your temperatures should start dropping. If the ambient temperature where you're doing the fermentation is balmy, you can turn the blanket off; if it's chilly, keep it on but turn it down. Reds can finish fermentation nicely at as low as 65°F (18°C).

To stay on top of just how well and how fast your fermentation is going, you need to check the temperature and the conversion of sugar to alcohol at least twice a day. Check the temperature with a glass-cased thermometer large enough to read easily when it's covered with sugary juice/wine.

Taking your wine's temperature involves several small steps:

1. **If you're checking a red wine fermentation, test right after a punch-down so that you're reading the overall temperature, not the temperature of the cap.**

   See the preceding section, "Punching down reds."

2. **Make sure the thermometer is clean — preferably dip it in a solution of SO_2 to sanitize it — to avoid spreading microbes.**

3. **Submerge the thermometer entirely into fermenting red grapes, or float it in the fermenting juice in a carboy, and give it 15 seconds to register the temperature.**

4. **Pull the thermometer out, read the temperature, and write it down in your winemaking log along with the date and time.** (See Chapter 3 for more about keeping a winemaking log.)

To make sure your thermometer doesn't get lost among the red grapes, or doesn't fall out of reach inside a white wine carboy, tie a string around it to hold on to. Trust me, this simple step prevents a great deal of irritation.

Disappearing sugar, emerging ethanol

Besides temperature, the other element to check twice a day is the progress of the fermentation. Is the sugar going away, and the alcohol arriving as predicted, or does all this sound and fury signify zilch?

The tool for tracking this transformation of sugar to alcohol is a *hydrometer* — a long necked glass tube that looks something like a thermometer but is calibrated and marked to indicate sugar and potential alcohol in liquids. The hydrometer sits inside a small cylindrical stand that holds the wine sample, and the level at which the hydrometer floats — the markings right at the surface level of the wine — give the relevant information. Figure 6-3 shows a hydrometer at work.

Technically, a hydrometer measures *specific gravity*, the density of the test liquid relative to water; but you're interested in how the hydrometer translates that into sugar and potential alcohol.

One line of graduated markings on a standard hydrometer is marked Brix (or perhaps Balling — a similar scale), and another scale next to it is labeled *potential alcohol* — the amount of alcohol that can be created by conversion of the full amount of remaining sugar measured on the Brix scale. If, for example, your hydrometer floats at 10° Brix, it will also indicate a little over 5 percent potential alcohol. The sidebar in this chapter on "Fermentation math" gives more technical detail about how hydrometers and alcohol conversion work; your key job is watching the Brix drop in your fermentation day-to-day.

Because you need to take hydrometer and temperature readings twice a day, doing both of these measurements at the same time is most efficient.

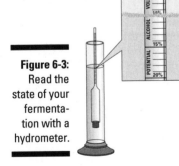

Figure 6-3:
Read the state of your fermentation with a hydrometer.

Here are the steps in a hydrometer reading:

1. **Make sure the hydrometer and its column stand are both clean before each use.**

2. **Do a punchdown if you're measuring a red wine fermentation.**

   Mixing the cap down into the wine makes the liquid more available for sampling. (See the earlier section, "Punching down reds.")

3. **Draw out a sample.**

   For white wine fermenting in a carboy or barrel, draw off a sample using a thief, like the one shown in Figure 6-4, and release it through a funnel into the hydrometer stand until the hydrometer floats freely. (You also use a thief to draw wine for tasting, which is what the figure shows.)

   For reds, scoop a sample with a measuring cup and drain it through a sieve into a small pail, then pour the liquid through a small funnel into the hydrometer column until the hydrometer floats freely.

4. **Note the Brix reading on the hydrometer at the surface level of the wine and record it in your winemaking log book, along with the date and time.**

5. **Return the wine to its fermenter and rinse the hydrometer and stand to have it ready for the next sample.**

Once a fermentation is established, white wines proceed slowly and gently, but steadily. As a rule, if you can keep the fermentation temperature cool, down around 55°F (13°C), your white should ideally convert 1 percent of its sugar to alcohol each day. So if you start with juice from grapes that are, for example, 22° Brix — 22 percent sugar — the gradual conversion of sugar to alcohol should take about three weeks, dropping 1 percent a day.

Figure 6-4:
Yes, it's a wine thief, but it's your wine thief.

Fermentation math

This book consistently uses Brix as the method of measuring sugar content in juice and wine. However, both the Balling scale and the Plato scale are used. All three are conventions for measuring *specific gravity* — the presence of varying amounts of dissolved solids (such as sugar) relative to pure water. They differ mainly in the standard temperature they assume for the liquid being measured. For home winemaking purposes, the differences are so minor as to be irrelevant. Brix it is.

The math for conversion of sugar to alcohol is slightly inexact, because different juices contain slightly varying amounts of irreducible, unfermentable sugars. As a wine industry rule, each percentage of sugar — each Brix degree —

converts to 0.55 percent alcohol. Grapes that arrive at 23° Brix, for example, will normally produce wine with about 12.6 percent alcohol. Grapes that show up at 29° Brix, however, will ferment out to nearly 16 percent alcohol — unheard of two decades ago, but not uncommon in high-end California wine these days.

Many of the yeast strains on today's market can tolerate high alcohol levels and continue working up to 17 or 18 percent alcohol. But that doesn't mean the yeasts produce more alcohol per chunk of sugar, just that they are willing to put up with more of it. Winemakers who blame the yeast for the high alcohol of their wines are most likely underestimating the sugar their grapes started with.

Most home red wine fermentations take about a week, give or take a day, but the pace and progress can be all over the map. The Brix level of red grapes and wine falls much more rapidly. For the first couple of days, the yeast will primarily be reproducing — called the *lag phase* — building up the population, and won't consume much sugar. Then, as the fermentation heats up, the Brix level will drop in a hurry, as much as 10° or more in a single day. Once the Brix is down into low single digits, the final conversion proceeds more slowly to the finish line.

Sniffing, slurping, and sensing your fermentation

Besides monitoring the rise and fall of temperature and the declining Brix level, put your own sensory equipment to work — your eyes, ears, nose, and taste buds. Seeing, smelling, and tasting the transformation is the best fun in winemaking — and a great early warning system for finding potential troubles.

You probably don't spend much time listening to wine; sure, you hear a cork pop here and a gurgle into the glass there, but we mostly listen to other people talking about wine. However, during fermentation, your ears give you the first clue that things are off and running. Wines in carboys start releasing carbon dioxide up and out through the airlocks, which makes a gurgling sound; all you have to do is walk into the room to hear the action. Red wine fermentations make a louder and louder fizz, like an overflowing glass of bubbly or beer, and for the same reason — carbon dioxide escaping through the cap of skins. If your wine doesn't make any noise, you have a problem.

Your eyes come into play watching the head of foam build on whites in carboys and seeing the cap of red skins puff up like a soufflé inside your fermenter. Figure 6-5 shows the not-so-pretty sight of fermenting whites and pinks. Even better, as you continue to pull samples to measure the progress of fermentation, the color of reds changes visibly day by day, from light pink to deep pink to serious red to nearly opaque purple-black. From a production control point of view, the color change lets you know you're making progress; from a purely sensory, hedonistic point of view, the first few times you witness this transformation are inspirational.

Your nose is without doubt the most important quality control tool in your winery. Fermentations announce how they are faring by the volatile aromatic compounds they spin off. Both reds and whites should dispense vaguely fruity aromas, some yeasty smells — like bread dough rising — and a heady bit of alcohol vapor, especially in reds, which ferment at higher temperatures. Fermenting wine doesn't smell as elegant as finished, bottled wine, but it smells clean, exuberant, and inviting.

Figure 6-5:
It's hard to believe that this unappetizing gunk becomes clean, clear wine.

Eileen Raphael

But if you start to pick up aromas that remind you of vinegar or nail polish remover or rotten eggs and spoiled garlic, and you get that whiff more than once, head for the "Troubleshooting a Stuck Fermentation: When the Fermentation Won't Ferment" section later in this chapter. Your nose can pick up troublesome aromas before any lab equipment and before any serious damage is done.

Your taste buds come in handy, too. Make sure to taste your grapes and juice before fermentation starts, and then check back every now and then as the drama unfolds. When you pull samples for hydrometer readings, take a little sip. No, you don't want to drink a glass of this stuff, full of yeast and pieces of grape skins and perhaps the occasional fruit fly. You can, however, and s of grape skins and perhaps the occasional fruit fly. You can, however, experience the day-by-day makeover of grape juice into wine, feel the alcohol coming on, taste the changing balance, and feel the acidity tingle in your mouth.

The changes that occur during the few days of fermentation are astonishing, like the changes a child goes through in the first year or two of life — learning to walk, learning to talk, learning to talk back . . . you don't want to miss this age.

Knowing when it's done and what to do then

Just as fermentation lets you know it's happening, it lets you know when it's done, too. The foamy scum on the top of white wines dies down, and starting at the top, the wine slowly begins to clarify, letting some light through and accumulating the sediment of dead yeast at the bottom of the container. Reds stop hissing, and the cap of skins starts falling back into the wine soup, while the temperature drops. These are all clear signs that your wine is nearing *dryness* — the complete conversion of sugar to alcohol.

Hydrometer readings are an important indicator of the stage of your fermentation. When the hydrometer registers that your wine is down to zero Brix and zero potential alcohol, you are close to dry — but not there quite yet. The hydrometer measures the density of your sample as compared to the density of water, and when your wine has 10 to 15 percent alcohol in it, it's less dense than water — below zero on the hydrometer. (Don't worry, the hydrometer has markings for this.) No precise formula exists for how far below zero you have to get, but something in the negative $1\frac{1}{2}$ to $2°$ Brix range is the ballpark.

A more exact test for dryness, which you can easily do at home and should, uses Clinitest tablets. (These tablets are designed for testing the sugar level in urine, but pay no mind.) Following the instructions that come with the tablets, put a few drops of wine, a few drops of water, and a tablet into a small test tube and compare the resulting color to a color chart to see if any sugar is still in the wine. Alternatively, have a winemaking shop do the analysis.

When whites get to dryness, let them sit a week or two so they can continue to clarify and more dead yeast can head for the bottom. Keep the airlocks tightly sealed and filled with water on carboys to keep air out and the remaining carbon dioxide in as a protective blanket. If you have a canister of carbon dioxide, shoot a little gas into the top of the carboy to protect the wine from oxygen. After a while, the partially clarified wine can be racked off the bottom sludge into a new container for further aging. (Chapter 7 covers the ins and outs of racking.)

Pressing Reds

Reds get pressed after fermentation is complete, since the fermentation needs contact time with the skins to extract color, flavor, and texture compounds, making the timing and techniques for pressing a little different.

Timing red pressing

Most reds are pressed when all the sugar is fermented and the wine has gone dry. Hydrometer readings are the best indication, and because the presence of alcohol changes the density of the liquid, the hydrometer reading should be just slightly into negative territory — as though the wine contained less than zero Brix. The last little bit of fermentation can continue in barrels or carboys, so the wine doesn't have to be absolutely dry at pressing time.

Sometimes, in fact, good winemaking calls for pressing before dryness, when the budding wine still has from 2° to 4° Brix of sugar remaining. By that point in a red fermentation, all the color compounds have been extracted, as well as all of the aromatic and flavor compounds; what continues to be extracted is tannin, an important component of the structure of sturdy red wines.

Sometimes, however, the winemaker — that would be you — wants a lighter wine, a juicy, summer-weight, picnic-style wine that has no need to age and no need for a lot of tannin. And sometimes, by continually tasting your red wine as it ferments, you may notice that it has already picked up plenty of tannin and is becoming unpleasantly astringent. In these cases, pressing a little before dryness is a good decision. The wine will still go dry, just without the tannin buildup. (More on early pressing in Chapter 11.)

Squeezing your reds

Home-style red wines are almost universally separated from their used-up skins and seeds with basket presses, equipment described in Chapter 3. Grapes and wine get scooped by the pailful from the fermenter and dumped into the press; the wooden or metal slats or screen keep the skins and seeds inside the press; and the wine flows through and into a bucket to catch it. More and more pressure is exerted by a ratchet gear and wooden plates, squeezing wine from the grapes. Reds get exposed to a hefty final dose of oxygen along the way, and that's just fine. They're young. They can take it at this stage.

Chapter 5 shows the parts of a basket press as part of the discussion of pressing white grapes, so you can turn there to see what the press looks like and the full detail of how things work. The basic steps for pressing a batch of fermented red grapes and wine go like this:

1. **Check that all the parts of the press that come in contact with the grapes and wine — the metal base, the wooden slats, the wooden half-moons that go on top of the grapes, the central pole on which the ratchet sits — are clean.**

   Rinse and scrub with water and a light SO_2 rinse as needed.

2. **Assemble the press, making sure that the wine can flow to the lip of the base and drain off into a container.**

3. **Place a bucket under the lip of the press base, and place a fine-mesh strainer over the bucket to strain seeds and skins out of the wine.**

4. **Scoop the fermented grapes and wine from the fermenter into the press; wine will immediately begin to flow through the slats, over the lip, through the sieve, and into the bucket.**

   Pay attention to how much wine goes into the press and how fast — too much too quickly can overrun your waiting bucket.

5. **When the bucket is mostly full, swap it out to the side, swap in another bucket and sieve, and empty the full bucket of wine into a storage container (most likely an empty, clean carboy).**

6. **Repeat Steps 4 and 5 until all the grapes and wine have been transferred to the press.**

   If some seeds are left at the bottom of the fermenter, leave them there.

7. **Use the half moons, wood blocks, and the ratchet mechanism to increase pressure on the grapes and squeeze the wine out and into waiting buckets.**

   Continue until the flow of wine has reduced to a bare trickle and it becomes quite difficult to keep working the ratchet.

8. **If more grapes and wine are left un-pressed, dismantle the sides of the press, remove the cake of skins and seeds, and start over.**

9. **Take everything apart and clean it before storage.**

The wine that flows out of the press without any added pressure — called *free run* — and the wine that comes only with the ratchet — called *press wine* — may have somewhat different characteristics. The free run portion may be lighter and fruitier, and the press wine heavier with tannins and pigments extracted from the skins in the final push in the press. If you have enough wine to fill two or more storage containers, it can be instructive to keep the two kinds of wine separate for a while, so you can taste the difference and possibly use the two batches in different ways — just remember to label them.

Put wine from a red pressing immediately into sealed storage containers to protect it from oxygen. That might mean a barrel — more on this option in Chapter 11 — or one or more carboys. My preference is to put red wine after pressing into carboys and let it settle out the gross sludge from the fermentation for a week or two, and then put the wine into its long-term home.

Troubleshooting a Stuck Fermentation: When the Fermentation Won't Ferment

The vast majority of home wine fermentations finish off just fine, going through their paces in a fairly routine way. This section deals with the rare case when that doesn't happen and the fermentation grinds to a halt before it's complete. With luck, you may never need to read this section.

Recognizing the signs and scents of trouble

Fermentation stops or slows to an unacceptable crawl when the yeasts come under too much stress. Excessive heat can cook them; excessive cold can shut them down. More likely, your yeasts might run out of necessary nutrients before their job of converting sugar to alcohol is done, or the yeast strain at work in your fermentation may no longer be able to tolerate the level of alcohol it has helped create.

One way to check for a stuck or sluggish fermentation is by monitoring the fermentation with hydrometer readings (see the earlier section "Disappearing sugar, emerging ethanol"). If the Brix level of your fermentation stops dropping, or slows unexpectedly, a problem could be developing. If this work stoppage persists, take action, as I describe later in this section.

Your nose is the other early warning system. As you sniff your fermentation — during punchdowns and sample testing for reds, when the airlocks come off for sampling whites in carboys — be alert for off odors. The telltale sign of a stuck fermentation is the aroma of hydrogen sulfide, an unpleasant substance that stressed yeast produces, which resembles the smell of rotten eggs — in fact, it is the smell of rotten eggs. If a fermentation stays stuck for several days, other unpleasant smells may join the aromatic chorus. When fermentation stops, bacteria can have a field day, generating sharp, vinegar-like aromas, or something resembling nail polish remover. I share techniques for getting rid of these and other forms of stink in Chapter 8; but step one is to stop their production by getting the fermentation going again.

Checking first things first

If your fermentation starts to stick, don't panic. Start by checking and treating the simplest possible causes immediately:

- ✔ **Temperature:** If your wine's temperature is out of range, or on the margin, do whatever it takes to get it on track (see the earlier "Checking temperature" section for tips).

- ✔ **More yeast:** Try again to build up a yeast population by re-inoculating with another dose of rehydrated yeast. If you used some yeast that had been lying around for a while, get fresh yeast. If you used a yeast with low alcohol tolerance, try one with a high tolerance.

- ✔ **Water:** Water may help, but only sometimes. If you started with grapes at a very high Brix level, and have already achieved a high alcohol level — 14 percent or more — and still have sugar left to burn, you may need to dilute the wine, which lowers the alcohol and gives the yeast a fighting chance. Math for water additions can be found in Chapter 5; use enough to lower alcohol by a percent or two; distilled water is best. This is a last resort, and you might as well go for a full re-start, which the following section describes.

Adding nutrients is likely *not* a good idea if your fermentation is stuck near the end of sugar conversion; by then, it's too late for nutrient therapy.

While you try these first-aid measures, make sure to protect your wine from oxygen and potential spoilage. Keep carboys sealed with airlocks with their water topped up, and keep the lids on your red fermenters. If you have a canister of CO_2, pump some in to fill the headspace in carboys and blanket the grapes in red fermenters.

If your fermentation doesn't move in a couple days, it's time for a full restart.

Re-starting a stuck fermentation

Fermentations get stuck when yeast undergoes too much stress. Re-starting a fermentation means giving some fresh yeast a truly supportive environment, so the happy yeast can pick up where the old yeast left off.

Start by removing a significant portion of the stuck wine — at least 5 percent, maybe ten percent. Remove wine only; leave any red grapes where they are. Put the wine into a container with a little headspace, room enough for a renewed fermentation to make some foam. Then treat the re-start wine according to the following steps:

1. **Add water.**

   Dilute the starter wine with a 20 percent addition of water, significantly lowering the alcohol level and relieving that stress on the yeast.

2. **Add fresh yeast.**

   To prime the re-start, use the appropriate amount of a yeast strain optimized for high alcohol and a strong finish — EC1118, Pris de Mousse, and Uvaferm 43 are good choices.

   Rehydrate as directed before adding.

3. **Add yeast nutrient.**

   Add a supply of broad-based yeast nutrient to the re-start wine, in a dosage corresponding to the volume of wine being doctored.

4. **Add sugar.**

   If your wine is stuck with a good deal of sugar left — registering a Brix still in the high single digits or higher — skip this step.

   If the wine is stuck at the end of fermentation, down around 1° or 2° Brix, bump the sugar in the treated sample up to 4° or 5° Brix. (Chapter 5 discusses calculating and dissolving sugar additions.) Test with a hydrometer to make sure your new yeast has plenty to gnaw on.

5. **Adjust the temperature.**

   The re-start wine, red or white, should be warm enough to get going quickly, at least at 65°F (18°C).

Expect the re-start wine to show the first signs of fermentation in 24 to 36 hours, in the form of bubbles around the rim. By two or three days, it should be bubbling away vigorously. Pour it into the stuck wine, either all at once for a small batch or in two or three staged additions over 24 hours. Within a day or two, the charged-up yeast from the re-start wine should kick-start the process and resume the fermentation. In truly hard cases, repeat as necessary.

Chapter 7

Doing the Post-Fermentation Tango

*Y*our white wines are dry, your reds are pressed, your winery space is tidy again, and the biggest part of the heavy manual labor is over. However, you can't sit back and pat yourself on the back just yet. Now is the time to consolidate all the gains you and your wine made during fermentation and ease onto the glide path of aging. Sure, celebrate the last pressing with a bottle of something or other — and then get out your checklist.

Cleaning Up Your Wine

Besides all the chemical changes and the replacement of sugar with alcohol, your brand new wine has something else it didn't have when it was grape juice — lots of sludge. The millions of yeast cells that made the wine for you are now dead, but neither gone nor forgotten: They expired smack dab in the middle of your wine.

Spent yeast is known as *lees.* The large volume of spent yeast (and sometimes particles of skins, seeds, fruit flies, and so on) right after pressing are the *gross lees;* after the worst of these leftovers have been removed, you still have the *fine lees.*

Whatever the amount of lees, you don't want them in your wine glass. Getting the lees out — and possibly making some use of them in the meantime — is a major theme in your winemaking from post-fermentation to bottling.

The first step on the road to clarification comes soon after fermentation completes: for whites, when the bubbling stops and gunk starts falling to the bottom; for reds, a few days after pressing, when the worst fermentation fall-out has settled. To better understand how your wine has fared, clean it up a bit with the first racking.

Practicing the art of racking

Thanks to our old friend gravity, the sludge problem mostly solves itself. Millions of yeast cells are suspended in the wine at first, but sooner or later, they fall to the bottom of the container. This process takes anywhere from a couple of months to a couple of years, depending on how dirty the wine is to begin with, how much wine you have, and how you store it.

Sucking up your siphoning skills

When the first thick, visible layer of lees collects on the bottom of your carboy or barrel in a week or so, move the clean(er) wine away from the sludge by *racking* — siphoning the wine into another container and leaving the grosser lees behind. This is a little more complicated than it sounds.

Home winemakers do their racking with a racking tube and a length of plastic hose. Racking tubes come with *anti-sediment tips,* thimble-shaped plastic covers at the end of the tube which extend upwards half an inch (1.5 centimeters) or so. When you insert the racking tube into the bottom of a sludgy carboy or barrel, the siphoned wine can only get into the tube over the brim of the plastic tip, not directly from the bottom of the container. So, the sludge stays put, because the wine is drawn from just slightly higher up.

For the hydraulics of siphoning to work, the source container has to be higher than the target container. Suck some air out of the end of the plastic hose, drawing wine up the racking tube and into the hose, and then insert the hose in the target. Once the siphon starts, the wine will flow until it's all transferred. Figure 7-1 shows this better than any written explanation could.

Because the purpose of racking is to leave the sludge behind, try not to stir things up with the tip of the racking tube. In carboy racking, the best spot for the tip of the racking tube is along the bottom edge, the crease between the bottom and side of the carboy. Once the wine is halfway siphoned, tilt the carboy slowly and gently until the racking tube is straight-up vertical; that way, you stir the lees less and get the most wine with the least sludge.

All of this may sound obvious, but getting the siphon flow to work, without letting air bubbles stop the suction, or spilling wine on your floor, or accidentally getting mouthfuls of wine, takes some practice. If you're not a veteran siphon sucker, practice with a carboy full of water and get the hang of it before you rack your wine.

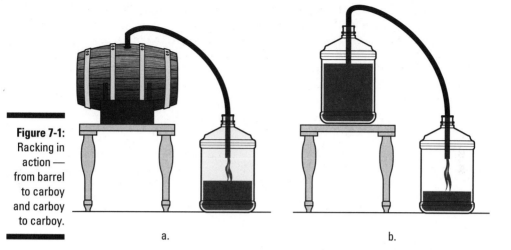

Figure 7-1:
Racking in
action —
from barrel
to carboy
and carboy
to carboy.

a.   b.

Guarding against air — or not

Once wine has been fermented and pressed, it needs to be protected against oxygen. Gassing the target container with carbon dioxide before starting the siphon helps with oxygen control; the wine flows into the target under a blanket of CO_2 and doesn't get exposed to air anywhere in the process.

Sometimes, however, aerating the wine during racking is a good idea. The prime example is when you are trying to get rid of rotten-eggy, hydrogen sulfide aromas, which could be left over from a sluggish fermentation. In this case — called *splash racking* — skip the gas, and don't insert the hose very far into the target container; let the incoming wine splash around the sides and bottom of the new container to get some fresh air.

Racking from barrels

Barrel racking has its own constraints. Commercial wineries rack their barrels using pumps to move the liquid along, not relying on gravity, and if your home operation gets sophisticated, you may do that, too. But for the rest of us, the first requirement for barrel racking is that the barrel has to be high enough for gravity to work. The bottom of the barrel has to be higher than the top of the target container, whether that's another barrel or a series of carboys. Keep this in mind before you fill the barrel in the first place.

Because of their rounded shape, barrels are hard to rack efficiently; you are likely to end up either transferring sludge or leaving good wine behind. My solution:

1. **Insert the racking tube vertically, with the tip at the low point of the bottom side of the barrel.**

2. **Siphon until the flow stops.**

3. **Turn the barrel upside down and drain the remainder, sludgy as it is, through a sieve into a bucket.**

   Put that dirty remnant into a gallon or half-gallon jug (2 to 4 liters), and after a day or two, it will separate into liquid and solid, letting you reclaim quite a bit of wine.

The good news about barrels is that, for reasons not well understood, wine clarifies faster in barrels than it does in tanks or glass. After a couple months, pull a barrel sample with a thief and look at it — you'll be surprised. White wines, done in carboys or tanks, almost always need more than racking to get crystal clear; barrel-aged reds often clarify themselves.

Experiencing the joys of lees

Dead yeasts don't ferment anything anymore, but they can still add something to the character of wine. In their new alcohol bath, yeast cells gradually surrender some of their stuffing through a process called *autolysis,* in which naturally occurring enzymes break the cells down and release certain compounds (mannoproteins and polysaccharides, if you must know) into the wine. The main impact of *sue lie* (on the lees) autolysis over time — for example, long barrel aging — is wine with enhanced, rounder, fuller mouthfeel and body. The enzymatic activity also plays an antioxidant role and can add complex aromatics.

Whether you want this in your wine or not is a stylistic choice. A squeaky-clean Sauvignon Blanc might be happier without the influence of lees, which would mean racking it earlier and more frequently. A rounded Chardonnay or a hefty red, on the other hand, might like the company of these yeast breakdown products, and benefit from having at least some lees around for a good long time. Lees are the constant companions of Champagne and other sparkling wines as they age, essential for producing creamy mouthfeel.

Doing the Post-Fermentation Checkup

Your wine just went through a tumultuous transformation, and its chemistry probably changed in surprising ways. Time for a health check-up — more or less the same tests and adjustments you made before the fermentation started.

Checking dryness

Chapter 6 discusses monitoring wine fermentation to track the rise in the level of alcohol and the drop in sugar, down to the point of *dryness* — where no sugar is left, or at least none that the surviving yeasties can chew on. When your wine is at least on the verge of dry, the Brix on your hydrometer drops down below zero — that is, lower than pure water, because the alcohol now in the wine is lighter than water. But reading a hydrometer is a less-than-precise method, so if you have not yet run a specific test for dryness, do it now.

A more sure test for dryness that you can easily do at home uses Clinitest tablets. Following the instructions that come with the tablets, put a few drops of wine, a few drops of water, and a tablet into a small test tube and compare the resulting color to a color chart to see how much, if any, sugar is still in the wine. Alternatively, take a sample to a winemaking shop for analysis.

Some wines take their sweet time, as it were, going fully dry. That last 1 percent of transformation can drag on for a while. This doesn't mean the fermentation is stuck, but with the yeast population down, the alcohol up, and the temperature down, finishing the job may take a while. If you pressed a red wine a little early, still at 3° or 4° Brix, that small remnant can take longer to ferment than the main part did.

Sooner or later you need to know that your wine is fully dry. Otherwise, it may spring back to life at the worst moment — say, after you've bottled it.

If you don't want the wine dry, but are aiming to retain some residual sugar, turn to Chapter 20 for advice on making sweet wines.

Adjusting pH

Chances are that in the course of fermentation, your wine's pH will rise slightly and end up higher than it was in the grape juice, and the total acidity will drop slightly. The reason is that some tartaric acid gets bound up in compounds that fall out of the wine.

The rise in pH may be small — only an increase of .1 or .2 — and the acidity drop likewise modest, perhaps half a gram per liter. But if your juice had a high or borderline high pH — up at 3.7 or higher — going into the fermentation, it could emerge unacceptably high. Ditto for the drop in acidity.

When the wine is dry, test the pH and the acidity — I tell you how in Chapter 3, and the proper ranges are in Chapter 6 — and make any needed adjustments to bring things back in line. Because the amount of sulfur dioxide (SO_2) needed to protect the wine from here on out varies with the pH, knocking down the pH means less need for dumping SO_2 in the wine.

Lowering acidity

Warm-weather grapes often need acid additions to get pH and balance into line; cool-climate grapes, especially North American natives and French-American hybrids, sometimes need to get rid of excess acid. If your wine's acidity is still painfully high after both primary and malolactic fermentation, *de-acidification* may be in order. Several small additions of Acidex can do the job, or one addition of potassium bicarbonate; 2 grams of potassium bicarbonate per liter will reduce total acidity by 1 gram per liter.

Adding and timing SO_2

Most, if not all, of the sulfur dioxide (SO_2) you added at the crusher before fermentation disappears by the time the wine is dry — bound up with other compounds, rendered ineffective, or just plain gone — leaving you with thoroughly unprotected wine.

The first winemaking decision here is whether you plan to put this particular batch of wine through a secondary or malolactic fermentation, discussed in "Exploring the Mysteries of the Malolactic" later on. If a malolactic is in this wine's future, do nothing about SO_2 at this point: Wait until the malolactic is completed. But if you want to forestall a malolactic fermentation — and for the majority of white and pink winemaking, that's the norm — then it's definitely sulfur time.

The post-fermentation sulfur addition (either at the end of the primary, alcoholic fermentation or the end of the malolactic) is by far the most important one in the winemaking cycle. The small addition before crushing is a routine procedure to discourage bad critters; the small addition just before bottling is insurance to keep the wine happy in its new home. The post-fermentation sulfur is the key to stabilizing your wine's microbial future.

After fermentation is complete — again, for some wines, that means after the malolactic fermentation — your wine has no further need for microbes. Their useful work is done; from this point on, live microbes can only cause trouble. Will the wine's chemistry keep changing and evolving? Yes, absolutely. Does it need any microbes as helpers? Nope. Your job is to put them to rest.

Fortunately, most of the bugs working on your wine's behalf have died off — they've run out of sugar, or expired from the alcohol, or met some other natural fate. But among the survivors may be sleeper cells, zombie microbes just waiting for a comeback, plus assorted uninvited life forms that happen to be in your garage. For these hangers-on, you need SO_2.

The effective, "killer dose" level for SO_2 additions varies with the pH of the wine, and the difference between one pH and another can be dramatic. A wine at pH 3.3 needs 26 parts per million (ppm); a wine at 3.7 needs 63 ppm. This is one of many reasons why accurate pH readings are essential for controlled winemaking. You can just toss in some sulfur dioxide and hope for the best, but getting a precise handle on sulfur chemistry is well worth the trouble.

Appendix D has detailed math for sulfur additions in relation to pH levels.

Exploring the Mysteries of the Malolactic

One of the first technical winemaking terms rank-and-file wine drinkers encounter is the mysterious malolactic fermentation. In a tasting room, or in the presence of a wine snob, "malolactic" or just "malo" will get tossed around, leaving half the people in the room blank-faced, afraid to admit they have no clue. After reading this section, you will be blank-faced no more.

Understanding what the heck malolactic fermentation is

Malolactic fermentation — or *malo*, or *MLF* — refers to the transformation of malic acid in wine into lactic acid. Wine grapes nearly always contain some amount of malic, although its highest concentration comes in apples, which are the source for commercial extracts of malic acid. Lactic acid shows up in milk and butter, which you may not think of as acidic at all. Gram for gram, lactic acid tastes much less sharp and strong than malic, so going through malo softens a wine. Figure 7-2 shows what goes into and out of lactic acid bacteria.

This acid trip is performed by a family of critters called *lactic acid bacteria*. They couldn't care less what your wine tastes like; they just happen to eat one acid and eject another in the course of the day. These critters float around in nature, as well as your garage, and do a more or less good job at remodeling the acid profile. Some, alas, produce truly stinky residues along the way.

The vast majority of commercial wineries, and nearly all homies, make sure to get the job done right by using a freeze-dried, carefully selected commercial strain of *Oenococcus oeni* — pronounced *E-no-caucus E-knee*.

Getting why malo matters

Turning malic acid into lactic acid changes the way a wine tastes, making it less sharp, and the way it feels in the mouth, making it smoother and fuller. You have two winemaking choices: either encourage malo or prevent it.

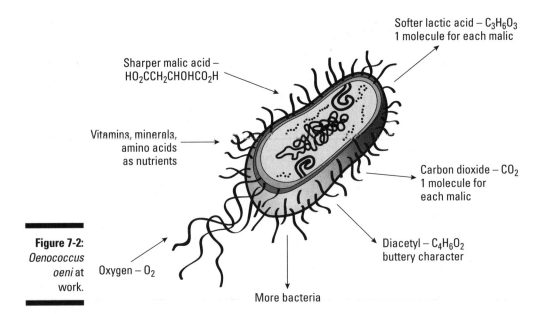

Softer lactic acid – $C_3H_6O_3$
1 molecule for each malic

Sharper malic acid –
$HO_2CCH_2CHOHCO_2H$

Vitamins, minerals,
amino acids
as nutrients

Carbon dioxide – CO_2
1 molecule for
each malic

Figure 7-2:
Oenococcus
oeni at
work.

Oxygen – O_2

Diacetyl – $C_4H_6O_2$
buttery character

More bacteria

Nearly every red wine in the world goes through malo for this reason, though a few winemakers resist in order to do something a little different. White wines are split: Many Chardonnays get the malo treatment for added fatness and buttery aromas, and many other whites — most Sauvignon Blancs, nearly every Riesling — don't.

Malo also produces *diacetyl*, a compound that gives a buttery aroma, something you may or may not want in your white wine. The impact of malolactic fermentation on whites is greater, since their relative delicacy shows off textural and aromatic changes more easily.

Choosing one route or another isn't a matter of right or wrong, but one of personal taste based on the wine styles you like to drink. If your wine contains a large proportion of malic acid, as much as a third of the total — and you can test for this at home — converting it to lactic will have a big impact, maybe more than you want. On the other hand, if your wine has only a tiny bit of malic, you may want to just turn it into malic, making your wine more stable.

To malo or not to malo is a major wine stability issue; you can't ignore it. Those same stray lactic acid bacteria that fermented spontaneous malolactics for centuries might do that in your winery, too, when you least expect it. My dear brother Byron, to whom this book is dedicated, is among the legions of home winemakers who made perfectly good wine for several years, never quite getting clear on the malo thing, and then had a vintage go through malo in the bottle, blowing out the corks. Finish it or stop it.

Doing the deed

To promote malolactic fermentation, add a freeze-dried bacterial starter to your wine after the alcoholic fermentation is complete — don't do both at once or you'll risk setting up a competition for nutrients. The standard packages from winemaking shops or online suppliers contain enough frozen bacteria to handle about 65 gallons (250 liters) of wine. While you're at it, add a bit of malolactic nutrient — not the same stuff as yeast nutrient! — to make sure the bacteria are cheerful and productive.

After you open the packaging on malolactic bacteria, any unused portion exposed to air may not be worth much for long. If you have more than one wine headed for malo, save money — these bacteria are more expensive than yeast packets — by waiting until all the wines are ready for inoculation and make good use of the standard 65-gallon (250-liter) capacity packet.

Besides being fond of malic acid, malolactic bacteria have other needs and preferences. They don't like low temperatures, and so rapid, successful malolactic fermentation works best at 65°F (18°C) or higher, and that goes for white wines as well as reds. Low pH, below 3.3, can also inhibit bacterial activity, as can high ethanol. Under favorable conditions, malolactic fermentation should complete in two to three weeks; under stress, it may take many times that long. Because you want to move on to making the major SO_2 addition and protecting your wine, the sooner malo is completed, the better.

Oak barrels that have been home to a malolactic fermentation in one vintage almost always provoke a malolactic the next time they're filled; getting rid of the critters would require destroying the barrel. Even so, inoculating barrel wines with a starter is good practice, to make sure a reliable strain is at work and that the process completes as soon as possible.

Sprinkling in some malo pixie dust isn't enough. You have to test the wine to make sure the malo actually finished completely; otherwise, it will bite you later. Strip tests and paper chromatography tests are readily available. And while you're at it, re-test the pH and the total acidity; malo typically drops acidity a small amount, and raises pH by 0.1 to 0.3 units.

Stopping malo in its tracks

Unfortunately, preventing a malolactic fermentation can be more difficult than encouraging it. Commercial wineries employ sterile filtration, using a filter medium that pulls out any lactic acid bacteria (as well as yeast and other things) that happen to be around, and the vast majority of the white wine in the world gets processed this way. Accomplishing a truly sterile filtration in your home winery is next to impossible.

Your first line of defense against malo is keeping wine pH low, down under 3.4 or less for whites. Right behind pH comes adding SO_2 at a level corresponding to the wine's pH promptly after the primary fermentation. Deliver that knockout punch, keep your containers topped up and away from air, and periodically refresh the SO_2 with small additions (25 ppm) at racking time, and you should be covered. Otherwise, you're taking your chances.

For my non-malolactic whites — which are the only kind I make — I also add 250 ppm of *lysozyme*, an egg-white-derived enzyme that kills most but not all lactic acid bacteria, after the alcoholic fermentation is complete. Yet another line of insurance.

Even if you take steps to squash the malolactic, test your wine after a month or so for signs of malolactic activity. You may be surprised. If a malo fermentation is happening despite your efforts, you may need to check your SO_2 levels or add the lysozyme you skipped earlier — or you may decide to just go with the flow, add some bacterial starter, and push the malo to completion. Either way, test and get your wine stable.

Two final cautions: If preventing malolactic fermentation entirely requires eternal vigilance, stabilizing a partial malo at home — for example, a blend of one carboy with malo and one without — is beyond risky. And if you're making a sweet wine and have killed off the yeast with potassium sorbate (see Chapter 20), unplanned malolactic activity will produce an extremely unpleasant, geranium-leaf odor — so be more than careful.

Evaluating Wine at the Yucky Stage

Even after a racking to clean up your post-fermentation wine, it's not a pretty sight. Especially in see-through carboys, white wines still look like vegetable purée and reds are impossibly murky. Infant wine is full of carbon dioxide from the fermentation, making it slightly spritzy in the mouth; strange, yeasty aromas linger; and the suspended dead yeast cells in your trial sip may make you want to floss. However, your job is to sniff and taste the wine anyway.

Sniffing out trouble

The first cut in post-fermentation tasting is sniffing out — or sipping out — trouble. At this point, problems are easier to identify and important to address. The sooner you fix any potential wine fault, the less work you have to do, and the happier both you and your wine will be.

Hydrogen sulfide

The most likely culprit right after fermentation is hydrogen sulfide, the rotten cabbage, rotten garlic, rotten egg family of unpleasant odors. Even if your fermentation went straight through to dryness without getting stuck, it may have hit a couple of hard patches along the way, and the yeast always leave little reminder aromas behind. The remedy is to immediately do another racking, this time a splash racking with intentional oxygen exposure, to neutralize the offending compounds and blow off the aromas.

 Copper neutralizes hydrogen sulfide, so some winemakers add a short length — perhaps a foot or 18 inches (30 to 45 centimeters) — of copper tubing to the end of the racking hose. The stinky wine benefits both from the cleansing power of the copper and the dose of oxygen. But depending on your wine, the rate of flow, and the nature of the copper, you could end up over-coppering your wine to the point it tastes metallic. If you try this, do a small batch first.

If one or two vigorous rackings don't clear up the problem, you need to take sterner measures. Details are in Chapter 8.

Microbial mishaps

Most of the trouble caused by rogue microbes — critters like *Brettanomyces*, a branch of the yeast family that smells like bandages and barnyards — shows up later on during aging. If your wine suffered through a long, drawn-out, stuck fermentation, lactic acid bacterial odors could linger (think sauerkraut odors); if your fermentation included moldy grapes, you could have something tasting earthy/musty/turnipy. Leftover aromas and flavors from fermentation mishaps don't easily go away and can't easily be removed; your best bet is preventing them from happening, or careful blending.

The most exotic microbe-related wine nightmare I have ever heard about is *ropiness*, in which malfunctioning bacteria produce slimy, greasy, fatty mouthfeel. This apparently happens often enough in France to have its own name, *graisse,* meaning fat. I have never had this happen, or met anyone who has had it happen; if your wine goes ropy on you, please send me an e-mail.

Tasting for trajectory

Tasting infant wine is great fun, but also frustrating. The wine exudes strange, temporary odors, good and bad, that will soon go away, and the texture is full of CO_2 bubbles and dead yeast. Making judgments about how the wine will taste in two months, let alone six years, involves considerable guesswork.

The starting point is a check-in on the wine's *balance* — how the elements of fruit, alcohol, acid, and sometimes tannin or sugar fit together as a whole package. (Oak, if it figures in the equation, comes later.)

The acid in the wine, even a Big Red, should be noticeable; your wine should not taste like grape juice any more. On the other hand, a wine that seems especially tart right after fermentation may need blending or some other action later on. Tasting at this point works in tandem with testing the acidity; you may want to take action immediately or just ride it out for a while as the wine emerges. But if acid promises to be an issue, take note of it now.

Tannin for reds should also be evident, another way to tell this isn't grape juice. Fruit juice makes a pleasant impression in the mouth; wine, red or white, should have a more forceful impact because of acid and/or tannin. If a red wine at this early stage is excessively tannic — producing a definite drying of the mouth and a scratchy after-feeling — take note of that, too. The tannin may balance over time, thanks to oak or mouthfeel goodies reclaimed from the lees — or, it may not. If tannin promises to be an issue, make a note.

The more you practice tasting wine in its infancy, and then tasting it again when it has grown up, the better you get at predicting wine trajectories and figuring out the answers to questions you may have: Did this wine come out a lot lighter than I was expecting? Should I rethink how much oak it can absorb? Did I use the right yeast? I planned to blend this wine, but should I consider bottling it on its own? Is this wine so tannic that I had better start learning about fining to remove tannin?

Speculate lightly; you have plenty of time to change your mind, and the wine will be much more revealing of its true self in a while. But the better you know your wine at every stage, the better care you can take of its future. The reason veteran winemakers are good at tasting infant wines, or even grapes, and predicting their futures is not better palates — just more experience.

Exposing to Oxygen, No; Topping Up, Yes

Through the end of fermentation, oxygen is mainly the winemaker's friend; most notably, it's one of the things yeast needs to do its work. Now things have changed. With a few important exceptions, from here on out, you have to keep oxygen at bay. You still need oxygen; your wine, not so much.

Excess oxygen can turn your white wine brown, adding amber notes to that pale yellow-green; that's fine for a well-aged white, which has been interacting with small amounts of oxygen for years, but not for wine you haven't yet bottled. Oxidized wine may develop aromas of roasted nuts or dried straw; these would be great in a sherry, not so much in a Pinot Grigio. And if large amounts of oxygen are getting to your wine, other things are getting there, too — the usual stray microbes hoping to crash your party.

The goal is not zero oxygen; wines that are entirely starved of oxygen become *reduced,* giving off vaguely sulfury aromas or perhaps no aromas at all. Fortunately, the chances that you can arrange for zero oxygen exposure in your home winery are zero. Racking, filtering, and bottling are bound to introduce some oxygen; barrel aging works its magic because of the trickle of oxygen that gets through the wood. Do your best to minimize the effects of oxygen, secure in the knowledge that enough will get to your wine, anyway.

Topping up and headspace

It is the duty of every wine vessel to be full of wine — unless it's off-duty, waiting for the next racking or the next harvest. Your wine shouldn't share its space with anything else, except perhaps for a few wood chips, and certainly not with air. Keep *headspace* — the area between the top surface of the wine and the top of the vessel or stopper — to a minimum.

For carboys, limit headspace to the narrow neck portion; in barrels, the wine level should come up to within half an inch (about 1.5 centimeters) of the bottom of the bung hole. In neither case should the wine fill absolutely all the headspace, because temperature changes make the volume of wine expand and contract slightly. Plus, you need a little room to insert a thief to sample wine or a tube for racking (check Chapter 6 for a view of a thief in action).

In carboys with airlock stoppers, essentially no wine evaporation occurs, so once a carboy is properly topped off, it stays topped off. (The water in the airlocks, however, does evaporate, and that needs refilling quite often.) Barrels produce constant, very slow evaporation, a good thing that means the remaining wine is more and more concentrated. Since evaporation enlarges the headspace, you need to top up barrels every two or three weeks, depending on temperature. Meeting this obligation to keep wines properly topped off provides endless puzzles to solve. What do you do with 4½ gallons (17 liters) of wine? You can't put it in a 5-gallon (19-liter) carboy and leave that much headspace. Putting it in a bunch of small containers helps the math come out right, but is a pain in the neck.

Filling that missing half gallon of space — *topping up* the carboy — means blending in something else, either one of your own wines or something from the store, which may subtly change the wine. However you solve the problem, it will come up again next time you rack the wine, because a bit will be left behind again. These logistical mini-challenges follow you right up to the last bottle at the bottling, which is guaranteed to be only half full.

There is no general answer to how to handle the intricacies of headspace and topping up; winemakers have to figure it out on the spot every time it comes up. My advice is not to be afraid to use good-quality commercial wine to round out your containers; it's not a crime against the laws of home wine-making. Commercial wineries buy and sell wine with each other all the time.

Today's wine marketplace features a vast amount of value-priced wine from all over the planet, and you should think of that as a resource, not a taboo area. It's still your wine.

Being careful what you top with

In choosing a topping wine, the first choice is usually matching the grapes; Chardonnay with Chardonnay, Syrah with Syrah. Topping within traditional grape "families" is a close second: filling out a Cabernet Sauvignon carboy with one bottle of Merlot is not only a time-honored addition but might well add a teeny bit of complexity. Rhône reds also work well with each other: a dab of Grenache in your Syrah, a dab of Syrah in your Grenache, and so on.

Be careful, however, not to introduce a sudden instability into your wine. Topping off a completely dry carboy with a bottle of off-dry wine will re-start the fermentation; adding a wine that has gone through malolactic to one that hasn't can start malo again. Depending on the amount of the addition, the combined wine could end up with a higher pH or more acidity, and an already tannic wine could become more tannic still.

Be sure to smell and taste every topping wine before you pour it in; one corked bottle of blending wine, reeking of mold, can undo an entire barrel. If you're making a large addition — maybe 20% of something to create a blend — it wouldn't hurt to test its TA and pH.

Getting gassed

One of the best forms of insurance against oxidation in your home winery is compressed carbon dioxide gas, available in canisters at very reasonable prices. If your entire output is one carboy, don't bother. If you're working on a larger scale, it's a good investment as one canister may last you two or three years.

Putting an inert gas like CO_2 between your wine and its container is the next best thing to having no headspace at all. Commercial wineries often use argon or nitrogen, but CO_2 is more readily available to home winemakers and brewers. Use gas when racking, when filling barrels, when topping off containers; some fastidious winemakers even *sparge* their bottles — displacing all the air inside with inert gas — just before filling them.

Chapter 8

Aging and Blending

*W*hat's great about wine is that it's continually evolving from grape to bottle and well beyond — it's never frozen in place. What's tricky about wine is that it's a living thing, continually subject to chemical reactions, external pressures, and microbial adventures — never the same from month to month.

Your wine doesn't ask for much, but it won't tolerate complete neglect. So after you've shepherded your wine through fermentation and maybe a malolactic fermentation, you can't just go off on a six-month cruise. This chapter covers how to age your wine, what to look for, and how to fix the wine as it matures. If fermentation is like childhood, full of swift transformations, then aging spans the teens — energetic, stubborn, sullen — and the onset of adulthood — ready to settle into the bottle.

Glass, Germs, and Steel: Carboy Aging

Home wine storage normally happens in one of two containers: glass carboys or oak barrels. Most home winemakers start by aging their white wines and small batches of red wine in carboys and later move up to barrels, at least for some reds. Either way makes excellent wine, with stylistic and budgetary differences. If your first wine is a modest experiment, a carboy or two is the way to go. For cases and cases of wine, barrels may be in your future.

Glass carboys (and their plastic cousins) are the default home winemaking containers. They have several advantages as a wine storage and aging solution when compared to barrel or stainless steel tank aging:

- ✔ Glass, unlike barrel oak, is inert, adding no flavors or aromas to your wine; if you want wood flavor, you can add oak chips.

- ✔ Inert glass can be sanitized better than barrels, which greatly reduces the survival chances of bad microbes.

- ✔ Glass provides a solid barrier against oxygen; the only air available is the tiny amount in the neck of the carboy and whatever oxygen gets introduced during racking. (I describe racking in Chapter 7.)

- ✔ Carboys are smaller than barrels and more portable for filling, racking, and cleaning. A 5-gallon (19-liter) carboy filled with wine weighs roughly 50 pounds (23 kilograms) — not light, but easier to move around than a full barrel, which can weigh several hundred pounds or kilograms.

- ✔ Glass lets you see your wine age. You can watch it clarify, change color, and build up sludge at the bottom, signaling racking time.

- ✔ You need less than a hundred pounds (45 kilograms) of grapes to fill a carboy with wine — perfect for small, experimental batches or for wine-makers on a tight budget.

Naturally, carboys have their downsides, too:

- ✔ Glass can crack more easily than plastic, steel, or wood, which leads to leaks and the occasional small flood.

- ✔ Glass does such a good job of keeping out oxygen that it can limit a wine's development; barrel aging allows a small amount of oxygen to creep in, helping to round out and integrate wines.

- ✔ When you're making larger volumes of wine, the forest of carboys can be a pain (and take up immense storage space when empty).

- ✔ Glass carboys got more expensive when their prime source shifted from Mexico to Italy, raising production and transportation costs.

For making white wines on a larger scale — 30 gallons (115 liters) or more — a small stainless steel tank may be a good investment. Most reds benefit from barrel aging, so when you're up to 15 gallons (55 liters) or more, barrels may get onto your shopping list. But carboys are part of every home cellar — and show up in most commercial wineries, too.

Barreling Down Your Wine

For some reason lost in the mists of time, winemakers don't talk about "putting wine in barrels"; they refer to "barreling down" a wine, regardless of the barrel's actual altitude. Choosing a term is simple compared to choosing a barrel: sizes, oak species, forests of origin, treatments as they get made. Like the topic of yeast, this could fill a book — *Wine Barrels For Dummies* — but the following sections cover everything the average homie needs to know.

Debating wood versus glass

Barrel aging contributes three things to wine that glass or steel don't:

- ✔ Most important, barrels allow a slow trickle of oxygen to come inside, and a slow process of evaporation to send small amounts of the wine — known as the *angels' share* — outside; this interchange helps concentrate the wine and round off any rough edges.

- ✔ Barrels, in their first years of use, impart flavors to the wine from the oak and from the techniques used to prepare the oak. Flavors may include vanilla, caramel, spice, or others. At first, a lot of flavor leaches in, and then less and less over time.

- ✔ Barrels contribute oak tannin, which supplements the tannin from grape skins and seeds in the wine, adding to structure and mouthfeel. This effect also decreases over time.

You can simulate the last two barrel effects — imparting flavor and tannin — by adding oak chips or powder or tannin additives to carboy wines. However, barrel aging remains unique because of the oxygen/evaporation dynamic, and there must be something to it: Most of the world's premium wines — virtually all the reds and a healthy slice of whites — are aged in barrels to benefit from a little evaporation.

Judging differences in new and old (er) oak

By the time an oak barrel shows up at your winery, the wood is already two or three years old, having spent time air-drying before the staves were fire-charred (called *toasting*) and assembled into a barrel. The first time a barrel is filled with wine, it is considered *new oak* or *first-fill*. By the next harvest, it's called *second-fill*, and so on. Most commercial wineries consider any barrel older than three years or three fills to be neutral, though barrels continue to impart a bit of flavor until their fifth or sixth fill.

The emphasis on new oak in winemaking is relatively new. All barrels are new for one year, but until recent decades, barrels were used for years and years, until they literally fell apart. Assuming they remain clean, free of microbial invaders, barrels perform the oxygen/evaporation dance for a very long time. The modern emphasis on new oak is all about flavor — and for my taste, often way too much of it.

Some grape varieties marry well with new oak flavors: Cabernet Sauvignon for one, and, remarkably, Pinot Noir, despite its lightness and delicacy. Sangiovese, however, gets buried in new oak rather quickly, as do most Rhône varieties such as Grenache and Mourvèdre. Rhône reds (see Chapter 13) work best with older oak, or a mix of old and new. Except for full-bodied Chardonnay, few white wines benefit from lashings of new oak.

Home winemakers who adopt barrels face particular challenges in managing oak influence. If you have only one new barrel, you'll get a lot of oak in your wine — which may be fine, or may be pushing it. Home winemakers also often employ smaller barrels — 15- or 30-gallon (55 to 115 liters) sizes — than the commercial winery norm — 55 or 60 gallons (210 to 225 liters). The smaller barrels give more wood contact per gallon of wine and build up oak flavors and tannins faster than the larger barrels.

Some wine drinkers like lots of oak, others only a hint — preferences are all over the map. Plenty of the world's great wines show definite oak influence, but you don't really want your pride and joy to taste like lumber. Personally, I want my wine to taste like its fruit, not like its storage container. Oak works best when it adds depth to a wine, but doesn't make it taste like . . . well, oak. Here's my low-oak winemaking philosophy:

- ✔ Use only as much oak flavor influence — from new barrels or chips — as your wine really wants.

- ✔ Go easy on the oak at the beginning of aging; you can always add more two or three or five months later.

- ✔ In the first year of a new, small barrel, rotate two or three batches of wine through it during the year to spread out the new-oak impact, and let the wines spend the rest of their time in old wood barrels or carboys.

- ✔ Keep your barrels clean, and re-use them forever.

Keeping and cleaning your barrels

Used barrels make terrific containers for wine storage and aging — but only if they're clean. Properly maintained barrels can be re-used vintage after vintage. Stick your nose in an empty barrel: It should smell like some combination of oak — sweet vanilla, caramel, spice — and healthy wine. If your sniffer picks up aromas of the barnyard or vinegar or a smell more appropriate for your first aid kit, you have a problem, one you don't want to share with your next batch of wine. Infected barrels — where funky microbes have taken up residence — have a future only as decorative planters.

The most vulnerable time in a barrel's life is between vintages, or between the time when wine A leaves the barrel and when wine B is ready to go in. Wine barrels want to be full; empty barrels offer the volatile combination of oxygen, traces of leftover wine, and endless nooks and crannies — all of them fertile ground for spoilage critters, instant wine vinegar, and other maladies.

Whenever wine is racked out of a barrel, the barrel should get a quick cleaning before refilling. Rinse the barrel thoroughly with water — hot water if you have it — and then rinse again with a mild solution of sulfur dioxide and citric acid — 10 grams of potassium metabisulfite and 5 grams of citric acid for each gallon (four liters) of rinse. Drain the barrel completely, then refill.

When a barrel takes a real break, the minimum protection plan is to hang an inch or two (2 to 5 centimeters) of *sulfur wick* — a paper strip coated with flammable sulfur — on a bent paper clip or other holder, light it, and let it burn out inside the barrel. Doing so fills the barrel with sulfurous gas that will discourage critters and reduce the amount of oxygen in the barrel. Don't sniff what you're doing: you'll learn quickly why any life forms, from microbes to winemakers, dislike the stuff! With the bung tightly back in place, your barrel should be good for a month or two.

For longer vacations from wine, several months at a time, rinse the barrel thoroughly with water to remove any wine residue. Fill the barrel with water, including a small amount of sulfur dioxide for sanitation and a small amount of tartaric acid to maintain wine-like pH. For each gallon (4 liters) of capacity, dissolve 9 grams of potassium metabisulfite and 5 grams of citric acid in a small amount of water, and mix in thoroughly. (Many winemakers use sodium bisulfate instead of potassium metabisulfite for barrel work, saving the latter for wine additions.) Seal the barrel with a bung, and top it up with water occasionally as the liquid evaporates.

The solution keeps the wood wet and the barrel watertight, and it also provides anti-microbial insurance. In a newish barrel, you'll lose some of the precious oak flavor you paid for to the water; but at least you won't lose your entire barrel investment to bugs. Filled with this solution, barrels can safely stay "empty" for months.

Identifying and dealing with barrel taint can be an iffy proposition. If a barrel has produced or stored a wine with microbial spoilage — like *Brettanomyces* or acetic acid bacteria, discussed in the section on "Sniffing Out and Snuffing Out Trouble" later in this chapter — that's easy: dump it. In less obvious cases, the only practical way to know a barrel is suspect or trustworthy is to sniff it. If something smells off — vinegar, barnyard — try rinsing it with a solution of sulfur dioxide and citric acid, drain the barrel, wait a day, and re-do the sniff test. If the problem was never that serious, your barrel may be refreshed. You can also try rinsing with chlorine-free sanitizing agents like sodium percarbonate as a last-ditch salvage strategy. My experience suggests it's better to get the saw out, convert it to a planter, and buy a new barrel.

Commercial wineries often get rid of their barrels after two or three years, as do some home winemakers, so you could get what seem like real bargains. Just be very, very cautious about buying or accepting used, empty barrels.

Make sure the barrels are clean; ask how they've been handled and treated; stick your nose in and sniff; then sniff again. The amount of wine ruined by other people's empty barrels is staggering. You can simply scrub used carboys; but you have to be very careful with barrels.

Choosing French or American oak

Forty years ago, the United States wine industry thought barrels were barrels, oak was oak, and for that matter, redwood vats were fine for aging wine. These days winemakers all over North America go to great lengths to pick and choose among a huge range of barrel types. Because your home winery probably only has room for two or three barrels, your choices are simpler.

The basic choice is between French oak and American oak. Controversy has raged for years over the comparative quality of these two options — see the sidebar on "Franco-American forest products" — so I offer you a few practical factors that are important for your decision:

- ✔ American barrels generally cost about half to two-thirds as much as French barrels of the same size, which can mean a difference of several hundred dollars even for half-size barrels.

- ✔ American oak barrels tend to impart stronger, more assertive flavors and aromas to wine, in particular lots of sweet vanilla. French barrels tend to contribute more restrained, nuanced spices.

- ✔ While French oak generally has a higher reputation in fine wine production, certain important winegrowing regions — France's Rhône Valley, Spain's Rioja, Australia — have traditionally used a lot of American oak, which suggests that grape variety and wine style are important factors in choosing your wood.

Other than the price, choosing a French or American barrel won't impact your winemaking much, especially compared to all the other factors in the process. Oak barrels from Hungary and other Central European countries are also available, priced and flavored somewhere between French and American.

Toasting barrel staves

Wine barrel staves are heated and charred by open flames — called *toasting* — just before assembly. The degree of toasting is nearly as important as the curing of the wood in shaping the flavors that go into the wine. Standard toast levels go from light, to medium, to medium plus, to heavy; the darker the toast, the more pronounced and assertive the oak.

Franco-American forest products

French and American barrel oak come from different species of the tree: *Quercus ruber* for France, *Quercus alba* for the United States. More important, French *cooperage* — the techniques of barrel-building — was vastly different from its American counterpart until recently.

When American wineries discovered the joys of barrel aging in the 1970s, they naturally turned to the nearest and least expensive supply — the same barrels used for aging bourbon in Kentucky. The barrels were slapped together out of young, green wood, without much curing, and rolled out for production. Bourbon loves strong oak flavor, so wines made in those barrels got oaky in a hurry. The best French coopers, by contrast, dried their oak staves two or three years before toasting the wood and assembling the barrels, resulting in a gentler wood influence. French oak built a reputation for refinement and elegance; American oak was simply cheap storage.

Bit by bit, cooperages in the United States adopted European curing techniques and explored the multitude of wood sources within the United States. To pick one prominent example, Ridge Vineyards in California, an ultra-premium producer of Cabernet Sauvignon, Zinfandel, and Chardonnay since the 1960s, has used American oak exclusively from the start, working with coopers and wood suppliers across the country, and few accuse Ridge of making clumsy wines. Even some high-end California Pinot Noir producers, the last holdout of French-only oak attitudes, quietly slip in an American barrel or two to round out their flavor profiles.

Someone, somewhere must use light toast barrels, but I've never come across anyone who does. Medium is an industry norm for mid-priced premium wines; medium plus is fashionable for higher-end red wines; and heavy toast is part of the mix for wineries that want an unmistakable statement in their wines. More isn't better; it's a stylistic choice.

My advice is to go with medium toast, for both barrels and oak alternatives (see the next section), until you gain some experience with what new oak does to your wines and how you like the results. Adding more oak flavor as a wine ages is so much easier than covering it up after you've gone overboard.

Exploring oak alternatives

If you're after flavor, oak alternatives can do the job just as well as a barrel, and with even more precise control. Non-barrel oak comes in a variety of forms:

- ✔ **Staves** to stick inside large containers (neutral barrels, tanks)
- ✔ **Chips** and **cubes** that you can add by the handful or measure into time-release tubes
- ✔ Powdery oak **sawdust**

These options come in French or American oak and various toast levels, giving home winemakers nearly the range of flavors available to commercial operations. Homies, however, have only a barrel or two, or perhaps a carboy or two, so achieving the complex mix of influences a commercial outfit gets with 1,000 barrels is impossible.

In my experience, the most useful form of oak alternative for home winemaking are cubes, roughly ¼ inch (25 millimeters) on a side, toasted any way you want. Add the cubes to neutral barrels or carboys and remove them during racking. Compared to whole staves, they're more convenient; compared to powder, the cubes impart far better flavor — powder tends to taste like pencil shavings — and release their flavor more slowly over time.

The standard dosage for giving noticeable but not overbearing oak flavor is 2 to 3 ounces (55 to 85 grams) of oak cubes for a 5-gallon (19-liter) carboy. Leave the cubes in the wine for three months. On a barrel scale, proportional additions are an excellent way to get a little oak flavor into wine aging in older or neutral wood. (Chapter 16 discusses using oak cubes in carboys to mimic barrel fermentation for white wines.)

Tasting, Topping, and Tweaking

Just as the furious period of fermentation requires a routine for checking on your wine's progress, slow-mo aging needs a routine, too. You need to drop in on your wine at least every two weeks, check its health, taste its development and maturation, and tweak anything that needs it.

Tasting, tasting, tasting

Regularly tasting your wine as it ages is one of the most enjoyable parts of home winemaking — and definitely the most revealing. Wine drinkers taste wine only after it's finished, cleaned up, and bottled, but a whole world of chemical and sensory changes happen before a wine gets there. Experiencing wine's evolution firsthand can be astounding, perplexing, satisfying, and inspiring — and that's just in a single tasting.

Evolving wines don't fit a standard pattern: vintages differ, grape varieties differ, even two barrels made from the same oak and filled from the same fermentation taste a little different. You can safely expect that your wine will change, over and over, even in short periods of time, before it begins to stabilize. Don't be alarmed: This part is fun and requires no manual labor.

One day, your wine may taste fruity, gushing over with raspberries or peaches or whatever. Two weeks later, the acidity or the tannin in the wine may be a lot more evident. Two weeks after that, all the wine's aromatic properties may seem to disappear, only to return a few weeks later. A seemingly thin wine in February may turn into a blockbuster in April. This is wine's adolescence, moody and changeable — you were young once, too.

Despite all the fluctuations, periodic tasting can clue you in on two things:

- ✔ The wine's basic character comes through, in and around all the changing details. Is this going to be a pretty wine or a sturdy wine, a simple and straightforward wine or a complex one, a candidate for blending or a star on its own? How close is this wine to what was in your head when you started? Your cumulative judgment of the wine as it develops informs later decisions about blending, filtering, and so on — topics I cover later on in this chapter and the next.

- ✔ Emerging problems, if there are any, show up as you taste, and particularly as you sniff your wine's aroma. The "Sniffing Out" section at the end of this chapter covers the most common issues that emerge during aging; tasting is the quintessential early warning system.

I always find it instructive to taste wines with other people — casual wine consumers and other winemakers alike. Nobody has a perfect palate every day of the year, and how a wine comes across to someone with a different background and different preferences can be enlightening — not to mention a great deal of fun for your friends who never get to taste a wine in progress.

And by the way, when you and your friends are done sniffing and sipping the samples, pour what's left back into the carboy or barrel. Don't feel compelled to drink it all, and don't worry about contaminating your wine with cooties. The alcohol neutralizes almost anything, and the more wine you put back, the less you have to add to refill the container. Commercial wineries do this when they taste through their barrels; act like a pro.

Topping and tending

Carboys full of wine closed with secure airlocks lose little or no wine to evaporation over time, but they can develop *headspace* — the gap in the neck of the carboy between the top of the wine and the airlock — when wine gets taken out for tasting or testing, or during racking. Barrels lose wine through sampling and racking, and a little each day to evaporation.

You want to keep headspace to a minimum, and you do that through a process called *topping off,* which is pretty much what it sounds like — adding more wine until the container is filled, leaving little-to-no room for air.

In a carboy, the wine should come up to the bottom of the narrow neck, so only a small circle of wine surface is exposed to oxygen. In a barrel, the wine should be no more than half an inch (13 millimeters) from the bottom of the bung hole. Neither container should be entirely filled right up to the stopper, because daily temperature fluctuations make the volume of wine expand and contract slightly, possibly knocking off an airlock or expelling a barrel bung.

The best wine to use for topping is the exact same wine that's in the carboy or barrel. Such purity, however, can get tricky. If your barrel needs a cup of wine to top it off, and that cup has to come from a small jug, which then has too much headspace, requiring several smaller jugs with their own stoppers . . . don't bother. Use reasonably similar, sound wine, your own or commercial, and you'll be fine. Just don't top with anything you wouldn't drink.

After struggling with topping strategies for several years, I recently discovered a handy solution: commercial bag-in-box wines. Several premium quality brands are on the market, filled with perfectly decent wine in standard varieties at bargain prices. Best of all, you can measure out exactly the amount of wine you need for topping, and the remainder in the box will keep for several weeks, protected from oxygen.

To aid in sealing out oxygen, if you have a canister of carbon dioxide gas, give your wine container a squirt before putting the airlock or bung back.

Getting the most out of dead yeast

With the fermentation completed, almost all of the millions of hard-working yeast cells who made your wine are spent, gone, dead. But like a gift that keeps on giving, spent yeast — known as *lees* — can still contribute to the development of your wine.

In the presence of alcohol, yeast cells start to break down — a process called *autolysis* — and release useful compounds into the wine solution. Lees may give some aromatic and flavor elements, but the chief contribution is to texture and mouthfeel — roundness, creaminess, and a softening of the astringent edge of red wine tannins. The most important compounds for the lees effect are mannoproteins and polysaccharides (you only need to know how to encourage them, not how to pronounce them).

Lees stirring is ridiculously simple: Use a sanitized long rod or spoon handle to gently uproot the lees on the bottom of a carboy or barrel of red or white wine. If you want to feel better about poking a stick in your wine, use the French term, *bâtonnage.*

Stirring the lees exposes all the cell surfaces to ethanol, extracting more goodies. Stirring your wine every two or three weeks for a few months can make a noticeable difference. After a wine has been racked once or twice, the volume of lees becomes so low that you don't have much to shake a stick at.

Timing the rackings

Home wine typically gets *racked* — a process in which you move clean wine off the sludge that collects at the bottom of containers — two to four times before the final finishing and bottling. Racking helps clarify the wine, makes the eventual job of filtering easier, introduces a small but useful dose of oxygen, and brings out the wine's inherent flavors and aromas. (Go back to Chapter 7 for a detailed description of the racking process.)

The amount and the timing of rackings is partially a matter of wine style, partially a matter of convenience. A white wine designed for quick turn-around and early bottling to capture maximum freshness could get racked three times at four- to six-week intervals and be ready for finishing touches four months from harvest. A red benefiting from long barrel aging could go six months or more between rackings. The timing may also depend on how many friends you have available on a given day to share the chores.

While racking pays off in clarifying wine, it can also introduce more oxygen than you want. Over-racking doesn't make your wine any cleaner, just more oxidized. If you can see a layer of sludge at the bottom of a carboy, it probably merits racking. But overall, my rule is to do the minimum number of rackings needed to clarify the wine.

Calculating aging time

First-time home winemakers are always tempted to bottle their wines as soon as possible in order to get to the drinking part — the point of the activity, after all. A wine from a happy fermentation with no funny microbial faults starts tasting like wine in a couple of months; why not just start the party?

Wine tastes pleasant well before it's ready to bottle. Fermentation produces a range of yummy, inviting, fruity overtones — known as *esters* — that sooner or later dissipate and fly away. These "tutti-frutti" or "baby wine" aromas are delightful, but transient. In addition, early on, your wine may still have a touch of residual, unfermented sugar in it, adding come-hither sweetness that you have to deal with sometime — so it doesn't re-ferment after bottling.

No hard and fast rules exist for when to bottle your wine. But it needs to reach three important milestones:

- ✔ **It must be biologically stable.** The alcoholic fermentation has to be complete, any malolactic fermentation has to be either complete or prevented, no uninvited bacteria should be blooming, and so on. Chemical changes will still happen; the biology should be over.

✔ **It must be clarified from aging and racking.** You can speed this process up with filtration, but the wine has to be fairly clear before that, so as not to clog the filter. Your wine has to look like something you would want to drink.

✔ **Its flavor and aroma profile are consistent from tasting to tasting.** Fermenting wine changes every few minutes; early in aging, wine changes noticeably from month to month. Gradually the pace of mutation slows down, and the wine settles into a groove. Wine never stands still, but you can taste when your wine has taken on a grown-up identity.

As a general rule, carboy-aged whites are ready anywhere from four to six months after fermentation. Reds in carboys take longer, perhaps six months to a year. Barrel-aged wines generally take a year or longer — but keep in mind, the smaller the barrel, the quicker the development. I offer some thoughts about how long different grape varieties need in later chapters.

The Joys of Blending

Blending is the home winemaker's best friend. Adding a little of this into a lot more of that can make your wines more interesting; round out the aromatics; expand the flavor complexity; improve the balance of fruit, alcohol, acid, and tannin; and turn an average wine into a head-turner.

Most commercial North American wine is labeled and sold by the name of the grape variety, encouraging the false impression that "pure" varietal wines are superior to blends. Tell that to the vintners in Bordeaux, who have used multiple grapes in their wines for centuries; or to winemakers in Châteauneuf du Pape, who choose among 18 permitted varieties; or to wineries in Chianti and Rioja who traditionally add a splash of something to the main grapes of those regions (Sangiovese and Tempranillo, respectively) to fill out flavors.

Even the 100 percent varietal commercial wines are often blends of the best batches or barrels from the vintage. For your home Merlot, you can't choose the most intriguing 30 barrels out of the 50 you have available; but you can give your one barrel more backbone with a little Cabernet Sauvignon, or deepen the flavors with a little Syrah, or make it livelier with a dollop of Zinfandel. The chances that your single barrel of 100 percent Grenache will come out spot-on perfect are daunting; the chances you might improve it with a small percentage of another wine are often worth exploring.

Sometimes home blends come together by accident, from tasting two or three unrelated batches of wine and tripping across a nice combination. Sometimes blending combines loose ends — the leftovers that didn't fit in the barrels — and produces something quite drinkable. When you get the blending bug, you may well do it on purpose, planning a Bordeaux red blend or a Rhône-style white blend from the time you order your grapes.

Winning combinations

As a home winemaker, you have the freedom to blend anything with anything, as long as you like the way it tastes. If a mix of Malbec, Gewürztraminer, apple juice, and Seyval Blanc works for you, go for it. This is one of the rare advantages homies have over the pros, who are far more hemmed in by labeling restrictions and market niches.

Some time-honored combinations, produced in well-known wine regions for decades or centuries, are likely to work in your winery, too:

- ✔ The Bordeaux family of red grapes and wines — Cabernet Sauvignon, Cabernet Franc, Merlot, Malbec, and Petit Verdot — often play well together in almost any combination of two or three or five.

- ✔ The main Rhône reds — Syrah, Grenache, Mourvèdre, Carignane — are almost joined at the hip, growing and blending together for centuries.

   Change the last three of those names to Garnacha, Monastrell, and Cariñena (same grapes), throw in Tempranillo, and you have combinations that have worked in Spain for centuries.

- ✔ Classic white blends include the Bordeaux duo of Sauvignon Blanc and Sémillon, both for dry and sweet wines, and the Rhône trio of Roussanne, Marsanne, and Viognier.

- ✔ Most California Zinfandel has had at least a splash of Petite Sirah in it since the two grapes hit the state more than a century ago.

Some common blending strategies aren't as famous, but they're quite useful. Mixing a small amount — maybe 5% — of an aromatic white — Riesling, Muscat — into a more standard fruity white — Chardonnay or Sauvignon Blanc — can add a hint of exoticism. A modest amount of Cabernet Sauvignon or Petite Sirah instantly deepens the color and enhances the structure of almost any red wine in need of firming up. Syrah is a blender around the world because of its ability to round out and fill in other wines. The proportions in all these combinations vary wildly; judge quantities by how they taste.

 I always make at least a small amount of Syrah and Viognier every harvest, even when those are not the wines I'm concentrating on. They may end up as useful blenders, and if I don't need them, I can always bottle them on their own. But those choices reflect my taste in wine; you might decide to have a little Chardonnay or Cabernet Sauvignon handy, just in case.

Table 8-1 lists some of the blending combinations with proven track records; these aren't rules, just suggestions to get your blending juices running.

Table 8-1	Winning Wine Blends	
Main Component	**Major (25 to 50%) Partners**	**Minor (< 25%) Complements**
Cabernet Sauvignon	Merlot, Cabernet Franc, Syrah	Zinfandel, Sangiovese
Merlot	Cabernet Sauvignon	Cabernet Sauvignon
Pinot Noir	Careful — can get overpowered	Zinfandel, Grenache, Syrah, Petite Sirah
Sangiovese	Careful — can get overpowered	Cabernet Sauvignon, Merlot, Cabernet Franc, Zinfandel, Barbera
Syrah	Grenache, Mourvèdre, Carignane, Petite Sirah, Cabernet Sauvignon	Viognier
Tempranillo	Graciano, Grenache, Carignane, Portuguese varieties	Graciano, Grenache, Carignane, Portuguese varieties
Zinfandel	Careful — can get overpowered	Grenache, Carignane, Mourvèdre, Petite Sirah, Barbera, Cabernet Sauvignon
Chardonnay	Sémillon, Sauvignon Blanc	Aromatic whites — Riesling, Viognier, Gewürztraminer
Pinot Gris/Grigio		Muscat, other aromatics
Rhone whites — Marsanne, Roussanne, Viognier	All work well with each other	All work well with each other
Riesling		Muscat, other aromatics
Sauvignon Blanc	Sémillon	Viognier, Muscat

Finding wine to blend

The obvious source for blending wine is your own, and using it can add extra satisfaction. But that's not the only option, especially if you're only making one wine or the alternatives you have in your cellar are not what you need.

Blending is a great reason to get to know other home winemakers. You can't sell your wine legally, but you can certainly trade a bit of yours for a bit of theirs. If you need some Merlot to smooth out a ragged-edged Cabernet Sauvignon, ask around. If some low-acid Chardonnay could help balance your overly tart Sauvignon Blanc, see if your local winemaking shop probably knows somebody who might have some to spare.

Please don't be shy about using store-bought wine to improve or fill out your home efforts. Commercial wineries buy wine from each other all the time, even though that information never shows on the label. Buying wine can be expensive, but if you only need a few bottles of something to improve several cases of your wine, head for the store.

Timing, tasting, and trials

Wines can be blended any time in the winemaking process, from fermenting two varieties together in the same vat to waiting until the last minute — or close to the last minute. Blending early gives the wines time to settle in, get to know each other, marry their flavors, and develop further in tandem. Blending later on allows for a fuller appreciation of each component wine and more confidence in how the combinations might work. The better you know your grapes — from having made wine from them before — the more confident you can be about blending earlier.

Do your blending a minimum of two weeks before bottling to give the newly created wine time to react to itself. Blending creates wine with a chemistry different from any of the components, and those changes in acidity, pH, and other variables can provoke unexpected reactions — the wine may suddenly show a haze, or some dissolved compound may now decide to fall out entirely. Make sure the new wine is stable before you bottle it.

The key to successful blending is running trials. Before you dump two batches of wine together, hoping for the best, make up a miniature version of the blend and concoct other samples of slightly different proportions. Even if you decide not to blend, the tasting trials can be a revelation — small additions make a huge difference.

Winemakers develop their own protocols for blending trials, but I offer my general suggestions:

- ✔ Recruit several tasters; many palates are better than one, even when you call the final shots.

- ✔ Have lots of clean, matching glassware on hand — nothing fancy, but matching glasses make for a level tasting field — as well as calibrated beakers for precise, reproducible measurement (see Chapter 3).

✔ Taste the candidate blending wines separately first, discussing what each might bring to the blend and what each might lack on its own.

✔ Prepare multiple small sample blends, differing by 5 or 10 percent in the mixtures; the range helps you zero in on the "sweet spot."

✔ Take the time to talk about each blend, identifying its aromas, flavors, tannin level, acidity, and so on, as well as rating how much you like it.

✔ Write down the proportions of the trial blends and keep notes on what the tasters find; you can't keep this much information in your head.

One additional method, called a *triangle test* because it involves three samples, is especially helpful for gauging the effect of very small additions. Give each taster two glasses of one wine, either the current wine or the proposed blend, and one glass of the other. Can they pick out the one that's different? If not, you may need a bigger addition, or decide not to bother.

A blending trial may produce a clear winner, or leave you scratching your head and trying another blending strategy. The perfect blend may be delicious, but not possible, because the proportions of the trial don't match the volumes of wine you have available. Whatever the outcome, blending trials are bound to be instructive — another way home winemakers can try things consumers who only know bottled wine never experience.

What blending can fix and can't fix

Blending is an excellent way to improve the balance of one or more wines. A wine with low pH can bring down the worrisomely high pH of another wine; a wine with higher acidity can brighten a dull, low-acid wine. When blending for balance, make sure to consider both how the blend smells and tastes and what it does for the wine's basic chemical parameters. (Appendix C has information for an online blend calculator that can help with the math, but basic wine chemistry testing after blending is a good idea, too.)

Blending *cannot* fix bad wine, especially microbe-infected and otherwise stinky wine. Adding good wine to wine you wouldn't drink doesn't hide the problem — it just wastes good wine and makes more bad wine. If you have a problem wine, fix it first; don't share it. Some tips on fixing delinquent wines are in the nest section.

Sniffing Out and Snuffing Out Problems

As it ages, wine develops new and interesting aromas, and sometimes, they're not aromas you want. Maintaining good winery sanitation and controlling exposure to oxygen should keep your wine on track. But, stuff happens.

Wine in barrels is more vulnerable than wine in carboys, because barrel aging involves more oxygen exposure, and barrel wood can never be as thoroughly sanitized as a glass carboy. Some problems arise during aging; others start during fermentation but only show up later. In all cases, the sooner you diagnose and deal with the issue, the happier you and your wine will be.

Your job, as the ever-vigilant winemaker, is to sniff out trouble. These sections cover the most common issues and remedies — not stray aromas here or there but stubborn things that can ruin your day — and your wine.

If you smell or taste something you really don't want in your wine, and you and your friends smell or taste it over and over, don't panic: Wines do weird things, and you can handle them.

Smelling sulfur and brimstone and rotten eggs — oh my!

The most common wine fault — at home and in commercial wineries — is the unmistakable odor of hydrogen sulfide (shorthanded as H_2S). The smell of hydrogen sulfide is similar to rotten eggs, spoiled cabbage, and rancid garlic. Sewer gas is another similar odor. In big doses, hydrogen sulfide makes wine positively reek; at lower levels, it covers up all the good, fruity aromatics with a mild layer of rot.

Hydrogen sulfide and its aromas are not the only sulfur-related odor that might show up in your wine, and it's important to keep them straight. An excess amount of sulfur dioxide can appear in your wine, but instead of smelling like rotten eggs, the odor is more like a burning match. If you add a bit too much sulfur dioxide to your wine, it eventually becomes bound and ceases being volatile and smelly.

The source of hydrogen sulfide is generally over-stressed yeast during fermentation, though the aroma may not be evident until later on. H_2S can also appear when grapes are treated with sulfur in the vineyard too close to harvest. Whatever the source, the sooner you deal with hydrogen sulfide, the better; over time, it morphs into related compounds (called *disulfides* and *mercaptans*) that are far more difficult to remove.

If you suspect H_2S, one way to validate your nose is to put a bit of wine in a glass, drop in a clean copper penny, or swirl the wine around with a copper-wire scrubber, and see (or smell) whether the odor goes away. Hydrogen sulfide binds up with copper and stops being volatile and stinky.

You can't bottle pennies with your wine, but you can use other methods, listed here in the order to try them:

- **Racking:** The first line of defense is to give the wine some air. Rack the afflicted carboy or barrel, encouraging the H_2S to blow off into the air. (Racking is covered in Chapter 7.)

  In normal racking, the goal is to minimize exposure to oxygen; here, you want to flaunt it, aerating as much as possible, splashing the wine around. If your normal practice is to rack wine under a cover of carbon dioxide, skip that here.

- **Running the wine through copper:** If the offending odors are still around after a well-oxygenated racking, the next escalation might be to insert a piece of copper tubing — 12 to18 inches (30 to 45 centimeters) long — into the end of your racking hose. When you rack, the siphoned wine flows through the copper as well as the plastic, hopefully binding enough of the H_2S to remove the stink. Depending on your tubing, however, this can add a metallic taste to your wine, so try this on a small sample first.

- **Adding copper sulfate:** For stubborn odors after two or three rackings, copper sulfate is the last resort. Try not to get to this stage: Copper sulfate is poisonous, though used properly, the small amounts needed to de-stink wine will bind up with the hydrogen sulfide and eventually settle to the bottom of the wine container, allowing the cleaned-up wine to be racked off safely.

  Bottles of copper sulfate solution from your local wine shop or web-based suppliers come with instructions, which you should follow carefully. The basic approach involves doctoring small samples of the wine with a drop or two or three of the copper sulfate solution in order to find out the minimum needed to clean the wine, and then calculating the dosage for the full volume of wine. This method is quite precise, and if done properly, completely safe

- After a week, rack the wine and go back to normal winemaking.

The good news about adding copper to your wine is that if you overdo it, your wine will taste terrible — spit-out terrible — long before the copper level becomes dangerous.

Getting too much air

The exposure of alcohol to oxygen during aging encourages the formation of compounds called *aldehydes*. Some aldehyde production is inevitable, but in large concentrations, oxidating aldehydes give wines the aromatic characteristics of sherry — odors that range from nuts to bruised apples to wet cardboard. These may be fine for sherry, but probably not in your Pinot Grigio or Cabernet Franc.

Like other off aromas, aldehydes often mask good aromas rather than jumping out and announcing themselves. They make a once-exuberant wine taste tired or stale. If your wine starts to smell dull and closed for no good reason, aldehydes created by alcohol and too much oxygen are a likely culprit.

The treatment for aldehydes is sulfur dioxide. If this issue comes up during aging, I recommend adding half the amount of SO_2 you added at the end of fermentation (see Chapter 7 and Appendix D). In other words, the remedial dose will vary by the wine's pH. Whenever you rack your wine later, freshen up the active, free SO_2 with another small addition — 25 parts per million. Minimize further exposure to oxygen by carefully racking and topping up containers.

A particularly nasty form of aldehydes — called *acertaldehydes* — can mushroom when *surface yeasts* — also known as *flor yeasts* — gain a foothold. These rogue yeasts love oxygen, which is why they float on the surface of wine, and can tolerate very high alcohol. Their aromas are in the roasted nuts and dry straw department. Flor yeasts can form a thick film on your wine, which you need to remove. Soak it into a paper towel, suck it out with a thief — get rid of it before treating the wine with SO_2.

Confronting bad news Brett

Benevolent yeasts made your wine; later on, your wine can fall victim to rogue yeast, the ringleader being *Brettanomyces bruxellensis*, also known as *Dekkera*, and usually referred to simply as *Brett*. Brett is the heart and soul of some types of Belgian beer, but for wine, it's trouble. Brett is a survivor, comes is many strains, has visited nearly every commercial winery on the planet, and can even use alcohol as fuel. Brett throws off a wide range of aromas, sometimes pleasantly fruity, usually barnyardy or medicinal, horse blankets or Band-Aids. Wet dog is a charming Brett descriptor.

Brett is controversial in the wine world. Some well-respected, high-priced wines carry its signature year after year; some influential critics seem partial to Bretty wines; most winemakers do everything they can to stamp it out. A hint of Brett, many people think, aids a wine's complexity, but the odds on micro-managing Brett in your home winery to just the right level are nil. Your job is to get rid of it whenever it rears its smelly head. If you check in on your wine and you immediately think of cows and horses, fix it.

Winery sanitation is the key to preventing and eliminating Brett: clean equipment, especially clean barrels, and proper additions of SO_2 to safeguard the wine. Even if signs of Brett aren't evident, sanitation and microbial control are critical, because low levels of Brett can bloom into high levels over time, even in the bottle. If Brett has taken hold, and you succeed in killing it off, you may still be left with its unfortunate aromatic by-products. Commercial wineries have ways to remove these compounds, but home winemakers don't — another reason to head Brett off at the pass.

Used, empty barrels are ideal breeding grounds for Brett, not to mention mold and other nasty things, so once a barrel becomes infected, it has no future in winemaking.

Calming volatile vinegar

Wine vinegar is a staple in nearly every kitchen, but it has no place in a winery. Your wine may pair well with salad, but shouldn't be confused with the salad dressing itself.

Leave a bottle of wine open to the air, and sooner or later it will turn to vinegar, thanks to a brand of bacteria called *Acetobacter* that float around freely. Short of full-scale vinegar, these critters produce sharp, prickly aromas described as *volatile acidity* or simply *VA* — and volatile they surely are. On the way to full vinegarhood, *Acetobacter* produces ethyl acetate, somewhere between nail polish remover and airplane glue.

Acetobacter love alcohol (which they turn into acetic acid) and crave oxygen, so an increase in VA means your wine has gotten too much oxygen — likely from barrels or other containers not being properly topped off and stoppered.

To control VA, you need good sanitation and the proper use of sulfur dioxide to kill off the perpetrators and limit exposure to the oxygen they require. Catch this problem early and a small amount of VA won't ruin your wine; let it go and your wine is in a pickle and good only for mixing with oil and drizzling on salad. Check out my forthcoming *Making Wine Vinegar without Trying For Dummies*.

Chapter 9

Finishing and Bottling

In This Chapter

▶ Fining for clarity, stability, and balance

▶ Filtering to make your wine shine

▶ Assembling the bottling line

▶ Finishing up in style

*T*he final stages of winemaking — cleaning up the wine one last time and getting it into bottles — keep home winemakers and their helpers nearly as busy as the opening flurry of the crush and fermentation. Lots of moving parts are in play, none of them all that complicated, but all of them require attention to detail. You've come this far: Finish it right.

Fining: Cleaning Up Wine's Act

Fining — adding various liquefied substances to wine in order to pull out something undesirable — often serves a purely cosmetic purpose, but sometimes fixes an issue that's truly getting in the way of enjoying the wine. More fining agents are on the market than the number of pages in this book; the following sections give you the highlights.

Winemakers differ in their opinions and practices about the order of multiple finings and what can be combined with what. Generally, the standard order is the order they appear here: bentonite before cold stabilization, tannin fining agents before closers like polyclar and sparkalloid.

Accounting for heat, cold, and protein

In your home winery, your wine has led its life in a narrow, moderate temperature range. In that happy environment, your wine has gotten clearer and clearer. But what happens when the bottled wine ends up in a refrigerator down around 40°F (4°C), or spends a few hours in your car on a sunny day and heats up to 90°F (32°C)? What could happen is *protein haze,* clumps of protein that come out of solution and show up as suspended particulate matter at stressful temperatures.

Most of your wines could be perfectly haze-free without fining. But then, when your prize Gewürztraminer comes out of the fridge looking like grapefruit juice, it's a bummer. Fining is preventive action, and worth doing.

The fining agent for protein removal is *bentonite,* a clay formed from volcanic ash (and first discovered near Fort Benton, Wyoming) that attracts protein molecules and keeps a grip on them as it sinks to the bottom of a wine vessel. Make the bentonite into a slurry by mixing it with a larger volume of hot water — the bentonite will expand rapidly and thicken into a pudding — and then pour the mixture into the wine, stirring to mix thoroughly. The bentonite, the protein, and whatever else it picks up should settle in about a week, and then you can carefully rack the cleaner wine.

Packaged bentonite comes with specific instructions on dosages, temperatures, and so on. Careful winemakers, commercial or home, do bench tests first, trying various dosages on half-bottles of wine, letting them settle, and then heating and cooling the samples to see what works. Trials can make sure you are using neither too much nor too little bentonite.

You can use bentonite on juice before fermentation as well as with finished wine. Bentonite included in wine kits often comes with directions to add it before adding yeast.

Getting bentonite out of carboy and barrels can be tricky; the sediment is all particles, not stuck together, and can be stirred up easily. Getting the wine clear may require more than one racking.

Stabilizing tartrates

Technically, stabilizing through chilling isn't a fining operation at all, because nothing but cold temperature is added to the wine. But this process also helps to get your wine clean, so I talk about it here.

Besides throwing a protein haze, cold temperatures can also lead to the formation of *tartrate crystals* — clear, odorless, crunchy little bits of tartaric acid that fall out of solution. You have probably encountered these "wine diamonds" in commercial wine; the crystals don't interfere with anything, they just look weird at the bottom of the last glass.

Commercial wineries routinely *cold stabilize* white wines, chilling them to near freezing for two weeks or so to force out the tartrate crystals before they appear in someone's refrigerator. If you have a freezer large enough to accommodate carboys for a few days, that's great. A halfway measure can also do a useful part of the job. Carboys of wine held at normal refrigerator temperature — around 40°F (4°C) — for two weeks will shed at least some of the tartrate crystals, reducing the chances that they'll show up later when the wine is served.

Fining reds to tame tannin

Fining for excess tannin improves drinkability, not just appearances. High-tannin grapes and wines — Cabernet Sauvignon, Tempranillo, Tannat — may end up unpleasantly astringent, even when they've had time to age in barrels or carboys. Ideally, restraint in winemaking keeps this problem from showing up, and in any case, a bit of excess tannin usually drops out of sight — or out of taste — when the wine is paired with food to absorb the scratchy astringency (the same feeling you might get from sucking on a tea bag).

But if too much tannin keeps you from enjoying the wine, or if you designed the wine for easy summer drinking and tannin was not part of the plan, fining can mitigate the problem.

The best and gentlest tannin remover is *isinglass*, made from sturgeon swim bladders and sometimes called *fish glue*. (See how much fun winemaking can be?) Dissolve freeze-dried isinglass in water at about a 1:250 ratio and stir into the wine, then rack the wine two weeks later.

Fining versus filtration

Fining and filtration both remove what you don't want in wine, but they operate in very different ways and can have very different consequences.

Fining agents work through electrical charges and the attraction of opposites: positively charged agents attract negatively charged compounds, negatively charged agents attract positively charged compounds. The fining agents aren't picky about what they attract; if the charge is right, they go for it. Consequently, fining can pull out good stuff as well as bad, stripping the wine of flavor or color or texture. Fining is quite useful — removing protein with bentonite is pretty standard practice, for example — but it can be a very blunt instrument.

Filtration, on the other hand, removes things based on size. Filter pads care no more than fining agents what those particles are, but sheer size turns out to be a pretty good criterion. Many microbes, which you don't want in your finished wine, are fairly large; flavor compounds, tannins and pigments are much smaller, and unlikely to get trapped in even the tightest filter.

Winemakers argue endlessly about filtration, and about whether it strips wines of vital ingredients, and whether it is somehow an affront to nature. In your garage — where your ability to do an extremely restrictive, truly sterile, possibly stripping filtration is zilch — filtration likely inflicts less collateral damage than fining.

Besides the sturgeon thing, fining for tannins is done with egg whites or liquid gelatin and with some chemical agents. Bench trials for any of these methods take time but are a good idea; you want to take out just enough tannin to restore balance in the wine, and overdosing will strip other desirable goodies at the same time.

Last resorts

These final two products qualify as last resorts because they are very broad-gauged fining agents, which have a tendency to pull out good stuff along with bad stuff — but they may come in handy.

If your wine has picked up some unpleasant mustiness, or turned a tad brown in the course of pre-bottle aging, you might freshen it up by fining with *polyclar* — poly-vinyl-poly-pyrrolidone, or PVPP — which goes after oxidized compounds and off-track pigments.

If your white wine absolutely refuses to get clear after several rackings, a dose of bentonite, and enough time to try your patience, my clarifier of last resort is *sparkalloid,* which contains silica derived from fossilized marine critters found in dry sea beds. (Someone should explore whether isinglass-sparkalloid wines pair well with fish dishes.) Sparkalloid is the true closer: It not only pulls junk out of your wine, but also tamps down any other fining agent you might have used into a nice, solid layer at the bottom.

Filtration: Making Your Wine Shine

Many home winemakers skip this step entirely, and their wines come out just fine. Filtration mainly serves a cosmetic purpose, making wine more brilliant and sparkling clear. As long as your wine has cleared thoroughly through time and gravity and is chemically and biologically stable, filtration is not required. But if you want to make wine that holds its own with the commercial competition, make filtration part of your arsenal.

Why bother filtering?

Filtration makes your wine look pretty and closer in appearance to the commercial wines you go out and pay good money for. Even a light filtration — and most of the time, that's all that's needed — makes a huge difference in clarity, in how the light dances through the glass, and in how appetizing the wine appears when it's poured and sipped. Rent a filter rig from your wine-making shop and push just one carboy of your wine through; the difference between before and after is startling. What you thought was pretty darn clear now seems like dishwater.

Filtration cannot do some things, like take out excess tannin or reduce volatile acidity. Nor can it reliably accomplish what commercial wineries call sterile filtration — removing everything down to .45 microns (millionths of a meter), guaranteeing your wine is microbe free. For home use, the tightest cellulose filter pads promise "sterile filtration" down to the ".5 micron" level (or even .2 micron). But this promise turns out to be "nominal .5 micron" — *nominal* as in "in name only," or more precisely, "most of the openings are right around .5 micron." And some of them aren't. True sterile filtration is not an option with home pad filters — but some serious cleanup is.

I started off filtering my wines, then gave it up for a while as just too much of a hassle, and then got back in the habit again a couple years ago. I'm never going back to unfiltered wine. Besides the vast upgrade in the visuals, my winemaking co-conspirators and I all think that the wines taste slightly cleaner, brighter, and fresher, with less interference from stray stuff that doesn't add anything useful. Maybe the effect is psychological; but then, what's wrong with feeling better about your wine?

Procedures and precautions

Filtration is the one step in home winemaking that always requires electrical machinery. Because of the pressure involved, you need a pump or some form of suction, to push or pull the wine, and for that, you need an electrical outlet. The exception is that winemakers who keep their wine in beer kegs can force the wine through a plate filter with gas pressure. Somewhere out there are home winemakers who have figured out how to rig up bicycle pumps to hoses and carboys and can filter their wine off the grid — but not many.

Dozens of options are available, spanning a wide range of prices, filtration capacities, and abilities to handle various levels of sludge. In all options, wine is sucked through a hose from a source container — a barrel or carboy — and then pushed through a filter medium that traps the sediment and lets cleaner wine through. The wine then goes through a second plastic hose into a target container or, in a very integrated setups, directly into bottling equipment.

The least expensive options are small canisters containing the filter medium that work with small pumps and a series of connecting hoses. At the higher end is the home winemaking standard, the Buon Vino Super Jet rig, which can pass larger volumes of wine through a set of three filter pads, available in varying degrees of tightness. A final, high-end option is the Enolmatic filler and filtration combination, in which a vacuum pump that is part of the bottle filler draws wine from its source through a filter housing and reusable cartridge and into the filler. All this equipment come with instructions.

Home filtration equipment usually offers three grades of cartridges or pads: coarse, rated at 5 to 8 microns; polish, rated at 1 or 2 microns; and sterile — again, that's what they are called, not what they accomplish — at about .5

micron or under. For most purposes, even with white wines where clarity is critical, coarse filtration makes a huge difference, enough to satisfy most of us. Polish filtration for whites and pinks makes them look absolutely gem-like. Home filtration at the .5 level makes wine even more brilliant in apearance, but is, in my opinion, not usually worth the trouble.

Even coarse filtration assumes that the incoming wine is pretty clear, not swimming in sludge; if the particulate load is too high, the filter will clog, the motor will overheat, and you'll have to bail out and start over. If you plan to do a polish or "sterile" filtration, start with a coarse round first to make the second round flow easier.

With all of the filtration setups, the first step is cleaning everything in the filter rig itself thoroughly by running through water, then a cleaning/sanitizing agent like sodium percarbonate, then a sulfur dioxide solution, and finally a citric acid solution — this last step readjusts the pH of the filter medium back from the pH 7 of water to something more wine-like, between 3.0 and 4.0. Then the wine itself gets pumped through. As soon as what's coming out looks like wine, put it into another container. When you're done, repeat the cleaning steps again to make sure that nothing left inside could breed microbes.

In all forms of filtration, be careful to limit the amount of oxygen the wine is exposed to. If the wine gets thoroughly aerated along the way, showing up with a foamy, beer-like head in the target container, that means a large amount of oxygen dissolved in the wine, which can adversely affect color, flavor, and longevity.

Make sure that the filtration device's fittings and connections are tight, its pads are securely in place, and that nothing is leaking air; if the target wine is full of foam, stop the process, tamp everything down, and try again.

The other trick in filtration is one that shows up in manual racking, too: getting a siphon flow started. Pumps seem like powerful things, and many are advertised as "self-priming." But the interaction between stretches of liquid and pockets of air in an enclosed tube are a wonder, so don't be surprised if it takes a while to get the knack of it. Try running clear water through your filtration setup before running your wine through.

Setting Up the Home Bottling Line

The bottling stage goes by surprisingly quickly, after all those months of waiting for your wine to come around. Half a dozen people in an assembly line can easily fill, cork, label, and capsule 30 or 40 gallons (115 to 150 liters) of wine — 15 or 20 cases — in a couple hours. That rapid assembly, however, depends on decisions and preparations in advance of The Big Day.

Bottles and fillers

To begin with, bottling requires bottles and ways to fill them.

Buying versus recycling

Most home winemakers start with the thought that they can save a little money by just recycling their own wine bottles and maybe those of their friends, cleaning them out and soaking off the labels.

Recycling your own bottles is indeed cheaper, and perhaps more environmentally friendly, and gives you something to do while your wine is aging and getting ready to bottle. It is also a tedious chore. You can soak off labels with everything from solutions of baking soda to ammonia, but you often need to scrape them off, too. You need to peel off the capsules — the foil wrappers at the top of the bottles — and that usually involves a knife or scissors. Then you have to rinse the bottles and rinse them again and perhaps clean them one more time with a sanitizing agent — and rinse them again.

If you have a teenager at home you want to punish, this might be a good fit. Scavenging bottles saves money — new, matching glass bottles generally cost about (USD)$1 each. But most homies who have made wine more than two or three times, or make more than a carboy or two a year, buy bottles.

The other downside of bottle recycling is that your bottles won't match. This may seem trivial, but to my mind, a Chardonnay poured out of a tall, dark, Bordeaux-style bottle loses some of its Chardhood.

Bottle shapes

Differences in bottle size — 1.5-liter magnums versus standard 750-milliliter bottles versus 375-milliliter half-bottles — can make a difference in how wines age over time. Differences in shape are simply a matter of traditional aesthetics in various wine regions, as are differences in glass color.

You can put your wine in any shape of bottle, but most homies gravitate toward the bottle shape a particular wine usually comes in. Cabernet, Merlot, and the rest of the Bordeaux varietals normally come in the high-shouldered bottles known as Bordeaux- or Claret-shaped; Pinot Noir, Chardonnay, and the reds and whites of the Rhône generally come in the slope-shouldered bottles known as Burgundy-shaped. However, Cabernet Franc wines from the Loire Valley come in "Burgundy" bottles, and many rosés from around the world, regardless of their base grapes, show up in tall, clear, high-necked German-style "hock" bottles. Figure 9-1 shows the most common bottle shapes; have fun using them.

Figure 9-1: Bottles, bottles, in many shapes.

German "hock" Bordeaux / Claret Burgundy / Rhône

Bottle cleaning and sanitation

Your bottles must be clean and free of any critters or substances that could undo your hard work. If you use personally recycled bottles, make sure they not only get clean, but stay clean over time as they wait for the actual bottling. If you buy bottles, you can assume they left the factory clean, and because they are normally placed upside down in their cardboard cases, they should be protected against the incursion of junk. If your cases of bottles get rained on or stuck in a moldy cellar, they may need another cleaning.

Fastidious bottlers rinse their bottles one more time, just before bottling, with a mild cleaning agent — preferably one that rinses off easily with just clear water. Standard practice on the bottling line itself is to flush each bottle with a light solution of sulfur dioxide, delivered by a spring-powered injector-rinser, and then place bottles upside down on the spokes of what's called a *Christmas tree* — the spiky rack for holding bottles shown in Figure 9-2 — to drain before being filled.

Figure 9-2: A Christmas tree, but don't expect to see Santa.

Wanda Hennig

Bottle fillers

You can hand fill bottles using a simple funnel and a measuring cup. However, hand filling tends to be inexact; you're always putting in a table-spoon too much or too little, pouring some off, and drizzling more in; after a case or two, it can get tedious. But if your total output is one carboy of wine, translating to two cases, a funnel and a cup can do the job.

For larger-scale bottling, two solutions are available. The simplest is a *bottling wand,* a thin plastic tube with a spring-loaded tip. When the tip is pressed — as against the bottom of a wine bottle — the wine flows, and when pressure is released, the flow stops. The space the wand itself takes up is just enough, after it's pulled out, to leave room for a cork and a bit of headspace. You can attach the wand to a length of plastic hose that drains wine by gravity/siphon from a carboy or other container.

Once you get to a dozen cases or so, the wand, like the funnel, gets tedious. For bigger volumes, manual bottle fillers with two or three spouts, like the one in Figure 9-3, make life easier. In this equipment, wine flows into a basin by gravity; an assembly much like a toilet float stops the flow when the basin is full; the weight of bottles hanging on the spouts tips them down enough to let wine flow through them; and the flow stops when the bottle is full.

Through the magic of hydraulics, the bottles hanging from the spouts fill only to the level of wine in the basin; they can't overflow. Once the full bottle comes off the spout, just enough room remains for a cork and a pinch of headspace. Half bottles, double-sized bottles, it doesn't matter; any bottle that fits on the spout fills correctly. (Doing a trial run on a basin filler with clear water is a good idea.)

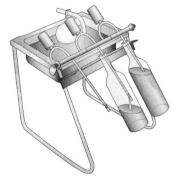

Figure 9-3:
You gotta love a piece of equipment this ingenious based on a toilet float.

Even though a basin filler does most of the work, be sure to inspect the bottles to see that they're being filled to the right level, with enough room for the length of the cork you're using (which can vary) and for about half an inch (about 15 millimeters) of air under the cork. Too low a level leaves too much oxygen in the bottle; too high a level can make wine squirt out of the bottle when the cork is inserted.

Although you can get wine into a wand or a basin filler in many ways, one good solution is to create a dedicated "filler vat." Take a small (20-gallon/75-liter) plastic fermenter and poke or burn a small hole in it on the side very close to the bottom. Insert a small plastic tap and its fittings, leaving an opening on the inside of the vat and some form of faucet/shutoff mechanism on the outside. Attach the hose that goes to the wand or to the basin filler to the tap. Place the vat high enough that gravity can do the work; siphon the wine to be bottled into the vat; open the tap and insert the wand into a bottle, or let the wine flow into the basin filler.

Fancier equipment for home bottling can be found, including specialized bottling tanks and integrated systems that combine filtration and bottling.

Corks and corkers

For home winemakers, the basic options for closing bottles come down to natural corks, synthetic corks, or for those with beer-making backgrounds, crown caps. Screwcaps, alas, require about (USD)$150,000 worth of equipment, which could seriously unbalance your home winemaking budget. The nearby "Closure complications" sidebar looks into the pros and cons of various wine closures; this section deals with the practicalities.

Natural corks are anywhere from five to ten times as expensive as synthetics, but get bonus points for being traditional. There is always some small chance of a "corked" wine — the unpleasant, intensely moldy result of a chemical known as TCA sometimes found in natural corks — but that likelihood is steadily declining. If you go with natural cork, spend the money on good ones, in either solid-body or agglomerate versions. I suggest making sure your corks come from one of the producers affiliated with the Cork Quality Council (www.corkqc.com).

If you choose synthetics, make sure your corker is happy with them; some corkers and some synthetic materials are not good matches; tiny, pinched tracks can get scored along the side of the cork, letting air in and wine out.

Both natural corks and synthetics come in a variety of lengths, from about 3/4 inch (15 millimeters) to 2 inches (51 millimeters). The general idea is that the shorter the expected bottle life, the shorter the cork; the greater the presumed longevity, the longer the cork. Somewhere in between is fine for home winemaking; quality is more important than size.

Crown caps are perfectly good as stoppers for wine that will be consumed within a year; commercial wineries use crown caps all the time for their own samples and trial projects. But besides being too air-leaky for wine that needs to age, crown caps also severely restrict the shapes and sizes of bottles you can use and make it likely your bottled wine will look a lot like bottled beer. But if you already have beer bottling equipment and know the ropes, crown caps are a perfectly practical solution.

Just before use, natural and synthetic corks should get a quick rinse with a mild sulfur dioxide solution to get rid of any stray cork dust or other flotsam, and then be drained or dried on paper toweling before insertion.

Closure complications

How to close a wine bottle has become one of the most contentious issues in the world of wine. For 300 years, the only answer was to put a cork in it; in the past two decades, synthetic corks, screwcaps, and other variations have made bottle-stoppering a highly charged debate.

Natural cork took a big hit in the 1990s over the prevalence of *cork taint,* a moldy, funky smell showing up in far too many bottles of wine. The funk was traced to a compound called *TCA* (trichloro-anisole), sometimes found naturally in cork and sometimes introduced inadvertently by the use of chlorine in washing and cleaning cork material. Synthetic corks quickly gained a large market share as a solution, particularly for mass-market wines, but hit their own bumps in the road when trials revealed that many let in too much oxygen over time, shortening wine life expectancy, and that some stuck to the bottle necks, becoming nearly impossible to remove.

Screwcaps, used for spirits and for low-end jug wines for decades, became the next new thing, promising to keep wine exactly as it was the day it was bottled. Screwcaps remain on a roll, rapidly gaining adherents, but also facing criticism for being almost too good. Research indicates wine needs a tiny amount of oxygen to age, and some screwcap-topped wines, starved for oxygen, end up with unpleasant sulfury odors or otherwise diminished aromatics. The screwcap folks say that the problem isn't the closure; it's deficiencies in the wine some people put under it.

To keep the pot boiling, the natural cork folks, who have greatly reduced the incidence of TCA in their stoppers in the past decade, have added another line of argument: environmentalism. Which do you prefer, they ask, a closure that comes from oak forests that trap carbon dioxide and preserve a traditional way of life, or artificial closures made from plastic and aluminum?

All the bottle closures have their advantages and disadvantages, and all are getting better by the day under competitive pressure. The perfect closure, like the perfect wine, is probably more an inspiring goal than an immediate prospect. Meanwhile, as we all worry more and more about carbon footprints, the problem may be the bottles, which get shipped all over the world, not the closures: what other product has packaging that often weights as much as the contents?

Corkers come in two basic styles. For small runs, hand-held cork inserters are fine: the cork gets knocked into the bottle with firm hand pressure or a small rubber mallet. Once you get beyond a couple cases, buying or renting a larger, stand-up manual corker, such as the one shown in Figure 9-4, becomes attractive. Taking advantage of leverage is a great relief to your hand, and stand-up corkers also give you more control over exactly how deeply the cork goes into the bottle neck.

The force needed to insert a cork also shoves extra air into the bottle, building up pressure. To let your bottles adjust, leave them standing straight up for a few days; the inside and outside air pressure will equalize. Then, for longer-term storage, put cases or bottles with natural corks on their sides or upside down, to keep the ends of the corks moist.

Figure 9-4:
A stand-up corker saves your hands and your back.

The finished look: Labels and capsules

Your wine will come across better to your bottling crew, your friends, and anyone who gets a bottle as a holiday present if it receives the final touches it deserves. Designing labels is fun, a chance to show off your sense of humor or your advanced wine geekiness, and a great place for photos of your family or your pets or the best blooms from your garden. Give your winery a fanciful name. You can mimic the label requirements for commercial wineries, specifying the alcohol level, the vintage, the growing area, and so on, or you can just make stuff up. All you need is a computer with basic word processing and graphics tools, and you can print out your labels on adhesive address labels in whatever size and shape you want.

Capsules do no earthly good in keeping air out of or wine inside a bottle, but they look cool, and only cost about a nickel each. The best part about these plastic/foil add-ons is watching them go on: slip a capsule over the end of the bottle neck, stick it into the steam coming from a bubbling tea kettle, and whoosh! The capsule shrink-wraps itself around the neck. (Figure 9-5 shows this process.) Alternatively, use a hair dryer and spin the bottle around. I guarantee that members of your bottling crew will fight to do this job.

Figure 9-5:
Using the power of steam to seal a capsule.

Bottling line checklist

Home wine bottling lines come in more configurations than anyone can count, so I won't attempt a comprehensive spec sheet. The following list offers pointers, especially for the first time you run a complex bottling:

- ✔ Finish up the work on your wine — the final racking, filtration, any other tweaks — the day before, or the morning before. Don't get crowded for time at the last minute and do something dumb when your bottling crew arrives and gets restless.

- ✔ Give your wine a final, farewell addition of SO_2 — around 25 parts per million — before bottling. This helps combat the oxygen introduced by bottling and helps with the wine's long-term stability.

- ✔ Think through the layout of your bottling line before you actually put it to work. Decide where you'll do it and see how much space you have; figure out how to get vessels and equipment close enough together or at the right elevation for gravity to work. Locate all the shims, props, and miscellaneous stuff you may need — a tea kettle or hair dryer for capsules, measuring cups, funnels, plenty of cloth and paper towels, and lots of buckets.

- ✔ Clean everything thoroughly before you use it — siphon tubes, fillers, corker innards, buckets, funnels. If a surface will touch wine, clean it.

- ✔ Set up the entire line before you start, even the space and equipment for the last bits like capsules, and decide where the cases will go. You'll have enough surprise decisions to make during the bottling run as it is.

- ✔ Start off slowly and deliberately, making sure everything works, all the equipment is in order, and everybody knows their jobs, then pick up the pace. A three-spout bottle filler processes bottles faster than one person at a corker can insert corks, for example, which could leave you with open bottles standing around sucking air and waiting to be tipped over.

When you're done, and before you have too much fun, clean everything again. Half the time at your bottling will be spent cleaning and re-cleaning, and half on actual bottling . . . plus the drinking part.

Closing the Deal

If you have more than a few gallons or cases of wine, bottling can get complicated with many small decisions and several people working in tandem. Especially with a boisterous crew, bottling can be just as intense as the craziness of the crush. It's also your last chance to hit the mark as the winemaker and give your wine a great sendoff.

Final oxygen and sanitation warning

The second that cork goes in, your wine is on its own, and so as your last official winemaking act, make sure to protect it from oxygen and unhelpful life forms.

The string of steps in bottling — moving the wine from barrels or carboys to a filler vat to a filler mechanism to the bottle to a corker — offers plenty of opportunity for oxygen exposure and sanitation lapses. Do everything else right, and then fill your bottles through filler spouts that have grown mold farms in the off-season? Not good. Increase the oxygen in and around your wine by aerated siphoning or leaky hose connections or leaving way too much headspace in the bottle? Don't go there.

During the bottling, periodically rinse your hands (all of you) in a sanitizing solution. Wear hats or hair nets — you really don't want hair in your wine. Clean your shoes. The time to let down your guard is five minutes after the last bottle is finished.

The bottling-day lunch

Amazingly enough, most other home winemaking books don't cover this essential point: The day you bottle your wine, you need to celebrate!

You will no doubt figure out your own rituals. Here at my garage winery, known as subterranean cellars, we've evolved a standard routine over a dozen years of three or four small bottlings per year. We invite a few folks over to work on the bottling, usually a few more than would be required for complete efficiency. We bottle the wine in a line that stretches out the door of the winery/garage and into the driveway, and then inside the house for capsules and labels. We all pause every now and then to pass around a glass of what's being bottled — purely for reasons of quality control, you understand — and tease each other about crooked label placement or the occasional minor spill. Then we adjourn to the backyard for a potluck lunch and begin removing the corks we just inserted, comparing our efforts with a commercial bottle or two. Life is good.

And over dessert, we start speculating about what new grapes we might try next year.

Chapter 10

Storing, Serving, and Starting Over

After your wine is bottled — especially your first wine — the urge to drink it immediately is powerful. Sure, open a bottle or two to celebrate, share some on the spot with your bottling crew, and pop a cork with one of your home winemaker pals. But just because your work on the wine is done, don't assume the wine itself is done — it's just entering a new phase of development. Remember how different it tasted from month to month while you were shepherding it along? Even with a cork in it, just wait.

You still need to monitor your wine and test it from time to time — only now that "testing" involves having a bottle with dinner. Keep your eyes, nose, and taste buds alert as the wine reveals more of its inherent qualities and the results of your handiwork. And while you're enjoying your creation, get ready for the next harvest — it's coming sooner than you think.

Storing and Tasting

Treat your own wine with the same respect you give commercial wine that you put down good money for — especially because you spent real money on your own wine, too, and a lot of hard work over many months. Give it a good home, give it some time, and give it some attention.

Beware bottle shock

The day you bottle your wine may be great fun for you, but it's probably the worst day your wine ever has. (Chapter 9 details the bottling process.) The wine has been resting peacefully for some time. Now it's getting squeezed through filter pads; absorbing a last dose of sulfur dioxide (SO_2); being run through tubes and hoses and pipes; and getting splashed into bottles. The bottles get corks and air pressure jammed into them, and then have their necks cooked to put on capsules. It's like a train wreck followed by a car crash.

Talking about tasting wine

Aside from winemaking, there's the fun part — wine tasting, which has its own lingo. This book isn't the place for the whole nine yards about how to taste wine. For that, you can consult *Wine For Dummies* by Ed McCarthy and Mary Ewing-Mulligan, both of whom can taste circles around me. But I do offer a brief list of wine-tasting terms you may want to become familiar with:

✓ **Appearance:** Both red and white wines should be *clear* — you should be able to see clearly through even the darkest red, with enough light. Finished wines that are *cloudy* (this is more obvious with whites) may simply be unfiltered, or they may be in the throes of unanticipated biochemical activity. If your own wine is cloudy, you need a good reason.

✓ **Aroma, bouquet, and nose:** Strictly speaking, *aroma* includes the smells produced by the grapes and by fermentation. *Bouquet* describes the smells that develop over time with bottle aging. The *nose* of a wine is whatever you pick up when you sniff a glass of it.

✓ **Body** and **finish:** These terms describe the wine's texture. *Body* is the apparent weight of a wine in the mouth, usually classified as *light-bodied, medium-bodied,* or *full-bodied.* The quantity of body isn't a measure of quality; some wines are supposed to be very light-bodied. *Finish* refers to the impression a wine leaves in the mouth, especially at the back of the mouth, and includes *persistence*, how long the impression lingers.

Wines with little or no finish are often called *short*; a long finish is a good thing.

✓ **Color:** *White*, *red*, and *pink* are self-explanatory. The various shades of red — ruby, garnet, and so on — aren't so important. But *purple* tones generally indicate young wine and *brick* or *brown* tones are a sign of age — and in a young wine, premature age from oxygen exposure. Whites can be extremely *pale* or *straw-like* or maybe *golden*; young whites with brown overtones are likely oxidizing before their time.

✓ **Flavor:** Deciding whether a wine tastes like blackberries or cherries is a small matter. What mainly counts is *balance*, the harmonious — or unharmonious — interrelation of several elements: the *intensity* of fruitiness; *acidity*, the tart edge of a wine, the quality that makes it refreshing; *alcohol*, the substance that makes it wine, but the level of which can be too low, making the wine taste like grape juice, or too high, making the wine seem *hot* and *burning* at the end; *sweetness*, desirable in some wines but not in others; *tannin*, compounds that are more texture than flavor, giving red wines bigger *structure*, denser mouthfeel, and perhaps *astringency*; and, sometimes, *oak flavor*, primarily *vanilla, spices,* and *smoke*.

✓ **Mouthfeel:** Texture of wine in the mouth, which may be full or thin, smooth or harsh and astringent, velvety, and so on, depending on the wine.

Not surprisingly, your wine may object to this type of treatment. All the jostling, the SO_2, and the sudden confinement in cramped quarters produce what's called *bottle shock* — a temporary deadening of the wine's aromas and flavors. The day after bottling is probably your wine's sensory low point.

The good news is bottle shock wears off in two or three weeks. Air pressure created by injecting the cork equalizes with the outside atmosphere. The SO_2 starts to get bound up and becomes less volatile, and your wine forgives you.

Storing happy wine

All wines — red, white, pink, dry, sweet, homemade, commercial — deserve a good home while they age in the bottle and wait to be consumed. The consensus for ideal storage conditions has four environmental aspects:

- ✔ **Temperature:** Somewhere between 55° and 60°F (13° to 16°C), and preferably constant, not swinging up and down.

  Temperature is the most important variable. Warm or hot storage — over 70°F (21°C) — for extended periods of time make wine age rapidly and not very well — the character gets slowly cooked out. Wine lore has it that one afternoon in the back seat of a hot car with the windows rolled up is like a year in a proper cellar.

- ✔ **Humidity:** Fairly humid, around 70 percent. Humidity keeps natural corks from drying out and limits evaporation. If the air outside the bottle is moist, the water in the wine has no incentive to roam.

- ✔ **Light:** As little as possible. Light shining through glass can accelerate certain chemical reactions.

- ✔ **Vibration:** As little as possible. Exactly why vibration is a no-no has never been fully explained, but it's on all the lists.

In the real world — your house or apartment — meeting these standards may be tough, but do what you can. If you have a lot of your wine bottled and no room to keep it, ask a friend with a cool basement or an air-conditioned garage. Trading wine for good storage space is a great deal that can pay off for years. If you have even more than that — as some prolific home winemakers do — consider putting it into commercial wine storage facilities, just as you would commercial wine.

Earmark a portion of your wine — maybe just two or three bottles, maybe two or three cases — for longer-term aging, two or three or five or ten years. You'll learn something from tasting them down the road, and you'll have occasions to pat yourself on the back (though not with the same hand that's holding the glass).

Tasting for quality and development

I'm not trying to talk you out of drinking your wine; but I encourage you to stretch it out enough to enjoy it fully. Home wines often get bottled a year or more sooner than commercial wines from the same harvest, so they deserve a little time to mature. As you dip into your output, you're simultaneously observing and enjoying the wine's development in the bottle and making sure nothing funny is going on.

Just as your wine went through changes as it aged, it goes through more transformations in the bottle — slower, but just as significant. First the wine gets over bottle shock and gets back to being the wine you remember. Over months — or years, depending on the wine — the fresh, youthful, fruity character pulls back and some of the exotic, floral aromatics disappear.

If the young-wine qualities are what you love about a particular white wine or rosé, drink it while they are in flower. Not all wines want to age.

Longer term, especially for bigger reds, the various elements of wine's balance — acid, tannin, fruit, oak — become more integrated. The wine takes on one overall taste definition, no longer a collection of moving parts. After some time in the bottle, perhaps two to five years, both reds and whites start to develop a new set of aromatic characteristics — called *bottle bouquet* — layered on top of the fruit and perhaps oak that went inside at bottling. The sky's the limit on what might arise: hints of leather, tobacco, nuts, dried fruit, petrol, mushrooms, truffles . . . . These bottle aromas aren't wine faults; they're part of the normal development over time. Fans of older wines seek out and revel in these aromas.

As the winemaker, your tasting and smelling have another component. You need to judge the impact of the decisions you made along the way, such as your choice of fruit, yeast, or oak; your handling of acidity levels; and your blending decisions. You may conclude that the fruit is fabulous, but the tannins are too much, or that putting the wine through malolactic fermentation was a mistake. Tasting one vintage helps draw lessons for the next. As you taste, make notes in your winemaking log for future reference.

But if you find something has gone wrong — seriously wrong — you may need to fix it, even at this late date. Read on.

Fixing Bottled Wine

Pulling out corks, pouring out wine, going back into remedial winemaking, and bottling all over again is no fun — but it beats having all your wine go bad and stay bad. If you get to this point — trust me, *not* very likely —

remember that you're in the good company of countless commercial wineries that have done some very public product recalls.

Don't undo your winemaking for something small — a wine that's not perfectly balanced, a blending decision you wish you had done differently, a dessert wine that isn't quite sweet enough. Low levels of wine faults are often quite tolerable, too, as tasting through your local wine shop will testify. If your wine is enjoyable to drink, drink it, and tweak your technique next time. But if the wine is definitely headed south — usually from unscripted microbial adventures — put your winemaking hat back on.

Diagnosing problems

You know those signs on fire hose cabinets in public buildings, the ones that say, "Break glass only in case of emergency"? Read this section only in case of a true cellar emergency.

Before you do a mass cork-pull, work with a sample bottle or two to narrow down the problem. The right diagnosis is the key to the right solution.

Some problems show up in how the wine smells:

- ✔ **Sulfides:** If your bottled wine's aromas are in rotten-egg country — caused by hydrogen sulfide, mercaptans, and their ilk — it's too late for the racking and aeration that might have worked just after fermentation. Do a trial with copper sulfate (as explained in Chapter 8), uncork the bottles, and fix it.

- ✔ **Barnyards and Band-Aids:** Foul, fowl-like, or medicinal smells are the aromatic calling cards of *Brettanomyces*, a rogue yeast that can go into high gear in the bottle. You should be able to kill it with sulfur dioxide (see Chapter 6), but the aromas may persist. Catch this early, and you're fine. If you can live with it, keep drinking.

- ✔ **Vinegar:** Highly unlikely, since vinegar-producing bacteria *(acetobacter)* require lots of oxygen. Treatment requires sulfur dioxide to kill bacteria (again in Chapter 6), but residual odors may persist. Again, if you catch this early, you can take care of it and move on.

Other issues reveal themselves through visual clues. If a white or pink wine is perfectly clear at normal storage temperature, but clouds up when chilled or heated, the problem is unstable proteins. You can just live with this — I certainly have — because it's purely cosmetic. Or you can uncork the wine, fine it with *bentonite* (a process I describe in Chapter 9), settle it, then rack it clean.

If the wine becomes cloudy at normal room temperature, or starts throwing a visible sediment soon after bottling, or shows tiny bubbles at the surface of the wine, microbes are on the move. This might indicate a final bit of yeast fermentation, the result of a small percentage of sugar and some live yeast still in the wine; or it might be malolactic activity, either the last gasp of a desired malolactic or the start of an unplanned, unwanted bacterial project.

The best way to diagnose the problem is to test a sample of the wine. Test for residual sugar, a clue that yeast fermentation may be going on. Test for malolactic activity and completion. (I talk about these tests in Chapter 7.)

Treat the wine depending on what you find. For wine you wanted dry but apparently isn't, add yeast and nutrient to finish the job. If the problem is a fermentation starting up in a sweet wine, treat it with sulfur dioxide and perhaps sorbate (see Chapters 6 and 20). For an incomplete malolactic, add malolactic starter and nutrient and get it done; but if malolactic wasn't part of the program, try SO_2 and perhaps lysozyme (see Chapter 7).

The clearest clue of all is audible: the sounds of corks popping out of bottles because of the buildup of internal pressure. Or the evidence may be less dramatic, and the corks may just start inching up above the rims of the bottles. The culprit is almost guaranteed to be *malolactic in the bottle*, one of the home winemaker's worst nightmares, and the solution is either to finish the malo with another inoculation of malo starter or stop it once and for all with SO_2 and possibly lysozyme.

Re-bottling all over again

When you know what's wrong with your wine, start pulling corks. Put the affected wine into clean carboys, not barrels, to make treating the wine and seeing how it responds easier. Proceed with whatever treatment is called for. As you open, decant, treat, and re-bottle your wine, do your best to minimize further exposure to oxygen.

If the problem is mild — a whiff of hydrogen sulfide — you may be able to fix it and re-bottle in a few days. More stubborn issues — like fermentations where the last bit of activity takes its sweet time — may run longer.

Test with your sniffer and your taste buds and your lab equipment to be sure the problem is truly fixed, and then let the wine sit a week longer just to be even more sure — you don't want to do this again.

You can rinse and re-use the bottles, and if you're careful, the labels will withstand the effort. The corks, alas, are history. Write down the experience, move on, and enjoy your salvaged wine even more — you've earned it.

Serving and Pouring with Pride

You've gone to considerable trouble to make your wines, waited months from harvest time, and now you get to reap the rewards. Enjoy the experience. Drinking your wine doesn't take a lot of effort, but presenting your wines under the right conditions is only fair — both to the winemaker and the wine.

Showing off your wine

The wine you made is not just another beverage, an alcoholic alternative to iced tea. You've produced something most of your friends probably think is impossible. Turning a bunch of grapes into well-made wine seems like magic. You have every right to pour your wine with satisfaction and a smile. Your wine isn't "just homemade." The proper description is, "Yeah, I made this."

Serving your wine to family and friends alongside the commercial competition is an excellent way to showcase your efforts. You might taste your Merlot with one or two premium commercial versions and compare them. For a dinner party where you're serving an appetizer wine, a main dish wine, and a dessert wine, use your own wine for one course as a way of saying, "My wine is in their league, too." Context is everything in tasting and appreciating wine, so putting your handiwork in the company of wines people expect to pay good money for is not only enjoyable, but — if you'll pardon the expression — good marketing.

Every time my friends and I bottle up some wine, I make a point of finding a bottle or two — usually in the $10- to $20-range — of comparable commercial wines, and we taste them all over lunch. For a recent bottling of a dry Chenin Blanc, I opened bottles from France's Loire Valley, South Africa, and California; for a three-grape blend in the style of Portugal's Douro Valley (my grapes, of course, were from California), I managed to locate an actual Douro made from the same varieties. The point of these exercises isn't to force people to tell me mine is better, but rather to put the homemade wine in context, showcasing the strengths and weaknesses of the whole lineup. It's the company you (and your wine) keep.

Gauging temperature and glassware

Temperature is a crucial part of wine fermentation, and it's just as important in serving wine — yours or anybody else's — to show off its best properties.

At least in the United States, white wines frequently get served a few degrees too cool, at temperatures that dampen the aromatic qualities. Whites tend to get opened straight from the refrigerator, at a temperature not much above

40°F (4°C). Wine this cold is certainly refreshing, but it's not all that it can be. The same wine at 50°F (10°C) shows more volatile aromatics that you can pick up via your nose and mouth. If your wine has been thoroughly chilled in the refrigerator, give it half an hour outside before opening it.

Red wines often get served too warm, which emphasizes the alcohol and throws off the balance of elements. Small restaurants sometimes store their wine too close to the kitchen, and the temperature in many houses is on the warm side, too. (The notion that red wines should be served at "room temperature" dates back to 19th century England, to foggy weather and houses without central heating — definitely not today's idea of room temperature.) Most reds should be served around 60° to 65°F (16° to 18°C), and lighter reds — Beaujolais, Pinot Noir — often benefit from being a few degrees cooler. If your chosen bottle has been sitting in a warm house, give it half an hour in the refrigerator before you open it.

Like any aspect of wine appreciation, temperature preferences are subjective; personal taste varies, and different grapes and wine styles can also show best at different temperatures. Find the temperature at which your wine sings the sweetest and try to serve it that way.

Serve your wine in good, matching glassware. Serving company in matching glassware is a nice touch; it makes you and your wine seem more professional and makes everyone's experience more consistent.

Unless you have unlimited storage space and an uncontrollable need to spend money, don't bother buying a dozen sets of different glasses allegedly calibrated to different grape varieties. The shape of a wine glass does affect how the aromatics rise out of the glass, but because the range of aromatics in a dozen Zinfandels varies as much as the difference between a Zinfandel and a Pinot, relax and use the same glassware for both (separately, of course).

A modest, 10- to 12-ounce (300- to 350-milliliter) glass is fine for whites. Use a slightly larger, 18- to 20-ounce (530- to 600-milliliter) glass for reds, both with the standard tulip shape. Use the smaller glass for dessert and sparkling wines. That's all you need.

Cycling from Harvest to Harvest

When you get into the winemaking habit — and I'm willing to bet that you will — the end of one harvest rolls right into preparation for the next. In fact, if you age reds for a year or more, the vintages start overlapping, with new grapes coming in before the old ones have been bottled. Whatever the timing, part of wrapping up each cycle is making sure both the winemaker and the winery's equipment are properly positioned for another go-round.

Applying lessons learned

Wine takes months or even years to show what it's made of — how good the fruit was, how careful the winemaking, how spot-on or clueless the various decisions about steering wine style were. Veteran winemakers with illustrious careers get only thirty, maybe forty chances in their lifetimes to get it right; compare that with how many times a professional chef gets to try making a perfect soufflé, or a musician gets to work on a new lick. The only way to get better is to milk every winemaking experience for all it's worth (pardon the incongruous beverage metaphor).

Start by evaluating the wine itself, including what you like and don't like about it. Did it come out balanced? Did the tannins provide enough structure, or too much? Did a little too much oxygen get into the act? How much fun would it be to do this wine again, only more of it?

Collect opinions from multiple tastings and ask your friends and family. With your judgment and theirs, try to get more than an up or down vote — "I really like this wine!" — and into more concrete description — "What's great about this wine is how complete it is: a beginning, middle, and finish in my mouth."

Look back over the log book where you took notes from the time the grapes arrived till you slapped on the last label. Try to find the connections between what you did and how the wine came out. Were you happy with the yeast choices, or did they give you fits? Did you pay scrupulous attention to adding and monitoring sulfur dioxide, or let it slide at a critical time? Would a couple gallons of grape X have made a better blend? Would it have been better to oak just one of the two carboys? Should I try another source for my next Vignoles? Think through a checklist of options — like the Red and White Winemaking Decision Trees in Chapters 11 and 16, respectively — and consider what you might do differently.

Whenever possible, I try to make any new grape variety or new wine style two years in a row, hopefully with the same fruit. It's a chance to undo any mistakes from round one, experiment with variations on a theme, figure out how good the fruit really is, and see, smell, and taste in sensory detail the impact of my work and decisions. The two vintages make great comparisons.

Giving your equipment a rest

Some winemaking equipment — scrub brushes, testing tools, a thief for pulling samples, all those buckets — stays in frequent, year-round use, so cleaning, maintenance, and replacement are routine parts of winemaking. The bigger-ticket items — in size and price — may not be equipment you use all the time, such as crushers, presses, filter rigs, and bottling rigs. Or else they sit holding wine for long periods, such as carboys and barrels.

Some suggestions for off-season care of your equipment:

- **Barrels:** Empty barrels invite trouble, as discussed in Chapter 8. A little leftover wine, a little moisture, a lot of air, and some ambient heat add up to a microbial field day. If your production schedule means a still-usable barrel can't be re-filled with wine soon, keep it filled with water and a mild solution of sulfur dioxide and citric acid instead.

- **Basket press:** Clean thoroughly, especially between the wooden slats (or in the mesh of a stainless steel cage), with a sanitizing agent and a brush. Rinse thoroughly. If you pressed red grapes, don't bother trying to get all the red out of the wooden slats, because you can't; if you plan to do both reds and whites, you need two sets of slats. Cover, if possible.

- **Bottling rig:** After use, rinse thoroughly to get rid of leftover wine. The trick is cleaning the filling tubes. Fill the basin with clear water and start a siphon into each filling tube, putting bottles on the ends to catch the flow of water. Then dissolve a small amount of a sanitizing agent in the basin water, and refill the bottles, leaving them on the filler and keeping some of the cleaning liquid in the filler tubes. After five minutes, rinse everything thoroughly. Store it covered.

- **Carboys:** Carboys that stay empty for a while, even just a week, should be cleaned thoroughly, rinsed with sulfur dioxide, allowed to dry completely, and then sealed — use an airlock, or a bit of plastic wrap and a rubber band around the neck.

- **Corker:** Use mineral oil and a paper towel to clean the top, bottom, and inside of the space that accepts corks; cover this area with a plastic bag.

- **Crusher:** After its final use of the season, clean thoroughly with strong water pressure, especially in between the rollers and around all the beaters or spokes that separate the grapes from the stems. Store the crusher with some kind of cover, even a shower curtain or trash bags taped together, to keep dust and junk from accumulating inside.

- **Fermenters:** Clean plastic fermenters thoroughly after use with a sanitizing agent and lots of water rinses. Get them thoroughly dry and keep them dry off-season, because moisture breeds microbes. If the thin plastic lining is torn (which happens eventually), cleaning gets compromised, so put another fermenter on next year's shopping list.

- **Filtration rigs:** After each use, clean thoroughly by rinsing with a sanitizing agent like sodium percarbonate, a sulfur dioxide solution, and clear water. Dry thoroughly and drain any water out of the hoses. Clean the ceramic plates by hand with a brush, as well. Store covered.

- **Leftover fermentation products:** Yeast sealed in pouches can spend a year in the refrigerator and work fine. Freeze-dried malolactic starter, if unopened, can stay viable in the freezer for another year. Nutrients for yeast and malolactic and most enzymes and fining agents can last a year at room temperature if tightly wrapped to keep moisture out.

Part III
Deeper Into Reds

"Okay, who wanted the glass of Pinot?"

In this part . . .

Most home winemaking books have sections about making red wines and sections about making whites. But nobody makes just "red wine." People make Zinfandel or Pinot Noir or Baco Noir.

While the universals of winemaking are, well, universal, different grapes require different strokes. This part traverses the various "advanced" techniques that can make Merlot memorable and Syrah sensational.

Chapter 11

What's Special about Red Wines?

Home winemakers are drawn to red wines the way women go for chocolate and little boys like to blow stuff up. Red wines are bigger, bolder, more bang for the buck, and make a big statement when you show off that first bottle. Muscle in red wines is fairly easy to produce, and so is muscle-bound — too much of everything. The art of the red wine is balancing power and finesse.

This chapter surveys a number of optional "advanced" techniques you can use for turning out tasty reds and some general considerations about red wine style. The common thread running through these techniques is playing fast and loose with the conventions of basic, routine red winemaking, yet doing so carefully. All of them pertain to the period of fermentation, when decisions matter most. Later chapters in this part match the techniques with particular grape varieties and pass on advice from professional winemakers. Go ahead: Go red!

Exploring the Deceptive Ease of Reds

This section discusses red winemaking philosophy. You don't need a philosophy to make wine, but for making good wine, it comes in handy.

Contrary to most people's hunches, red wines are generally easier to make at home than whites. Whites seem lighter and simpler and take fewer steps; reds, however, are more forgiving, more tolerant of slight mess-ups. A hint of funky unseemliness in a white can be fatal; in a red, it could become a feature, drawing praise for "earthiness." Red grapes come with lots of stuffing that spills out easily into the fermenter; white grapes need coaxing. Check your mental photo gallery of old-time home winemaking: All those European immigrants in the New World fermenting wine in their basements and sheds, without a trace of formal training. What are they making? Red wine.

 The fact that red winemaking can be a little more casual, a little less compulsive, can also set a trap for the novice winemaker. The only thing easier to do with red grapes than making wine is overdoing it and making a red wine so over-extracted it's mean.

Balancing power and finesse

Red winemaking is the eternal quest to balance power and finesse. *Power* and *finesse* are handy catch-words, and every winemaker on earth is in favor of them, but neither is easy to define. You can measure alcohol, acid, and sugar. But what instrument tests for the percentage of finesse? What scale quantifies power? The answer is that the wine drinker rates these subjective qualities.

Power in a red wine should mean the following (at least):

- ✔ An intensity of flavors
- ✔ Enough complexity to offer some sensation to every part of your mouth, front to back
- ✔ An edge, a structure, a sense of definition that comes from acid and tannin and makes it wine, not fruit syrup
- ✔ Sensations that linger (pleasantly, one hopes)
- ✔ The impression of an integrated whole, not a bundle of components

Qualities associated with *finesse* in a red wine — a truly slippery term — include the following:

- ✔ Continuity between the wine's smell and taste
- ✔ A harmonious balance of elements, nothing — not oak, tannin, acid — overpowering the rest
- ✔ No irritating, distracting sour notes or off aromas
- ✔ A refreshing quality, even in a massive wine, that makes you want to take another sip (not just stare at it in awe)

A few red grapes and styles — like early drinking Beaujolais made from Gamay, perfect for a picnic — revolve around fresh fruit and youthful exuberance. And while they're delightful, they are, alas, rarely considered "serious" wines. The big names in Big Reds — Cabernet Sauvignon, Merlot, Zinfandel,

Syrah, Tempranillo, even Pinot Noir — deliver a full-size mouthful of wine, or at least they're expected to. But if they're only big and are also clumsy, top-heavy, or dumb-as-a-post — in other words, lacking finesse — these reds don't impress anyone.

To develop your own sense of what makes for power and finesse, try a lot of wines, from different places, grapes, and producers, and judge for yourself. In your winery, despite the lack of guaranteed techniques, the starting point is this: Your grapes will deliver the elements of power; your job, as winemaker, is nurturing the finesse.

Getting a high from sugar, alcohol, and pH

For centuries, winegrowers in Europe struggled to get their grapes ripe, with plump fruit flavors and enough sugar to produce the alcohol for full-bodied, balanced wine. Today, throughout many of the major New World wine regions — California, Australia, Argentina, and Chile — winemakers battle the opposite problems: overripe grapes, super-high sugar levels, unbalanced alcohol percentages, and pH readings that no textbook would tolerate.

Cooler-climate regions have less trouble with these basic parameters of juice and wine chemistry. New Zealand, Canada's Okanagan Valley and Niagara Peninsula, New York's Finger Lakes and Long Island, and Oregon — these areas have different issues. But because California is the major supplier of grapes for home winemakers in North America, and because sugar levels are creeping up elsewhere, super-ripe grapes may show up in your home winery.

High sugars don't automatically translate into big, powerful wine; all they do with certainty is generate a lot of alcohol. The volume of sugar can outpace the intensity of the fruit, the complexity of the flavors, or the roundness of the mouthfeel and produce that unlikely wonder: A wine that is both huge and thin. Trying to compensate with great lashings of oak flavor just makes the wine weirder. To achieve some finesse, you may need to rein in the power.

If you're working with a trusted fruit source, and you know the grapes can create balanced wine despite elevated sugar or alcohol, fine. But if some unknown fruit lands in your lap (or your crusher) with a Brix level up in the high 20s, the best course is to deal with it immediately — that's what water is for. Similarly, if your juice or your just-fermented wine has an inflated pH, anywhere up near 4.0, get ready to add some acid, maybe a lot of acid.

It's not the grapes' fault; they didn't decide when to get picked. The sooner you align the building blocks of balance, the better your chances of ending up with a winning wine.

Tannin truths and tales

The standard folk wisdom about tannins, inside the wine industry and more broadly, goes something like this: Tannins in grapes are either green or ripe; tannins in wine are either hard or soft; skin tannins are better (softer) than seed tannins. Also, over time, tannins form longer and longer chains, becoming smoother and less astringent, until finally, after long aging, they become so large they just fall out.

Recent research suggests every one of these propositions is dubious.

No one has yet been able to produce a sample of "green" or "ripe" or "hard" or "soft" tannins. Tannins are pretty much tannins. The perception of "hard" tannin in a wine is mainly the result of more tannin, not a different kind.

Longer tannin chains (tannins have a fondness for binding with each other) turn out to be more astringent, not less, in sensory trials. Which only makes sense: Larger particles are more abrasive than small ones. A mouthful of sand is bad enough; a mouthful of gravel . . . .

Therefore, it's intriguing that seed tannins are generally shorter — and thus less astringent — than skin tannins. Seed tannins average ten units in length, while skin tannins average a little north of thirty units, which makes them three times as "hard."

Over time, tannins form longer chains — and then break up into shorter ones, and then play tag in a seemingly haphazard fashion. But they do not go away: When researchers at the Australian Wine Research Institute (AWRI) looked at a 50-vintage run of one particular Cabernet Sauvignon, they found vintage variations in tannin content, but no overall decline with age.

"One thing that is good about being a tannin scientist," says Paul Smith of the AWRI, "is you know you've got a job for life — if the funding keeps coming in!"

Managing tannins

Tannins come with the red wine territory. Every red grape contains some; every red wine ends up with some. *Tannins,* found in the skin, seeds, and stems of grapes, give red wine a structure, a substance, and a character that distinguishes it from free-floating fruit juice (similar to what acidity does for whites). Tannins also help preserve red wine color, binding up over time with the anthocyanin pigment compounds, and play a key role in maturation and longevity.

Tannins do their work best when they don't make their presence known — certainly not in a harsh, astringent finish. Some tannins are necessary to promote full, round mouthfeel; too high a concentration of tannins makes wine downright painful.

Managing tannins isn't an issue in white winemaking, because the grape skins are usually out of the picture. Extracting excess tannins is harder to accomplish on a home scale than a commercial scale; but homies are less likely to produce the temperature, the punchdown pressure, and the hard, mechanical pressing that can lead to a tannin overdose. Commercial operations test for the tannin levels; you have to rely on your taste buds.

My rule is this: For grapes that are naturally rich in tannins — including Cabernet Sauvignon, Petite Sirah, and Tempranillo — take it easy during fermentation and try to get to the fruit, not the tannin. For lower-tannin grapes (often also lower-color grapes) — like Pinot Noir and Grenache — aim for as much extract and structure as you can. The next section looks at techniques.

Thinking oak is oaky-dokey

Wine and oak have a classic love-hate relationship. In the proper amount, the flavors of oak fill in a wine's profile, make it seamless, and add richness. In an overdose, oak makes wine stupid; it is, hands down, the most common enemy of finesse. If lumber is your thing, consider forestry, not winemaking.

Suitable oak treatments for different red grapes and styles vary widely. Oak is surely one place where formulaic, one-size-fits-all winemaking makes no sense. Some grapes love new oak flavors; some just want the tiniest hint of wood, if that. The chapters in the rest of Part III offer suggestions about using oak to its best effect.

Playing with the Rules — Options, Alternatives, and Experiments

A great deal of very tasty commercial red wine is made using the basic techniques described in earlier chapters of this book: crush the grapes, add yeast, ferment the must, press the wine, age it (usually in wood), clean it up, and bottle it. Some truly interesting, more modern wines make use of additional techniques and options, all of which depart from the standard conventions about temperature or oxygen or fermentation time.

Some of these alternatives are especially well suited for certain grape varieties and wine styles, and some might just be fun to try in your winery when you have a handle on the basics.

Taking a cold soak

The main extraction of goodies from red grape skins — pigment, tannin, flavor compounds — normally occurs during fermentation in the presence of rising ethanol and warm temperatures. Some winemakers, particularly in the world of Pinot Noir craftsmanship, try to get some of that extraction done early, before the alcohol and heat show up.

The technique

The technique is called a *cold soak* — letting the crushed red grapes and their juices sit and stew for anywhere from one to three days before adding yeast or allowing "wild" yeast to take hold. (Turn to Chapter 6 for a discussion of yeast.) In a solution of just water and sugar, grape skins yield up their contents, though at a slower rate than they do in a warm bath of alcohol.

A proper cold soak requires temperature control and protection against oxygen. The must should be kept under 60°F (16°C), preferably closer to 50°F (10°C). Keeping the temperature this chilly usually requires either a chilled room or food-grade dry ice. The must should be shielded from oxygen to discourage microbial activity, which means covering the container with plastic sheeting and blanketing the must with carbon dioxide or some other inert gas. The soaking grapes should receive an initial dose of SO_2 at 50 parts per million for protection.

Creating these conditions may be tough in your garage, but if you're a Pinot Noir zealot, you're likely to try at least once. Users of frozen red grapes get a bit of an automatic cold soak; the fruit takes two or three days to thaw.

The pros and cons

Opinions vary on the benefits of cold soaking:

- Advocates claim that the gentler extraction brings out delicate flavors, better color, and softer tannins. And by doing some of the work early, you have the option of pressing early, not waiting until the fermentation has gone completely dry, thus avoiding over-extraction at the end.

- Skeptics note that there isn't really any scientific validation for these claims, just anecdotal testimonials, and that letting crushed grapes sit around for a few days is an invitation to spoilage.

The cold soak controversy is another indication that winemaking isn't an exact science — which just makes it more fun.

Pulling off pink

Chapter 19 extols the virtues of rosé and other forms of pink wine. Here the point is that drawing off some juice — 5 to 10 percent of the total — from recently crushed grapes can be a tool in *red* winemaking. For enhancing power, what could be simpler than reducing the ratio of liquid juice to solid skins, thus enhancing concentration?

The best part is that later on, you can not only thank your rosé for its contribution to your red wine program; you can drink it, too.

Multiplying yeast strains

The first duty of a yeast strain is to get your wine dry, and the heart of being able to do that is handling the temperatures and alcohol levels your winemaking creates. Beyond that, different strains of yeast offer different effects, ranging from extracting certain aromatic compounds to encouraging chemical reactions that promote structure in wine. In my experience, what yeast suppliers claim about their various strains and their capacities is real. That is, in a laboratory setting, that strain truly did produce those effects.

The same results may or may not happen in your garage, of course. Your grapes aren't the ones they used in the lab and may not have the same pH, the same nutrient levels, and so on. Many of the apparent differences in the by-products of yeast strains that are striking right after fermentation tend to diminish over time, within six months to a year.

Still, if you have enough grapes to split the batches, experimenting with multiple yeast strains can be instructive. The later chapters in Part III suggest commonly available strains, and you can unearth more with a little research. Try combinations that emphasize different types of fruit character, or one that maximizes fruit and one that maximizes structure. Even if it all ends up in the same final wine, tasting the differences along the way is usually a revelation.

Multiple strains of yeast work best with multiple batches of wine, not mixed together as a cocktail in one fermenter. One of the strains will reproduce faster and come to dominate within a day or two, canceling your experiment.

Fermenting a multitude of grapes

Combining two or more grape varieties in a single fermentation has a long tradition in winemaking, stretching back to when growers planted multiple varieties in the same vineyard and harvested everything at once. In the more precise modern age, joint fermentation is less common, but still practiced.

Co-fermentation makes sense in situations where you know the wines will be blended later on, anyway — the constituents of a Bordeaux blend or a Rhône blend or your own invention. Blending two or three wines after they've finished fermentation and malolactic and developed some character allows for more control of the proportions and the resulting flavors; blending the grapes in the fermenter marries the flavors from the beginning. If possible, ferment a small amount of each grape on its own so that you can tweak a final blend.

Fermenting grapes together, of course, requires having them arrive at the same time. (Frozen grapes have the advantage that you can schedule when they're ready.) The timing doesn't have to be absolute. No harm will come in adding Grape Two a day, or at most two days, after the fermentation of Grape One kicks off. But make sure that Grape Two is at the same temperature as Grape One so as not to shock and kill the yeast population.

One intriguing variation on co-fermentation is the practice of mixing white grape skins with red grape fermentations. The most prominent example is the common practice in the southern Rhône of adding Viognier skins (after those grapes are pressed) to fermentations of Syrah and other reds; the result can be both enhanced aromatics in the red wine and, paradoxically, better red wine color. The technical basis for this practice is known as *co-pigmentation*, in which certain compounds in the white skins help stabilize the color pigments from the red skins. If you try this, add no more than about 10 percent white skins — that is, skins from 10 pounds (4.5 kilograms) of pressed white grapes — to 100 pounds (45 kilograms) of crushed red grapes.

Fermenting with whole grapes and clusters

Most red wine fermentations feature crushed grapes in a juice/wine soup, allowing the yeast to get their hands on every particle of skins and seeds. Sometimes, winemakers choose instead to include some portion of either whole clusters or just whole grape berries in the mix.

Whole clusters allow you to extract some additional tannin from the stems, so a little can help beef up a lighter wine, such as a Pinot Noir, but a lot of stems get harsh and green in a hurry, so use them sparingly. Whole clusters also help to hold down the temperature of a red fermentation, and can contribute some spicy flavor notes. Do this by putting a layer of whole clusters at the bottom of your fermenter, then adding the crushed grapes on top.

Commercial wineries are moving more and more towards using whole berries, simply destemmed without crushing. This method adds a fruitier element to a red fermentation. The yeast can get to the innards of the grapes through the openings created in destemming, but extract a bit less tannin and color from both the seeds and the intact skins. However, getting the grapes off the stems can be a neat trick at home. If your crusher-destemmer will allow you to remove the rollers, you can let all the clusters fall through to the destemming level (see details on destemmer-crushers in action in Chapter 5). You may be able to invent other ways to strip the berries by hand.

Fermenting inside the grapes — carbonic maceration

Whole clusters of intact grapes sometimes undergo an entirely different fermentation process known as *carbonic maceration*, in which the fermentation takes place inside the grape berries. Without yeast and without oxygen, enzymatic processes in the grapes find alternative ways to turn sugar into alcohol, meanwhile doing much less extraction from the skins.

Carbonic maceration is used primarily for making wines designed for young drinking. The process emphasizes soft fruit flavors and downplays tannins. The practice is fairly common in the wines of Beaujolais and for some wines from the southern Rhône; it also plays a role in Pinot Noir production. Carbonic maceration is often applied to a small number of grapes, which then get blended with the batch made the standard way.

To do a carbonic maceration at home requires keeping the fruit quite cool, down around 50°F (10°C), in a closed container fully flooded with carbon dioxide to protect the fruit. It's a risky business, which can leave fruit exposed to oxygen and all manner of critters. When it works, it adds a lovely, youthful dimension.

Talking temperature

Standard advice for red winemaking (including in this book) is to aim for at least a day or two of fermentation at around 85°F (30°C) or slightly higher, and to stay away from anything over 90°F (32°C). The warm target temperature helps with good extraction; the suggested upper limit is a precaution against cooking the yeast, killing it off, and burning off fruitiness.

Some winemakers, naturally, break the rules. Pinot Noir producers frequently let their fermentations go above 90°F (32°C); for some reason, Pinot seems prone to fermenting hot, anyway, and with open-top fermenters without cooling jackets, temperature control may be hard to come by. A short time at

90°F (32°C) won't kill most of the yeast; a prolonged plateau at 100°F (38°C) almost surely will. High temperature fermentations are winemaking on the edge: When it works, it's delicious; when it backfires, it's a mess.

Cooler temperatures also have their fans. "Cooler" here doesn't mean white wine cool, but rather peak temperatures at 80°F (27°C) or a little below that. The advantages claimed by proponents are slightly longer fermentation times on the skins, thus extracting more goodies, and softer, fruitier wines. In other words, you get some of the same benefits claimed for cold soaks, which I talk about in "Taking a cold soak" earlier in the chapter.

Controlling fermentation temperatures with this much precision in your garage is no mean feat. It's more a matter of trying to push temperature toward the high end or keeping it from dropping below the lower end.

One situation where temperature surely does matter is with high-Brix, high-alcohol fermentations. The danger of stuck fermentation with these grapes is high already, and very hot temperatures simply add more stress to the poor, struggling yeast. For red grape with a Brix over 25°, holding the temperature down a few degrees is an excellent precaution. Be nice to your yeast.

Deconstructing wine: Rack and return

Winemakers in Australia and some parts of France use a technique the Aussies call *rack and return* and the French call *délestage*. Wine in mid-fermentation is separated from the cap of skins and seeds. On a commercial scale, the fermentation tank is drained into another tank; the cap is exposed to air for an hour or two; and the wine is then pumped back into the original tank, re-soaking the skins.

The first thing the procedure accomplishes is an intentional exposure to oxygen. The juice or wine picks up some oxygen during transfer, and the cap sits exposed for a time. This timely oxygenation helps revive the fermentation and eliminate reductive, sulfur aromas that tired yeast generate. In addition, if the mass of skins is removed from the fermenter, some of the seeds that have fallen to the bottom may be eliminated, reducing what some winemakers feel is the danger of bitter influences from the seeds.

Doing rack and return at home is easy. Simply scoop up the cap from the current fermenter with a sieve, leaving the juice behind; put the skins into a new, clean fermenter; wait an hour or two to give it some air; then pour the wine from the old fermenter into the new one, leaving many seeds behind.

Pressing early

Red musts normally get pressed when the wine is dry and all the sugar has been converted to alcohol. In some cases, pressing a little earlier produces a softer wine.

The reasons for pressing early generally fall into one of two categories:

✔ To encourage soft, fruity characteristics

✔ To prevent the buildup of astringent, excess tannins

During fermentation, all the color that can be extracted comes out in the first few days, as do most of the flavor compounds. Near the end, the main thing pulled out is more tannin. You may want it; you may not.

Commercial wineries can test for the level of tannin and other phenolic compounds in wine; you probably can't. Which means you should taste the wine day-to-day as it progresses — something worth doing anyway. If you pick up a lot of tannin in a near-dry wine — a dry, scratchy finish at the back of your mouth despite the sugar remaining in the wine — it may be time to press. Fermentation continues to completion just fine without the skins.

Pressing early — with anywhere from 2° to 6° Brix remaining — can also be a technique for emphasizing fruitiness, even when no danger of tannin overload exists. It makes for younger-drinking wines, and lets you hedge your bets on future blends by having at least one softer batch of wine in the mix.

Pressing way later

The mirror image of early pressing is *extended maceration* — leaving the dry wine on the skins for two or three weeks, sometimes more, after the fermentation is complete. The theory behind extended maceration — not very well documented — is that the longer the skins stew in the finished wine, the more the tannins soften and the rounder the wine becomes.

Some winemakers have had nothing but bad luck with extended maceration, ending up with wines that have tannins off the charts. Some have had wine go bad from spoilage. And some have made excellent wines, particularly from high-tannin grapes like Cabernet Sauvignon. I have no experience in making wines this way, only in drinking them. I don't recommend this technique for home winemakers, but I mention it because it's fashionable.

Don't bet your whole fermentation on extended maceration. Extended maceration at home is even more of a dice roll than it is for commercial wineries. The chances of encouraging spoilage are good, as are the chances of losing fruit character. For the first two weeks, perceived tannin will surely increase, making it tempting to press the wine at just the wrong time. The process works, when it works at all, only with enough time for tannin issues to get resolved.

If you insist, keep the temperature down and oxygen away from the wine. Use a container with as little headspace as possible; blanket the wine with carbon dioxide or some other inert gas; and cover tightly with plastic sheeting.

Going to barrel clean or dirty

After you press your wine, you transfer it into containers for long-term storage. The question is whether you put it there as is or clean it up first.

As always, opinions differ. At one extreme are those who suggest filtering the wine immediately to get rid of all the remaining solids; why should your expensive barrels waste their flavors on dead yeast cells? At the other pole are fans of going to barrel dirty, putting wine with all its resident gunk right into the barrel, letting the wine continue to extract useful things from the spent yeast. Critics of the squeaky-clean school say those wines have less character and no soul; critics of the dirty school warn of the risk of stinky, sulfur odors from stuff you always get rid of eventually.

For most of us, the important distinction is between *gross lees* — the entire mass of particles of stuff that gets through the press — and *fine lees* — what's left after the first wave of sludge settles. Two or three days of settling, maybe a week, allow for racking wine into its permanent home with only fine lees remaining. And since the wine is nowhere near clear yet, enough yeast cells remain to make an ongoing contribution. Safe winemaking says it's better to boost your chances of making good wine by reducing the risk of funk.

Addressing Aging

Even for big-name commercial wineries, predicting how well a particular bottling will age, and for how long, is a less-than-exact science. Longevity clearly has something to do with the presence of polymeric chains of tannins and other phenolics, which combat oxidation and allow flavors to develop without going flat. Many winemakers (and researchers) believe that relatively low pH (in the 3.5 range) and good acidity (a total acidity of 5.5 or higher) also contribute to age-worthiness — and that the new breed of high pH, low-acid reds have no staying power. In 100 years, this dispute may be settled.

To make successful aging more likely, your job as winemaker has four parts:

✔ Get good flavor extraction from your fermentation through high-quality fruit, yeast strain selection, and temperature control — so the wine has more in it to preserve.

✔ Keep the pH under control and the acidity reasonably brisk.

✔ Make sure the wine is stable — protected from microbial adventures — through sulfur dioxide management and clean bottling practices.

✔ Remember that the only wines that stay balanced are wines that go into the bottle balanced in the first place, with all the elements in harmony.

You should be following these practices for sound winemaking, anyway. Put aside a few bottles of everything you make — white, red, or otherwise — and taste them over time. At a minimum, you'll learn more about how wine matures, and you may create some pleasant surprises for yourself.

Make sure you like to drink older reds before you go to a lot of trouble trying to create and store them. The fashion today is for drinking wine, even Big Reds, early on, maximizing the hedonism of all that youthful fruit. Some red wine styles are purposely designed for drinking right after bottling, and they deliver plenty of fun. Well-aged wines can taste quite different from young ones, full of aromas and flavors that not everyone craves — tobacco, cigar box, leather, dried flowers, cured meats, for example. As part of your wine drinking homework, seek out older vintages from friends or wine shops. You may decide that you're in love, or you may decide not to bother.

Making Decisions, Decisions

From choosing grapes to labeling bottles, winemaking involves one decision after another. Figure 11-1 lays out the steps in red winemaking — required ones like pressing, optional ones like blending — in a decision tree (an outline of all the choices you can make, or not make, along the way). You can refer to this decision tree again and again as you ferment your reds.

RED WINEMAKING DECISION TREE

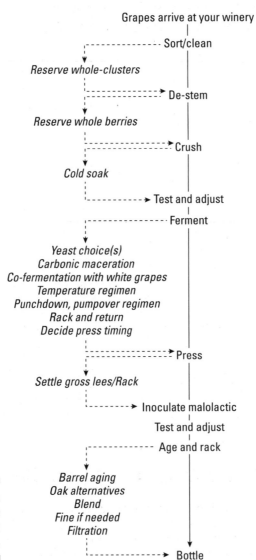

Figure 11-1:
Red wine
decision
tree.

Chapter 12

Bold Bordeaux Reds

- -

- -

*F*or two centuries, the red wines of Bordeaux have reigned as the kings of the international fine wine hill. The careers of wine critics rise and fall based on how well they call a particular vintage in Bordeaux. Cabernet Sauvignon, a Bordeaux mainstay, remains the most popular red wine variety from North American producers, after a short period in which Merlot topped the charts.

The Bordeaux varieties are home winemaker favorites, singly and in combination, and for good reason: Their names are familiar, and they're generally not all that hard to make. All the Bordeaux reds are good candidates for making big, bold wines — indeed, just be careful not to overdo it.

From Bordeaux to London to the World

Like the rest of France, the Bordeaux region has grown wine grapes nearly forever, certainly since Roman times. Varieties that originated there now show up in most of the winegrowing areas of the globe. If you ask the Bordelaise why that might be, they would likely say it's because their grapes and their wines are so far superior to the rest. Well, maybe.

Bordeaux's climate is considerably cooler than many New World Bordeaux grape-growing areas. The Napa Valley's temperature profile, for example, is more like that of Tuscany than Bordeaux; Washington State is actually more comparable. Besides its moderate temperatures, Bordeaux's humidity means plenty of disease pressure. And the danger of damaging rains occurring right around the fall harvest is a source of annual anxiety.

To cope with nature's whims, growers in Bordeaux have always relied on planting multiple grapes. If one gets clobbered by the weather or mildew, another one can carry the load. And in a good year for all or even most of the vines, blending promotes enormous complexity. In many of the ever-sunny New World growing regions, every grape gets ripe — and sometimes overripe — every year, so little need exists for the Bordeaux-style insurance policy of multiple varieties. But with the turn to mono-varietal wines, the complexity that made Bordeaux famous can get lost in other places.

The most widely planted variety in Bordeaux is Merlot, not Cabernet Sauvignon; Merlot ripens earlier and can avoid bad Fall weather more often. Generally speaking, wines of the Left Bank — the western side of the Gironde River as it flows toward the Atlantic — emphasize Cabernet Sauvignon, the wines of the Right Bank — the eastern side of the Gironde and its tributaries — Merlot. With notable exceptions, the other Bordeaux grapes — Cabernet Franc, Malbec, and Petit Verdot — play smaller roles.

How the Brits made Bordeaux famous

Bordeaux has fine grapes, but the region owes its pre-eminence to the Brits. The relationship was first established through a famous dynastic marriage, when Henry Plantagenet and Eleanor of Aquitaine got hitched in the 12th century. That made Aquitaine (including the Bordeaux region) officially part of England and provided a massive new market for the area's wines. Bordeaux went into boom mode in the 18th century, dramatically expanding population, vineyard acreage, and wine production. Again, the Brits, having no wine grapes of their own but ruling the world at the time, were the major standards-setters in the wine world. And did they ever love their *Claret* (their Bordeaux reds)! Affluent Englanders also had the resources — and the chilly climate — to stash cases of Bordeaux in their cellars, where well-made Bordeaux aged for decades.

When the barons of Bordeaux arranged for the famous Classification of 1855, dividing producers into First Growths, Second Growths, and down the line, the basis was the prices commanded by the various chateaux — that is, what the Brits wanted most with dinner.

The *phylloxera plague* in the middle of the 19th century — caused by a root louse accidentally imported from the United States — wiped out nearly all of France's vineyards. So the Bordeaux houses went elsewhere, especially Spain, to fill the void, thus spreading winemaking talent and grape preferences in many directions. A century later, when New World wine regions got serious about competing on the international level, they naturally tried to stake their claim with Bordeaux grapes, with or without the soils and climate of Bordeaux. Soon Cabernet, and to a lesser extent Merlot, was getting made everywhere, from Tuscany to Hungary, from Long Island to Chile to Greece. If a lot of the world's wine seem to taste the same these days, you can thank the Brits.

King Cabernet

Full disclosure: Cabernet is not my favorite red grape — that would be Grenache. But in deference to the fact that the rest of the world apparently disagrees, Cabernet Sauvignon is where this survey starts.

Small berries, big wines

Aside from the shifting sands of popular taste in wines, Cabernet Sauvignon has one built-in advantage in the quest for great grapes: small berries. Cabernet grapes don't have more flavor compounds, or better ones, or tannins with superior pedigrees: They have a higher ratio of skin to pulp. And that means the juice in a Cabernet Sauvignon fermentation has a higher volume of skins to work with, resulting in more goodies (color, tannin, and so on) per gallon. Smaller berries, bigger wines. That's not the whole story, but . . .

The natural advantage of the high skin-to-pulp ratio has a downside: the danger of over-extraction. Some grape varieties need to be worked over and heated up and punched and pummeled to locate their inner winehood; with Cabernet Sauvignon, the grapes can be generous to a fault, especially with more tannin than anyone needs. In my experience tasting and judging home-made wines, the highest proportion of unbalanced, unpleasant bottles have been Cabernets. Cab is plenty powerful; be careful how you use it.

Cabernet for fruit, age, or both

The challenge in Cabernet Sauvignon winemaking is taking advantage of the grape's natural assets without being buried by them. You want to revel in the depth of color, the powerful, dark flavors, and the aging potential that comes with the tannins. But if you end up with lots of color and lots of tannin and not much fruit, the wine can come out thin and hard at the same time.

Grape quality and composition, as always, are critical. When Cabernet Sauvignon is underripe, some green, bell-peppery flavors can be pronounced. A slight herbal, vegetable streak in Cabernet — or any Bordeaux variety — can please some palates (including mine), but a wine that shouts "Green!" won't do. Monterey County in California produced Cabernet with too much of "the veggies" for years, to the dismay of wine critics, until new vineyard practices got the green out. The Finger Lakes region in upstate New York struggles to ripen Cabernet Sauvignon, but has better luck with Cabernet Franc, which requires less heat to ripen fully. In hot climates, Cabernet makes flat, boring wine.

Cabernet Sauvignon provides another example of how sugar level and ripeness level are not always in synch. In cooler climates, Brix levels rise slowly, and flavor development reaches optimum level with comparatively modest sugar. In warmer climates, sugar spikes more quickly, and can get quite high before flavor catches up. In new-wave California winegrowing, fear of any hint of green flavors and a fondness for high-octane wines keeps grapes on the vine well beyond the time they need to develop sugar or flavor.

If your taste in wine tends toward the California blockbuster, fruit-bomb style — and many people have that taste — you'll want to start with big-wine grapes, likely from a warmer region and likely with a Brix at 26° or above. If your taste runs toward leaner, more European, food-friendly wines, look for a cooler region and hope for ripe flavors at a Brix of 23° to 25°.

Because of the small berry size, Cabernet Sauvignon wines are often on the high end of tannin extraction. This provides structure and mouthfeel to the wine and plays an important role in Cabernet's fabled longevity. Too much tannin, of course, means astringency. When winemakers talk about "soft tannins," what they really mean is that a particular wine has either fewer tannins or something else — residual sugar or *polysaccharides* (carbohydrate structures) — helping to mask the tannins' bite. (Find more about tannin management in Chapter 11.) Your mission as a Cab winemaker, should you accept it, is either to moderate tannin extract or ramp up balancing elements.

In my experience, when making Cabernet Sauvignon, aim to get to the fruit; the *phenolics* (color, tannin) will take care of themselves.

Styling your Cab

At the crusher, be nice to your Cabernet Sauvignon grapes. The more the skins get shredded, the more *jacks* (bits of stem) end up with the grapes, and the rougher the extract during fermentation. If you have a way to simply destem the clusters, while crushing them barely or not at all, so much the better.

Cold soaks (which I describe in Chapter 11) are not common in commercial Cabernet Sauvignon winemaking. But choosing to use this technique can give you an advantage in tannin management. Beginning the extraction of color and tannin early, at cool temperatures and without yeast or ethanol, gives you the option of pressing early, 2° to 4° Brix before dryness, stopping any further tannin extraction while the fermentation completes.

Depending on the initial wine chemistry, your Cabernet may need some adjustments. If the sugar and potential alcohol are just too high, pull off some juice for pink wine (yes, Cabernet Sauvignon makes excellent rosé in Bordeaux) and use water to adjust the red must (targets and methods in Chapter 5). Super-ripe grapes also tend to have elevated pH, which you need to get under control early on. Cool-climate, slightly underripe fruit — down around 20° Brix — may need to get bulked up with sugar to, say, 22°.

In making Big Red wines, the effects of different yeast strains — assuming they can get the wine dry — doesn't matter that much, especially after a year or more of barrel or carboy aging. Still, if you have enough Cabernet to split into batches, it can only help to use one yeast that promotes structure and mouthfeel and one that delivers fruitiness — for example, the Bordeaux yeast strain in one fermenter, RC-212 in the other — to create a final blend.

Cabernet versus Merlot: Pros on the top dogs

Given their broad consumer popularity and the vast range of climates, soils, and environments they are grown in, Cabernet Sauvignon and Merlot are made in more ways than you can skin the proverbial cat. Here's a sampling of thoughts from good winemakers with different backgrounds, goals, and grapes to work with:

✔ Dan Duckhorn, a Napa pioneer in serious Merlot, says that up into the 1970s, Merlot was regarded only as a blending wine, a way to leaven Cabernet Sauvignon. (This was an era in which California Cabernets were often unbearably tannic.) Figuring that Merlot could stand on its own, Duckhorn and others decided to treat Merlot much the same way they treated Cabernet: low yields, similar soils, similar winemaking, longer maceration than it usually got, and full barrel aging. Since Merlot has larger berries than Cabernet, he figured that even with the big treatment, Merlot would come out softer, but still far more than a blender — and he was right. Now he says that differences between batches of each grape are more important to how they get treated at Duckhorn Vineyards than the variety itself.

✔ Roman Roth at Wolffer Estate on Long Island says he can pull out all the stops making his Merlot, that region's flagship red, but he exercises some restraint on his Cabernet. Merlot gets fermented at a higher temperature and macerated

somewhat longer, even beyond dryness. He's happy to produce both varieties at a final alcohol under 14 percent.

✔ In Washington State, Mike Januik, former winemaker for Château Ste. Michelle and now with his own label, says his Merlots are often mistaken for Cabernets, both showing the structure that comes from a long growing season. His Merlot is rarely a candidate for extended maceration, which would likely produce over-extraction. Merlot gets less new oak.

✔ Cold soaks are almost mandatory in the world of Pinot Noir, rarer with Cabernet, but Ted Edwards at Napa's Freemark Abbey is a fan of the technique for Bordeaux varieties. He thinks they give him better color extraction and brighter fruit, and that some important flavor compounds extract better in an early watery solution than later on with high ethanol.

✔ Chimney Rock Winery, in Napa's famed Stags Leap District, aims for food-friendly wines and elegance with its Cabernets, not raw power. Winemakers Eilsabeth Vianna and Doug Fletcher take wines home at blending time and try them with food. Vianna says Chimney Rock's wines can be both age-worthy and still "feminine" because they carry good acidity and low pH, not just tannins for longevity.

Fermentation temperature makes a noticeable difference. The *high-extract strategy,* in which you do frequent and aggressive punchdowns, calls for very warm temperature — 85° to 90°F (30° to 32°C) or even a couple degrees higher for a day or two — preferably early in the fermentation cycle.

The combination of high temperature and high sugar/alcohol can be a double whammy for the poor yeast, heightening the risk of a stuck fermentation, so keep a watchful eye. (If your wine gets stuck, turn to Chapter 6 for tips on restarting it.) For more fruit and less phenolic extraction, set the thermostat (or the electric blanket) down to 80°F (27°C). When it's time to press, keep the wine that just runs off and the wine that has to be pressed separate, at least for a few days while the wine settles. That way, you can taste and compare the results, with much less suspended sludge, and taste whether the press fraction is excessively harsh and needs special treatment down the line.

Well-grown, well-made Cabernet Sauvignon certainly has the capacity to handle new oak flavors, whether from barrel aging or oak chips in carboys. But that doesn't mean it has to be oaky, unless full-frontal oak is high on your winemaking agenda. You can add character incrementally as you continue to taste, taste, taste. If the flavors from an older barrel or chip-enhanced carboy need an oak boost, add some more chips. If you're using a new, small barrel — one-half or one-quarter the size of a standard 55-gallon (210-liter) commercial barrel — the higher ratio of surface area to wine volume develops flavor more quickly. Give the wine three or four months in the barrel, taste it, and if the oak is obtrusive, rack the wine into carboys for a breathing spell.

Malleable Merlot

Merlot was on a seemingly unstoppable roll in the United States in the 1990s, briefly reigning atop the red wine sales charts. And then, almost overnight, a lot of people discovered that a lot of truly mediocre Merlot was on the market. The public slam came in the movie *Sideways,* the foil for its celebration of Pinot Noir. But the movie only confirmed what wine drinkers and sommeliers and critics were discovering on their own.

Making bad Merlot is easy; you don't even need this book. For tips on making really good Merlot, read on.

Getting beyond generic

There are no bad wine grapes, only grapes abused in the vineyard or the winery that then take their revenge on innocent wine drinkers. Merlot's meteoric rise came because many people saw it — or tasted it — as a softer, less tannic alternative to Cabernet Sauvignon. The expanding fan club led to more and more planting of Merlot, in less and less appropriate places — many way too warm — and to higher and higher yields, diluting concentration. Worse, wineries compensated for thin, flabby fruit with more oak — and an appearance of sweetness — and higher ripeness levels to supply more alcohol.

The first step in Merlot rehabilitation is recognizing that it performs better in moderate climates, not warm ones. Bordeaux, where Merlot is the top grape, is cooler than a lot of New World growing regions. Where the growing season temperatures are too warm, sugar accumulation outpaces flavor development. And if the vines are also carrying too high a crop load, things only get worse, opening up the possibility of both green flavors and high alcohol. Yuck!

Finding and selecting good Merlot grapes is especially critical. If you have several fruit source choices, concentrate on those from relatively cooler climates — not Yukon cool, but not sun-baked, either. Grapes that have to work at getting fully ripe before the Fall weather turns bad generally develop more character than grapes that ripen early and easily every year. And find out all you can about vineyard yields and practices. I can't offer a magic number for how many tons per acre or kilograms per hectare, since vineyard conditions vary so widely. But what's more important is whether your grower is aiming for quality fruit — and likely charging for it — or for volume.

In your winery, Merlot should be treated as a serious wine, with techniques designed to coax as much flavor and structure from the grapes as (reasonably) possible. If the cautions for making good Cabernet Sauvignon at home are "Take it easy," and "Don't over-extract it," the Merlot mantra would be something like, "Go for it!" I have no quibble with soft, fruity wines; I drink them all the time. But Merlot has more potential, and even if you crank up the winemaking a notch, your Merlot should still come out slightly softer and more accessible at an earlier age.

Merlot's revenge for being dissed in *Sideways*

Most wine lovers know the legend about how the movie *Sideways* in 2004 took a bite out of Merlot by panning it and venerating Pinot Noir instead, making Pinot a hot seller (true) and knocking Merlot off the sales charts (not really). Close watchers of the film, however, noted that Miles (Paul Giamatti) consoles himself at one point by knocking back a bottle Cheval Blanc, a Bordeaux icon made largely from . . . Merlot.

Much of the film was shot at the Hitching Post, a longtime Santa Barbara wine country dining and watering hole, whose owners also make their own wines, including several Pinots.

Naturally, the film's popularity meant that Hitching Post wines started to sell out before they were bottled.

Two years later, owners Frank Ostini and Grey Hartley set the record straight, releasing two vineyard-designated Merlots under the Hitching Post label. They explained that they had both always loved the wine and thought that selling Merlot in a Pinot-crazed market might be a hoot. Plus, they think that Merlot actually pairs better with the Santa Maria-style barbecue they serve up at the restaurant.

Nurturing Merlot style

The trend in commercial winemaking these days is toward very, very gentle crushing — sometimes destemming without crushing at all. For your Merlot grapes, standard, home-grade crushing and destemming is fine — although you don't want to put them through a juicer. You want to get as much as you can from the grapes, and cracking and squashing them a bit on the way to fermentation can help.

A two-day cold soak, for perhaps half of your grapes, can add another layer of flavors to the final blend down the road. That is, *if* you're able to do a cold soak safely at all: The crushed grapes have to be kept away from exposure to air and stray bacteria with plastic sheeting, and the temperature should be well under 60°F (16°C). (Cold soaking gets attention in Chapter 11.)

To enhance the concentration of your Merlot, bleed off a small portion of juice — about 5 to 10 percent of the potential total — a few hours after crushing. Some dubious alcoholic beverage products on the market are labeled "White Merlot," but dry rosé made from Merlot grapes can be terrific — ask the fancy chateaux in Bordeaux who make it.

As with any grape variety, make sure the basic juice/wine chemistry is in a reasonable range before starting the fermentation. Depending on where your grapes come from, you may need to make different adjustments:

- ✔ California grapes are likely to come in with high pH and low acidity, so add tartaric acid.

- ✔ Cooler-climate grapes — perhaps from New York or the Niagara Peninsula — may arrive with too little sugar (under 22° Brix) and too much acid (more than 8 grams per liter), suggesting some amendment with sugar and water.

In pursuit of complexity, if you have enough grape material, try splitting the fermentation into two or more batches and using different yeast strains. Where Cabernet Sauvignon sometimes needs the help of a yeast that pulls out fruit, not tannin, Merlot could use at least one strain that emphasizes structure and mouthfeel.

Fermentation temperature should be on the warm side, spending a day or more between 85°F (30°C) and 90°F (32°C) as early as practical during the week-long fermentation cycle. Merlot generally gets pressed at dryness, not before, though if you can taste an onrushing tannin buildup, pressing slightly before dryness makes sense. Two or three vigorous punchdowns a day help get the stuffing out of the grapes and into the wine.

Merlot, like most reds, should go through a full malolactic fermentation. Aging in one or more barrels makes a big difference for mouthfeel and concentration, but for oak flavor, carboys and oak chips do just fine. Merlot can't soak up quite as much oak flavor as Cabernet Sauvignon and still retain its personality; however, the fuller and more intense the wine, the more oak can play a role. Oak flavor is a matter of personal taste: Add more oak influence in stages, tasting as you go.

Marvelous Minor Players

Cabernet Sauvignon and Merlot have the biggest public relations budgets in the world of Bordeaux reds, but three other grapes are well worth seeking out; I cover each in the following sections.

Cabernet Franc: Cab on a smaller frame

Genetically speaking, Cabernet Franc is the "father" of Cabernet Sauvignon; the *sauvage* (French for "wild") streak captured in the latter's name comes from the "momma," Sauvignon Blanc. Yes, Cabernet Sauvignon, the biggest bruiser on the block, is the result of a spontaneous vineyard fling between lesser-known Cabernet Franc and a white wine grape.

Cabernet Franc has all the attributes of Cabernet Sauvignon: a similar flavor profile, deep color, and good tannin content without as much danger of abrasive tannins emerging from fermentation. Same package, slightly lighter frame. On top of lots of red and black fruit, Cabernet Franc is the most aromatic of the Bordeaux varieties. It thrives in cool climates — like upstate New York — where Cabernet Sauvignon fears to tread, as well as moderately warm ones. In Bordeaux itself, Cabernet Franc is generally used in small proportions as a blending wine, although it is (along with Merlot) the backbone of the famous wines of Cheval Blanc. Cab Franc plays the starring role in France's Loire Valley, including the wines of Chinon and Bourgeouil.

In a too-cool climate, or a too-cool year in a good climate, Cabernet Franc may retain a touch of green, bell-peppery flavors. Outside of California, this is not regarded as a crime, and many of the best of the Loire wines include a hint of grass or herbs in their complexity. In an overly warm climate or year, Cabernet Franc can fall prey to the usual over-ripeness: high sugar/alcohol, low acidity, high pH.

I get my Cabernet Franc from places on the warm West Coast of the United States, and usually go for the coolest choice I have.

Carménière: From Bordeaux to Chile, but probably not to your garage

In the old days, Bordeaux had six red varieties, not just the five that make up its grape toolkit today. Carménière was part of the old mix, but for whatever reason, when Bordeaux was replanted after the phylloxera epidemic in the mid-nineteenth century, nobody replanted Carménière.

Meanwhile, pre-phylloxera, Carménière vines went to Chile with the rest of the Bordeaux mix to establish that country's modern wine industry, and then folks forgot what it was.

For decades, Carménière plantings in Chile were identified, vinified, bottled, and labeled as Merlot. But in the 1990s, scientists realized this was another variety entirely, giving Chile its own signature grape.

I have consumed my share of Carménière, in blends and on its own, and it's a fine entry in the Bordeaux family. But I've never gotten my hands on any grapes for making wine. If you get lucky, my only suggestion is to think of it like Merlot — like the Chileans did for 150 years.

If you want to make Cab Franc as a solo wine, or the main event in a blend, give it the usual, Big Bordeaux treatment: warm fermentation temperatures, yeast that goes for structure and mouthfeel, pressing at dryness, and a possible cold soak. If your Cab Franc is going to spice up a blend, use a fruitiness-friendly yeast strain and ratchet down the fermentation temperature a few degrees (80° to 85°F [27° to 30°C]). That way, you will emphasize fruit qualities and engaging, almost floral aromatics.

Cabernet Franc gets along fine with wood, but use a light touch. Even though this is Cabernet Sauvignon's daddy, it makes wines with more prettiness and less muscle, so oak flavors should add to the charm, not the bulk and power.

Malbec: From Cahors to Mendoza

Malbec has been a bit player in the blends of Bordeaux for ages. In France, Malbec gets center stage in the region of Cahors, east of Bordeaux, where it's known as "the black wine of Cahors" in honor of its deep color. But what made Malbec a household word — well, in wine-drinking households, anyway — is its New World home in Argentina. Malbec from the Mendoza region, high in the eastern foothills of the Andes, has made a big splash in the international export market. The vintners of Cahors are busily trying to remind the world where Malbec got started.

Besides its legendary contribution to color — its thicker skin means more pigment — Malbec delivers plenty of fruit flavors, from red fruit to black, from blueberries to blackberries to plums. It works in climates slightly cooler than those Cabernet Sauvignon prefers. Its wines are generally ready to drink a little younger than some of their Bordeaux compatriots. Wherever they come from, the wines have a quality I can only call juiciness — something very mouth-watering and inviting that makes you want another sip.

Malbec is not a highly tannic variety, but certainly contains enough to make solid wine. Color takes care of itself. Which means your job is mainly to concentrate on coaxing out fruit flavors. Doing a cold soak with part of the grapes is one option, assuming you control the conditions carefully; using a portion of whole berries or a small amount — from 5 to 10 percent — of whole clusters is another.

If you try whole clusters in a fermentation, the stems should be brown — which is how they look when they're "ripe — and not green. Green stems taste about as good as the name suggests.

Fermentation temperatures in the low 80s Fahrenheit (high 20s Celsius) should do the job; punchdown twice a day; press at dryness. Extended maceration is frequently done in Bordeaux, but rarely in Argentina, where many Malbecs are geared toward fairly early drinking, not French-style aging. Barrels are always nice for red wine development, but Malbec is a fine carboy red, benefiting from just a touch of oak, not a death grip.

You'll never meet a nicer grape.

Petit Verdot: Bordeaux's mystery ingredient

Petit Verdot is the last of the five common Bordeaux red varieties to emerge from the shadow of Cabernet Sauvignon and Merlot and the anonymity of blends. Only now are winemakers around the world realizing it may be Bordeaux's secret weapon.

Just as Petite Sirah is anything but petite, Petit Verdot packs a wallop of its own. The name translates roughly as "small green"; the "green" part refers to its need for a long growing season to ripen properly, which is easier to accomplish in the New World. Pound for pound, it may be the champion in sheer intensity: strong, focused fruit, plenty of tannin, color to spare, and enough flavors and aromas to make a big impact with a small presence.

Bit players and the winemakers who love them

Winemaker David Whiting at Red Newt Cellars in New York's Finger Lakes says that in the area's frigid winters, Cabernet Franc is a hardy survivor. In a cool growing season, vigilance about limiting crop load and opening up the grapevine canopy to sunlight is essential for ripening. He aims to get the fermentation temperature up to 90°F (32°C), even 95°F (35°C) for a short period early in the cycle, reasoning that the yeast can handle the strain of high temperature better when the alcohol is still low.

Chuck Reininger at Reininger Winery in Washington's Walla Walla Valley notes that Malbec can sometimes hide its flavors in the vineyard, revealing them only after fermentation. He says it's important to taste Malbec all along the way during fermentation and make punchdown and pressing decisions based on whether harsh flavors are accumulating. Reininger has pressed lots at anywhere from 8° Brix to entirely dry. His Malbec is happy in 100 percent new French oak.

Lucien Dimani's family makes Malbec at Domaine Le Bout du Lieu in Cahors in France, but I caught up with him while he was working at Afton Mountain Vineyards in Virginia. His commentary on Malbec's color is that the minute the grapes hit the sorting table, the table turns deep purple. In Cahors, where Malbec is the centerpiece, the grapes get the full treatment: destemming without crushing, cold soaks, lots of whole berries in the fermentation, temperatures around 80°F (27°C) or slightly higher, and extended maceration for as long as 52 days.

Among the enthusiastic fans of Petit Verdot is Brendan Eilason of Periscope Cellars in Emeryville, California, one of the many San Francisco Bay Area urban warehouse wineries (in this case, a former submarine repair facility). He says Petit Verdot "is like Cabernet, only more so" — plenty of color and tannin, good mouthfeel. Cabernet's color, he says, is dark red; Petit Verdot is inky purple, and its aromas resemble Cabernet Franc, redolent of violets. He makes it as a solo varietal and blends it with such unlikely bottle-mates as Pinot Noir.

As a background blender, Petit Verdot fills in holes, bolsters color, and ensures tannin structure. Put more in the spotlight, it shows a broad range of flavors beyond primary fruit, things like cigar box, leather, peppers, and smoke, plus spicy, floral aromas. A little goes a long way; Petit Verdot by itself can verge on massive — but an intriguing massive.

Because Petit Verdot is such a powerhouse, winemaking requires no tricks for getting good extraction. Treat Petit Verdot like Cabernet Sauvignon, the other Bordeaux variety that can become too much of a good thing if you're not careful. Crush gently; use a fruit-oriented yeast strain; peak the fermentation at 85°F (29°C); punchdown gently; press at or just before dryness. Petit Verdot, like Cabernet Sauvignon, may need fining for excess tannin if you've over-extracted it during fermentation.

Petit Verdot takes some work to find on the home winemaker market, but if you spot some, it's fascinating stuff.

Blending Strategies

Somewhere, sometime, somebody has tried every possible combination of the Bordeaux varieties, and nearly all have succeeded at least once. Cabernet Sauvignon and Merlot get blended frequently outside the Bordeaux family, with everything from Sangiovese to Syrah to Zinfandel. Merlot is probably the most versatile blender, behaving well in almost any company, whereas Cabernet Sauvignon tends to take over a blend quickly.

Blending possibilities just within the Bordeaux Big Five include:

- **Napa Fruit Bomb:** Base it on low-yield, high-Brix Cabernet Sauvignon; do very careful sorting and gentle crushing; bleed some juice for pink wine and increased concentration; some whole berries; high-temperature fermentation with extractive, structure-oriented yeast; press at dryness; age with plenty of oak influence; add a little Merlot and/or Cab Franc to soften any rough edges.

- **Bordeaux Left Bank:** Similar to the Fruit Bomb, except with more modest sugar/alcohol grapes; typically a slightly lower pH (3.5, not 3.7) and higher acidity (6 grams per liter, not 5); ratchet back the wood a bit; blend proportions might be 75 percent Cabernet Sauvignon, 20 percent Merlot, and 5 percent Petit Verdot.

- **Bordeaux Right Bank:** Merlot, Cabernet Franc, and Cabernet Sauvignon, in that order, even with a bit of Malbec or Petit Verdot if you have them; aim for extraction in the Merlot, since it's the main driver; make sure to get fruit from the Cabernet Sauvignon; moderately warm fermentation temperatures; restrained but present wood.

- **Serious Merlot:** Even good Merlot can benefit from a small proportion — 10 to 20 percent — of Cabernet Sauvignon or perhaps a shot of Petit Verdot; without killing Merlot's rich fruit, the bolstering can ensure structure and perhaps a longer life in the cellar.

- **"Fruity Bordeaux":** I put this in quotation marks because the idea of fruity may not match the stereotype of age-worthy Bordeaux. But this family of grapes is quite capable of making delicious early drinking wines. Concentrate on Malbec and Merlot; water down the sugar/alcohol and bump up the acid, if needed. Pick fruity yeast strains, and keep fermentation temperatures modest. Maybe press one component just before complete dryness and go easy on the oak. Your grandchildren will forgive you for making one wine they'll never taste.

Making Yeast and Style Choices

When you ferment Bordeaux wines, you can go for a big, structured, "Left Bank" style or a softer, fruitier, "Right Bank" style. Table 12-1 suggests yeast choices for the style you choose:

Table 12-1	Yeast Choices for Bordeaux Varieties
Grape Variety	**Yeast Strains**
Any Bordeaux red, for big, structured style	Bordeaux Red (BDX) for classic profile; MT For tannin and floral aromas; D254, D80 for volume and mouthfeel; RP15 for concentrated fruit
Any Bordeaux red, for softer, fruitier, fresher style	D21, GRE, RC212 for fresh fruit; CSM to reduce herbaceous flavors in low-alcohol wines

Table 12-2 lists the style options to consider. Because this is winemaking, these are not recipes, just some advice you can take or leave.

Table 12-2	Style Options for Bordeaux Reds	
Options	**Structured, "Left Bank" Style**	**Softer, "Right Bank" Style**
As single variety or main variety in blends	Cabernet Sauvignon	Merlot
Whole clusters/berries	Berries	Berries
Cold soak	Consider a portion	Consider a portion
Carbonic maceration	No	No
Co-ferment with whites	No	No
Temperature regimen	85°F (30°C) or higher	80° to 85°F (27° to 30°C)
Punchdown	3 times daily	2 times daily
Rack and return	Rare	Rare
Press timing	Dryness	Dryness or slightly early
Oak style/influence	High proportion new wood	Small proportion new wood
Fining	May be needed for tannin	May be needed for tannin

Chapter 13

Ravishing Rhône Reds

*F*ull disclosure: I love Rhône grapes. I am beyond being objective about them, although I've made every effort not to go overboard.

Just as the grapes made famous in Bordeaux now grow on every continent, the varieties lumped together as Rhône reds span the globe. Most of them didn't start life in France, and some that did have moved on to better days elsewhere. Read the fine print on the labels of international-style wine blends today, and you're likely to find at least one Rhône grape on the list. For versatile home winemaking and blending, you can't beat 'em.

End of editorial. On to a discussion of the best grapes in the world (oops — last rave, I promise).

Sipping Syrah around the World

Some grape varieties, like Pinot Noir, grow well only in a fairly restricted climate range. Syrah grows like a weed almost anywhere, except for the very coolest regions. It's one of the less troublesome varieties in the vineyard and one of the more dependable varieties in the cellar. Plus, it tastes really good and blends well with nearly anything red.

Syrah shows up in a range of styles, which can be both an advantage — freedom of expression for winemakers — and a disadvantage — confusion for consumers.

Exploring origins and name changes

Most of the prominent red grapes of France's Rhône River Valley originated in Spain; some of them were likely brought by Phoenician explorers and already in cultivation when the Romans arrived. Since these grapes flourish in a warm Mediterranean climate, it was natural for them to spread northward and eastward into southern France.

The migration produced some very similar names for the grapes. Spain's *Garnacha* is France's *Grenache*; Spain's *Cariñena* is France's *Carignane*; Spain's *Monastrell* (and Portugal's *Mataró*) is France's *Mourvèdre*. Showing signs of the relocation, *Mourvèdre* is named after a town in Spain, although one not located in a traditional *Monastrell* growing region. This one transplanted grape has several dozen names in different Mediterranean locations.

France has bragging rights for being the birthplace of Syrah (see the sidebar on "Syrah, Shiraz, Sirah"). Syrah-based Rhône wines were already famous in Europe when they became the adopted red grape of Australia in the nineteenth century, getting a name change to Shiraz in the process. The entire Rhône entourage came to California at about that same time, underwent some more name changes, got planted in many mixed-variety vineyard plots, and became part of the backbone of mass-market California red wine.

Closing the circle, Syrah made its way to Spain in the great global grape exchange of the last few decades, where it has been greeted by Cariñena, Garnacha, and Monastrell grapes like a long-lost cousin. Some of the best Rhône wines in the world today are made in Spain's Priorat region.

Broadly, the two poles of contemporary Syrah winemaking are the Northern Rhône style, which is dark, intense, and dry, and the Australian Shiraz style, which is warm, engulfing, and fruity to the max. I cover both in the next sections.

Unpacking the Northern Rhône style

Syrahs from the northern parts of the Rhône — Côte Rotie, Hermitage, Crozes-Hermitage, St. Joseph — don't gush fruit; instead, they exude character. The best wines from here have a definite, noticeable tannin structure, fairly strong acidity (for red wines), a peppery finish, and often something smoky or meaty along the way, on top of intense black fruit flavors. Fruit punch, they're not.

Getting the grapes

The hardest part about emulating this style in your garage is that your grapes, alas, will not be coming from the Northern Rhône. Next best thing is to find grapes with a similar profile:

✔ Grapes from vineyards where the yield is kept low, or where older vines naturally produce lower yields, making good concentration more likely.

Yield numbers are not magic, but 2 or 3 tons to an acre (4.5 to 7 metric tons per hectare) is a ballpark range.

✔ Fruit harvested with ripe flavors at European-style Brix levels — 25°, not 28°.

Ultra-ripe, blockbuster fruit is more suited to the Aussie style; if you're leaning Rhônewards, you may need some water.

Processing the grapes

Cold soaks are commonly used to enhance extraction before ethanol comes onto the scene, and you may want to extend maceration after dryness as well. (Chapter 11 covers cold soaking and maceration.) Keep acidity slightly on the high side for reds — 5.5 to 6.5 grams per liter — and pH down to 3.5 or 3.6. Fermentation itself should be fairly warm — 85° to 90°F (29° to 32°C) — with frequent punchdowns.

Many of the leading yeast choices for Syrah — including one strain named simply Syrah — were isolated in the Rhône, making them a natural fit.

For Northern Rhône Syrah — and reds from the Rhône generally — go easy on new oak, because this style benefits primarily from used and slightly used wood (or if you're flavoring with oak chips, not too many). Save the prominent new oak for the Aussie style.

Even if your aim is a single-varietal Syrah, a pinch of blending with Grenache or Viognier may be worth exploring. The Viognier option is quite common in the Côte Rotie, probably the most prized of the Northern Rhône regions.

Getting down (under) with Aussie style

Mainstream Aussie Shiraz winemaking is focused on fruit: lots of it, gobs of it, pure and clean and fresh and right in the wine drinker's face. Some critics complain that the Aussie Shiraz style is too brash, too simple, but because it served as the main vehicle for transforming Australia into a global wine export powerhouse in the 1990s, Aussie Shiraz must have some appeal. As with any first-class wine, low yields in the vineyard are a better bet than high yields. Australian fruit tends to come in opulent and quite ripe, somewhere around 25° Brix or higher, with the final alcohol often above 14 percent.

Unlike some California producers in that same Brix range, the Aussies are more insistent on getting the pH down to traditional levels, around 3.5 or even 3.4. If the grapes don't come in that way, the winemakers fix the chemistry with acid additions so the pH at the start of fermentation is in that range.

The Pros on Syrah

One reason for Syrah's rise in popularity is that it seems, at least in the New World, to be fairly trouble-free in the vineyard and idiot-proof in the cellar. "There are not too many ways to screw it up," says McDowell Valley Vineyards winemaker Bill Crawford, whose Mendocino County ranch has what may be the oldest Syrah plantings in California. And California Central Coast Rhône pioneer Gary Eberle of Eberle Winery says, "I just wish everything I make was as easy to work with."

Veteran California-Rhône winemaker John Buechsenstein says that cooler-climate Syrah is a better candidate for bottling as a single varietal, while warmer-weather Syrah is more likely to benefit from blending partners. "Cool-climate Syrah can be like Picasso in his 'blue period' — lots of intrigue and diversity, but all blue. The warmer the region, the more you need the mixed box of crayons." On the Picasso track, he suggests using a combination of methods on small batches and blending them together: some cold soak, some not; some whole clusters; different yeast strains; different pressing timing, and so on.

"Australian winemakers are looking for complexity and age-ability and so on," says Michael Scholz, who got his training in Australia's Barossa Valley and now presides at St. Supéty in the Napa valley. "But they work to ensure domination by the fruit, to reflect the vineyard." Techniques that may have a following in France or California — wild yeast fermentations, for example, or extended maceration on the skins — are rarely employed in Australia, he says, because they can undercut fruit clarity.

Australian reds also frequently receive a small pre-fermentation addition of oak tannin; at home, this might mean adding 3 to 4 ounces (100 grams or so) of oak chips per 100 pounds (45 kilograms) of grapes to the fermentation.

The winemaking for this style is very straightforward: crush the grapes, inoculate immediately with a yeast that tolerates high alcohol, and try to get the temperature up to about 90°F (32°C) as soon as possible (crank up that electric blanket around your fermenter). The idea is to extract as many of the goodies as possible before the alcohol level rises very high and to encourage an overall short period of fermentation.

Midway through fermentation, Australian Shiraz often goes through the process of rack and return — separating the cap of skins from the fermenting juice/wine, exposing both to some air briefly, then putting the wine back together. In your winery, this means lifting off the floating cap with a sieve, putting the grapes in a clean fermenter, waiting a couple hours, and then pouring the wine from the original fermenter into the new one. This gives the wine and the must a shot of oxygen and hastens the last bit of fermentation.

Australian Shiraz is frequently pressed before full dryness, with anywhere from 2° to 6° Brix remaining. By that time, the wine has extracted all the color and tannin it needs, and pressing early avoids any chance of adding something harsh at the end. The fermentation finishes in carboys or barrels. Extended maceration is rarely used.

If lowering the pH during fermentation results in excessively high acidity afterwards, consider de-acidification with potassium bicarbonate. Reducing the acidity by 1 gram per liter — say from a too-tart 6.8 grams per liter to a smoother 5.8 grams per liter — requires an addition of 2 grams per liter of potassium bicarbonate.

Aging for Aussie Shiraz is often done in American oak, and for high-extract wines, a lot of new wood. Australia acquired the American oak habit initially because transportation costs were lower, but over time, they found that the stronger American oak flavors married well with their fruit-bomb style.

Here's a great project: Split your batch of Syrah grapes in half, do one Northern Rhône style, one the Aussie way, and see what happens.

Using the "improving variety"

The worldwide boom in Syrah production in the past two decades has put a lot of bottles labeled Syrah (or Shiraz) on people's tables. But it means even more Syrah is getting blended with other wines, often behind the scenes. The use of Syrah as "the improving variety" has a long history in France; the dependably ripe grapes of the Rhône, especially the Southern Rhône, bailed out far too many weak, under-ripe vintages in Burgundy and Bordeaux to count. Syrah and sometimes Grenache could be counted on to add at least alcohol and often color and flavor.

Today Syrah plays an analogous role on several continents, filling in the holes in incomplete wines, pumping up the color, adding fleshy fruit, reining in excess acidity — the universal fixer. The downside of Syrah's popularity is that it contributes to a growing "sameness" in too many international-market wines.

The take-home lesson for home winemakers is that a little Syrah in your garage winery can be a very versatile blending friend.

Living Large with Petite Sirah

Petite Sirah gets its very own major heading in this chapter for two reasons. First, to reinforce the idea that this much-maligned and misunderstood California entry belongs with the more traditional Rhône varieties. And second, to emphasize that Petite Sirah — which is anything but petite — is a really great variety for home winemakers to get their hands on.

Rising from field blender to solo act

When Petite Sirah got to California at the end of the 19th century and proved to grow well, it sort of disappeared into the mix. (Read about the origins of Petite Sirah and its relationship to Syrah in the "Syrah, Shiraz, Sirah" sidebar.) Like winegrowers in Europe who hedged their bets with multiple grape varieties, California vineyardists planted a little of this and a little of that, not only in the same vineyard but in the same row, to increase the odds that enough of the crop would ripen successfully. Harvested all at the same time, these "field blends" produced wine that was not only dependably sturdy, but surprisingly complex.

In the mix, Petite Sirah (whatever it might be called) could be counted on to add color and tannin to a blend. Every now and then, someone would try the grape on its own, with mixed results. In 1964, Concannon Vineyard in the Livermore Valley released the first varietal-labeled Petite Sirah, and the grape started its long, slow rise to respectability. When it was good, it was very, very good; when it was bad, it was simple and nothing but tannin.

Petite Sirah was a natural partner for that other only-in-California grape (or so we thought) — Zinfandel. Blending a small amount of Petite into Zin was established as a standard California winemaking practice. Zinfandel gives the gushy fruit; Petite holds it all together.

Eventually, scientists demonstrated Petite Sirah's lineage from the Rhône, where it was crossed by and named after a breeder, Dr. Durif. All that Syrah in the DNA only confirmed what winemakers had discovered: Petite Sirah acted and tasted like a member of the Rhône family.

The Rhone Rangers, a promotional organization for producers of Rhône-style wines in the United States, decided to add Petite Sirah to its list of approved grapes. And finally, the little grape variety that could got its very own organization — P.S. I Love You (www.psiloveyou.org).

Taming the beast

Petite Sirah is a great home winemaker grape. You're guaranteed to get deep, dark color; good structure; and the flavors of strong black fruit and, most of the time, blueberries. Plus, the grapes are usually picked ripe enough that alcohol and body are no problem.

The wine works by itself and is a very handy blender. The only thing to watch for with Petite Sirah is tannin buildup.

TECHNICAL STUFF

Syrah, Shiraz, Sirah

It was confusing enough when wine lovers had to scratch their heads about the relationship between Syrah and a mysterious grape called Petite Sirah. Then the Australians invaded the world wine market with something called Shiraz (pronounced *sure AS,* not *shi-ROZ*). (Not as confusing as those six-syllable German vineyard names, but close.)

The easy one is Syrah versus Shiraz: two names for the same grapevine. Some different clones are planted in France and some in Australia, but it's the same variety.

Exactly when and how the Shiraz name variation got coined and popularized is still the subject for detective work, but the term Shiraz has been common in Australia for over a century. Even in France, Syrah was long thought to have a Persian connection — with the city of Shiraz in Iran — but that still doesn't explain why only the Aussies adopted the name. Speculation abounded about how Syrah/Shiraz made its way to the Rhône from Egypt, Cyprus, or Persia, by way of the Romans or the Crusaders. Then science got into the act, and so much for romance. According to genetic marker research conducted by Jean-Michel Boursiquot of the wine research faculty at Montpellier, France, and Carole Meredith of University of California Davis in 2001, Syrah is the offspring of two undistinguished local grapes from the south of France — Dureza and Mondeuse Blanche. No Persian connection, no Roman Legions, no Crusaders, just a couple of willing vines enjoying a pollen frolic in the vineyard. Both parent grapes exist in collections and scattered field plantings in France, but neither has been intentionally cultivated for some time. (Mondeuse Blanche also figures in the lineage of Viognier.) Because the happy parents and endless relatives are also indigenous to the south of France, a distant origin for Syrah is highly unlikely.

The confusion about Petite Sirah went beyond the name and its offbeat spelling. Vines carrying that name showed up on record at the end of the 19th century in California, but the term eventually got applied to a miscellany of "black grapes" planted around the state (inducing some misidentified Syrah). To make matters worse, the most highly regarded Syrah vines in France were those that bore small grape berries — that is, the *petit* Syrah.

DNA sleuths sorted this one out, too, and confirmed that California's Petite Sirah was the French grape Durif, a cross between Syrah and Peloursin (another red), named after the viticulturist who developed it in the 1880s. Dr. Durif's project proved to be mold-prone under French skies, but it became a workhorse in California.

Petite Sirah winemaking closely follows Syrah winemaking — same options, same desirable grape characteristics, same handful of suggested yeast strains, and so on. It works just fine in both of the Syrah styles discussed in "Sipping Syrah around the World" earlier in the chapter.

Modern winemaking has largely overcome the problem of excess tannin by emphasizing gentler crushing and less shredding of fruit. Don't overdo the number or aggressiveness of punchdowns, and consider pressing just before dryness to stop the accumulation of tannin. American oak is the obvious choice. If, during aging, the wine seems too astringent with tannins out of balance, a gelatin fining can smooth out the edges. (I talk about fining in Chapter 9.)

Introducing Marvelous Minor Players

In the Northern Rhône and New World regions like Australia and California, Syrah often stands alone as a star. But in the Southern Rhône, Spain, and elsewhere, Syrah is just one member of a family of grapes and wines that all have their claims to goodness, singly and in riotous combination.

You say Garnacha and I say Grenache

Grenache is generally the go-to grape in the Southern Rhône and the South of France, and equally important in Spain as Garnacha. It serves as the base for lots of blended wines and adds a bit of complexity to higher-status varieties. And in both countries it makes a ton of pink wine every year.

A variety that makes good base wine often gets grown badly, maximizing the yield in the vineyard and the alcohol in the final product. That, and a lot of really inferior rosé, gave Grenache a bad name. But any grape has to be judged on its best examples. The legendary wines of Châteauneuf du Pape and the newer, near-cult wines from Spain's Priorat region both rely on Grenache, proving without a doubt that Grenache/Garnacha had a date with greatness.

Great Grenache grapes have at least two interrelated characteristics: relatively low yield and full ripeness at harvest. Over-cropped Grenache never gets ripe enough, unless it's grown in a region so hot that it gets cooked; well-cropped Grenache develops fruit intensity and relatively high sugar/alcohol levels. Cutting back yields in the vineyard and working with very ripe fruit is well worth doing if you're a grower as well as a fermenter.

Be aware that much of the Grenache planted in the United States (at least in California) is from a clone known as Grenache Gris, the Grey Grenache, rather than Grenache Noir, the Black Grenache. Grenache Gris makes great pink wine, but struggles to make a full-bodied red.

If you have the real-deal Grenache/Garnacha grapes to work with, full-strength winemaking is in order: fairly high fermentation temperatures, the same robust yeast strains that work with Syrah, and nearly anything from the Rhône bag of tricks. If the Brix is ridiculously high, add some water.

Grenache has two notorious vulnerabilities:

✔ A tendency to not have or to lose color — not as bad as Pinot Noir, but common.

The main solution to the color problem is low grape yields. But you can't control that if you don't have your own vineyard. So your Grenache may be a candidate for adding a color-fixing enzyme during fermentation.

✔ A tendency toward *oxidation* — a particular fondness for glomming on to oxygen and becoming slightly brown and a bit dull.

The danger of oxidation makes Grenache a poor candidate for rack and return (which intentionally brings in oxygen) and means that racking and barrel-topping have to be done carefully.

Keeping sulfur dioxide (SO_2) levels up to snuff helps fight oxidation, as does blending with Mourvèdre, a wine that eagerly seeks oxygen.

Always a somewhat lighter wine, Grenache needs very modest contact, if any, with new oak: The *fruit* should sing, not the timber.

If your Grenache grapes are on the light side, try pulling off a large percentage — perhaps 20 percent — of the juice after a few hours to make into pink wine, and don't try to over-extract what's left. For blending, what Grenache/Garnacha needs is cheerful fruit, good balance, and bright acidity, not massive fruit — a wealth of blending partners can handle that chore.

Moody, mysterious Mourvèdre

First, on the pronunciation: *moor-VED-ruh* is close enough, though in France, it's more likely just *moor-VED*. (It is not *MOO-ved-ruh*, which is more likely a product made by or from cows.)

Mourvèdre is the wild card grape of the Southern Rhône; as Monastrell, it has long been a jug wine blend staple in Spain. In California, where it has been around for more than a century, Mourvèdre spent decades on the jug wine track, and some winemakers claim it was the reason that Gallo Hearty Burgundy, a wine that had nothing to do with Burgundy, was such a terrific, tasty value wine in the 1960s and 1970s.

Mourvèdre needs a warm climate to get properly ripe, and with controlled crop levels — old vines keep yields down automatically — it makes big, dark, deeply flavored, age-worthy wines. Bandol in the South of France is one benchmark area; Spain's Jumilla is a close second.

Wherever it's grown, Mourvèdre is full of surprises as you ferment it. A Mourvèdre that is perfectly on track will taste like blackberries one week, neutral, fruitless red liquid the next, and something between frying bacon and smoldering newspaper the next. In my experience, and that of a lot of commercial winemakers, Mourvèdre is second only to Pinot Noir in how changeable it is over time.

You need no special winemaking tricks for this one. Treat it like a big Rhône red, try some cold soak, get the temperature up, try more than one yeast strain. Aerate through rack and return. And take your time.

I have two pieces of advice for working with Mourvèdre:

- ✔ Be patient. If the wine is sound, it will come around.

- ✔ Be aware that Mourvèdre has tendencies toward reduction, oxygen starvation, and a sulfur-like stink. If that develops, give the wine some air: rack it less than carefully, let the wine splash, give it a breather, and the reductive quality should go away. (I address racking in Chapter 7.)

When the wine comes to terms with itself, it's likely to offer more than simple, primary fruit — which is why it makes for truly interesting wine. Smoky/gamey/meaty is a possibility; herbal/tobacco could show up; throw in a little bit of oak flavor, and you could end up with chocolate on top of the dark berry fruit core.

Cinsault is just a bowl of cherries

Most Cinsault (pronounced *san-SO* and also spelled Cinsaut) in France gets made into very fine rosé. The fruit yields the essence of red cherry, sometimes candied red cherry, and if it tends toward the simple, it's the cheeriest, most Spring-like form of simple in any grape I know.

Cinsault rarely gets made into a single-varietal wine, though with low-yield grapes, some juice bled off for pink wine, and perhaps a little stiffening with some Syrah, it can be done.

Unless you make it all into rosé, handle Cinsault grapes in a way that brings out that lovely fruit; don't pretend it's a Big Red. Crush as gently as possible; use some whole berries or even clusters; use a yeast strain that aims for fruit, not structure; keep the fermentation temperature slightly low for reds; keep acidity up and oxygen away. To recycle an old insight about how much women really need men, Cinsault needs oak like a fish needs a bicycle.

The "other" Rhône reds

Some thoughts from winemakers who are well versed in the ways of the "minor" Rhône reds:

✔ **Mourvèdre:** Cline Cellars in California was one of the first to recognize the value of old-vine Mourvèdre planted along the shores of the Sacramento Delta, an almost moon-like sandscape dotted with ancient vines. Fred Cline, founder of the winery, recalls the day he was convinced that someone was smoking in the barrel room — only to discover it was just the ambient aroma from racking barrels of Mourvèdre. Simple fruit, it's not.

✔ **Carignane:** Jeff Brinkman, winemaker for Husch Vineyards in Mendocino County, says, "We're not aiming for something over the top, highly extracted; we want fruit expression. It's more like making a Pinot Noir than making a Cabernet."

✔ **Cinsault:** Bill Frick — a former home winemaker whose first Zinfandel from a kit years ago was, he says, "a disaster" — is one of the few California winemakers who does a solo Cinsault, from his winery in Sonoma County's Dry Creek. The large berries, he says, with lots of pulp for the amount of skin, mean wines with not much tannin and not much color — which is, for him, "no big deal." He treats it like Pinot Noir, uses yeast strains on the fruity side, punches it down often to get extraction, and ages it in neutral barrels.

Carignane, or is that Kerrigan?

In Europe, it's pronounced *CAR-in-yahn*, except in Spain where it's Cariñena, *car-i-NYEN-ah*. In California, growers gave up and started pronouncing it more like *Kerrigan* — sounding like the first noteworthy Irish wine grape.

The first red wine I ever made was a Carignane. My local winemaking shop was sold out of everything else that year, and they assured me that, yes, I could produce actual wine from these grapes. I ended up making 3 gallons of a delightful rosé and, to my amazement, 10 gallons of a drinkable red. I was hooked. Whenever my wife tells me this hobby of mine is out of control, I say, "Blame it on that first Carignane."

Many grapes get no respect, but Carignane gets the prize in the no-respect stakes. In early editions of the *Oxford Companion to Wine*, Jancis Robinson made it sound as if Carignane was to winemaking in France what the Black Plague was to life expectancy.

As with any grape, Carignane is all about the viticulture, the crop load, the farming, and how much attention the grapes get. This time, the proof that the grape had merit came from Spain, where ancient, gnarly, barely yielding

Cariñena from the sun-baked, desolate Priorat region teamed up with the local Garnacha (another low-reputation variety) to make some of the most stunning wines on the world market.

In California, Carignane used to be a Central Valley jug wine staple. For a couple of decades now, it has been leading the pack for the most acres ripped out and replaced with something else each year. Pockets of old-vine, low-yield Carignane still exist, mainly on the North Coast, and those grapes make perfectly wonderful wine.

When not made from abused grapes, Carignane arrives with color, tannin, alcohol, and black fruit flavor — the basic red wine checklist. Blockbuster material? No. As complex and snazzy as Syrah? Hardly. More fun than generic Merlot? Probably. Put it in your Rhône blending kit.

Blending? Of Course

Rhône reds were born to blend. Not because the individual grape varieties are so lacking in merit that they need emergency help, but, as with the Bordeaux varieties, the whole of a blended Rhône is much more than the sum of its parts.

The point of blending is always to add what's missing to the current mix: refreshing acidity, firm structure, dark fruit, light fruit, a longer finish.

The following list contains suggestions for blending strategies, not recipes. How well they work, and with what modifications, depends on the fruit you have. But they may help to get your thinking and blending juices going:

- **Basic Côtes-du-Rhône:** Base 80 percent of the blend on Grenache, Syrah, and Mourvèdre — or any two out of those three — and fill in with smaller percentages of two or three other Rhône varieties and maybe a splash of Viognier for softness. Minimal oak, maximum freshness. Blends along these lines make great, versatile, food-friendly, early drinking wine with more character than most of the competition.

- **Mock Châteauneuf:** The wines of Châteauneuf du Pape are similar to the rest of the Southern Rhône Grenache-based blends, but almost always based primarily on intense, full-flavored Grenache — maybe 80 percent — with a host of other grapes in smaller quantities. Among the Southern Rhônes, they show greater concentration and more structure and get longer aging before release. Depending on the quality of your Grenache, your blend could come out like a muscular Châteauneuf or a lighter, perfectly pleasant, Côtes-du-Rhône.

✔ **Picnic Special:** Built for summer, not posterity. Using Cinsault, Carignane, and Grenache, keep the alcohol down, the acidity up, highlight the fruit in the winemaking, skip the oak, and bottle it young.

✔ **Syrah Plus:** Even the best Syrah may benefit from a pinch — 5 to 10 percent — of Grenache to brighten the fruit, or a dollop of Viognier, either from fermenting with Viognier skins (see Chapter 11 for a discussion of co-fermentation) or blending in wine to enhance the nose.

✔ **Syrah/Petite Sirah:** Because these two grapes are genetically parent and child, the family resemblance makes for good blending. Proportions can vary all over the place. One of my favorites, stolen from a California commercial wine, is roughly equal, 40 to 50 percent portions of each, with 10 percent Zinfandel to make it thoroughly Californian.

✔ **Shiraz/Cabernet:** This is an Australian staple. Combining these two Big Reds in one bottle sounds like a train wreck, but especially with fruit-forward Aussie-style winemaking, the combination often comes out more elegant than either component. Fifty-fifty is a good starting point for a blending trial. This strategy offers accessible early drinking, courtesy of the Shiraz, and the ability to age, courtesy of the Cabernet.

✔ **Going Spanish:** Take your Grenache and Carignane, re-purpose them as Garnacha and Cariñena, and blend in Syrah or Cabernet as a minority partner to mimic wines from Spain's Priorat region; or blend with Tempranillo for the full Spanish makeover.

Choosing Yeasts and Other Options

The variety of Rhône wines leads to a multitude of choices when it comes to choosing yeasts and deciding on processing steps. Table 13-1 shows yeast choices:

Table 13-1	Yeast Choices for Rhône Varieties
Grape Variety	*Yeast Strains*
Syrah	Syrah yeast for classic aromas; D21 for tannin structure and high pH fruit; D80 and D254 for body and structure; BM45 for mouthfeel and spice; RP15 for concentrated fruit
Petite Sirah	RP15, D80, D21, Syrah
Grenache	GRE, RC212 for fresh fruit; 71B for soft, young-drinking fruit; D80, D254, BM45 for big style
Mourvèdre	D80, D254, Syrah
Cinsault, Carignane	GRE, RC212, 71B

Table 13-2 walks you though some of the decisions you need to make about your wine's style and some of the technique options that might work toward that end.

Table 13-2	Style Options for Rhône Reds	
Options	*Big Style Syrah, Petite Syrah, Mourvèdre*	*Grenache, Cinsault, Softer Blends*
Whole clusters/berries	Some portion	Some portion
Cold soak	Some portion	No
Carbonic maceration	No	Some portion
Co-ferment w/whites	Small portion Viognier skins in Syrah, Petite Sirah	Not common
Temperature regimen	85°F (30°C) or higher	80° to 85°F (27° to 30°C)
Punchdown	3 to 4 times daily	2 times daily
Rack and return	Consider for Syrah, Petite Sirah	Not common
Press timing	Consider early press for Syrah, Petite Sirah	Dryness
Oak style/influence	Small portion new wood	Older/neutral wood
Fining	Petite Sirah may need fining for tannin	Not common

Chapter 14

Handling the Hard Cases

Some grapes are trickier to grow than others, and some are trickier to turn into good wine when they're in the winery. The Holy Grail of winemaking is achieving balance in the glass, and grapes that threaten to go out of whack, time after time, can be challenging. That doesn't mean that winemakers, professional or amateur, love them any less; it just means that these grapes need a little more TLC.

The four grapes this chapter covers don't comprise the whole list of grapes with special handling requirements. But they're all well-known varieties and the source of some of the world's greatest wines, so they merit a closer look. The issues they raise can also pop up in a normally well-behaved variety when you least expect it.

Treating Pinot Noir with Kid Gloves

At its best, Pinot Noir is transcendent stuff: intoxicating in the nose, light on its feet, exploding with flavor, never heavy or clumsy. But of all the grapes ever made into wine, it has the most intimidating reputation. Legend goes that Pinot Noir is impossible to grow, is totally cranky and unpredictable in the winery, and is as fickle as the day is long. In short, some say that making Pinot Noir is a project only for winemakers with masochistic tendencies. Now, most of this reputation is baloney, with a whiff or two of or self-serving whining by winemakers thrown in. Pinot, however, isn't your average grape.

How not to make Pinot

Early North American Pinot vintners made the mistake of treating the grapes as if they were going to make Cabernet Sauvignon — a recipe for disaster, akin to confusing pork chops with pea sprouts. The grapes were manhandled the way Cabernet likes to be treated: vigorous crushing that verged on shredding and using methods to extract color that those skins never had in the first place. If the wine didn't cooperate, it got extra oak to fill in the gaps. The result: Boring wines, high in alcohol, short on acid, unbalanced in tannin, and lacking in the lively, racy, ethereal qualities that make a good Pinot.

Eventually, winemakers figured it out. Winemaking techniques moved from brutal to gentle: barely crushing the fruit, moving it around by gravity and as little as possible, and letting the wine more or less make itself.

Everybody, winemakers and drinkers alike, had to get their heads straight about Pinot Noir color. The variety lacks one whole class of *anthocyanins* — the phenolic pigment compounds that give wine its color — and no amount of over-extraction will make Pinot look as opaque as Cabernet. Which, for Pinot lovers, is just fine; better to look at light dancing through your wineglass than stare at a crystal inkwell.

Less is more

Once winemakers stopped trying too hard with their Pinot Noir, most settled on a philosophy that can be summed up as "less is more." The less the grapes get beaten up, the more flavors and aromas they reveal. The less you mess with the grapes, the more you'll like the wine. In other words, if you do it right, Pinot Noir winemaking is actually *easier* than most — not impossibly difficult.

Grading grapes

Try to find Pinot Noir grapes from a fairly cool climate, or at least a cool pocket inside a warmer climate zone. The longer the grapes spend ripening on the vine, the fuller their flavor development and the better their balance.

One bewildering thing about Pinot grapes is that everyone — growers, winemakers, even wine drinkers — is clone-happy, rattling off strings of numbers that identify exactly what combination of plant material went into a particular wine. But because how any given *clone* — a variant of a particular grape with slightly different characteristics — performs in different settings is highly variable, don't get obsessed with the numerology. Tasting wine made from the vineyard is much more important than knowing its clone matrix. (I talk more about clones in the nearby sidebar, "Bring in the clones.")

Pinot pioneers tell all

Growers and winemakers in California and Oregon in the 1950s, '60s, and '70s learned the secret codes of Pinot Noir the hard way: by growing and making it wrong for years, producing some seriously bad wine. Pinot was planted in places — like the Napa Valley — that were far too warm for good fruit development. The grapes came in too ripe (leading to too much alcohol) and too low in acidity (leading to flattened flavors).

Finally, growers took cues from Burgundy, where everyone agreed the best wines were mind-boggling, and found that planting in cooler climates — Oregon's Willamette Valley, California's Santa Barbara, and the Carneros at the southern end of Napa and Sonoma — produced better grapes.

But veterans of the struggle have battle scars and lots of stories. Their self-critical descriptions of how these poor, innocent grapes were mistreated are often harsher than any complaints handed out by smug wine writers who never got their hands dirty making wine:

✔ "At the beginning," says Dick Ponzi, one of the early winemaking pioneers in Oregon's Willamette Valley, "(Pinot Noir) was a monster. We thought you just needed to ferment it on the skins, and it didn't much

matter how it got there, how you crushed it and destemmed it. We treated it like any red grape. Over the years, we realized that was damaging the fruit, and modified the process."

✔ Josh Jensen, founder of Calera Winery, high in the Pinnacles mountains in California's San Benito County, had enough tales to fill a book, *The Heartbreak Grape*, the title of which gives you a clue about how much fun Pinot was. "In the bad old days," says Jensen, "Pinot was made through the standard red wine formula — crush, destem, filter, age it in tank, filter it again. Or if it was in barrel, rack it over and over, and so on. Since the wine had no color left, wineries would add in Alicante or Petite Sirah absolutely finishing off the wine. It had no resemblance to Burgundy at all."

Wineries that were paying attention eventually learned that Pinot Noir does not like being pushed around. "It's a grape with a memory of how it's been handled and processed," says Ponzi. "Unlike most reds, which can be abused a bit, Pinot remembers everything you do to it — and so the less you do, the better the expression."

Compared to most Big Reds, Pinot grapes frequently get harvested with slightly lower Brix — more like 24° than 28° — and slightly higher acidity — 7 or 8 grams per liter. The pH is likely to be lower, 3.5 or under. In cooler places like the northeastern United States and parts of Canada, the harvest numbers could show even less sugar, more acid, and lower pH. These numbers don't mean the Pinot is anemic; they mean that it's cool-climate Pinot, ripe for the picking.

Destemming and (barely) crushing

Pinot grapes need to be destemmed — and that's about it. Many winemakers use whole berries, or a high proportion of them. If you can't do that, separate the rollers on the crusher as much as possible to lessen the impact. Some whole clusters, still on their stems, can go on the bottom of the fermenter before the crushed grapes are added, contributing to the wine's structure — but only if the stems are nicely brown and mature, not green. Some producers put a portion of the grapes through full carbonic maceration (discussed in Chapter 11).

Doing a cold soak — the Pinot must-do . . . maybe

The practice of *cold soaks* — letting crushed grapes sit for two or three days, soaking in their own juices, before fermentation — enjoys an almost religious status among Pinot Noir producers. Fans claim that different goodies can be pulled out of the skins in the absence of ethanol; skeptics say all that stuff would come out eventually, anyway. Nobody has much rigorous scientific data on this topic. However, much of the color extraction can be done before fermentation, and getting a head start gives you the option of pressing early before the wine is entirely dry, in case too much tannin is building up.

You might try a cold soak and judge for yourself, but be very careful about the possibility of spoilage. Give the (barely) crushed grapes an initial protective dose of sulfur dioxide — 25 to 50 parts per million; keep them cool, certainly under 60°F (16°C); blanket them with CO_2 and cover whatever container they're in with plastic sheeting. If the grapes show signs of premature fermentation, warm them up and hit them with yeast.

Speeding through the fermentation

Pinot fermentations, for some reason, tend to be slightly quicker than other reds; in your home winery, maybe a day shorter than it takes your Syrah or Merlot. And Pinot winemakers like to push the heat envelope while they can, getting temperatures up near 90°F (32°C). At that level, flirting with a heat spike could kill off your yeast; careful temperature monitoring and thorough stirring of the must during punchdowns are essential.

Pinot's sensitivity to handling extends to punchdowns; the more frequent and more aggressive, the more tannin extracted, so be careful. Taste the wine as it ferments, and keep in mind the option of pressing a day early and finishing off the last few Brix in carboys or barrel.

Yeast strains that emphasize fruit are normally used for making Pinot Noir.

Pairing Pinot and oak

Once your Pinot goes through malolactic, the question is, "How much oak?" The answer depends on your personal taste in wine and whether you find oak obtrusive or a natural match for the flavors of wine. All I can offer is the observation — not mine alone — that Pinot Noir, for all its lightness and delicacy, marries very well with oak, absorbing more oak flavor than you might think without getting buried in it. If your Pinot ages in barrel, some time in new oak is a good idea; in carboys, try oak cubes in successive additions and stop when the balance suits your taste.

Tasting a moving target

Just as Pinot Noir grapevines constantly change, throwing off new clones, Pinot wines go through more than their share of changes in the cellar. Taste the same wine twice, two weeks apart, and it may be hard to recognize: fruit character up; fruit character down; perceived acidity up; perceived acidity down; and so on. Mutability is Pinot's idea of steady state, a trait that can carry through even after the wine is bottled. Don't worry; just roll with it.

Blending? Oh, the horror! (Oh, get over it)

Along with cold soaks, the other quasi-religious belief about Pinot Noir is that it should never be blended: Any less-elevated grape could only drag it down. This attitude is silly, considering the centuries-old practice in Burgundy of beefing up thin vintages with heftier wines smuggled in from the Rhône. If you like your Pinot just the way it is, fine; if you want to fool around, that's fine, too.

Bring in the clones

Pinot growers and producers seem fixated on grapevine *clones* (natural mutations), and with reason. The Pinot grape is the most changeable variety around, given to spontaneous mutations in the vineyard; Pinot Noir, Pinot Gris, Pinot Meunier, and Pinot Blanc are all simply different *clones* — slight variants but with the same genetic makeup — of a single grape variety, even though two of them are red and two are white. All those numbered Pinot clones — 115, 667, 777, and on and on — do in fact have their own characteristics, such as different berry size, disease resistance, and ripening timing.

For thousands of years, grapevines have been propagated by taking cuttings from one vine to start another, not by growing from seed. With seeds (sexual reproduction), the new plants are entirely unpredictable, and could have any combination of characteristics of the *vinifera* species. With cuttings (vegetative reproduction), the offspring vines are identical to the donor vine. In choosing planting material, growers don't just want Merlot or Chardonnay; they want to know what clone they're buying.

The weak link in clone-worship, however, is that knowing that clone X shows a particular set of characteristics in a particular soil-climate-nutrition setting doesn't predict how it will perform halfway around the world. Many of the Pinot Noir clones certified and popularized in France, for example, were selected for their ability to ripen early, useful in Burgundy's cool climate. However, transplanted to sunny California, where ripening was never a problem, they can produce top-heavy, overripe grapes — with great clone pedigrees. Luisa Ponzi, winemaker and daughter of Dick Ponzi (see "Pinot pioneers tell all"), says that the very French clones that made Oregon famous in the 1990s aren't working as well today, due to climate change. The old-timer clones are getting a fresh look.

For firming up a light Pinot, small amounts of Syrah, Petite Sirah, or Grenache are all good choices. If you're blending the other way — using some Pinot to liven up a bigger, but duller, wine — most any combination is fair game.

To my palate, Pinot works *least* well with the Bordeaux family of grapes.

Zinfandel: Wine on the Wild Side

One of my dearest friends from prehistoric times — the 1960s — is a wine-hound in Massachusetts and has a palate trained on Bordeaux and Burgundy. During a California visit, I served him a big, fat, ripe, exuberant, alcoholic Zinfandel. He took a sniff, took a sip, wrinkled his brow, set the glass down carefully, as though it might explode, and said, "This stuff is . . . wild. It's savage. It's . . . out of control." Eventually, he finished the glass, still fixated on its feral quality, still shaking his head.

That's exactly why we Californians love this outlaw grape. Zinfandel is possibly the most expressive — or, depending on your taste, hyperactive — red grape in the *vinifera* catalog. Zin is California's signature, a perennial candidate for the official state grape, despite its origins in Croatia, where it got created in a random vineyard mating in some other century as the variety Crljenak Kaštelanski.

Home winemakers love to start their garage wineries with Zinfandel, the same way kids with 55cc motorbikes like to dream about Harleys. Zin is almost guaranteed to make you a big mouthful of wine; trouble is, it may be too big.

Standing up to scary-ripe grapes

Current-day commercial California Zinfandels take a lot of heat for being *hot* — over-the top alcohol levels, often 15 percent and counting. What's more, many of these high-octave Zins have already gone through alcohol reduction, in which semi-combustible finished wines undergo *reverse osmosis* (an exotic form of filtration) that puts out some of the flames. Imagine what the next 15 percent Zin you buy would have been like at its original 17 percent.

Although winemakers could take steps to rein in the high-alcohol trend, they're not entirely at fault — the grapes share the blame.

Two unfortunate tendencies are wired into Zinfandel's DNA:

> ✔ **Sudden, last-minute jumps in sugar level can occur right around harvest time.** The well-meaning winegrower may go to bed, secure in the knowledge that the grapes are coming along nicely, right around 25° Brix, ready to harvest in a day or two; and wake up to find them at 29°.

✔ **Clusters ripen unevenly.** A single bunch may contain some grapes that have barely turned from green to pink, some that are nicely ripe, and some that have shriveled to raisins.

Zinfandel clusters often grow what are called *shoulders* or *wings*, sub-clusters that grow outwards at the top of the cluster and ripen on their own schedule. If that's the story, row after row, exactly how ripe are those grapes? When do you pick? While some grapes are still green, or after everything has gone to raisins?

Most California winegrowers opt for making sure Zinfandel blocks are fully ripe, because dealing with high sugar/alcohol is easier than dealing with green flavors. But the result is raw material that poses a number of challenges in the winery: alcoholic balance, the danger of stuck fermentation, and microbial management issues that come with super-high pH.

Taming the wild thing

Because Zinfandel's challenges often develop in the vineyard, your most important work as winemaker starts right at the beginning, before fermentation kicks off. If all starts well, the rest of your Zin's development shouldn't cause you to lose sleep.

Finding and fixing balance

Zinfandel's propensity to arrive with high sugars and high pH puts a premium on getting accurate wine chemistry numbers from the beginning. Even growers who claim they're trying to avoid extravagant ripeness often end up harvesting Zinfandel at 28° Brix, a pH of 4.0, and a total acidity level down around 4 grams per liter. That's a different reality from the textbook prescription for Big Red wines of 24° Brix, a pH of 3.5, and a starting tartaric acid around 6 grams per liter.

Getting good numbers is complicated by Zinfandel's uneven ripening, and in particular by the frequent presence of raisined grapes. Raisins contain a super-high percentage of sugar, because nearly all their water has evaporated; but that sugar may not show up in a quick field sample, because it doesn't go easily into solution. Grapes harvested at 28° Brix — already enough to yield a wine with 15.4 percent alcohol — may turn out, after crushing and soaking in their own juices for a day or two, to be closer to 30° Brix — portending a wine with 16.5 percent alcohol. The pH and acidity measurements can be thrown off, too.

However the harvest numbers were advertised, re-check them a day or so after crushing and stir and mix the must thoroughly. If your Zinfandel has more or less normal numbers, consider yourself lucky, and proceed with straightforward red winemaking. But if the numbers are off the charts, or right on the edge, you need to intervene.

If your grapes have a sugar overload, bring on the water. To keep the acid balance correct, add water containing 6 or 7 grams per liter of tartaric acid. Yes, you (like many commercial wineries) are diluting your precious grape juice with mere water — to save the wine. Fortunately, Zinfandel grapes contain enough intense fruit flavor to survive a little adulteration.

The best way to prevent diluting the grape juice too much is to pull off some juice and turn it into rosé, then replace that volume with water to lower the sugar in the red fermentation. For example, if you have a potential of 20 gallons (76 liters) of liquid — juice to turn into wine — and a Brix of 30°, adding 2 gallons of water yields 22 gallons (83 liters) of liquid at just over 27° Brix — still high, but much more manageable. If, however, you divert 2 gallons (8 liters) to rosé, then replace the lost juice with water, you end up with the original 20 gallons (76 liters) of potential wine right at 27°. Same final alcohol, but in the meantime, the goodies from the grapes get extracted into a smaller volume of wine that is more concentrated. (The rosé will need some water, too.)

Similarly, don't be afraid of dramatic intervention on the pH and acidity. Flagrantly high pH is trouble, a chemical imbalance that can turn your wine into a lab experiment in spoilage. Add dissolved tartaric acid to knock down the pH. The hypothetical ratio — an educated guess because other things in a particular wine can affect the acid/pH connection — is that every additional gram per liter of tartaric should drop the pH by 0.15. For a particular batch of wild-eyed grapes, you may need an addition of 2 or 3 grams per liter. Make an addition; taste it; test it to see where the pH has landed; maybe add more.

Following winemaking protocols

Although huge, jammy Zins have the biggest reputation — positive or negative, depending on your taste — Zinfandel adapts well to other styles, too:

- ✔ Reined in, elegant, "Claret"-style wines with brighter acidity and firmer tannin

- ✔ Light, young-drinking, almost Beaujolais-style summer beverages

- ✔ Fabulous dry Zinfandel rosé (despite the low-life status of White Zinfandel)

Where to go with your Zinfandel depends on your grapes as well as your drinking preferences. If you have fat, ripe grapes from low-yield vines, go for big and concentrated. If you have more modest fruit, perhaps from young vines or a slightly cooler climate, aim for elegance — even if "elegant Zinfandel" sounds self-canceling.

Legend has it one reason so much Zinfandel was shipped across the country during Prohibition, the heyday of home winemaking in the United States, was that the grape's thick skins traveled well. In fact, most Zinfandel is on the thin-skinned side. Nonetheless, normal destemming and crushing should be fine, though some winemakers use a portion of whole berries or line the bottoms of fermenters with a layer of whole clusters. Because obtaining accurate sugar readings is difficult, many winemakers give their Zins a day or two of cold soak, largely for time to get to know the fruit and tweak it.

Depending on what you hope to accomplish, go with a yeast strain that promotes structure or one that promotes fruit. Another option is to try a strain that helps bring out Zinfandel's spice notes. Better yet, separate the grapes into two batches and use two strains, giving some complexity to the wine. Big styles want higher fermentation temperatures, up in the high 80s Fahrenheit (low 30s Celsius); more modest, fruitier styles benefit from temperatures in the low 80s Fahrenheit (high 20s Celsius).

If you're dealing with extremely high sugar/alcohol levels, the danger of a stuck fermentation is increased. Prized old-vine Zinfandel fruit also tends to be naturally low in nutrients, making stuck fermentation more likely. Use an alcohol-tolerant yeast strain; make multiple, small additions of yeast nutrient along the way; monitor the fermentation carefully; avoid heat spikes; and cross your fingers.

Make sure your Zinfandel is dry — tested dry — before inoculating for the malolactic fermentation. If some sugar is still around, the malolactic bacteria may take away nutrients from the yeast that are attempting to finish the job, which could generate unwanted volatile acidity.

Zinfandel rarely ends up overly tannic, so pressing at dryness is the norm. As with any red, barrel aging helps round out the wine, but carboy Zin with a few oak chips is still a Zin. The current fad for high-alcohol Zins generally favors large lashings of new oak, but for my palate, Zinfandel's inherently intense fruit and natural spice shine through best with modest oak — a small percentage aged in new oak, or a second- or third-use barrel, or small, incremental oak chip additions in carboys. Zinfandel has plenty to flaunt without encouraging deforestation.

Basking in the blender's paradise

Zinfandel is a versatile blender. It welcomes other wines into its company and offers its energetic fruit to a broader world. California's long Zinfandel tradition has been built on judicious blending, either from growing other varieties alongside it or tinkering in the cellar by good winemakers. A splash of Petite Sirah is almost the default option for Zin; Syrah and Cabernet also work well in the same way to give the high-flying, free-thinking Zin more of an anchor. Zin and Cab in a fifty-fifty mix gives explosive fruit and age-worthy structure.

Blended the other way around, an infusion of 10 to 15 percent Zinfandel can liven up and energize a heavier, possibly duller red. Read the fine print on the back of most proprietary, odds-and-ends red blends from California, and you'll likely find Zinfandel on the list.

Secrets of the Zin masters

Successful Zinfandel winemakers have a variety of opinions for style and winemaking techniques: native yeasts or commercial yeasts; very little oak or lots of oak; big, jammy wines or restrained, elegant wines. But ask the pros what makes Zinfandel special, and they'll all say it's the maddening unevenness in how the grapes ripen.

After making a little bit of everything at Windsor Vineyards, Carol Shelton started her own label that focused on Zinfandel from all over California. "The biggest bugaboo," she says, "is deciding when to pick. Because of the raisins, you can't just sample berries; you have to sample whole clusters, destem and crush them, check the sugar, then let them settle overnight and test again. The Brix will likely go up 2° or 3°." And after the picking decision, she notes, you make the water decision.

At Dashe Cellars in urban Oakland, California, Michael Dashe makes Zins from several vineyard sources. Because he tries to stay away from the high-alcohol style, he puts a lot of effort into picking locations and worrying about viticulture. Dashe thinks cool nighttime temperatures and a little fog help slow ripening and keep acid up. Low yields, nipping off green clusters when most of the grapes have ripened, and pulling leaves to let dappled sunlight through all help minimize uneven ripening. One of his Zins, for example, comes from a tiny vineyard in the middle of acres of Riesling and other cool-climate grapes — not your standard Zinfandel growing area.

Duane Dappen at D-Cubed Cellars works with fruit from several Napa vineyards, and joins the chorus warning about uneven ripening and the need for accurate sugar-level readings. He frequently does at least short cold soaks, mainly to get accurate sugar numbers, and warns that the Brix can go up after pressing, when the last bit of sugar is squeezed out of the last raisins.

After dealing with the sugar/ripeness issues, Zin-makers go their separate ways. Dashe does only natural yeast fermentations; Shelton does some wild ferments, but advises home winemakers not to go there; Dappen uses commercial yeast inoculations that can safely handle the sugar/alcohol. Dashe likes fermentation temperatures that get up near 90°F (32°C) more than once in the cycle; Dappen and Shelton prefer theirs under 85°F (29°C). Shelton thinks the high-spirited fruit of "America's grape" can absorb a fair dose of new American oak; to showcase that same fruit, Dashe goes for very limited oak, using large casks or used barrels for aging.

Taming Temperamental Tempranillo

Tempranillo is the great red grape of Spain, the backbone of the wines of Rioja and Ribera del Duero and, under a hundred local names, also the grape behind the wines of Valdepeñas and La Mancha (Cencibel), Toro (Tinta de Toro), and several other regions. In nearby Portugal, it's called Tinta Roriz.

Tempranillo delivers intriguing flavors, not only plum, cherry, and strawberry fruit, but earthy hints of tobacco and leather. It works in styles from light and lively to brooding and age-worthy, blends well with others, and offers an unusual combination of delicacy and depth — qualities that often get it compared to Pinot Noir. It may also bring tons of tannin and stratospheric pH values to the table — or the winery. I used to think these factors were oddities of California vineyards, until I attended a conference on Tempranillo, replete with Spanish winegrowers — all anybody talked about was tannin and pH.

Grapes with gratuitous grip

Tempranillo's thick skins contain fairly high levels of tannin, but certainly no more than Cabernet Sauvignon or Tannat. The difference is that Tempranillo generally makes medium-bodied wines, wines whose restraint makes them more comparable to Pinot Noir or Sangiovese than to Cabernet or Merlot (let alone Tannat). Tannin buildup, therefore, sticks out more easily in Tempranillo than heavier wines. Managing tannin is one reason that the wines from Rioja tend to spend more time in barrel and then in bottle before release than most high-profile reds — often a year or more longer than a comparable Bordeaux.

Tempranillo's pH problem stems from the vines' voracious appetite for potassium in the soil. Wine grapes need some potassium to grow up big and strong; Tempranillo's potassium addiction may make the vines happy, but it drives winemakers nuts. The longer the grapes stay on the vine, developing nice, ripe flavors, the greater the potassium uptake. The elevated potassium translates into elevated pH — often too elevated. Worse, the potassium concentration makes acid additions somewhat less effective than usual in reducing pH, so that ratcheting the pH down far enough can make the wine overly tart.

Don't let a little tannin and pH scare you; folks have been making good Rioja for a thousand years.

Tricks to managing tannins

With Tempranillo, you need to manage tannins throughout the winemaking process. The following tips work for any tannin-prone wine:

- ✔ Keep the crushing gentle, just enough to let the juices flow, not so much pressure that the grapes get shredded.

- ✔ Ferment in the low 80s Fahrenheit (high 20s Celsius). Try to reach that peak temperature as early in the fermentation as possible, extracting color and flavor goodies before the alcohol level rises very far. Let the ferment finish down in the high 70s Fahrenheit (mid 20s Celsius). That way, some extraction is done mainly with heat and some mainly with ethanol, rather than both at the same time.

- ✔ Do a rack and return in mid-fermentation to get rid of most of the seeds and their tannins and to lower the final tannin tally. You can also press just a bit early, with 2° to 4° Brix remaining.

- ✔ Forego extended maceration. Given the looming tannin, few winemakers even consider putting Tempranillo through an extended maceration after the end of fermentation.

- ✔ Stir the lees every week or two during the early stages of aging, either in barrel or carboy. Stirring can improve the roundness of the wine's mouthfeel and cover up rough tannin edges.

- ✔ Try fining to dampen down tannins. But try not to get this far, because fining always pulls more out of wine than just the compounds it is prescribed for.

Expect Tempranillo to take a little longer to come around during aging and to benefit more than many reds from a little bottle age.

Tempranillo grapes tend to show comparatively low acidity by the time they ripen, alongside the high pH. The earlier you can change the numbers, the better. Don't be afraid to add 2 or 3 grams per liter of tartaric acid, possibly more, to get the starting pH under control. If the pH remains high after fermentation and your taste buds indicate it can tolerate more acidity, dose it some more. You may still have a higher pH than you'd like, but the more control you exert, the less room marauding microbes have.

Touching up Tempranillo

Aside from dealing as needed with high pH and too much tannin, Tempranillo winemaking is pretty standard. Once the newly minted wine has gone through malolactic and headed into aging, stirring lees to enhance mouthfeel is a useful technique. Tempranillo's earthy streak resonates well with a little wood (emphasis on *little*); Tempranillo does better with a long time in used barrels than a short time in new barrels that gush oak flavor.

A bit of blending is standard procedure in Rioja, where the bottle-mates are usually a bit of Garnacha (Grenache), or a bit of Graciano, or both.

Taste to see if your Tempranillo has any holes in it and consider some touch-up work. If it needs to be brighter, Grenache might be just the ticket; if it needs to be firmer, with more bass notes, a small percentage of Cabernet could help — that's the norm in Ribera del Duero. But take it easy: Tempranillo is delicate enough that any additions over 10 or 15 percent can make it almost unrecognizable, even if tasty.

Trial by Tempranillo

The first world-class Tempranillo I ever tasted from a producer in the United States came from an unlikely place: Oregon. But in southern Oregon's Umpqua Valley, Abacela Vineyards found the right package. Founder Earl Jones says the area resembles Rioja because it has a long, cool, dry period in September and October to finish ripening the grapes without cooking them. He's happy with a harvest Brix of 24° and with picking "before the acid drops off the scale." And unlike most Tempranillo producers in Spain and elsewhere, Jones bottles 100 percent Tempranillo — not on principle, but because he hasn't found that adding any other wine makes it better.

Louisa Lindquist of Verdad in Santa Barbara tried various fermentation techniques at first, in hopes of taming Tempranillo's tannins. She tried long and slow, resulting in "searingly tannic" wine; she tried really hot and fast; and she finally decided to live with "whatever nature gives us" in open-top fermentations. Her blenders of choice are Grenache and Syrah.

In the Livermore Valley, Murrieta's Well makes an Iberian blend of Tempranillo, Touriga Nacional, and Souzão (and sometimes other things) called Zarzuela. Winemaker Karl Wente has used blending as a tool for dealing with Tempranillo's pH, and the usual option of acid additions, but he also emphasizes the necessity to make sulfur dioxide additions correspond to the pH, even when you're not happy with the pH. He employs a form of rack and return as a winemaking tactic to enhance aeration and reduce seeds.

"Don't despair," says Earl Jones, "when the young wine is so tannic at crush, or after three, six, nine or twelve months. It will eventually calm down. Bottle age does wonders for Tempranillo."

Savoring Sharp-Edged Sangiovese

Sangiovese is Italy's best-known grape, mostly because it's the prime ingredient in Italy's best-known wine, Chianti — not to mention Brunello di Montalcino, Rosso di Montalcino, Vino Nobile de Montepulciano, Morellino di Scansano, Rosso Piceno, and a host of other designations.

So if Sangiovese is Italy's most-planted red grape, how can it be a hard case? Because it took the Italians several hundred years to figure out how to handle its combination of high acidity, plentiful tannin, and iffy color stability — a puzzle North American growers and winemakers are still figuring out. Sangiovese's beguiling flavors make the effort more than worthwhile; you, too, can be part of the solution.

Centuries of solutions

Since Sangiovese is grown in many different soils and climates, and comes in many clones, the grapes at harvest aren't identical. Sangiovese, in fact, is regarded as one of the more site-sensitive varieties. But far too often, the fruit arrives at the winery with higher acidity than most reds; the skins lack one of the pigment compounds (anthocyanins) most other red grapes enjoy; and the variety's delicacy (like that of Pinot Noir and Tempranillo) allows for a tannic edge to stick out assertively. Instead of full, robust wine, Sangiovese can come out thin and mean.

Over the past several centuries, numerous strategies have been employed to make Sangiovese more user-friendly. In the mid 19th century, Baron Bettino Ricasole promoted the virtues of blending in a little red wine for color and a little white wine to soften the acid/tannin edge; this became a kind of recipe, enshrined in formal regulations for the Chianti region until quite recently. The breakaway "Super-Tuscan" innovators of the 1970s dumped all that old-fashioned Canaiolo, Colorino, and Trebbiano — the traditional blenders — and pumped up their Sangiovese with Cabernet Sauvignon and Merlot.

Other winemakers experimented with limiting vineyard yields, altering fermentation temperatures and times, and layering the wines with sweet oak to smooth it out. Some of these efforts have produced wines that are rich, dense, Bordeaux-dark, and California-oaky — but they don't taste much like Sangiovese. Some of them are wonderful.

Pretending it's Pinot

The starting point for successful Sangiovese is, of course, good grapes, and in particular, grapes from vines that are not over-cropped. Too large a crop means more difficulty in achieving ripeness, which just makes the acidity higher, the color paler, and the tannin issues that much more complicated

When the grapes arrive, remind yourself that they will grow up to be Sangiovese, not Cabernet Sauvignon or Syrah. These grapes are not destined for blockbuster status; but they can, instead, produce what may be the world's most versatile, medium-bodied food wine. Think of Sangiovese in the same breath as Pinot Noir, or Nebbiolo (Barolo and Barbaresco), or Tempranillo —wines that work because of their complexity and lightness, not because of sheer power. Treat them gently and coax out all their charms; don't try to beat them into becoming something they aren't.

Gentle handling from start to finish is the key to tannin management. Take it easy at the crusher; consider using some whole berries; try a brief cold soak to get a head start on extraction; keep fermentation temperatures on the low side of 85°F (29°C); and consider pressing just before dryness if you begin to taste a tannin buildup.

Surprising Sangiovese

Sangiovese was supposed to be the next-new-thing grape in California in the 1990s; instead, its name got put on a lot of over-priced, mediocre wine. Two producers who got it right from the start are Monte Volpe in Mendocino County and Vino Noceto in Amador County in the Sierra foothills.

On vineyard sites, Monte Volpe owner/winemaker Greg Graziano says, "It's more about the grapes and the location than the winemaking. Buy grapes from a hillside vineyard with shallow soils and rocky ground; you don't want good soils, that makes it much more challenging." Vino Noceto winemaker Rusty Folena concurs: "Sangiovese does not like fertile soil, it grows best in concrete, the rockiest, crappiest soil you can find. Otherwise, it's too vigorous."

Both winemakers use analogies to another famously cranky grape. Graziano advises, "Treat it like Pinot Noir. We use a gentle punchdown or pump-over, and try to get as long a fermentation as we can. Temperature is needed for color extraction, but not too hot." And Folena says, "One day you'll like it, one day you won't. It changes a lot — in fermentation, in the vineyard, in barrel, in the bottle. Don't panic; it's just temperamental."

Both advise going light on the new oak.

What's the hardest thing about making Sangiovese? Folena: "Getting used to the ever-changing flavors in the vineyard and the cellar." Graziano: "The temptation to do too much to it."

On the color issue, one thought is simply not to worry about it; not every wine has to be inky to be enjoyable. If you insist, consider adding a color-stabilizing enzyme before fermentation. Blending in a very small percentage of Cabernet, Merlot, Syrah, or Zinfandel can do wonders for color without overpowering the Sangiovese flavors; drawing off some juice before fermentation for a Sangiovese rosé, further concentrating the red portion, may be the best course of all.

With the tannin under control, Sangiovese's acidity is a virtue, not a drawback, unless your grapes are an extreme case. Having 7 or 8 grams of acid per liter at harvest is fine. It will drop a bit during fermentation, drop some more with malolactic, and end up making the wine refreshing and deliciously food-worthy.

Relax. You and several thousand Italian winemakers can handle it.

Pairing Yeasts and Making Choices

Table 14-1 suggests widely-available yeast strains that have proven to work well with this chapter's hard-case grape varieties. Some of the yeasts share names with some of the grapes.

Table 14-1	Good Yeasts for Hard Reds
Grape Variety	*Yeast Strains*
Pinot Noir	RC212 for ripe, bright fruit; Assmanshausen for fruit and spice; GRE for red fruit; RA17 for young drinking
Zinfandel	RP15 for berries, spice, and alcohol tolerance; D21 for mouthfeel; D80 for tannin, pepper, and spice; Assmanshausen for spice; Syrah; BM45
Tempranillo	MT, Syrah for fruit and florals; D21 for berry fruit and high pH; RP15 for color and mouthfeel
Sangiovese	BM45 for big mouthfeel; D80 for volume and floral notes; D254 for round tannins; MT for color intensity

For a quick reference, Table 14-2 summarizes techniques that can help improve one or another of these tricky but tasty grapes.

Table 14-2	Care and Feeding of Hard Reds			
Options	*Pinot Noir*	*Zinfandel*	*Tempranillo*	*Sangiovese*
Whole clusters/ berries	Very common	Small portion berries	Small portion berries	Small portion berries
Cold soak	Very common	Brief	Consider	Consider
Carbonic maceration	Portion	Not common	Not common	Not common
Co-ferment w/ whites	Not common	Not common	Not common	Consider
Temperature regimen	85°F (29°C) or higher	All over the map	80° to 85°F (27° to 29°C)	80° to 85°F (27° to 29°C)
Punchdown	2 to 4 times daily	2 times daily	2 times daily	2 times daily
Rack and return	Not common	Not common	Consider	Not common
Press timing	Early if tannin buildup	Dryness	Early if tannin buildup	Early if tannin buildup
Oak style/ influence	Handles new oak	Handles new oak	Modest oak	Modest oak
Fining	Not common	Not common	For tannin, if needed	For tannin, if needed

Chapter 15

Up-and-Comers and Off-the-Radars

A handful of grape varieties dominate wine sales and consumption in North America, and the New World generally. Add up the figures for Cabernet Sauvignon, Merlot, Zinfandel, Syrah, Pinot Noir, Chardonnay, and Sauvignon Blanc, and you have over 90 percent of the premium varietal wine market — and more than 90 percent of home winemaking production as well.

All are worthy grapes. So, however, are several dozen other varieties, some just now being planted in North America, some trapped in the low-glamour zone for a century or more. Finding a good Cabernet or Syrah at your nearest wine shop is a snap. But think about trying grapes beyond the usual suspects.

A Mouth-Filling Miscellany of Reds

The world is your grapevine. In these sections, I fill you in on a toothsome handful of "other" red grapes, all part of the standard *vinifera* species, all with charms of their own. This is a tiny fraction of a whole list; just enough to wet your whistle.

If you come across a grape variety you don't know well but have reason to believe can make good wine — let's say you've tasted a commercial bottle of it — a little detective work on the phone or the Internet can go a long way. Ask someone who is proud of their Teroldego, or their Charbono, or their Negrette how they made such an interesting wine, and you'll be amazed how much winemakers, amateur or professional, will share.

Savoring Northern Italian specials

Sangiovese is the biggest and best-known grape from Italy, but it shares the soil and spotlight with a couple hundred other varieties, many of which make great wine. Despite the importance of Italian winemaking families in the United States, their native grapes have had a hard time finding a market. But for anyone who knows the wines, they are definitely worth the effort.

Waiting for Nebbiolo

Nebbiolo is the grape behind the great wines of Barolo and Barbaresco in the Piedmont section of northern Italy, wines that age and age and age and command a pretty penny. In the Piedmont, since the wines are designed to be held for several years before they are released, let alone consumed, winemaking methods go for full extraction.

What's compelling about Nebbiolo wines is that for all the hard, tannic edge of their youth and their legendary longevity, mature Barolos and Barbarescos can be delicate, almost ethereal wines — more like Pinot Noir than Cabernet.

Finding fully ripe Nebbiolo grapes for your winemaking can be a project in itself. Even in toasty California, growers struggle to get the grapes ripe, and when they fall short, winemakers have to deal with a hard, acidic edge as well as the propensity for tannin. But oh, what lovely flavors and aromas!

If you get your hands on some Nebbiolo grapes, make sure you're on top of the basic wine chemistry — sugar content, acid levels, pH — from the start.

For your first try, I'd suggest toning it down: crushing as gently as possible, keeping fermentation temperatures on the cool side, possibly pressing a bit early to avoid tannin buildup. That way, you'll get a better sense of the fruit within your lifetime.

Appreciating everyday Barbera

While the Piemontese wait for their Barolos to come around, their everyday red is Barbera — lots of it, paired with anything that might be on the table. Barbera can be serious wine, but even at its most formal, Barbera is always rich, hearty, juicy, and inviting — a candidate for the ultimate red food wine.

In most growing areas, Old World and New, Barbera grapes tend to come in with acidity slightly on the high side, one of the reasons Barbera makes for such a lively, refreshing companion to food.

As always, check your numbers, and if nature (or the grower) has somehow gotten the acidity down, fix it up; or if it's too high, bring it down. For good color, pull off some juice for excellent, flavorful rosé. (Find out more about pink wine in Chapter 18.) No tricks needed in the winemaking.

Doing double duty with Douro treasures

Spanish wines made a big splash in North America in the last decade, and Portuguese wines are the next wave, bringing plenty of grape varieties, plenty of winemaking history, and plenty of great new flavors at bargain prices.

The region that has gotten the most attention is the Douro Valley in northern Portugal. The area has long been known for growing the grapes that go into Portuguese port, but — the Portuguese knew this all along — these same grape varieties make knockout dry reds, as well.

Dry Douro reds are generally blends of several grapes you've probably never heard of: Touriga Nacional, Touriga Franca (or Francesca), Tinta Roriz (Spain's Tempranillo), Tinta Cão, Tinta Baroca, Tinta Amarela, Bastardo, and who knows what else. With changing consumer tastes, not to mention climate change, these warm-climate varieties are getting planted in California, north-western Georgia, and Virginia. They make gutsy red wine and, as a bonus, give you the raw material for making a port-style wine modeled on the original. For a solo dry red, Touriga Nacional is the best bet.

Laying in some Lemberger

One of the prime red varieties of Central Europe, Germany's Lemberger is Austria's Blaufränkisch, Croatia's Frankovka, and Hungary's Kékfrankos, where it serves as the staple grape of Egri Bikavér, the famous Bull's Blood wines. Lemberger has found New World homes from Washington State to New York's Finger Lakes and places in-between. Everywhere Lemberger grows, it makes wines with plenty of color, tannin, spice, and cherry-berry aromatics.

Modern European and New World winemakers are experimenting with this versatile, generous variety: style it young-drinking and fruity or give it the full barrel-aging treatment; use it for blending or let it go solo. The variety isn't difficult and makes tasty red wine. Get in on the ground floor.

Taking care with tannic Tannat

Tannat has one of the most menacing reputations in grapedom: so tannic that wines can be borderline undrinkable. Tannat's homeland is the Madiran region in southwest France, and the grape's legendary ferocity helps explain why Madiran is where the modern technique of *micro-oxygenation* (bubbling tiny amounts of oxygen into young wine to soften it quickly) was developed.

How and where Tannat vines grow, however, has a lot to do with how the grapes come out. The slow spread of Tannat in warmer California isn't generally showing the same mean streak. Plenty of tannin and accompanying dark pigment, sure, but nothing you can't handle.

Be gentle with your Tannat. Don't go out of your way to provoke it, and you'll discover a flavorful wine, rich and deep, full of warm black fruit, just the ticket for cassoulet or maybe goose. Blend in a little Cabernet for fuller flavor. If any other wine in your cellar needs punching up, think Tannat.

Searching Out Homegrown Hybrids

Full disclosure: Although I've had many tasty wines made from French-American hybrid grapes, and even judged a few flights of them at competitions, I have never turned one into wine. I confess to being trapped in the California wine vortex, which may not be a liability, but it's a blind spot. Some general traits of hybrid reds are well established, and additional insight comes from commercial winemakers who do a superb job with these varieties.

Surviving phylloxera

The story of the devastating vineyard scourge of phylloxera and its eventual control changed the face of winegrowing all over the world in crucial ways.

In the mid 19th century, French botanists began importing the native vines of the United States. In 1863, vineyards near one of the experimental stations in the Southern Rhône began to wither and die inexplicably, and soon the plague spread across all the great grapegrowing regions of France and far into the rest of Europe. Before the tide turned, more than two-thirds of Europe's vineyards were destroyed.

The culprit was a tiny, sap-sucking louse, *phylloxera*, inadvertently introduced on the roots of the imported American vines. The louse's bizarre, 18-stage life cycle made it difficult to understand or control. For a decade, a string of crackpot measures — burying a live toad under each vine, or fumigating the soil with vast amounts of sulfur — were implemented to try to stop it.

The eventual solution came in the 1880s, thanks to the work of botanists in France and the United States, built on the observation that the louse co-existed just fine with native North American grapes, an evolutionary adaptation that had never occurred with *vinifera*. By grafting European varieties onto rootstocks from American species, vines could survive the louse and bear grapes from the familiar European varieties. All of Europe was eventually replanted in this fashion.

By the end of the 19th century, phylloxera had spread to the *vinifera* plantings in California, forcing a near-total replanting of the state's vineyards. A century later, a widely popular rootstock, AxR1, which had a bit of *vinifera* in its lineage, fell prey to a new phylloxera strain, requiring yet another makeover of California's grape industry in the 1990s.

How come hybrids?

When Europeans first cruised over to the New World, they were amazed at the abundant native grapevines — enough that Vinland was proposed as a name, or at least an advertising slogan. Settlers in what became Eastern Canada and the East Coast of the United States tried for centuries to make good wine from the local grapes, with brief success but mostly frustration and misfortune. At the same time, attempts to import European grape varieties, generally seen as tastier, had equally mixed results; most of the plantings, like Thomas Jefferson's vineyards in Virginia, succumbed to disease and frozen winters.

One solution was mixing and matching — creating hybrids between the European *vinifera* species and the locals. Intentional cross-breeding became common by the mid 19th century, with most of the mainstays of today's hybrid winegrowing developed in France.

With advances in grape growing starting in the 1960s, much of the territory of the United States and Canada that had been hybrid-only began sprouting bigger and bigger plantings of European varieties. The *vinifera* juggernaut has not, however, made hybrids and natives irrelevant. They remain a worthwhile option, not simply a climatological necessity.

Constraints and conventions

As a rule — and an over-generalization — hybrid reds are likely to show higher acidity and lower tannin than the *vinifera* norm. But, in winemaking, you can lower acidity (or balance acidity with sweetness) and enhance tannin.

Further, many of the native grapes from the *labrusca* species, white and red, and their hybrid descendants carry a telltale aromatic element described as "foxy." It took me years to figure out what this term meant, since I had smelled few foxes. Today I think of *foxy* as a noseful of artificial, candied strawberries laced with a tiny whiff of musty urine — a feature with limited crowd appeal. Concord grapes and wine are the benchmark; some French-American hybrids carry the trait, and some show no trace at all.

Before this list of potential shortcomings scares you off, think about how, in the *vinifera* world, Scheurebe wines routinely smell like cat pee, and Sauvignon Blanc can taste like puréed green bell peppers, and both Tempranillo and Tannat frequently contain more tannin than winemakers want to deal with. Hybrids and native grapes are not the only ones that are hard to grow and vinify well, or that take getting used to for wine drinkers.

The commercial winemakers I've spoken to who do a good job with hybrids all share the view that hybrids often suffer from poor farming — over-cropping in particular. The underlying logic seems to be that since the wines won't ever be as glamorous as the *vinifera* wines, anyway, you might as well get a big crop and make a lot of wine. But carrying too heavy a crop compounds the problem: Vines carrying excess fruit can never get it ripe, which dampen flavor and keeps acidity far too elevated.

How the pros handle hybrids

To get the full scoop on hybrid and native grape winemaking, I got in touch with award-winning, professional winemakers who know their stuff. All of them have experience with both *vinifera* and hybrid grapes, and all of them emphasized the importance of vineyard sites and practices in producing fruit that contains a reasonable balance of sugar, acidity, and pH.

✔ **Norton:** David Johnson heads the winemaking team at Stone Hill in Hermann, Missouri, which was founded in 1847, producing over a million gallons a year in 1900. Closed by Prohibition, Stone Hill re-opened in 1965 and has produced Norton as its flagship wine ever since. Johnson says these all-American grapes don't have many of the issues *labrusca* hybrids are prone to, but they do often present the twin troubles of high acidity and high pH. Letting the grapes stay on the vine longer helps drop the acidity. Since Norton includes a very high proportion of malic acid, putting the wine through malolactic makes for a comparatively large acid drop — and a pH rise, which may need to be countered with a subsequent tartaric acid addition. Balancing starts early and goes straight through.

Johnson suggests, only half in jest, that one way out of the Norton acid/pH bind is to make it into a port-style wine. Sugar will mask the high acid, and the high alcohol will handle any spoilage danger from the high pH. Plus, it tastes really good in that style.

✔ **Chambourcin:** Harmony Hill Vineyards in Bethel, Ohio makes award-winning Chambourcin. Winemaker Bill Svarka is almost apologetic about not having to do all that much different in the winery to make the grapes work just fine. Long hang time in the vineyard — it's not unusual to harvest in early November — creates reasonable acidity and full, varietal flavors; a fruit-oriented yeast like RC-212 brings out the character; the addition of some stems back into the fermentation gives a small tannin boost. If some acid reduction is required, he's a fan of potassium bicarbonate as the treatment. The wines are barrel-aged. "If you treat any grape with respect," Svarka says, "you get that back twofold."

✔ **Baco Noir:** Giradet Vineyards in southern Oregon's Umpqua Valley has the distinction of being a hybrid-focused producer in the middle of a *vinifera*-happy state. Swiss-born founder Philippe Giradet knew these grapes from home and decided they were worth a try in Oregon. He was right. His son Marc, now the winemaker, says that in Oregon's climate, with enough time on the vine, the hybrid varieties develop wine chemistry in the normal *vinifera* range. Giradet's prize-winning Baco Noir stays on the vine late, since it tends toward high acid; fermentation may use slightly cooler temperatures and shorter extraction time before pressing. Oak tannin from barrel aging makes up for the grapes' natural tannin shortfall. Filtration removes the high concentration of solids, which can lead to off flavors.

Home winemakers must be vigilant in sourcing hybrid and native grapes. Find out who grows the fruit, and how they treat their vineyards. Does the grower try to keep vines in balance and limit yields? If the grapes go to commercial wineries, taste their wines. If you find a commercial example you like, try to trace your way back to the grower and see if you can get some fruit.

Reduce acidity, if needed, with several small additions of calcium carbonate or Acidex, or a single addition of potassium bicarbonate (more on de-acidification in Chapter 7). If you want to re-introduce sweetness, first do tasting trials, then treat the wine with potassium sorbate (a chemical compound discussed in Chapter 20) to halt renewed fermentation activity.

Be prepared to roll up your sleeves, to be alert to the basic chemistry of your fruit and wines, and to intervene when you need to. Don't be afraid to adjust acidity or, with some varieties, to have a little sugar in a red wine. You may have to work harder than homies who deal with perfectly ripe, nicely balanced *vinifera* grapes from the benign West Coast — be proud!

Proven winners

The following list just scratches the surface of indigenous and hybrid reds. This selection includes varieties that perform well enough, over and over, to win competitions against the *vinifera* crowd:

- **Baco Noir:** Baco is a hybrid of the French *vinifera* grape Folle Blanche — a neutral white variety used mainly in making Cognac and Armagnac brandy — and American *Vitis riparia* stock. It makes a good deal of red wine in cooler North American climates — Ontario, New York, Michigan, Pennsylvania, Wisconsin, and Oregon. Expect bright acidity, black fruit flavors, and not much tannin.

- **Chambourcin:** Chambourcin's hybrid parentage is not well known, but its breeding seems to have happened in France in the 1860s, though the variety only became commercially available in the United States a century later. Chambourcin has none of the *labrusca* foxiness and, when grown right, makes deeply colored, flavorful, aromatic dry red wine. If the grapes come in out of balance, you may need to reduce the acidity.

- **Concord:** Talk about a grape with a bad reputation. Many people first encountered wine made with Concord grapes in sweet, bland, mass-produced kosher wines from Manischewiz in their childhoods. Most folks think of Concord as a grape for jelly or juice, not wine, and indeed that's where most of the production goes.

  Nonetheless, Concord is a contender. Its *Vitis labrusca* origins put it high on the foxy list, but then, candied strawberries can be charming. On the rare occasions when Concord is grown for winemaking and allowed to get fully ripe, it can make dry wine, but at least a touch of sugar is more common. Standard home technique is to ferment the wine dry, then add sugar to taste and treat with potassium sorbate to kill off the yeast.

✔ **Marechal Foch:** Hybridized in France and named after Marshall Ferdinand Foch, a negotiator in the armistice after World War I, this grape works in styles from young-drinking to barrel-aged. Commercial bottlings come from eastern Canada, British Columbia's Okanagan Valley, the eastern United States, and Oregon. Small berries mean big color; acidity is normally low for a hybrid. Flavors can go beyond pure fruit to meaty-gamey — which some of us think is a plus.

✔ **Norton:** By far the best of the indigenous red grapes, Norton — also known as Cynthiana — is a variant of the *Vitis aestivalis* species, with the possibility of some other ancestral species in the genetic stew. Norton was the country's dominant red grape for a time; it's the official state grape of Missouri; and the Riedel crystal company, makers of glassware for the leading *vinifera* grapes, has a Norton glass as well.

Making good Norton, however, isn't easy, as the "How the pros handle hybrids" sidebar indicates. It tends to bring both high acid and high pH. So steps to cut the acidity — including malolactic fermentation — can bump the pH even higher, requiring attention to microbe control.

Turning to Teinturier Grapes: Red All Over

One more category of grapes, back under the *vinifera* umbrella but still in a world of its own, is *Teinturier* (French for "to dye" or "to stain"): grapes with red pigment in the pulp and juice, not just the skins. While this characteristic seems like a bonanza for red winemakers, the *teinturier* varieties also tend to carry a high load of tannins, often rendering their wines too harsh to make the cut as solo varietals. But for blending, a little goes a long way.

The most common Teinturier varieties are Alicante Boschet, a French variety often found in Zinfandel-based California blends; Souzão, a Portuguese variety used in port winemaking; Saparavi, the main red grape of the nation of Georgia; and Rubired, a cross developed through the viticulture program at the University of California at Davis that gets used for blending, food coloring, and producing grape concentrate to add color to red wines.

Handled very carefully and fined as needed to remove excess tannin, these varieties can make deeply colored, sturdy, rustic red wines. Having 50 pounds (23 kilograms) around can provide 3 or 4 gallons (11 to 15 liters) of very useful blending material.

Part IV
Deeper Into Whites

The 5th Wave   By Rich Tennant

"What do you mean you didn't make any white wine?
You know darn well I can't serve fish without white wine!"

In this part . . .

*B*oth Chardonnay and Riesling grapes grow on vines and make good white wine, but that's where the similarities end. Bringing out the best in each requires thinking like a grape, which is more fun than it sounds.

Pinot Blanc, Sauvignon Blanc, Seyval Blanc, Blancety-blanc . . . . Catch the nuances of whites in these chapters.

Chapter 16

What's Special about White Wines?

Red wines rule the roost for home winemaking. For the 2009 harvest, my local winemaking supply shop, which brings in grapes from all over the place, offered 19 different selections of red grapes and just three whites. The old wine drinker's saw, "The first duty of every wine is to be red," seems to apply with a vengeance in home winemaking.

But if white wine shows up on your table, make a place for it in your home winemaking. The grapes cost less; the winemaking takes less work; and the wine is ready to drink sooner. But the real reason to try whites is that they put your winemaking skills and devotion to the test — they're actually tougher to make *well* than reds.

This chapter surveys a number of optional "advanced" techniques to turn out tasty whites and includes some general considerations about pursuing white wine style.

Whites: Harder Than Reds?

Even veteran wine lovers are surprised when I tell them that white wines are harder to make well than reds. But most winemakers would agree with me, even the ones whose livelihoods depend on making nothing but red wines. How can that be? Well, I talk about some of the reasons in the next sections.

Make sure your whites don't become an afterthought — wines you make because you think you have to, or because your sister likes white wine, or because you need something alcoholic to drink while the "real" red wine ages. Whites are sensitive; they can tell when you're taking them for granted.

Shrinking the margin of error

White wines are lighter than reds — not simply in color, but in body and texture. Many successful and enjoyable whites are built for refreshment, not complexity, and for drinking right now, not for aging. Nearly all white wines are ready to bottle and drink sooner than any red. Whites cost less at every step along the way, from the average price of the grapes to the average price of the bottles. So what's hard about that?

White wines are challenging to make because the margin of error is much smaller than with reds:

- ✔ A touch of some strange bacterial by-product will disappear into a hearty red — and jump out of the glass for a white.

- ✔ Red wines, full of tannins and other compounds, can absorb lots of oxygen — which can turn a white flatter than a pancake.

- ✔ A tiny haze in a dark red may go entirely unnoticed; hazy whites make you wonder what you're drinking.

Avoiding these shortcomings doesn't require fancy winemaking tricks: you just have to pay close attention to keep your white wines happy.

The very delicacy that makes white wines lively and a pleasure to behold and drink also makes them vulnerable. The useful obsessions I discuss in Chapter 4 — controlling temperature, managing oxygen, and practicing good sanitation — all count double for making whites.

For most white varieties and styles, cool-temperature fermentation pays big dividends, while letting white wines get overheated may be too much for their delicate sensibilities. Too much oxygen after fermentation dampens white aromatics and can shorten the wine's life span dramatically. Funkiness from a badly cleaned carboy or a dirty stopper sticks out like a sore thumb.

Enough scare tactics — you get the picture. White wines aren't so much hard to make as easy to mess up. Pay close attention to detail and make good use of your own built-in sensory equipment — that all-important nose and those ever-helpful taste buds (unlike elaborate equipment and arcane additives, they're free).

Making whites with character

Making your white wines come out clean is important, but not the whole story. Squeaky-clean white wines can be thin and boring, something we all encounter far too often in commercial wines. White wines need to show just as much character as reds.

 Starting with good fruit is extremely important. White grapes grown with too big a crop load make watery wines, and no amount of winemaking trickery or oak injections can make up for diluted grapes. Many — but not all — whites do better in cool climates where they take longer to ripen and don't turn into sugar bombs from unrelenting heat. Too much sun can sunburn white grapes, which throws off the flavor.

Options, Alternatives, and Experiments

Most commercial white wine is made very much the way you'd do it at home: destem and crush the grapes, press them, ferment the juice at cool temperatures in stainless steel (glass at home), clean the wine by racking, filter it, and bottle it young. A good portion of sought-after, distinctive, high-end whites, however, depart from these conventions, usually in a very controlled way. Once you have confidence in your winemaking, the following sections offer some "rules" to break and some options to try.

Pressing whole clusters

Some high-end whites benefit from *whole-cluster pressing* — skipping the destemming and crushing altogether and squeezing the juice right out of the grape bunches under pressure. After the juice is collected, it gets processed like any other juice.

Advocates of whole-cluster pressing cite two main advantages:

- ✔ Because the juice spends very little time in contact with the cracked, split grape skins, it comes out purer and cleaner, with no trace of the harshness that can get picked up with longer skin contact.
- ✔ The transition from grape cluster to juice all happens within a closed system of presses, pipes, and tanks, reducing the oxygen exposure that comes with the standard crushing process.

The technique fits a wide range of grapes, from Chardonnay to Riesling to Sauvignon Blanc, and has been gaining popularity around the world. The limitation, commercially and at home, is the cost of the pressing equipment.

For home purposes, whole-cluster pressing with a small basket press isn't very satisfying. Creating enough pressure with a manual-crank ratchet is difficult, and you're likely get low juice yield per pound of grapes. You may have better luck with home-scale enclosed stainless steel bladder presses — which, unfortunately, cost more than twice as much as basket presses for the same capacity. If you make a major commitment to home white winemaking, a small bladder press may be worth the investment.

Savoring the skins

While most winemakers jump through hoops to minimize fraternization between white grape skins and juice, others swear by *skin contact* — letting crushed whites stew in their skins for several hours before pressing. Some wineries, looking for blending options, do both: whole-cluster pressing one batch of grapes and letting another pick up goodies through skin contact.

White grape skins don't offer any color pigment, but do contain some tannins, as well as aromatic and flavor compounds. Skin contact can extract elements that bolster a wine's character and complexity. Too much skin contact can produce harsh, bitter, astringent qualities that undermine white wine's charms. A little contact goes a long way, so skin contact is more common with assertive, strongly flavored varieties — Sauvignon Blanc, Muscat, Viognier — than with more restrained or neutral varieties — Pinot Gris/Grigio, Chardonnay, Chenin Blanc.

Trying a bit of skin contact in your winery is simple to do and can contribute to wine complexity. Take a small portion of your crushed white grapes and their juice — 20 to 25 percent. Let the mixture sit, in a covered container, under cool conditions (preferably under 60°F [16°C]) for three to six hours, and then press the grapes. Depending on the volume, the skin contact juice may just go in with the rest, or it may go through fermentation in its own carboy (the second scenario is ideal for tasting the differences after fermentation and for gaining a sense of what the skin contact adds). I've used the skin contact method with Muscat and Viognier, with excellent results.

Fermenting in barrels

Fermenting white wine in barrels was once a rarity. But it's becoming more popular and is almost obligatory for higher-end Chardonnay. Fermentation in new or newish barrels builds in oak flavors from the start, and both new and older barrels contribute oak tannins that encourage rounder, bigger mouthfeel.

Barrel fermentation changes two of the standard parameters in white wine-making: The fermenting wine gets exposed to slightly more oxygen than it would in a sealed carboy or stainless steel tank; and the fermentation temperature runs higher, usually up around 65°F (18°C) or a good deal higher — no convenient way to cool barrels exists (other than air-conditioning an entire room). You may lose some aromatic delicacy, complexity, and freshness, but the trade-off comes in bigger, more powerful wines.

Barrel sizes from 15 gallons (55 liters) and up are preferable; smaller than that, they may be more trouble than they're worth.

Many commercial wineries use barrel fermentation for a portion of white wine production and blend it with tank-fermented wine for a balance of fruit and body. Assuming you have enough juice/wine to work with, this is a great strategy in your home winery. You get the benefits of greater complexity and less risk of creating an unbalanced, one-dimensional wine.

Barrels used for white wine fermentation need to be new or previously used *only* for white wine. Barrels that aged reds leave color behind, and you can find a better way to make a rosé. (I tell you what you need to know about pinks in Chapter 19.) Used white wine barrels are fine for reds.

After pressing, let the juice sit for 24 hours to settle out some of the solids. Then fill the barrel about 80 percent full, leaving ample room for fermentation headspace. Inoculate with yeast and nutrients, gas with carbon dioxide (CO_2) if available, and use a large-diameter carboy-style airlock stopper to release bubbling CO_2. (A solid bung won't let CO_2 out, so the CO_2 will simply blow the bung out of its way.)

When the wine is dry, rack it off the *gross lees* — the dead yeast at the bottom of the barrel — and transfer it to whatever container — barrel or carboy — you choose for aging. If the wine goes back into barrel, the barrel should be entirely filled to prevent oxidation — so make sure you have enough wine available.

I do all my white wines in carboys — sometimes way too many of them — and I've had success with what I call *mock-barrel fermentation*. Add a small amount of oak cubes — perhaps 2 ounces (55 grams) — to one or more carboys when you add yeast, and leave the cubes in until the wine is dry and gets racked. One option is untoasted oak cubes, which simply add a bit of tannin and no flavor. This simple home method isn't exactly like barrel fermentation, but it adds some tannin and flavor to the wine. Mock-barrel fermentation is similar to the commercial practice of adding wood tannins to white wine tank fermentations, just on a smaller scale.

Multiplying your yeast

Every yeast strain is unique. They all convert sugar to alcohol, but yeasts differ in small ways:

- ✔ How they react to different temperatures.
- ✔ How much they need certain nutrients.
- ✔ Which aromatic and flavor compounds they interact with in the juice.
- ✔ How they affect a wine's chemical balance.

Some yeast effects are highly transient, and some last straight through till bottling and beyond. (I talk about yeast in more depth in Chapter 6.)

Yeast suppliers occasionally make extravagant claims, but for the most part, when they talk about specific yeast strains, they're pretty accurate. So, for example, a certain strain was indeed tested and proved to be good at pulling out *terpenes,* important aromatic compounds in Riesling and similar varieties, and another really did stabilize red wine color. But these claims were proven to be true *in the research lab.* Whether the same yeast performs that service on your batch of fruit is another question and well worth a few experiments.

Because yeast in home winemaking quantities is so cheap — a dollar or two for enough to ferment several hundred dollars worth of grapes — trying out new strains and mixing multiple yeasts is an excellent investment. Consider making yeast trials a regular part of your home winemaking, and be sure to take notes about the effects of each strain, for future reference. (Later chapters include specific yeast suggestions for white grape varieties.)

Whenever practical, think about dividing a batch of white wine juice into multiple small fermentations and try two or three or four different yeast strains. Take 15 gallons (55 liters) of juice, for example, split it between four carboys for fermentation, and use two of the tried-and-true white wine yeasts and two of the trendy strains that claim great benefits for the variety you're fermenting. Check their performance, especially the differences in smell and taste after fermentation — you may be amazed.

If you're using multiple yeast strains, use multiple containers, as well. Joined in a single fermentation, yeast strains compete, sometimes kill each other off, and leave you unclear about what effect each strain contributed. Some multistrain yeast "cocktails" claim predictable results, but if you're doing your own yeast trials, don't mix.

Some differences fade over time, and the wines may all end up in a single blend. You may fall in love with one strain; you may banish another from your winery forever. Your wine will end up more complex, and your notes will record your own tested ideas — not just the yeast vendor's advertising copy — for the next time around.

If you're feeling extremely adventurous, try letting one carboy go into *spontaneous* or *wild fermentation,* allowing whatever yeast strains that happen to be hanging out in your winery or on the grapes have their way with your juice. Sometimes wild fermentation produces amazing wine; sometimes it produces vinegar. A safer variation is to let a small batch of wine go on its own for a few days, starting a wild fermentation, and then add a commercial yeast strain guaranteed to finish the job. Proceed with caution.

Cooling down, warming up

White wines are more temperature-sensitive than reds, especially during fermentation; a few degrees up or down makes a difference. My general recommendation — and the norm for modern commercial winemaking — is to keep white fermentations in the 50° to 60°F (10° to 16°C) range, and bring the temperature up a few degrees (into the 60s Fahrenheit or high teens Celsius) toward the end for a dry finish. The goal is to keep the wine fresh and preserve all the fruitiness.

But in white barrel fermentations (see "Fermenting in barrels" earlier in this chapter), temperatures run quite a bit higher, 65°F (18°C) and higher. The resulting wines — certainly the barrel-fermented Chardonnays — receive critical acclaim and fetch impressive prices.

Before the advent of stainless steel and refrigeration in the 1960s, white wine was made for centuries at whatever temperature prevailed. The cool school is a recent phenomenon. Research demonstrates that yeast, even cold-tolerant strains, are happier at slightly higher temperatures. Cool fermentation may be a rule you want to break — carefully.

If you have multiple carboys of a white wine, try letting one of them ferment 10° to 15°F higher (3° to 6°C higher) than the rest, and compare the results. At a minimum, this adds another element to your wine. You may even discover that you prefer warmer fermentations for certain varieties.

To malo or not to malo

For many centuries, *malolactic fermentation* — the transformation of malic acid into lactic acid by various strains of bacteria — just happened to wine, or didn't, depending on the local microbial population. The mechanics of malolactic, the critters who perform it, and the techniques for encouraging or discouraging were figured out only about 40 years ago.

Attempting to match the biggest white wines from Burgundy, producers of California Chardonnay jumped on the malolactic bandwagon in the 1970s. The fat, buttery mouthfeel and aromas that resulted became defining features of the California style. Soon, everything was getting put through malo, too, with mixed, even peculiar, results. These days, malolactic fermentation for white wines is no longer a fad, but a conscious stylistic choice.

Malolactic fermentation for whites can serve two useful purposes:

- ✔ The first is stylistic, adding heft and roundness and a bit of popcorn-butter aromatics. Chardonnay is a good candidate, because its relatively neutral fruit can use the added dimension. But for aromatic wines like Gewürztraminer and Riesling, malo usually gets in the way.

- ✔ Malo improves balance, taking a too-sharp edge off a wine with excess acidity, especially excess malic acid; the change from malic to lactic acid reduces the perceived acidity of the wine.

For many whites, *partial malolactic* can be a nice compromise, which you achieve by putting part of the wine through malo or halting the malolactic fermentation of the whole batch in mid-process. Either way, this is highly tricky for home winemakers. It increases the chances that malolactic bacteria will loiter in the wine and decide to go for the full malo later on. Commercial wineries solve the stability problem through *sterile filtration*, which removes all the bacteria; you don't have that option. Malo control at home relies on additions of sulfur dioxide sufficient to kill the bacteria and, as insurance, the use of lysozyme. My personal taste in white wines is skewed toward bright acidity and zingy mouthfeel, so for my own whites, I almost always suppress malolactic activity, even with Chardonnay. But your taste is your taste, and partial malo may be one of your tools.

The bottom line with malo, as I explain in detail in Chapter 7, is that you have to make a conscious choice to encourage it or prevent it; if you just let it slide, a posse of microbes may very well ruin your day.

Oxidation on purpose

Modern white winemaking calls for keeping oxygen away from the wine at all costs — sometimes called *reductive winemaking.* Most of the time, keeping oxygen away should be high on your own home winery checklist. But as with any other winemaking precept, bending the rules can make interesting wines; in this case, purposely giving your wine some air.

Before and during fermentation, white juice needs oxygen, and so does the yeast that handles the fermentation chores. Once the wine has fermented, however, oxygen can flatten out flavor and encourage unwelcome microbes, so oxygen usually gets shut out. But oxidation can also do for white table wines a bit of what it does for sherry by adding complex, nutty flavors. Intentional oxidation of a fermented wine is an experiment you might try sometime on a small batch of wine, or a small part of a larger batch.

Slow, intentional oxidation is part of an old-fashioned wine style called *rancio,* still practiced in some parts of Spain and France. The main technique is neglect: You age the wine in barrels, but without topping them up or using sulfur dioxide to protect against oxidation. The resulting wines are fascinating, if not exactly mainstream.

Planned oxidation is not the way to make your first homemade white wine, but you might keep it in mind as an experiment down the road. If you don't want to risk a whole barrel — and I don't — simply age some wine in a small carboy and leave some headspace full of air.

Finishing touches

You can make yummy white wine by letting gravity do the work of clarification. You rack the wine nice and clean, and bottle it. All the finishing touches of cold stabilization, fining, and filtering are optional. They take a lot of extra work and equipment, but these additional steps give you sparkling clear wine that stays that way over time and at any temperature. The longer you make wine, the more important these small touches may become. Some finishing touches you can try include:

- ✔ **Cold stabilization:** This process prevents the formation of tartrate crystals in chilled wine by getting rid of them before the wine is bottled. Cold stabilization works best when wine can be held at temperatures down near freezing for several weeks, which is hard to accomplish at home.

Putting carboys in a 40°F (4°C) refrigerator for two or three weeks, however, does a good part of the job. More on this in Chapter 9.

✔ **Filtration:** Filtering your wine removes solids still suspended in the wine after most of the yeast and other sludge has settled out. It creates wine with great transparency and brilliant color — wine that seems to dance in the glass.

The pads for home filter rigs vary in the size of particles they trap, letting you choose between getting your wine clean or squeaky-clean. Most commercial white wine goes through sterile filtration, pulling out every conceivable microbe. True sterile filtration isn't practical at home, but you can make your wine look a lot prettier by filtering it.

✔ **Fining:** Fining white wines with bentonite stabilizes the wine's reaction to temperature changes in later life. *Fining* removes specific compounds from wine with the addition of a fining agent. In this case, bentonite takes out proteins that can come out of solution and create a haze in response to both hot and cold temperatures. Find more on this in Chapter 9.

All these cleanup techniques are useful and optional, and apply to any grape variety. In terms of the dazzling payoff in the glass, I'd rank filtration first, bentonite fining second, and cold stabilization third; in terms of the difficulty of doing them well at home, the order is probably reversed.

The White Wine Balancing Act

Beyond the specific techniques applied to white wines, the key element to pursue is balance. *Balance* is the harmonious combination of the elements that make up how a wine tastes — fruit, acidity, alcohol, tannin, oak, and so on. But balance is ultimately subjective, defined by each wine drinker's taste buds, preferences, and wine-drinking background. Your wines should reflect your idea of balance.

Red wines, with their big blast of flavor, get away with small balance infractions; white wines show them off. The most common imbalances in whites, home or commercial, come from too little acid and too much oak.

Keeping acidity up

White wines need good acidity to bring out their full range of flavors, to be refreshing, and to be a counterpoint to food. Flabby white wines with no bite are boring. Bright acidity also lowers pH, helping wine stability.

Acidity gets measured both by the numbers and by your tasting. Total acidity (TA) for whites should generally be in the range of 6 to 8 grams per liter, generally higher for off-dry and sweet dessert wines. Test acidity when the grapes or juice arrive, again after fermentation, and again before bottling, and adjust as needed (details in Chapter 5).

As the character of the wine emerges, tasting for acidity is crucial to the final wine; doing tasting trials with doctored samples can be instructive. White grapes and wines from warmer places routinely require additions of tartaric acid. Cool-climate grapes, on the other hand, typically have better, higher acidity, and winemakers sometimes need to reduce their acid levels, using potassium bicarbonate (something I cover in Chapter 7).

Acidity is one wine adjustment where my advice is, "Don't be shy!"

Easy on the oak

A few white wines marry well with oak flavors, but frankly, not many. Oak can clobber delicacy in a hurry, making wine into liquid lumber. Oaky flavors also fight with the food you'd think of pairing with white wine.

The full oak treatment — barrel fermentation, aging in small oak barrels — is a style that can work well for Chardonnay, but not so well for the more aromatic whites (Chapter 18 tells you more about the aromatic white crew). This is largely because Chardonnay's fruit flavors aren't that distinctive. On the other hand, oak flavor can trample and mute the delicate and seductive character of the aromatic whites. That's why the use of oak is somewhere between rare and non-existent in aromatic whites. In between lies some wiggle room for a judicious touch of oak to give your wine some complexity.

How you handle oak depends most of all on your own wine-drinking preferences. To explore oak and white wine in your own winery, I would suggest starting oak-free, then try a small batch with oak cubes, and take it from there.

Aging Your White Wines

These days, most white wines are consumed right after they're bottled, emphasizing the fresh, fruity qualities. Many whites, however, can continue to develop in the bottle for a few years, and they reveal more about themselves over time. Many would argue, in fact, that the greatest white wines — like the best German Rieslings — can out-age the best reds.

To make successful white wine aging more likely, your job as winemaker has three parts:

- ✔ Get good flavor extraction from your fermentation through high-quality fruit, yeast strain selection, and temperature control.
- ✔ Keep the pH low and acidity relatively high.
- ✔ Make sure the wine is stable — protected from microbial adventures — through sulfur dioxide management and clean bottling practices.

That's it — all things you'd be doing anyway. Put aside a few bottles of everything you make, white, red, or otherwise, and taste them over time. You'll learn more about how wine matures, and you may create some pleasant surprises for yourself.

Making those Decisions, Decisions

The next two chapters tackle particular white grape varieties — all the major ones and some intriguing less familiar ones — and suggest ways to mix and match the techniques from this chapter to achieve various wine styles.

I'm dividing the world of white grapes — somewhat arbitrarily — into varieties that are fruity and/or herbal, and varieties that are mainly known for their floral aromatics. All grapes show fruit; all grapes are aromatic. But since the dominant winemaking styles tend to differ, that's the division between Chapter 17 (fruity/herbal) and Chapter 18 (aromatic).

Figure 16-1 lays out the steps in white winemaking — required ones like pressing, optional ones like blending — in a decision tree, an outline of all the choices you can make (or not make) along the way. The upcoming chapters will discuss where the options fit or might not fit, as well as suggesting appropriate yeast choices.

WHITE WINEMAKING DECISION TREE

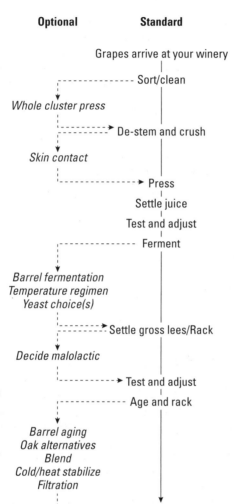

Figure 16-1:
The basic steps and many options of making white wine.

Chapter 17

Fruity, Herbal Whites

. . . .

In This Chapter

▶ Making Chardonnay, style by style

▶ Savoring Sauvignon Blanc, with and without grassiness

▶ Traveling the wide world of *vinifera* whites

▶ Harmonizing with hybrid whites

. . . .

All white grapes — all wine grapes, period — are fruity, and plenty of them have something herbal in the aromas or flavors. What this catch-all category does is *exclude* certain grapes — the ones mainly known for their floral aromatic qualities (I give you info on them in Chapter 18).

The fruity-herbal universe has two overwhelmingly dominant entries: Chardonnay and Sauvignon Blanc. Those two staples get their due in these pages, but so do a long list of other whites definitely worth a try and a taste.

Chardonnay: The Perils of Popularity

Chardonnay is the planet's most popular white wine and the dominant white in North America by every measure — acres planted, tons harvested, cases produced, boatloads consumed. Massive popularity, as always, is a double-edged pruning knife: The grape must have some endearing qualities to draw such a crowd, yet the sheer volume of output and drinking guarantees that a lot of questionably made wine is on the market.

Checking its changeable characteristics

Chardonnay grows reasonably well in a broad range of climate zones and makes pleasant, drinkable wine on every continent. Yet left to itself, truly great, distinctive Chardonnay only comes from a very few places. How could that be?

The answer is that Chardonnay's inherent aromatic and flavor profile is, well, pretty neutral and generic. Vague fruitiness is always present, and most often hints of apple or green apple, but often not much more. At the same time, Chardonnay generally arrives with more body than many whites, a combination of texture compounds and, certainly in warmer climates, comparatively high alcohol. More body makes it bigger, but not necessarily more interesting. I'm not saying Chardonnay isn't agreeable; but compared to Muscat, with its intoxicating floral fumes, or Sauvignon Blanc, with its assertive grassiness, Chardonnay is downright meek.

Chardonnay's lack of sharp sensory elbows is, of course, a major reason for its popularity; the analogy with light beer is impossible to resist. More to the point, Chardonnay's blank canvas almost begs for winemaking artistry — winery tricks and techniques to mold this modest grape into something better.

Take yeast choices, for example. A great deal of high-end Chardonnay comes from wild, spontaneous fermentations, as winemakers hope that less-domesticated yeast strains might add a bit of complexity. When choosing commercial yeast, winemakers often go for exotic, so-called *aromatic* strains, which accentuate things like tropical fruit aromas and flavors not usually prominent in the grapes themselves.

More often than any other white wine, commercial Chardonnay regularly goes through malolactic fermentation, fattening texture and layering in buttery flavors.

And then there's oak. Chardonnay tops the list of barrel-fermented whites, gaining body, texture, and — with new oak — a first step toward oak aromas and flavors. Barrel aging is common, again often with a large proportion in new oak; wood chips in bulk are a mid-priced mainstay. A major factor in Chardonnay's rise to the top in California was the extensive use of new oak, which gave the wine its signature aromas: Not anything from the fruit kingdom, but vanilla and butterscotch. All that oak — and sometimes a pinch of residual sugar — is what made Chardonnay generic and spawned the ABC — Anything But Chardonnay — reaction. Few grapes earn their own protest movements.

If you've never had one, it turns out that simple, bare-bones Chardonnay, made in glass or stainless, without oak or malo, is a remarkable, refreshing adult beverage. None of the common added treatments is inherently evil; none is a betrayal of the "true" Chardonnay; all have contributed to terrific wines. But it's easy to see how winemaking manipulation can overpower an unassuming grape, and why Chardonnay is known in the commercial industry as a winemaker's grape *par excellence*.

Matching fruit to technique

The challenge with Chardonnay is to select from among the available wine-making techniques based on the fruit you have. Putting the grapes in charge is good practice with any variety, but Chardonnay offers a particularly good example. Some fruit is cut out for barrel fermentation, some isn't. Some grapes benefit from malolactic fermentation, some are happier without.

The only way to find out for sure what the fruits of a particular vineyard can do is to take some grapes, make your best guess, apply some winemaking knowledge, and taste what happens. Commercial winemakers run trials on the side every year to evaluate different approaches, and house styles change over time. In that spirit, a slice of Chardonnay winemakers have backed off the oak and are even flaunting un-oaked, no-malo bottlings.

Climate, crop load, and harvest grape chemistry give important clues to what a particular batch of Chardonnay grapes can handle. Chardonnay is at its most intense in cooler-climate regions — the prime example is Burgundy. But the same influence shows up in Chardonnays from New Zealand, the Finger Lakes of New York state, the winegrowing regions of British Columbia and Ontario in Canada, and the upper Midwest of the United States.

More intense fruit can handle more winemaking magic. Warmer climates generally yield grapes that are diluted in flavor and short on acid, which make better candidates for simple fermentations and everyday drinking.

Like any other grape, Chardonnay performs best when the crop load is limited to a volume of grapes the vines can ripen. The cooler the climate, the lower the crop load has to be to fully mature; some places — much of German Riesling country, for example — are too cold for this cool-climate grape. (This is advantageous in Champagne, where the Chardonnay for sparkling wine isn't supposed to get very ripe.) In warmer spots, more crop is possible; but when the vines are in noticeably warm spots — including much of Australia and California — sugar levels shoot up and acid levels decline precipitously, long before full flavor expression. High-crop Chardonnay can be perfectly drinkable — your local wine shop has a shelf or two available right now — but will not likely be memorable.

The final indicator of what your Chardonnay can take is *harvest chemistry,* the basic numbers your grapes or juice arrive with. Cool-climate, low-crop, high-intensity Chardonnay often shows no more than 23° Brix, total acidity (TA) of 7 or 8 grams per liter, and a pH down around 3.2 to 3.3. Tens of thousands of acres of California Chardonnay test out at more like 26° Brix, 5 grams of acid, and pH up around 3.6 — fine numbers, but usually associated with Big Red wines.

Continent-wide Chardonnay

Although the Chardonnays that dominated the market and the magazines in the 1990s came from California, great Chardonnay comes from all sorts of low-profile places, done in every combination imaginable.

In the Okanagan Valley of British Columbia, Ian and Matt Mavety at Blue Mountain Vineyard do Chard in what Ian calls "not a very New World style," starting with picking fruit around 22° Brix, concentrating on acidity and not sugar. Half the wine gets fermented in one- to four-year-old barrels, half gets fermented in-tank; a small portion of the barrels go through malo, and all the barreled wine stays put on the gross lees until blending time in April.

Across the continent on Long Island, New York, Macari Vineyard consulting winemaker Helmut Gangl says wineries should mix multiple Chardonnay clones to avoid "monotonous" winemaking. Macari uses different viticultural techniques and picking dates to put together four Chardonnay styles: fresh and fruity, normal stainless, fuller-bodied, and sticky-sweet — truly a winemaker's wine.

Smack in the middle, near Traverse City, Michigan, Spencer Stegenga at Bowers Harbor Vineyards loves all the snow they get in wintertime, because it protects the vines from winter kill. The climate leads to lots of malic acid in the grapes, but enough overall acidity to put them through malo and give them the benefit from French oak. His rule on yeast: "No perfumy stuff."

More balanced wines with more Chardonnay character tend to exhibit the first range of harvest parameters. Grapes with the second chemical profile will have a hard time absorbing oak flavors, won't have the acidity to benefit from malolactic, and will gravitate toward the flabby. Ironically, those numbers are found not only on low-end, mass-market Chardonnay grapes, but on the fruit that becomes the over-priced, overblown, over-treated Chards. Small wonder that winemaking fingerprints are all over them.

The next two sections outline polar-opposite approaches to making Chardonnay: one lean and clean, one fat and rich. They're called *faux*, (French for "false"), because your grapes won't come from France. The "*faux* Chablis" route is safest, focusing on the fruit and minimizing the clutter. "*Faux* Montrachet" is harder to pull off in your one-barrel garage, but can make much bigger wine. Even at the lean end of the technique spectrum, I encourage you to experiment. Try using more than one yeast, ferment some wood chips in one carboy, and learn which tools work with your fruit.

Channeling "faux Chablis"

The Chablis region of Burgundy has an international reputation for bright, steely, mouth-cleansing, food-friendly wines — all made from Chardonnay and most carrying price tags normal humans can afford. The popularity of these wines in Europe and North America explains why the United States wine industry called nearly anything white "Chablis" for decades, regardless of grapes or winemaking.

Following is a start-to-finish overview of tips for achieving a Chardonnay in the Chablis style:

- ✔ **Sort fruit carefully.** Pick over the fruit (if you're starting with the fruit instead of juice), pull out anything broiled, bug-eaten, raisined, or moldy, as well as leaves and other stray material. After you crush the grapes, pick out any leaves and stem shards before pressing. This style leaves no room for off-flavors.

- ✔ **Press pronto.** Whole-cluster pressing is ideal. The next best is to minimize the time the crushed grapes spend extracting compounds you don't want from the skins; press them quickly.

- ✔ **Pay close attention to grape chemistry.** If the grapes come in with excessively high pH and/or low acidity, address the imbalance immediately by adding tartaric acid to reach about 7 grams per liter; if that means lots of acid, perhaps use a softer acid blend with some malic and citric in it, which may stick out less later.

- ✔ **Take pre-emptive measures.** When you have juice, dose it with 25 to 50 parts per million (ppm) of sulfur dioxide to knock back rogue microbes and 75 ppm of lysozyme to extend the un-welcome mat for malolactic bacteria.

- ✔ **Settle the juice.** Let the juice sit for 24 to 36 hours, keeping it as cool as possible — at least under 60°F (16°C) — and away from oxygen. Blanket the juice with carbon dioxide, if available.

- ✔ **Rack into fermenters.** Carboys are made for *faux* Chablis style; leave a few inches of headspace in each for the foaminess of fermentation.

- ✔ **Use a fruity yeast.** Table 17-2 lists a number of choices; aim for a strain that tolerates cool temperatures, finishes bone-dry, produces very little hydrogen sulfide, and is *neutral* — it extracts fruit, but doesn't put its own stamp on the aromatics.

- ✔ **Cool fermentation.** Keep the fermentation temperature down under 60°F (16°C) to hold on to Chardonnay's modest aromatics and slow the fermentation so that it takes two to three weeks to complete. If this means carboys in tubs of ice or outside in the chilly night air, so be it.

- ✔ **Test for dryness.** When the dead yeast and other yucky solids begin to fall toward the bottom of the fermenter, make sure the wine is dry. Start with the hydrometer reading as a clue, but verify with Clinitest tablets. The reason for doing this promptly is to get to the next step ASAP.

✔ **Prevent malolactic fermentation.** Get an accurate pH reading for the fermented wine, and make the corresponding sulfur dioxide (SO_2) addition to prevent malolactic. As insurance, adding 250 ppm of lysozyme helps beat up bacteria.

✔ **Rack carefully to clarify.** Once the wine is largely settled, rack it off the gross lees into a fresh container, using carbon dioxide (CO_2) gas to reduce oxygen pickup during the transfer. Top up the new container to minimize headspace, and keep oxygen out with a water-filled airlock.

✔ **Clarify quickly.** Because *faux* Chablis is a fairly short-turnaround wine, rack twice more, every few weeks, until the wine is reasonably clear. Taste along the way to make sure everything is in order.

✔ **Fine for protein.** Treat the wine with bentonite to remove protein and minimize the risk of protein haze.

✔ **Do a cold stabilization.** If you have access to refrigeration and containers small enough to fit in the refrigerator, let the wine spend a couple weeks at or below 40°F (4°C) to get rid of *tartrate crystals* (clear, granular bits of tartaric acid); this way, you don't end up with crunchy bits in the bottle when you chill it later.

✔ **Filter.** After the wine has been racked enough to be quite clear — including getting rid of the residue of the bentonite and cold stabilization — filter it for a final cleanup. Even a light filtration will make it look better in the glass. On this schedule, you may not have time for gravity to do all the work.

✔ **Bottle.** Add a final dose of 25 ppm of SO_2 just before bottling, keep everything sanitary, and have the grapes that were harvested in September into the bottle by April.

On this model, 5 gallons (19 liters) of juice or less than 100 pounds (45 kilograms) of grapes, one carboy, an airlock, a racking tube, a packet of yeast, and some chemicals can get you two cases of great wine in under six months.

Consider trying these variations on *faux* Chablis:

✔ Use multiple fermenters with multiple yeast strains for complexity.

✔ In one or more small fermenters, add 4 ounces (115 grams) of oak cubes, either toasted or untoasted, during the fermentation, for additional mouthfeel.

✔ Consider a small amount of blending, adding a pinch of something with more forceful aromatics — Muscat, Viognier, Sauvignon Blanc — if your blending trials indicate the addition improves the wine.

California woodlands

I will never forget watching veteran California wine writer Bob Thompson try his first sip of a highly regarded $75-a-bottle Sonoma Chardonnay, reflect briefly, and then announce, "This wine is a crime against the environment, for all the trees that had to be cut down." Oak and lots of it made California Chardonnay into a juggernaut, and then into a punching bag for many wine writers and critics. The consensus among those same detractors — myself included — is that in the past few years, a lot of wineries have eased off the gas and moved mainstream Chardonnay away from lumber and towards crisp fruit. (At the same time, entirely un-oaked Chardonnay has become a mini-trend of its own.)

What I discovered talking to winemakers and barrel suppliers, however, is that every bit as much wood is being applied; it's just that everyone has gotten better at marrying fruit and oak. Incremental changes include vineyard practices to produce better fruit; whole-cluster pressing; more concern for crisp acidity and controlled pH; endless oak trials; and malolactic bacterial strains that produce much less overt butteriness.

"We have a better understanding of barrels," says Buena Vista winemaker Jeff Stewart, speaking of the high-end industry as a whole, "and we're working with fruit that can handle barrels. The fermentation regimes themselves aren't all that different."

Mastering "faux Montrachet," or the Big Chardonnay treatment

The greatest of White Burgundies — which often have the word Montrachet somewhere in the name — are based on the same modest grape as the Chardonnays of Chablis, but show amazing complexity and nearly as much longevity as great Rieslings. Montrachet-style wines get the Big Chardonnay treatment — indeed, they invented it in France, not California — but have enough stuffing to hold their own against the winemaking overlays. If you have confidence in your fruit and love the style, go for it. (Yours may not be worth $400 a bottle, but what is?)

Many parts of the Big Chardonnay approach are identical to the *faux* Chablis method (see the preceding section), but some crucial differences crop up:

✔ **Pre-fermentation:** Pick through the fruit, press the juice off the skins quickly, and settle it overnight.

Make sure to adjust the wine chemistry as needed, particularly if you have low-acid fruit. Because you put this wine on the malo track, which lowers acidity, it needs enough acidity to start with. A modest initial dose of SO_2 and a bit of lysozyme are fine; some winemakers, however, prefer to hold off on the SO_2 until fermentation is complete. If you're doing a fermentation on the wild side, skip these additions.

✔ **Barrel fermentation:** New oak imparts more flavor and tannin during fermentation, older oak — in this case, oak previously used for white wines only — still contributes roundness. Either way, make sure the barrel is clean. Barrel fermentation can theoretically be done in very small barrels — down to 5 gallons (19 liters) — but in practice, full-size 60-gallon (about 225-liter) and half-size barrels are preferable, because they have a lower wood-surface-to-wine-volume ratio.

Fill your barrel(s) with settled juice, leaving four or five inches (10 to 13 centimeters) of headspace below the bung hole of the barrel. Gas with carbon dioxide to protect the wine until the fermentation kicks in and produces its own CO_2 cover. Close the barrel with an airlock and stopper, to allow fermentation vapors to escape.

✔ **Yeast picks:** Ask ten winemakers about yeast and you will get two dozen answers. Spontaneous fermentations are common in *faux* Montrachet style, but not recommended for your garage. Use a yeast strain that can finish dry for your Brix/potential alcohol level, without much risk of sticking and generating hydrogen sulfide. Ironically, the widely available Montrachet strain, isolated in that very place, is notorious for producing hydrogen sulfide and its rotten-egg odor — go figure.

✔ **Higher temperature:** Barrel fermentations run at higher temperatures than tank or carboy fermentations. The only way to cool a barrel is to cool the barrel room. Where stainless steel Chardonnay gets fermented somewhere below 60°F (16°C), barrel fermentations typically register somewhere between 65°F (18°C) and 70° (21°C). That temperature difference is enough to affect which kinds of volatile aromatics get produced and retained, and preferences vary. But there is a limit: White wine barrel fermentation in a garage at 85°F (20°C) is not a good idea.

✔ **Promoting malolactic:** Once the wine is dry, inoculate with a malolactic bacteria starter culture and a small dose of malolactic nutrient. Here the slightly elevated temperature of barrel fermentation is good, making the malolactic complete more easily. Malolactic activity continues to produce some CO_2, but at a much lower rate than alcoholic fermentation, so top the barrel up to leave an inch (3 centimeters) of headspace.

✔ **Testing for completeness:** In unheated wine caves in chilly parts of France, the malolactic might not complete until sometime in the Spring. In warmer climates and within insulated facilities, the malolactic should be done in two or three weeks. Test for completeness of both the alcoholic and malolactic ferments, and when the wine is officially wine, dose it with SO_2 according to the wine's pH.

✔ **Barrel aging:** You can age Big Chardonnay-style wines many ways. Some winemakers simply let the wine, the dying yeast, the whole business stay put in the same barrel, topping it off and leaving it for months before racking. Others rack out the fermented wine, get rid of the gross lees, and put the wine back into barrel. As the wine rests, some winemakers swear by frequent lees stirring to enhance mouthfeel, some don't like to overdo it. The pace of racking is slower than for the *faux* Chablis, spaced out three or four months at a time.

In *faux* Montrachet style, the wine spends longer in barrel than it might in glass or stainless; several months of slow, steady barrel influence can give incredible richness to the wine. But be on guard for off odors: If your barrel of Chard starts to smell funky or rotten-eggy, rack it off the lees ASAP, get rid of them, and let your wine get a bit of clean air in the process. Make sure to monitor and adjust free SO_2 levels to prevent oxidation and the formation of stale-smelling aldehydes.

✔ **Finishing:** When the wine is nearing the time to bottle, fine it in the barrel with bentonite for protein stability, then rack it out. Long-term barrel aging does wonders for wine clarity, so decide for yourself if you want to increase the dazzle through filtration. Bottle with a final 25 ppm dose of sulfur dioxide.

You may try a couple variations on *faux* Montrachet:

✔ Do half your Chardonnay in barrel, half in carboys with different yeast strains, then blend them together for a more complex package.

✔ Try to keep the carboy portion non-malolactic, accentuating the fresh and fruity contribution to the blend; when you combine the two, be prepared that the malo might kick in for all the wine anyway.

Sauvignon Blanc — Edgy and Otherwise

Sauvignon Blanc is the perennial number-two white wine grape — definitely second fiddle to Chardonnay — but still widely planted and eagerly consumed from France to New Zealand, Austria to California. It makes wines in multiple styles and climates, but all are uniformly refreshing and always identifiable. In contrast to Chardonnay, which often seems to beg the winemaker to give it shape and meaning, Sauvignon Blanc tends to announce its intentions, take it or leave it.

Sauvignon Blanc exhibits just as much aromatic intensity as the Muscat-Riesling-Gewürztraminer cohort, but not the same aromatics: herbs, not flowers; grassiness, not perfume. That grassiness — based on compounds called *pyrazines* — is the central winemaking issue for the variety: flaunt it, incorporate it, or try to hide it.

Climate-driven styles

Generally, the cooler the climate in which Sauvignon Blanc grows, the higher the concentration of *pyrazines* — grass, bell pepper, green pepper aromas — and the greater the formation of volatile compounds called *thiols* — the chemicals behind grapefruit, gooseberry, cat pee (honest!), and passion fruit aromas — during fermentation. The same elevated levels can be created, clumsily, in a warmer climate through vineyard practices that block sunlight and give lots of shade. Well-grown, warmer-climate Sauvignon Blanc still has these aromatic traits, but they steadily recede behind more conventional aromas of melon and pear.

The wines from New Zealand's Marlborough region are the poster kids for full-throttle Sauvignon Blanc, unmistakable in a lineup with other growing areas. Taking advantage of a very cool climate, and aided by research into thiol-happy yeast strains, the Kiwi producers decided to let it all hang out — and saw soaring sales in the export market.

Two or three decades earlier, winemakers and consumers in California decided that grassy was out — in this case, often grassiness-pepperiness from grapes that simply never got ripe. A movement began to turn Sauvignon Blanc into the New Chardonnay, growing it in warmer places, putting it through malolactic, and slathering it with oak. Some of the resulting wines were quite tasty, but somehow didn't seem like Sauvignon Blanc.

Elsewhere in the world, on the cool side, are South Africa, where Sauvignon Blanc is overtaking Chenin Blanc as the dominant white, and Austria's Styria region, definitely an international up-and-comer. On the warmer end, the Bordeaux region of France specializes in Sauvignon Blanc, usually barrel-aged and often blended with Sémillon. And this wine is a fixture in the Loire Valley, generally in a style halfway between New Zealand and Bordeaux.

The upshot of this survey is that you can only do so much to make a grape taste like it was grown somewhere other than where it was actually grown. Making a New Zealand-style Sauvignon from California fruit is more than a stretch, though winemakers can nudge things in that direction. When New Zealanders put their wines through malolactic and into barrels, they still somehow come out tasting like New Zealand. Once again, grapes rule. Keep this in mind while sourcing your grapes.

Sauvignon sensibilities

Veteran California winemaker John Buechsenstein has made a lot of wine from a lot of grapes, in several parts of the state, at different price points. His most recent project — now, alas, a victim of the Great Recession — was the Sauvignon Republic, producing Sauvignon Blanc, and only Sauvignon Blanc, from prime grape-growing regions around the world such as New Zealand, South Africa, and California's Russian River.

No surprise: John B. has a number of opinions about this grape. Cool-climate grapes, he says, make for cool-temperature winemaking,

fermenting in the 50° to 55°F (10° to 13°C) range in inert containers, slowly, so the yeast can convert all the "Big Five" thiols — pineapple, grapefruit, passion fruit, cat pee, and sweat. Picking grapes across a range of ripeness levels mixes up the aromatics. The alternative, barrel-fermented route shuts down Sauvignon's pyrazine/veggie character, and works best for people who have done this style for a long time.

Skin contact, he says, can improve juice yield, and so can pectic enzymes; but with machine-harvested fruit, where the skins are already sliced up, just get thee to a press.

Options, options, options

What's the best way to make Sauvignon Blanc? You name it: grassy or melony, oaky or oak-free, malo or no malo, bone-dry or sticky-sweet and flavored with botrytis (a fungus I discuss in Chapter 20). Sauvignon is a great wine to experiment with in your home winery. Try different tricks every year, mix up the yeast strains, toss in some oak cubes, blend it with other wines, or make it solo. Sauvignon Blanc is an almost can't-fail variety.

The two ends of the stylistic spectrum for Sauvignon Blanc are almost identical to the two takes on Chardonnay in "Chardonnay: The Perils of Popularity" earlier in this chapter. Rename them "*faux* Kiwi" and "*faux* Graves" (the top Bordeaux white wine region), and cut and paste — with a few variations.

Sauvignon Blanc traditionally comes into the winery with relatively high acidity and leaves in the same condition; an edge of crisp acidity should be present in any style. Chardonnay works — at least for some people — soft and mellow; Sauvignon Blanc, however rich it is, should wake up your mouth.

Yeast choices overlap, but some strains that maximize Sauvignon aromatics are widely available and worth a try. Maximizing thiols has been a major thread in yeast breeding for a decade; you might as well take advantage of it.

My taste — if you haven't noticed — runs toward Sauvignons that taste like Sauvignons. But short of the full Big Chardonnay treatment, you have plenty of options that go beyond the simple and squeaky-clean:

- **Skin contact:** More common with Sauvignon than Chardonnay, but best done in moderation — let only part of your grapes sit a few hours between crushing and pressing.

- **Multiplying yeast:** Do two or three or four carboy fermentations, each with its own dedicated yeast strain. Try one standard workhorse strain, a couple aromatic strains, and one from the Chardonnay family.

- **Mock-barrel carboy:** Put toasted or untoasted oak cubes in one or more carboys during fermentation, and keep them around for part of aging. This can improve mouthfeel, and oak flavor at a very modest level increases the feeling of richness and fullness without tasting like trees.

- **Lees:** For fatter mouthfeel, instead of barrels and malo, stir the post-ferment lees every two weeks for three or four months.

- **Partial malo:** Want a little taste of butterfat? Put one carboy through malolactic, suppress it in the others, and blend it all together, making sure to keep the combination stable with sulfur dioxide and lysozyme.

- **Blending:** Pump up your Sauvignon with 10 percent Chardonnay; liven up its nose with 5 percent Riesling or Muscat.

White Wine Wonderland

After you get past Chardonnay and Sauvignon Blanc, the commercial popularity of whites drops off sharply — as does the supply of grapes and juice for home winemakers. In recent years, Pinot Gris/Grigio has joined the top ranks of popular whites; however, most of it is imported from Italy, and you can't import Italian grapes — they'd either be raisins or rot when they arrived.

Nonetheless, dozens of white varieties planted all over North America make very good wine — if you can hunt down the grapes. Your nearest winemaking shop may have an angle on Viognier, or Riesling, or white hybrids; but no shop is likely to have them all.

Good news is on the horizon for home white winemakers. As part of the BWC movement — Bored With Chardonnay, not to be confused with Anything But Chardonnay — growers are trying out varieties from Spain, Italy, Austria, and elsewhere. Meanwhile, wineries are popping up in every state and province, often featuring grapes beyond the usual suspects. Maybe you know a grower;

maybe you can befriend a winery and talk them out of a couple hundred pounds, if you promise to stay in their wine club. The hunt is half the fun.

Because I can't know which whites you might get your hands on, I give you a lightning survey of some worthwhile grapes and categories of grapes, with pointers about styles.

Pinot Gris/Grigio

Pinot Gris — French for Italian Pinot Grigio — is a grape that can go either way: clean and lean, or rich and fat. The leaner Grigio style emphasizes retaining fruit and aromatics, which is why the main discussion of this variety is in Chapter 18 on aromatic whites. But in many places, the bigger Gris style works just fine.

Big-style Pinot Gris (PG) travels the same road as described in the "Mastering '*faux* Montrachet,' or the Big Chardonnay treatment" section earlier in this chapter. The two requirements for nudging your PG in this direction are

✔ You like the flavor of oak in your white wines.

✔ The grapes themselves have enough oomph to stand up to wood and malolactic fermentation without losing their charm.

Pinot Gris/Grigio, like Sauvignon Blanc, is a great grape for home wine experiments — multiple yeasts, a few oak cubes here, one carboy of malo there. And it plays well with others as a versatile blender.

Pinot Blanc

The Pinot family goes on and on, doesn't it? Pinot Blanc (PB — not to be confused with the jelly accompaniment) is just another clone in this mutation-prone variety — which also counts red Pinot Noir among its manifestations. Pinot Blanc (also called Pinot Bianco) gets its color-coded name because the skins stay white — that is, yellow-green — at maturity without taking on the pinkish hues of Pinot Gris/Grigio.

PB, presuming it gets ripe, makes full-bodied white wine with citrus, apple, and sometimes floral aromas. It's another entry in the Alsace stable of whites, where it also gets made into sparkling Cremant d'Alsace. PB is common in Germany, Italy, and most parts of the former Yugoslavia.

Pinot Blanc's full-bodied character would seem to make it a candidate for the Big Chardonnay treatment, but that rarely happens. Most PB is fermented and aged in tanks and not put through malo, so it retains a bright acidity. Neutral wood for fermentation and aging is a high-end practice. In all its guises, Pinot Blanc usually gets consumed young and fresh.

Marsanne and Roussanne

These two mainstay whites of both the Northern and Southern Rhône frequently appear in the same sentence, mostly because they often show up in the same bottle. Traditionally, the pairing followed the same logic as the combination of Sauvignon Blanc and Sémillon in Bordeaux: Marsanne, like Sémillon, contributed the heft and body, while Roussanne, like Sauvignon Blanc, added the racy, more aromatic edge. For grapes grown in New World soils and climates, that formula may or may not apply. Either grape can make a satisfying bottle on its own or blend with the more distinctly aromatic Viognier, another Rhône stalwart.

Marsanne flavors run to things like nuts, honey, pears, and melons. The color is often deeper than the white wine average. The grapes can attain fairly high alcohol without being out of balance. Marsanne is a good candidate for barrel fermentation and barrel aging, or for oak-cube flavoring in carboy production. As with any white, the oak can easily be overdone, but some oak influence is certainly worth a try.

Roussanne is another white grape that develops reddish-brownish skin tones at ripeness. The warmer the growing climate, the bigger and richer the potential wine; the cooler the climate, the more delicate and floral Roussanne becomes. Highly aromatic versions come from the small French region of Savoie, where Roussanne is known as Bergeron.

Commercial treatments vary widely, depending on the fruit. If I could get my hands on some Roussanne, which I haven't yet, I would probably start by making it in a fairly lean style, to get a better sense of the fruit and aromatics. Then I would fatten it up appropriately on a second pass.

Spanish whites

Wines from Spain have made a splash in the world export market in the last decade. The most popular have been red wines based on Tempranillo, Monastrell, and Garnacha grapes. Spanish whites developed — and deserved — a bad reputation for being flat, oxidized, and pretty boring. Then well-made Albariño arrived on the scene and became a wine list darling (see Chapter 18 for more about this semi-aromatic white).

Transplanting Rhônes

Bob Lindquist, owner/winemaker at Cal-Rhône flagship Qupé in Santa Barbara, is a fan of cool-climate grapes and of the vintages where acidity is high and sugar is under control. His Marsanne comes from the Santa Ynez Valley, slightly warmer than the Bien Nacido Vineyards in the Santa Maria Valley where his Roussanne grows. If the norm in the Rhône is that Marsanne is the fatter and Roussanne the brighter and zingier, Lindquist's story is the reverse.

He picks his Marsanne slightly early, often at 21° to 21.5° Brix, keeping the pH low and the alcohol in balance. "It may not have the weight it could have, but that's not the point." He gives the juice a good, long, 48-hour settle before fermentation, because the solids tend to produce aromas of wheat and canned corn (not in the plan). The Marsanne is barrel-fermented in neutral barrels with clean, temperature-tolerant native yeasts, and has the acidity to go through malo.

The Roussanne gets the Chardonnay treatment: The fruit holds its acidity at higher sugar levels; the juice solids are friendlier, so the settling is shorter; the barrels for fermentation are newish, though rarely brand new; and enough acidity is present for malolactic.

Turns out Albariño is just the tip of the Spanish white iceberg. The country is loaded with tasty, inviting varieties that just need modern viticulture and winemaking techniques, such as limited yields in the vineyard and temperature control in the winery. New Spanish white varieties are beginning to get planted in warmer North American climates, so keep an eye out for Godelo, Garnacha Blanca, Loureira, Macabeo, Torrontés (which started life in Spain, before moving to Argentina), Treixadura, and Verdejo.

Spanish whites generally want the clean and lean winemaking approach — little or no oak, malolactic not likely, and cool temperatures to retain freshness and beguiling aromatics.

Italian whites

Pinot Grigio is not the only Italian white grape. Italy being Italy, hundreds of different grapes are scattered around the country. Like Spanish whites, Italian whites built a shaky reputation in the market. This was partly because so many of them were made from Trebbiano — not the world's most interesting grape — and partly because careless winemaking led to premature oxidation in the bottle.

But don't blame the grapes: Italian white grapes make lovely wines. At a time when growers are looking for warmer-climate varieties (as a hedge against climate change) and looking for alternatives to the reign of Chardonnay, Italian whites are getting attention. Drink your way through commercial examples of wines made from grapes like Vernaccia, Vermentino, Verdicchio, Friulano, Malvasia, Fiano, and Arneis, and then look for the grapes.

German whites

Riesling is the German icon and generally the model for the country's white winemaking style, but it's not the whole story. Plenty of good wine comes from grapes better known by their French names, such as Pinot Gris *(Grauburgunder)* and Pinot Blanc *(Weissburgunder)*. Ditto for local varieties like Sylvaner and Traminer.

German vine breeders in the 20th century created a whole roster of hybrids, crossing one *vinifera* with another, hoping to cope with the chilly climate in which even Riesling had trouble ripening. Important offspring from these efforts include Müller-Thurgau, Kerner, Scheurebe, Siegerrebe, Huxelrebe, and Ortega.

Why these relatively obscure varieties might matter to North American home winemakers is that, by design, they flourish in cool-to-cold climates, from British Columbia to Oregon, and in chilly eastern climates, as well. The fact that the critic crowd doesn't rate many Kerners or Siegerreben doesn't mean you can't make a fine bottle of wine from them. Add to the list Madeleine Angevine, another crossbreed developed in France that is doing quite well around Puget Sound in Washington state, thank you.

Grüner Veltliner

Grüner Veltliner *(GREW-ner felt-LEAN-er)* is Austria's major white grape, though the country is deservedly proud of its Rieslings, too. Grüner — sometimes just called GV or *GROO-vay* — shows the power of broad-minded, inventive sommeliers and wine list designers to take a variety that was obscure in North America and make it into a trendsetter for the wine-savvy set. We owe them thanks, because Grüner is a fascinating variety, capable of making everything from simple quaffers to complex, deep-flavored, ageworthy wines frequently compared to (or mistaken for) white Burgundies.

Grüner falls very much at the herbal end of the white wine aroma continuum. a little short of Sauvignon Blanc, but still quite savory, not flowery, and often with a small bite of black pepper on the finish. Grüner is one of the great food wines on the planet. Fortunately, forward-looking growers in Oregon, Washington, New York, Maryland, and California are starting to plant Grüner, and domestic bottles are showing up in stores.

Winemaking should be on the cool-temperature, low-or-no oak, non-malo side. Get the richness from ripe Grüner grapes, lees stirring, and maybe neutral wood.

Hybrids that Hold Their Own

I must confess (as I did in the comparable section on red hybrids in Chapter 15) that I've never made wine out of any of the grape varieties in this section. But I have tasted a ton of hybrid whites, and they have nothing to be ashamed of in a *vinifera*-dominated wine world.

A couple years back, I judged at the *San Francisco Chronicle* Wine Competition, and the panel I was on got the flights of both red and white hybrids/natives. (Our cohort signed up for the offbeat wines — the thought of three straight days of tasting generic Merlots wasn't appetizing.) The reds, all from the northeastern United States, included several wines in the "nice try" category. The whites, perhaps two dozen Seyvals and Cayugas and Vignoles and Diamonds, were mostly wines I wished I had a case of.

The consensus view, in fact, is that white hybrids and North American natives are easier than red hybrids to make into good-to-very-good wine. Red hybrids struggle to develop sufficient tannins; whites don't need any tannins. Red hybrid winemakers often fight with high acidity; white winemakers crave acidity, and have the option of holding on to some residual sugar for balance. And that *foxy* quality that allegedly plagues natives and hybrids, the hard-to-define, artificial-candied strawberry flavor? Not as evident as with reds.

Among the indigenous, native North American wine grapes, Delaware, Diamond, and Niagara can do an excellent job. Best-performing hybrids include Seyval, Vignoles, Vidal, and Cayuga. Catawba, apparently a natural inter-species hybrid, is a thoroughly pink grape that begs to be made into sparkling and blush wine. If the only Catawbas you've had were over-sweet and sappy, blame the winemakers.

Even at a distance, I can safely advise this much about hybrid winemaking techniques:

- ✔ All these varieties benefit from cool-temperature — under 60°F (16°C) — fermentation.

- ✔ None of these grapes gets much useful mileage out of oak.

- ✔ Even though these varieties are not candidates for Big Chardonnay-style winemaking, using malolactic fermentation to reduce excessive acidity is worth considering.

- ✔ Depending on growing region, viticulture, harvest grape chemistry, and a few other things, almost all of these varieties (excepting Catawba) have been and can be successfully made into dry table wines.

- ✔ Several hybrids are excellent candidates for off-dry and dessert-wine styles, certainly including Vignoles, Cayuga, Niagara, and Vidal. If you like your drink a little bit on the sweet side, hybrids can be stunning.

Choosing Yeasts and Styles

Table 17-1 suggests some commonly-available yeast strains to maximize different qualities in fruity-herbal whites.

Table 17-1	Wine Style and Yeast Choices
Stylistic Goal	**Yeast Strains**
Get the ferment done, find the fruit	CY3079, EC1118, D47, GRE, Epernay2, Montrachet
Develop pyrazines, terpenes, thiols	QA23, BA11, VL3, K1
Achieve tropical tones, mouthfeel	T306, BA11, D254, Rhône 4600, R2

Table 17-2 summarizes this chapter's discussion of techniques that give rise to big, full whites — think California Chardonnay — and lean, clean wines — think New Zealand Sauvignon Blanc.

Table 17-2	Options for Fruity-Herbal White Wines	
Options	**Big Style**	**Lean Style**
Whole-cluster press	If possible; otherwise, gentle	If possible; otherwise, gentle
Skin contact	Common only with Sauvignon Blanc	Almost never
Barrel fermentation	The signature of Big Style	No — except for big, neutral wood
Temperature regimen	Ambient, 65°F (18°C) or more	Keep under 60°F (16°C)
Malolactic fermentation	Pretty much obligatory	Not really
Oak style/influence	From ferment through aging	None, or very discreet
Lees contact/stirring	Common	Optional
Blending	Rare	Why not?
Residual sugar	None	None (with some dessert exceptions)

Chapter 18

Aromatic Whites

· ·

· ·

*F*ull disclosure: I love these grapes, and it's more than an effort to be entirely objective about them. Still, in the spirit of *For Dummies*-ism, I've made every effort to limit this chapter with true statements and limit the hyperbole. The boundaries of the category "aromatic whites" are arbitrary: After all, every wine grape and every wine has an aroma. Some varieties not included in this chapter — Sauvignon Blanc, for example — can be as aromatic as they come. But by the informal conventions of the wine world — and for this book — the definition of *aromatic whites* combines both grape type and winemaking style, covering varieties that

✔ Have strong, distinctive aromatic qualities, usually including floral and/ or spice notes along with fruit characteristics

✔ Almost always receive winemaking treatments that emphasize and preserve those aromatic attributes, which means avoiding both malolactic fermentation and oak flavors

This chapter looks at the five "aromatic All-Stars" — Chenin Blanc, Gewürztraminer, Muscat, Riesling, and Viognier — and a slew of semi-aromatic varieties.

Stylistic Preliminaries

These generalizations about winemaking technique apply (nearly) across the board for aromatic whites, so I've assembled them in one place for your reading convenience. This style — cool temperatures, no oak, no malo, quick turnaround, fending off oxygen at every step — is sometimes described as *reductive winemaking* because it discourages oxygen rather than welcoming it into wine processing.

Critics say reductive winemaking yields predictable, safe, fruity wines, without much distinctive character. They argue that letting in lots of oxygen makes for wines that are more complex and alive. However, I've found that in the context of home winemaking, where your control of oxygen is compromised to start with, hewing to the reductive approach is a safer bet, giving you more control of the wine as it develops. And it is especially well-suited to the aromatic whites.

My advice with these aromatic grapes is to get your feet wet on the standard, reductive model. As you get comfortable with the style, tweak it to taste.

Keeping cool

Cool temperatures at every step in the winemaking process are the norm for aromatic white varieties. The grapes thrive in cool climates and get harvested in the morning before the sun heats them up. They should stay cool in the winery during crushing and pressing, go through fermentation under 60°F (16°C), and remain chilled by refrigeration or ambient temperatures until they get bottled. Keeping it cool emphasizes the purity of the fruit and encourages tropical fruit aromas and flavors. Are there exceptions? Of course.

Crushing, pressing, and skin contact

The trend in commercial production of aromatic whites is toward *whole-cluster pressing*, which minimizes the skin contact and oxygen exposure that comes from separating the crushing and pressing steps. At home, unless you lay out the cash for a small bladder press, whole-cluster pressing isn't an option. But you can keep temperatures down and move rapidly from de-stemming and crushing to pressing. Then quickly hit the juice with an initial dose of 25 to 50 parts per million of sulfur dioxide (SO_2) and fill any container headspace with neutral gas.

For all these varieties, a few producers allow a few hours or even a day of skin contact after crushing. The benefit is you extract more of the goodies that make these grapes so compelling and distinctive; the downside is you could extract more harsh, bitter *phenolic compounds* from the skins — the tannins that give red wines their backbone, but can seem out of place in a white.

When skin contact works, the wines come out more forceful and structured; when the phenolic content gets obtrusive, a bit of sugar — 0.5 to 1 percent — can mask it without throwing the wine out of balance. Trying skin contact on a portion of one of these varieties to create a blending component is worth a try.

Strategizing about yeast

In the aromatic world, winemakers differ over what qualities to look for in yeast strains. In regions that have produced these wines for centuries — Riesling in Germany, Chenin Blanc in the Loire — natural fermentation with the yeast strains that reside in the vineyards and wineries is quite common.

Because your garage doesn't have nearly as much history on its side as Germany's Mosel region, where many wineries date back five centuries or so, you have two remaining choices: Use a yeast strain that encourages fuller production of exotic aromatic compounds, or go with a neutral yeast strain, often one of the Champagne varieties, and rely on the grapes' own aromatic properties.

Either way, the ideal for aromatic whites is a slow fermentation, with the Brix dropping a degree or less per day. To ensure dryness help your yeast finish its job by bringing the temperature up a bit, perhaps to 65°F (18°C), for the final degree or two of Brix.

The fundamental requirement for aromatic whites is to use yeast strains that work well at cool temperatures and that do not tend to produce hydrogen sulfide (H_2S). (You don't want to have to aerate these wines to blow off stinky H_2S.) Navigate the yeast maze by doing small batches, trying more than one strain, tasting the results, and getting smarter the next year.

Preventing malo

Aromatic whites rarely get put through malolactic fermentation — at least not intentionally. Some malolactic bacteria strains produce their own signature aromas (think "buttered popcorn"), while others are relatively neutral. But malolactic fermentation always reduces wine acidity, and bright acidity is a hallmark of the best aromatic white grapes. Furthermore, successful malolactic generally requires warmer temperatures, which means that some of those nifty aromatics can get lost. Finally, malolactic fattens mouthfeel; aromatic white producers generally prefer to accomplish a similar effect by lees contact and lees stirring.

The main situation in which malo makes sense for an aromatic white is extremely high acidity — 9 or 10 grams per liter or more — in which softening would make the wine more appealing. If converting all the malic over-softens the wine, adding a pinch of tartaric acid can bring it back. The alternative strategy in the high-acid case is to hold on to or re-introduce some sugar, balancing the excess acidity with a bit of sweetness and retaining a crisp finish. Are there examples of malolactic aromatic whites? Sure.

Embracing acidity

By and large, aromatic whites arrive in your glass with bright, above-average acidity, and they normally start that way at harvest, too. Although finding a California Chardonnay that comes in with as much as 6 grams of acid per liter is hard these days, the aromatic crew in their Old World haunts routinely show up at 8 or even 9 grams per liter of total acidity.

The acidity will drop a bit during fermentation and again if the wine goes through cold stabilization before bottling. But maintaining 6 to 8 grams per liter in the finished wine is standard procedure.

The point isn't the numbers: The aromas and flavors of these wines jump out of the glass with good acid support, which also plays a role in their remarkable longevity.

Establishing an oak-free zone

Wine lovers expend lots of energy debating the proper role of oak in Cabernet Sauvignon or Zinfandel. But in aromatic land, oak is for furniture. If you are fortunate enough to have inherited huge, old, squeaky-clean, malo-free, neutral barrels from your winemaker grandfather, go ahead and ferment a special lot of Riesling there, clarify it by gravity, and bottle it. (The wood allows a tiny bit of beneficial oxygen into the wine, without adding flavor.) Some super-sweet dessert wines also get aged in thoroughly neutral wood. But aging or fermenting these wines in new oak barrels is like putting hot sauce on ice cream.

Stirring lees or not

With malolactic fermentation out of the picture, and barrel fermentation and aging uncommon, the remaining option for enhancing mouthfeel is extending lees contact and stirring the lees. Getting the most out of dead yeast does wonders for texture and body. Some producers do prefer to keep a laser-like focus on fruit purity and aromatic intensity, in which case the plan is to get the fermented wine off the lees as soon as possible. Up to you.

Sugaring to taste

Every one of the five Aromatic All-Stars (you meet them in more detail in the upcoming section "Noseworthy Nobility") works well at a range of sweetness levels. Noteworthy entries can be entirely dry, just off-dry, seriously sweet, and astonishingly sweet. The floral/honey/tropical/exotic aromatic package naturally lends itself to a bit of sugar, and the intense fragrance can stand up to the competition of the sweet taste just fine. In fact, thoroughly dry versions of these wines often "smell" sweet — the aroma makes a potential drinker expect to hook up with sugar in the glass, even when it isn't there.

How you handle the sugar in these wines is up to you, but try some absolutely dry: The combination of bright acidity and perfume can be spine-tingling.

Finishing

Because aromatic whites are generally bottled young to hold on to their freshness and more elusive qualities, they benefit strongly from finishing techniques. Bentonite fining for protein stabilization is simple and well worth doing, and some level of filtration will make sure the wines are clear and sparkling. (I talk about both processes in Chapter 9.)

Barrel-aged whites can get quite clear on their own, and may not need so much work at the end; quick turnaround whites risk looking cloudy and murky without that final finishing effort.

Noseworthy Nobility

The Aromatic All-Star Team has five starting players and a deep and versatile bench. They thrive in different countries, regions, and climates; show up in styles from bone-dry to super-sweet; and get blended in more ways than even the most dedicated wine connoisseur can count. All these wines are at least as much fun to sniff as to swallow.

Aromatic whites, Asian food

The tide of Southeast Asian immigrants and restaurants that flowed into North America in the wake of the Vietnam War produced a wine and food pairing breakthrough: aromatic white wines, notably Gewürztramlner and Riesling, and spicy Southeast Asian cuisine. Who knew?

The surprising fact about this now-routine pairing is that the wines developed over centuries alongside cuisines (German, Austrian) that are anything but spicy, and the homelands of the zingy foodstuffs (especially Vietnam and Thailand) are not now and have never been wine-producing countries. The fortuitous combination only came together because of prolonged military conflict, mass migration, and globalization.

On a wine tasting trip through Austria, I dined out in the Kremstal countryside at a restaurant focused on traditional fare — schnitzel, potatoes, that sort of thing. My winemaker companion noted that all the critics and writers agreed that a particular wine he was pouring made a great match with spicy Southeast Asian food. I looked out the window at the bucolic countryside, looked at my homey, comfort-food plate, and asked, "Rudi, where's the closest place you could get some of that spicy Southeast Asian food?"

He thought for a minute, and then said, "London."

Riesling: White wine royalty

In a poll of wine experts — writers, sommeliers, Masters of Wine — Riesling might well top the charts. Sip for sip, Riesling packs more fruit intensity, aromatic intrigue, flavor complexity, and potential for longevity than any white. (The possible exception is top-tier White Burgundy, which none of us can afford.)

Wide-ranging Riesling

Riesling is closely identified with Germany, but the Alsace region of France produces its share of great ones, and Austrian Riesling enjoys a higher regard than the more plentiful Grüner Veltliner. You can also find first-rate Riesling from Australia, New Zealand, Eastern and Western Canada, New York's Finger Lakes, Washington, Oregon, and even California.

Two general observations about this marvelous profusion of Riesling:

- ✔ All the great Rieslings come from cool climates with conditions that let the grapes get ripe at fairly low Brix while retaining strong natural acidity.

- ✔ Most of the world's Rieslings are made entirely dry — contrary to the widespread perception in the United States that Riesling is always a little sweet.

> For the U.S. market, a great deal of German Riesling is at least a bit off-dry. But the bulk of German Riesling, for domestic and international consumption (outside the U.S.), is fermented dry.

Riesling aromatics are endlessly captivating. They run the gamut of flowers, spices, and fruits. My choice for Riesling's most remarkable fragrance is the occasional whiff of red fruit — strawberries, raspberries — highly unusual for a white grape. While most of the aromatic whites specialize in one family of aromatic compounds, Riesling tends to have a little of everything, giving it an edge in complexity. With aging, Riesling can give off a signature aroma usually called *petrol* that is admired by Riesling fans and considered pretty darn freaky by others. Nothing is mundane about this variety.

Winemaking

Riesling fits the mold — perhaps it created the mold — for aromatic white winemaking practices. Harvest the grapes with Brix in the low 20s, while the acidity is still fairly high and the pH low. Keep the grapes and wine cool from start to finish. Crush, press, settle for a day or two, and ferment cool — 60°F (16°C) is the top of the normal range. Inhibit malolactic with sulfur dioxide and lysozyme. Rack the wine, clean it up, filter it for sparkling clarity, and bottle it young — three to six months after harvest — to preserve its freshness.

Modern German Riesling is the standard-bearer for the reductive, oxygen-phobic style of aromatic white winemaking. When you get the hang of Riesling, try expanding your repertoire by using multiple yeast strains; let the fermentation temperature go a little higher (perhaps in one carboy); and flesh out the wine's body with lees stirring.

Muscat: The power of perfume

Muscat is the hands-down aromatic champ, packed with more volatile stuff than any grape around. Tastes are split the way they are about certain stinky French cheeses: Some people love Muscat madly, and some people back away from the glass in a hurry. A clue to my own opinion is my adopted persona for the blogosphere: Blind Muscat Patterson (http://blindmuscat.typepad.com).

Fragrant family

The complex aromatic cocktail Muscat gives off includes the usual flowers, spices, and fruits, but also something close to, well, the smell of pheromones and truffles — think "musque" in the perfume world. Any way you cut it, Muscat often has a funky streak, and some of us think that's just fine.

Riesling revelations

The Finger Lakes region in upstate New York is recognized as prime Riesling country, worthy of appearing on the same wine lists as the best of the Old World. For decades, the chilly climate was considered appropriate only for hybrids, but starting with the pioneering efforts of Dr. Konstantin Frank and a few others in the late 1950s, *vinifera* varieties found a home, with Riesling as the pre-eminent icebreaker.

Riesling producers in the area agree about most aspects of Riesling winemaking: cool temperatures, no malolactic, no oak flavors (though some thoroughly neutral oak is used for aging), and early bottling. The reason this minimalist winemaking yields terrific wines lies in the grapes, not the winery: The climate allows Riesling to develop ripe flavors at 19° to 22° Brix, with good natural acidity, and the winemaking lets the fruit shine through. Styles tend toward drier and drier.

Finger Lakes Riesling makers differ from their Old World counterparts in matters of yeast.

Natural fermentation with resident yeast is the European norm, but Finger Lakes winemakers typically prefer known commercial strains, fearing that Riesling's delicacy may be violated by uncontrolled stray critters. "It's something to consider," says Morton Hallgren of Ravines, "but then there's the comfort level issue, and I just don't want to risk it." Like many wine producers, Hallgren builds complexity using a long list of yeast choices on different batches.

As in Germany, the Finger Lakes has a vocal minority of winemakers who swear by skin contact in making wines with greater aging potential. Steve diFrancesco, winemaker for Glenora Wine Cellars, says he discovered the potential one year at another winery when the press broke down. The malfunction created three days of unplanned skin contact, and a wine that went on to win a Double Gold in competition. Glenora's own practice includes 12 to 24 hours of skin contact, yielding "more intense flavors without getting harsh phenolics."

Muscat's aromatic complexity is matched only by the numbers of its sub-varieties. White Muscat, also known as Muscat Canelli, also known as Muscat Blanc à Petits Grains or Muscat de Frontignan, is the top pick in France and Italy; Yellow Muscat (Gelber Muskateller) gets the nod in Germany. Muscat of Alexandria, Muscat of Hamburg (Black Muscat), and several other variants make decent-to-excellent wine. So does Orange Muscat, apparently not a genetic relative.

Most aromatic whites mainly make dry wine, but can do well with sugar. Muscat tends to come sweet, though it works dry, too. Most wine drinkers first encounter Muscat either sweet and fortified — Muscat Beaumes de Venise in France, Spanish and Portuguese Moscatel, or good old-fashioned Skid Row Muscatel — or sweet and fizzy — like Italian Moscato d'Asti. All worthy wines, but dry Muscat is worth seeking out (or making), too. Muscat also departs from the aromatic white norm because it can thrive in warmer climates; California's Central Valley, for example, is a great Muscat-producing zone, as is Mediterranean-balmy Provence in the south of France.

Winemaking

The main thread in Muscat winemaking is the aromatic standard: keep it cool, keep acidity up, hold the malo, skip the oaky lumber. Doing a long, slow, cool fermentation all the way to dryness gives you options. You can fortify Muscat and sweeten it up, charge it up with carbonation (see Chapter 20 for more on both practices), or just bottle it dry and enjoy it as you would a dry Riesling or Gewürztraminer. In the dry mode, try the following experiment on your friends: Have them sniff the Muscat first, ask them if they think it's sweet, and then surprise the heck out of them.

Muscat grapes bring the whole controversy over skin contact to a head: The danger of harsh phenols and other unpleasantries is greater, but the lure of additional aromatic and structural stuffing is powerful. Allowing a few hours of skin contact for a portion of your Muscat is worth a try. If the wine crosses the line into abrasiveness, add a little sugar.

Gewürztraminer: Spice in a bottle

Though the name is undeniably Germanic, Gewürztraminer has its roots in northern Italy in the Alto Adige, which admittedly has a lot of German speakers. Its benchmark region is Alsace, a part of France which also has its share of German speakers. It pops up in lots of New World venues, usually cool places, frequently in areas in which almost no one speaks German.

Gewürztraminer presents the winemaker with a challenge that is unusual in white wines: The possibility of making a wine that is flat-out *too big*.

Embarrassment of riches

Gewürztraminer's spice-rack nose can be delightful, refreshing, and appetizing. The *gewürz* part of the name literally describes a spicy variant of the Traminer vine, though "perfumed" is probably closer to the reality — roses, gardenias, and lychee, along with nutmeg and cloves. But Gewürztraminer can also come out heavy, dense, and overpowering — too much of a good thing. As Jancis Robinson says in *The Oxford Companion to Wine*, "Gewürztraminer's faults are only in having too much of everything."

The grapes require full ripeness for proper flavors, which can mean alcohol levels higher than the aromatic white norm, on top of full body. With some residual sugar, increased viscosity gets added to an already formidable brew. Gewürztraminer skins usually contain a bit of pinkish-reddish-brownish pigment, which can bleed its way into slightly reddish white wine. More often, the color resolves to golden, maybe coppery, maybe peachy. (This characteristic is, by the way, a great clue for picking the Gewürz out in a blind tasting.)

Niagara Gewürz

At Cave Springs on Ontario's Niagara Peninsula, Angelo Pavan says that acidity is key for deciding when to pick Riesling, but that "Gewürztraminer has nothing to do with acidity." Gewürztraminer, he says, is all about texture, oiliness, and weight, so you have to wait until the classic flavors — rose petal, lychee — are there. The coolest years are the best, drawing out the ripening and enhancing the flavors. Made bone dry, he thinks Gewürz loses its character and has a bitter edge; 2 percent sugar is just right.

Winemaking

White winemaking usually requires you to coax as much out of the grapes as possible; Gewürztraminer requires restraint, and a steady eye (and nose and mouth) on our old friend, balance.

The grapes should be ripe, but not stupid ripe. Grapes grown in a cool climate — much of Canada, California's Anderson Valley, the Finger Lakes of New York State — can have mature flavors with a Brix in the low 20s and an alcohol somewhere in the 12.5 to 13.5 percent range.

If your Gewürztraminer grapes contain super-high sugars, consider watering down the must — you'll have plenty of aroma and flavor to go around. Or consider stopping the fermentation early to retain some sugar limit alcohol.

Skin contact would seem to be a risk for this semi-pigmented grape, certainly for bone-dry styles. Nonetheless, 12 to 24 hours of skin contact between crushing and pressing — with the grapes held at temperatures well under 60°F (16°C) and kept away from oxygen — is common among higher-end, smaller-batch Gewürztraminer producers. For truly sweet, late-harvest dessert styles, which tend toward richer color anyway, skin contact can work.

The most important parameter is acidity: The bigger the Gewürztraminer, the more important strong acidity becomes for maintaining balance and taming the impulse to excess. I have no magic total acidity number to reveal here, but simply a reminder to taste, taste, taste — don't be afraid to add acid if required. Gewürztraminer tends to come in with lower acid and higher pH than Riesling; the problem with slightly sweet, seriously flabby mass-market Gewürztraminer isn't that is has some sugar in it, but a lack of acid. If your Gewürz ends up too tart, or undercut by skin phenolics, use a pinch of sugar — many winemakers in Alsace, home of famously "dry" Gewürztraminer, do just that.

Cool, slow, long fermentation is the norm for Gewürz, along with avoiding malolactic fermentation and oak flavors, and maintaining good oxygen control. (One notable exception: some producers in Alsace put their Gewürz through malo, making very big wines, indeed.) Keeping oxygen at bay is standard for white wines, but Gewürz is a clear-cut case: Too much oxygen exposure makes wine taste flat and pushes color down the path to brown — a road Gewürz already travels. Clean it up with bentonite and a light filtration. Gewürz works well dry, slightly off-dry, sticky-sweet, or sparkling.

Viognier: Volatile and voluptuous

Viognier is the Rhône's contribution to aromatic whites. Until a few decades ago, it was confined to corners of the Northern Rhône, bottled on its own in tiny Condrieu (and tinier Chateau-Grillet), and sometimes blended in small quantities into reds from Côte Rotie. Then this nifty grape got "discovered" by winemakers in California and Australia, and now it's a household name — at least in serious wine-lover households. Elsewhere, it's still likely to be pronounced _vee-OG-knee-err_, not _VEE-o-nyay_.

As New World winemakers scrambled to figure this grape out, they made, of course, their share of mistakes — perhaps more than their share. If Viognier is made too lean, too tart, too austere, it comes out as bad Sauvignon Blanc and reveals an unpleasant bitter streak. If Viognier is made too fat, too gushy, too aromatic and fruity, it tastes like canned fruit cocktail juice.

Did I mention balance is important?

Getting good grapes

Since Viognier has only a 20-year record in North America, firm judgments about where it grows best are premature. Because it comes from the Northern Rhône and belongs to the aromatic white fraternity, you might expect fairly cool climates to work best. Indeed, some very good grapes come from Santa Barbara and Monterey in California and parts of Canada. But warmer spots with big nighttime temperature drops — the Sierra foothills, Paso Robles, and the northern end of California's Central Valley — produce good, balanced fruit, as well. For that matter, the largest concentration of quality Viognier producers may not be in any part of market-dominant California, but in Virginia. Viognier is a planting work in progress.

The trick is to get fully ripe flavors (with all those enticing aromatics) without losing the fruit's acidity. Viognier grapes, certainly from the warmer regions, often show harvest numbers more like red wine values: Brix up to 25°, total acidity (TA) down to 5 grams per liter, pH at 3.7 or higher. The winemaker usually needs to bring the acid and pH back into range — more like 7 grams of acid and a pH of 3.4 — to avoid flabby wine.

Viognier grapes often end up, pressed or unpressed, in Syrah fermentations, where they add complexity, smooth out the package, and help stabilize the red wine color. Making Viognier and Syrah the same year is a win-win.

Winemaking

Of the major aromatics, Viognier is the aromatic white that is most amenable to the "Big Chardonnay" treatment I describe in Chapter 17 — barrel fermentation, malolactic fermentation, oak aging, the whole nine yards. Sometimes Viognier made this way comes out entirely goofy. But it can work, if the grapes have enough flavor intensity to stand up to the treatments and retain enough acidity to make crisp wine. My advice is to start with the standard, minimalist approach to aromatic whites (which I describe earlier in this chapter) — glass or stainless fermenter, low-temperature fermentation, no malo, no oak, no fooling around. But when you find a reliable fruit source, consider branching out.

Old World Viognier winemakers often swear by a small amount of skin contact; most New World winemakers swear *at* the idea. Some winemakers play with the newer, more exotic, more aromatic yeast strains, some stick with the tried and true. I think using some of each is a good idea. Try fermenting one carboy with oak cubes, a kind of mock-barrel fermentation; do another one squeaky-clean, and blend the results.

In North America, Viognier is mainly known in its dry form. But like the rest of the aromatic pack, it can flourish a bit off-dry and in dessert forms.

Virginia Viognier

Viognier made its debut in the United States by way of California, but its more permanent home may be Virginia. Thomas Jefferson's Constitution-drafting came out better than his winegrowing, but today his home state turns out fine wine, with Viognier as one of its signature grapes.

The founding father, as it were, of Virginia Viognier is Dennis Horton (who also makes a first-rate Horton Norton wine), a onetime home winemaker. Horton decided to do Viognier on a large scale — a few thousand cases a year is a large scale for Viognier — and distribute it beyond Virginia to make a point about the state's potential. It worked.

Blenheim Vineyards doesn't have Horton's output or visibility, but it does have an interesting owner: rocker Dave Matthews. Matthews doesn't do a lot of hands-on barrel washing, leaving the winemaking chores to university-trained Kirsty Harmon. Harmon says Virginia's clay soils work well with Viognier, and the grape's loose clusters suit Virginia's humid climate.

Finally, says Harmon, Virginia Viognier works in multiple styles, from sweet to dry. Both Blenheim and Horton make their Viogniers dry, using a mix of barrel- and tank-fermented wine, and both rely mainly on relatively neutral, straightforward yeast strains — D47, GRE, EC1118 — on the theory that the grapes themselves produce enough aromatic goodies.

Chenin Blanc: Honey and flowers

Chenin Blanc is a great grape fallen on hard times, at least in North America. Chenin had a good run as the White Zinfandel of its era (1950s and 1960s) — pleasant, refreshing, light, slightly off-dry, perfect for quaffing on a hot day or as an entryway to more advanced wine drinking. Certain unnamed friends of mine found it a painless, inexpensive way to get happily inebriated, which was the problem: Because it was so charming and uncomplicated, Chenin developed a low-life reputation. Sales plummeted and thousands of acres got ripped out and replaced with . . . almost anything. Chenin in California is now on the wine lover's Endangered Cultivar list.

A handful of producers and growers kept the faith, making terrific wine year after year. The French, whose Loire Valley Chenins — from zingingly dry to seductively sweet — never missed a beat, scratched their heads about the fickleness of American wine drinkers. Do your part: Keep Chenin Blanc alive.

Endearing allure

Of the five Aromatic All-Stars, Chenin is the most modest, the least in-your-face, the unlikeliest candidate for a big-statement wine. It excels in making the kind of wine normal people drink most of the time.

Chenin's nose full of honey, citrus, and flowers rarely jumps out of the glass, but it does invite you to stick your nose back in again and again. Chenin generally arrives with high acidity, medium body, and a fruity palate — unless it is badly over-cropped and verges on entirely neutral. The range of styles in which it can excel — both from Loire appellations like Savennières, Saumur, Anjou, and Vouvray and from South Africa (where it is known as Steen) — puts it on a par with Riesling among the planet's most versatile varieties.

When infected at the right time, in the right vineyard, with a timely case of botrytis, the noblest of fungal rots (turn to Chapter 20 for a full discussion), and then made in a dessert style, Chenin's standard honey tones get amplified, spiced up, and balanced with a hint of bitterness in the finish. And leave it to the boisterous South African wine industry to offer a fortified variant, along the lines of Muscat Beaumes-de-Venise. And simply on its own, entirely dry, Chenin outperforms most of the competition.

Winemaking

Look for grapes grown for quality, not sheer tonnage. If Chenin is grown with a reasonable crop load, in a moderate to cool climate, it develops nice, ripe flavors at 20° to 22° Brix — it doesn't need Big Sugar and the consequent Big Alcohol, and in fact doesn't much like them.

Clarksburg Chenin

If Chenin Blanc in California is an Endangered Cultivar, the area around the Sacramento Delta town of Clarksburg is its last remaining habitat. In vineyards that are at — or a couple of feet below — sea level, circled by levees and river roads, and cooled by breezes from the river delta, Clarksburg grows thousands of tons of premium grapes — and a few hundred tons of ultra-premium Chenin Blanc.

Some excellent Clarksburg fruit reaches the market under the local winery brands — Bogle, Ehrhardt Estate, Wilson Farms — but more emerges from the wineries of such high-profile places as Napa's Pine Ridge and Sonoma's Dry Creek Vineyard. Both wineries started making Chenin from locally grown fruit in the 1970s, but when it became economically loony to grow Chenin in the upscale North Coast, both switched to Clarksburg grapes and never regretted it. Among the newer Napa practitioners of Chenin Consciousness is Vinum Cellars, where co-owner/winemaker Chris Condos learned the trade at Pine Ridge.

Winemaking at Pine Ridge and Dry Creek is minimalist: cold fermentation, all stainless, no malolactic, bottled before Christmas. "I remember bottling it once before Thanksgiving," says Pine Ridge winemaker Stacy Clark. Vinum does some fermentation in barrels, occasionally using a new one. Malolactic fermentation is not invited to the party — except, okay, for Vinum, which may do a small bit for added complexity. Pine Ridge and Vinum blend in about 20 percent Viognier; Dry Creek sticks to 100 percent Chenin.

Perhaps because its aromatics are slightly less aggressive than the rest of its fragrant cohort, Chenin gets a variety of treatments in the commercial world. Lots of producers use skin contact; lots don't. Barrel fermentation — typically in used or neutral oak — is common, though stainless tank fermentations are the norm. New World winemakers tend to keep fermentations cool, while many producers in the Loire like to get temperatures well up into the 60s Fahrenheit (the high teens Celsius). No one aims to produce oaky Chenin, but barrel aging in neutral wood can promote a satisfying roundness. Whatever techniques you try, keep the acidity bright.

The best clue about what style might work best with your Chenin fruit comes from tasting wines made from that same source, or at least the same region. As with the rest of these aromatic varieties, when in doubt, keep it simple — ferment the wine cool, dry, and oak-free — and then come back around the next year with a twist or two.

Blending

Aromatic whites make great blenders. Two or three or five percent of Riesling or Muscat or Gewürztraminer can transform a generic Chardonnay into something much more appealing (ask the folks at Kendall-Jackson); a splash of Viognier can make Syrah much more interesting (ask a few hundred producers in the Northern Rhône); and in at least one case, a benchmark California Cabernet Sauvignon was the beneficiary of judicious adulteration with canned Muscat concentrate.

Riesling, Gewürztraminer, and Muscat rarely have anything else blended into them; going solo is the best way to show off the full force of their personalities. Viognier gets blended with other Rhône whites (Marsanne, Roussanne) and, in California, often with Chardonnay, as well as figuring in some Rhône reds and blends. Chenin Blanc and Viognier play well together.

Aging potential

Among all white wines, the aromatic varieties — especially Riesling — show the greatest capacity to develop with age. Gewürztraminer, Viognier, Chenin Blanc — especially if made with a bit of residual sugar — can benefit from a decade lost in your cellar. Fortified Muscats from Spain get better decade after decade; well-made Riesling can outlast the *First Growths* — yes, the red wines of Bordeaux. What explains the remarkable longevity is still speculation, but high acidity and low pH are clearly part of the picture.

Your first try at a carboy aromatic may not be the one to will to your grandchildren. But with any of these Aromatic All-Stars, in any style, make sure to tuck a few bottles away for a few years. You'll be amazed at how your own handiwork evolves.

Semi-Aromatic Whites

If the aromatic white category is a little arbitrary, the semi-aromatic category is even more so. Semi-aromatic whites do have the potential for intriguing sniffing, don't tend toward the herbal or grassy, and generally benefit from the same cool, gentle, oak-free winemaking as the hard-core aromatics.

Pinot Gris/Pinot Grigio

Pinot Gris and Pinot Grigio (PG) are the same grape — or perhaps, the same part of the family of closely related clones of the ever-changing, split-personality Pinot grape. Both the French (Gris) and Italian (Grigio) names denote the greyish — sometimes blueish, brownish, or pinkish — tone to the skins. (In Germany, it's *Grauburgunder*, once again grey, though it doesn't come from Burgundy.) The two most common names have also come to be shorthand for two schools of winemaking. PG is one of the fastest growing white wine segments in the North American marketplace.

Grape expectations

Pinot Gris/Grigio is apparently not the best-behaved citizen of the vineyard, given to uneven cropping and sudden sugar accumulation at harvest time, wiping out natural acidity. A delicate grape, not a power player, PG can quickly turn boring with over-cropping or over-ripening. (You may have consumed some examples of this viticultural misfortune yourself.)

PG is not built to make blockbuster dry whites, so it doesn't need high Brix; in a cool growing region, it ripens happily with a sugar percentage in the low 20s. The exception is for a style known in Alsace as *Vendange Tardive* — late harvest — in which Pinot Gris gets picked at a Brix of 30° or more and converted into a wine with 15 percent alcohol and maybe 3 percent residual sugar — not a dessert wine exactly, more like a colossal appetizer wine. Try a glass with some foie gras and a ripe melon, and you'll have a new entry for your list of last meals before they haul you in front of the firing squad.

Assuming proper cropping and ripening, Pinot Gris/Grigio grapes have one additional problem: the namesake grey skins. Unlike the pigment in Gewürztraminer, which translates into an appetizing golden hue, PG skins turn wine pink, and not a nice, full, vibrant rosé pink, more like a rash. Consequently, Pinot Gris/Grigio needs gentle pressing — whole-cluster pressing if you can arrange it — and isn't a good candidate for skin contact. (A tip for picking PG out of an anonymous line-up of wines: It's the one with the merest hint of pink.)

Winemaking

Because this variety, under various names, grows up to be wine in many divergent places — several parts of Italy, Alsace, Germany, Canada, Oregon, California — it receives nearly every treatment known to winemaking. The two broad camps, though, are the Grigio producers — aiming for light, bright, zingy wines — and the Gris faction — shooting for fuller, rounder, more substantial wines. Technically speaking, only the Grigio-style PG belongs in this chapter; full-bore, California Chardonnay style, barrel-fermented, total malo Gris is more at home in the preceding chapter on the fruity-herbal whites.

Lean, vivid Pinot Grigio starts with gentle crushing and pressing to minimize the grey matter. Don't wring every last ounce of juice from the grapes; that final push could extract the pigment you don't need. Keep everything cool from start to finish; skip the malo, skip the oak, get it to bottle pronto. Make sure the acid is plentiful, up around 7 grams per liter or a tad higher.

To richen Pinot Grigio a bit, without producing a truly fat wine, do a mock-barrel fermentation by including a few ounces of wood chips in a carboy fermenter; and fatten the mouthfeel later by stirring the post-fermentation, post-racking lees every few days for two or three months before cleaning the wine up for bottling.

Amazing Albariño

This Spanish grape (Alvarinho in Portugal) hit New World wine lists in a big way a few years back, part of the advance guard of a phalanx of tasty Iberian wines. While most of us think of Spain and Portugal as downright hot winegrowing regions, both have their cool zones, located close together. These wines are vibrant thanks to marine influence and plenty of chilly wind.

Because of its unstoppable vivacity, Albariño is gaining acreage in cooler parts of California and showing up under more and more labels. If you get your hands on some, and if you have read this chapter from the start, you know the drill: relatively low harvest Brix (down in the low 20s), cool fermentation temperatures, no malo, no oak.

Blending Albariño with sympathetic varieties is fine, but tarting it up isn't. Possibly the worst white wine I ever tasted was an Albariño in a commercial tasting, which the pourer informed us was unusual: barrel-fermented, full malolactic, lots of new French oak. Another writer and I tasted it, looked at each other, and checked that style off our personal lists forever.

And a cast of thousands . . .

More and more of these semi-aromatic whites are making their way to North American vineyards, as winemakers and wine drinkers inch away from bigger, heavier Chardonnays to lighter, livelier wines. Vermentino from Spain; Torrontes from Argentina; Falanghina, and Fiano from Italy; and more varieties than you can count from Greece (starting with Assyrtiko, Moschofilero, and Roditis): Watch for these on the shelf as a consumer, and snatch a batch if you can as a home winemaker.

Choosing Yeast and Style Options

Table 18-1 offers some suggestions for yeast strains for various aromatic/semi-aromatic styles.

Table 18-1	Noseworthy Yeast Choices
Grape Variety	*Yeast Strains*
Any aromatic	For clean, straightforward fermentations: EC1118, D47, 71B, GRE, Epernay2, R-HST
Any aromatic	For added aromatic emphasis/extract:QA23, BA11, R2, W15, VL1, VL3
Semi-aromatics	D47, GRE for straightforward ferment; BA11, VL3 for more intrigue

Table 18-2 summarizes this chapter's discussions of how various techniques go with aromatic and semi-aromatic white varieties.

Table 18-2	Aromatic Style Options	
Options	*Aromatics*	*Semis*
Whole-cluster press	If possible; otherwise, gentle	If possible; otherwise, gentle
Skin contact	Common, if tricky; good for off-dry	Almost never
Barrel fermentation	Rare, and then only with neutral wood	Rare, and then only with neutral wood
Temperature regimen	Keep under 60°F (16°C)	Keep under 60°F (16°C)
Malolactic fermentation	What part of "no" don't you understand?	What part of "no" don't you understand?
Oak style/influence	None	None
Lees contact/stirring	Your choice	Your choice
Blending	Don't blend others into these; blend these into others	Sky's the limit
Residual sugar	Can go dry, off-dry, or sticky	Rarely

Part V
Beyond Red and White

"Brother Dom Perignon, everyone really enjoys your sparkling mayonnaise and blanc de turnip soup, but could there not be something else you could make with these grapes?"

In this part . . .

Some of the most fun in home winemaking — and home wine drinking — comes from categories outside the dominant red/white paradigm.

Don't be an old prune (or a raisin, in this case) and just make Cabernet year after year. Loosen up a little and experiment with pink wines, bubbly wines, fortified ports and sherries, sweet late-harvest wines, or whatever else floats your boat — or fills your glass.

Chapter 19

Thinking and Drinking Pink

*P*ink wines — *rosés, blushes, vin gris, rosado, rosato* — occupy a broad, varied, fascinating territory between whites and reds. Along Europe's Mediterranean coast, boatloads of pink wine get swallowed every summer. In North America, rosé is just now crawling out from under the rock of a terrible reputation — disdain brought on, ironically, by the smashing success of a pink wine —White Zinfandel. However, if you look in your local wine shops and on the wine lists at upscale restaurants, you will definitely notice rosé making headway. Don't miss the wave; help make it!

Ask a commercial winemaker, and you almost always find a fan of rosé wines. I know several who make a little bit for themselves and the staff on the side, even if the winery itself wouldn't get caught dead peddling pink wine. Dry rosé is refreshing in warmer weather, a versatile match with a wide range of food, and — from a home winemaking perspective — a great way to enhance the quality of your red wines.

Why Make Pink Wine?

Rosé is what you get when you apply white winemaking techniques to juice from red grapes. The result has some of the best characteristics of each: the crispness, delicacy, aromatic intrigue, and mouth-refreshing quality of a white, with a hint of the color, flavor, heft, and tannin of a red. Win-win. Plus, pink wines have the most gorgeous color spectrum of any wine category, hands down. Rosé is built for fun, for quaffing and casual meals, for sunny afternoons and beach picnics. How can you not want a wine like that?

Chances are no home winemaker ever started out with the goal of making great rosé. Most home winemakers start out trying to make big, hearty, red wine. Over time, some homies learn the value of restraint and start working with lighter red grapes and styles. A few home winemakers — more on the East Coast and in Canada than in California — sooner or later try their hand at white wines, perhaps even sweet dessert styles. And then there's pink.

Of course, unless you like to drink pink wine, you won't be tempted to make it. If it isn't already on your rotation, give it a try. The broader the range of wines you explore, the better your own winemaking will become.

Now for the final argument, the appeal to your self-interest as a home winemaker: Making rosé will enhance the quality of your reds. By removing a portion of the juice from crushed red grapes — the *saignée* method I discuss in "Stepping through a Saignée," later in this chapter — and reserving it for pink wine, you lower the ratio of the volume of liquid to the volume of grape skins. Presto! You get more concentrated red wine, because all the color, flavor, and texture goodies go into a smaller amount of wine.

Surveying Pink Wine Methods

Pink wine is made from every known red wine grape. Some grape varieties — Grenache, Tempranillo, Pinot Noir — get the pink treatment more often than others, but the rosé style knows no varietal boundaries. Whatever the grapes, pink wine, bottled early in the spring, offers a preview of the vintage's reds and rarely fails to come out delicious.

I usually take a small amount of juice — maybe 5 or 10 percent — from each of the red grapes I'm working with (several every harvest) and ferment them together as a mongrel rosé. The mix changes; the fun never stops.

Three basic methods exist for making rosé, on a commercial scale or in your garage. Winemakers differ on the best method for making good pink wine. The direct-press camp insist that they make "rosé by design" — using grapes grown for just that purpose — rather then as an afterthought for a red wine program. But saignée-style winemakers are just as insistent that their riper grapes make perfectly serious wine (serious, that is, for rosé). I give a brief overview of each of the three methods in the next sections.

Pressing pink directly

In the *direct-to-press method*, you press red grapes as whole clusters, or as destemmed whole grapes, without crushing them first. (The same technique is used on some white wines; see Chapter 16.) Because the contact with the red skins is brief, direct-press rosés tend to be very light in color. The classic is French *vin gris* — literally "grey wine" — from Pinot Noir grapes in Burgundy.

The method is also widely used in the south of France. Once the juice is extracted, winemaking proceeds along white wine lines.

Direct-to-press has its advantages (marked +) and disadvantages (marked –):

+ Because the grapes are used just for rosé, not for red wine, they are grown for the qualities pink wine needs — a relatively low sugar level (more like 20° Brix instead of the 24° for reds) and brighter acidity.

+ The process is simpler than the *saignée* method and doesn't require separating juice from crushed fruit, using multiple containers, or worrying about when to draw the juice.

+ Because the juice is available immediately for processing, it receives necessary additions and yeast inoculation earlier, which reduces the risk of spoilage bacteria.

– Home winemakers rarely want to pay red grape prices for pink wine.

– Whole-cluster/whole-berry pressing with the usual home winemaking equipment (a basket press) yields very little juice.

Bleeding off juice — saignée

The *saignée* method — "bleeding" in French — is used for making rosé around the world, especially by wineries that make a small amount of pink wine alongside a lot of red wine. (I cover this method in detail in "Stepping through a Saignée" a little further on.)

In a *saignée*, you crush red grapes, then allow them to sit for a short time — a few hours to two or three days. You drain off a small portion of the unfermented juice (which by now has picked up some color) for rosé and use the bulk of the grapes and juice to make red wine. Winemaking for the pink fraction uses white wine techniques.

The *saignée* method has advantages (marked +) and disadvantages (marked –):

+ The main value of *saignée* lies in raising red wine quality, by reducing the amount of juice in the red fermentation and increasing concentration.

+ The method is easy to do at home and requires no fancy equipment.

– Red grapes harvested at high, ultra-ripe sugar levels and low acidity can produce flat, high-alcohol rosé, which may require rescue work. If you have high-octane juice, add some water, please.

– Turning one batch of grapes into two wines might be too much for some home winemakers to deal with.

Blending whites and reds

Many people think pink wine is made by blending white wine and red wine. Sure enough, put some of each in a glass and — *voilà!* — pink wine. But people familiar with the standard direct-press and *saignée* methods for rosé generally think of blending pink wine as cheating.

Blending does play a legitimate role in rosé winemaking, including some pretty fancy bottles. In Champagne and other premium sparkling wine regions, Brut Rosé — sparkling dry pink wine — is often based on blending a little red wine into a lot of white wine before fermenting in the bottle. Fans of the direct-press method often fine-tune the color of the final wine with a dab of a full-colored red. So even if blending isn't the norm, you might consider dropping a bit of your own homemade white or red wine into a rosé blend for added dimensions in aroma and flavor.

Making rosé by blending has pros (marked +) and cons (marked –):

+ Blending allows more precise control over wine color.

+ Blending can make odds and ends of wine into something tasty.

– Blending gets done late in the game with finished red and white wines, which were probably not made with rosé style in mind.

Balancing blush

Some winemakers get mad when *blush wines* — pale pink and a little on the sweet side — get lumped in with "serious" dry rosé. What can I say? Blush wines are pink wines, too, and they sell like crazy.

Commercial blush wines like White Zinfandel (and White Anything Else) are generally made with grapes harvested very early, just barely ripe, and comparatively low in sugar and high in acid. The grapes are crushed and immediately pressed — picking up a mere hint of color — and fermented at cool temperatures. The wine ends up slightly sweet, either by stopping the fermentation with some sugar left or adding unfermented juice back in afterwards, and lower in alcohol. The color is tweaked as needed with red wine. Juice concentrate from aromatic white grapes — Muscat above all — gets added for extra intrigue. The wine is filtered and bottled young and fresh.

Sound like manufactured wine? Sure. But blush wines can still be quite drinkable and enjoyable. The art of the blush is balancing the sweetness with good, strong acidity. That way, the wine hits your mouth as refreshing, not cloying.

Getting opinions on pinks from the pros

Most commercial winemakers agree that most rosés tend to converge in a common aromatic and flavor profile, which Chris Phelps at Swanson Vineyards in Napa describes as "bright cherry, strawberry, rhubarb, and raspberry, with plenty of estery [floral aromatic] stuff." Phelps, a direct-press devotee, thinks that picking grapes early for rosé mutes varietal distinctions. French-born Jerome Cherry, winemaker for Saintsbury Vineyards in Napa, thinks rosé doesn't really show off *terroir,* the place the wine is from. Wine sensory analyst and educator John Buechsenstein, who has made a lot of rosé, says a pink wine may offer clues about what grapes it came from, "But mostly you can't tell, and who cares?"

Even the most passionate rosé producers warn against getting too worked up about the end result. Jeff Virnig, winemaker for Napa's Robert Sinskey Vineyards, says their pink wine is for refreshment, not meditation: "If someone wants to open a second bottle, we've accomplished our mission." But no one captures the spirit of rosé better than Jon McPherson, winemaker for South Coast Winery in southern California's Temecula Valley. "The trouble with rosé is that too many people drink it with their clothes on," he says.

Blush winemaking is more a style than a technique. But know that you can make excellent rosé with a little residual sugar, so if you like to drink wines in that style, you can do a good job at home. Chapter 20 covers wine with residual sugar.

Stepping through a Saignée

Making pink wine through a *saignée* from red grapes is by far the most likely home approach, so the steps merit a closer look.

Soaking the skins

Your pink wine starts with destemmed, crushed red grapes. Juice from just about any red grape can work, or a combination from two or more red varieties.

Saignée rosé can be made in any quantity, but to make the effort worthwhile, I recommend a minimum of 3 gallons (11 liters) of juice — enough for a little over a case of wine. The volume of pink juice should be somewhere between 5 and 10 percent of the expected total red juice volume; more than about 15 percent could affect your red. So to make 3 gallons (11 liters) of pink wine, you need to be making about 30 gallons (114 liters) of red wine.

Red and pink wine fermentations typically use different yeast strains, so don't add yeast to the crushed red grapes before you pull off the juice for your pink. You can add a routine, precautionary dose of sulfur dioxide (SO_2) to the whole batch of grapes, and make any needed adjustments — acid, water, sugar — as discussed in Chapter 5, but hold off on the yeast.

Your first decision is how long to let the juice and skins sit and stew before drawing off the juice for the pink project. You can wait anywhere from a couple hours to a day to get the color you want; some rosés soak longer, but I wouldn't start that way.

Three variables determine how pink the juice gets, and how fast the color develops:

- ✔ The longer the juice stays in contact with the skins, the more color comes out.

- ✔ Grape varieties that make deep-colored wines — Cabernet Sauvignon, for example — will produce color in the juice faster than varieties that make lighter-hued wines — like Pinot Noir or Grenache.

- ✔ The cooler the temperature of the crushed grapes, the slower the color extraction.

Your own preferences are important, too. Do you want something very pale pink, just a pretty touch of springtime color? Or are you aiming for a deeper, more substantial pink that could almost pass for a red?

For a first venture into saignée, six hours of skin contact is a good start. Double that to 12 hours if you know you want lots of color. That timing might mean you have to pull off your pink juice at 2 a.m., or time it longer or shorter — welcome to winemaking! Remember that if the color isn't quite what you wanted, you can lighten it by blending in a little white wine or deepen it with a little red.

Home winemakers find their own ways to draw off juice. My standard routine is to put the crushed red grapes and juice into the container where they will soon be fermented; do any necessary additions, amendments and tweaking, including an initial dosage of SO_2; keep the lid on the fermenter and fill the top space with carbon dioxide to limit oxidation; and keep the grapes as cool as my garage allows. When the time comes to pull off juice, I drain scoops of grapes and juice through a fine-meshed sieve into a bucket, and pour the bucket of juice into a carboy for fermentation. For larger volumes, you can push a strainer into the grapes, and siphon juice from the pool that collects inside the strainer into a carboy. From then on, red and pink move along very different tracks.

If your pink juice needs to wait a while before fermentation — for example, if you're using two or three red grapes, and not all of them have been harvested — you can put the juice into a refrigerator, which greatly slows the start of fermentation. Or, you can even freeze the juice and thaw it later. Or, as I often do, just add the juice from grape number two to the already fermenting juice from grape number one.

Making pink like white

When you have your pink juice, forget about its red origins and start thinking like a white winemaker. Table 19-1 summarizes the techniques:

Table 19-1	Processing Options for Pink Wine
Technique Options	*Rosé Style*
Whole-cluster press	Used in direct-press method
Skin contact	Used in *saignée* method
Barrel fermentation	Rare for any rosé
Temperature regimen	50° to 55°F (10° to 13°C)
Malolactic fermentation	Rare
Oak style/influence	Slim to none
Blending	Common in all methods
Heat/cold stabilization	Common in all methods
Filtration	Common

Checking acid, adding yeast

Before doing anything else, check the acidity of your potential pink. Many red grapes from warm climates are deficient in acid, and rosé needs to be tangy. Taste your juice and test it. Your taste buds are in charge, but total acidity should be up around 7 grams per liter, or even higher, so make adjustments at the start.

Good yeast strains for rosé are typically white wine strains, capable of fermenting at lower temperatures and adept at producing fruity, floral aromatics. Some strains particularly suited for aromatic whites — Riesling, Gewürztraminer — may not work so well, because red grapes rarely contain the same compounds these strains find in aromatic white varieties. Readily available choices include Côte des Blancs (formerly known as Epernay II), D47, 71B, BA11, and a strain called, appropriately enough, Rosé.

Going for a slow, cool fermentation

Rosé should be fermented slow and cool. Keep the temperature a little below 60°F (16°C), using the same methods you use with white wines — find a cool place, put carboys in tubs of ice water, swap them in and out of the refrigerator, and so on. Rosés are a little sturdier than whites, but they still need to keep cool.

A slow pink fermentation may take two to four weeks to go completely dry. If you're using more than one red grape for your rosé, and the second batch of juice shows up when the first batch has been fermenting for a while, no problem. Add the new, unfermented juice to the half-fermented juice — no new yeast needed — stretching out the joint fermentation.

Forestalling malolactic and making use of lees

After the alcoholic fermentation is complete, pink wine generally doesn't go through a secondary malolactic fermentation. The style direction for rosé is lean and crisp, and the fatness of a malolactic rarely goes with the program.

To keep malolactic fermentation at bay, make sure to measure the wine's pH and add the appropriate amount of sulfur dioxide to discourage bacterial activity. I also suggest adding about 250 parts per million of lysozyme, which holds back malolactic action. (Chapter 7 gives more detail on controlling the malolactic fermentation.)

Although you want to avoid fatness in pink wine, you can enhance mouthfeel by *lees stirring*. When the fermentation is complete and the wine has been racked into clean containers — glass or stainless steel, almost never barrels — stir the remaining yeast lees that continue to settle to the bottom every week or two with a long stirring rod. Over two or three months, the enhanced lees contact helps round out the wine without taking off the zingy edge.

Bottling it up and enjoying it

Rosé gets bottled early, after two or three rackings. It should be ready in six months or less from harvest. I usually bottle mine around April 1st, matching the whimsical nature of pink wine with the spirit of April Fool's Day.

Rosé's charming color palette shows through best if the wine gets cold and heat stabilized and goes through at least a light filtration before bottling. You want this wine to sparkle in the glass.

Drink it soon, fresh, and young, while it still gives off a gush of fruity perfume. Don't worry if you drink it all up; you can always make more.

Chapter 20

Dessert, Fortified, and Sparkling Wines

· ·

In This Chapter

▶ Breaking winemaking rules

▶ Controlling residual sugar, ensuring stability

▶ Hanging around for late-harvest sticky wines

▶ Fortifying port, sherry, and *vin doux naturel*

▶ Bestowing bubbles on your wine

· ·

*W*elcome to Home Winemaking Graduate School! The wine styles this chapter covers are quite different from the dry table wines that are the main focus of the book. All contain high levels of sugar, high levels of alcohol, or bubbles — and possibly a combination of these traits.

When you have the hang of basic winemaking, these wines are a ton of fun to make and drink. You can easily make late-harvest and fortified wines in very small quantities — perfect, because most people drink them in small quantities at, say, dinner parties and special occasions. Making these wines at home exactly like the best of the commercial producers is hard; making reasonable approximations that taste terrific is quite possible.

Making Exceptions for Exceptional Wines

The special qualities of dessert, fortified, and sparkling wines require special winemaking techniques, most of which violate the basic precepts of making standard dry table wine.

Table wines demand clean fruit; the most prized late-harvest-style dessert wines revel in flavors obtained from moldy grapes. A central goal of table winemaking is ensuring that the fermentation goes dry; all these specialty wines have some sugar in them, either from stopping the fermentation or re-introducing sugar later on. Table wines are not supposed to continue fermenting in the bottle, but for sparkling wines, that's the whole point.

With grapes harvested riper and riper, with higher and higher sugar levels, table winemakers struggle to keep alcohol in balance; for fortified wines, they dump in extra alcohol with abandon. While most white winemaking shuns oxygen, sherry thrives on intentional oxidation. For other sweet styles, instead of rushing the grapes to the crusher, they spend weeks or months on straw mats turning into raisins before winemaking begins.

Dealing with Residual Sugar

Sugar is essential to winemaking: no sugar, no conversion to alcohol, no wine. But sugar left in wine, or added to wine, is highly unstable, and more critters than you can count are looking for a sweet snack.

Wine styles that include some element of *residual* (unfermented) sugar require a different balancing act of elements — acid and alcohol as well as sweetness — to taste right. They also call for different production procedures to ensure stability in the bottle. So, you need to be able to adjust your winemaking techniques appropriately.

Taking many roads to sweetness

For those people who claim not to like sweet wine, let me ask you this: Do you like other sweet things — ice cream, chocolate, pie? If so, why not wine?

Besides being sweet — a taste most humans are quite fond of — sweet wines succeed because of other attributes — notably acidity. If you balance the sugar and acidity, you can produce a wine that's refreshing, not cloying. The same is true of pastry or candy: Sweetness alone is gag-worthy and off-putting, but sweetness tempered with the acidity of fruit or the bitterness of chocolate is a joy.

For late-harvest wines, acidity makes the equation work. For fortified wines, both acidity and the elevated alcohol balance the sugar. For sparkling wines, the naturally high acidity of the grapes, combined with creamy mouthfeel elements, performs the balancing act.

Sugar gets into these wine styles in two ways. One is by stopping fermentation while some sugar is still in the mix. The other is by adding sugar (often unfermented grape juice) to a dry wine, and occasionally, adding more sugar to an already sweet wine.

In late-harvest wines, fermentation gets shut down by a combination of chilling and sulfur dioxide (SO_2). In fortified wines, adding high-proof spirits in mid-fermentation kills the yeast. In sparkling wine, small amounts of sugar get added at two different stages of the complicated winemaking process.

Different options exist to keep these wines stable. Fortified wines, with alcohol levels in the 17 to 20 percent range, provide hostile environments for yeast and for spoilage microbes, so they're pretty safe bets. Sterile filtration removes any remaining viable yeast from commercial late-harvest wines, even though filtration can be difficult in wines thick with the viscosity sugar adds. Sparkling wines shed their yeast through gravity, not filtration, so a final pinch of sugar can safely be re-introduced at the end. Some of these methods work in your garage, and some don't.

Ensuring stability at home

At home, with home equipment, stabilizing fortified wines is easy. You can balance the sugar and alcohol — in round numbers, 6 percent sugar and 20 percent alcohol — either by dumping in high-proof *neutral spirits* (distilled grape alcohol with no flavorings — ask for it at your local wine shop) while grape sugar is still around, or by fermenting the wine dry and then adding both sugar and more alcohol. Either way, the final wine is biologically stable.

Sparkling wines offer two solutions, both straightforward. Using the traditional *méthode champenoise* technique, described in "Putting Bubbles in Your Bottles" later in this chapter, spent yeast collects into a plug in the neck of upside-down bottles, gets briefly frozen, and is physically removed to make the wine safe for a final smidgen of sugar. And if a stray yeast cell or two remains, so what? The wine has bubbles, anyway. Alternatively, you can treat dry base wine with potassium sorbate (I talk more about this chemical compound in a second), filter it for clarity, and then give it artificial bubble implants with CO_2 under pressure in a keg. Either way, stability control should not be a major issue with sparkling wine.

Late-harvest wines are the hardest to stabilize. Alcohol levels for these wines tend to be lower than table wines, usually 10 percent or less, so that's no help. While I highly recommend filtration for clarity, you can't do sterile filtration in your garage. And controlling yeast activity only with sulfur dioxide (SO_2) additions is risky in two senses: It may not completely subdue a vigorous yeast strain, and a high level of SO_2 can ruin the wine's aromas and flavors.

Which leaves the home winemaker with the option of *potassium sorbate*, a chemical compound that will kill off yeast and stabilize the wine. Careful treatment with sorbate leaves few sensory traces. Use other control methods as well — filtration cuts the yeast populations down somewhat, and sulfur dioxide is essential — but sorbate closes the deal.

Waiting for Late-Harvest Wines

Late-harvest dessert wines are some of the priciest and most sought-after bottles on the planet: German Trockenbeerenauslese made from Riesling and French Sauternes made from Sémillon and Sauvignon Blanc. Hungarian Tokaji, made from grapes you've probably never heard of (like Furmint and Hárslevelú), is explicitly mentioned in the Hungarian national anthem. Bottles of well-aged Sauternes from Chateau d'Yquem are willed to the next generation in some families. Your wines in this style will be priceless — especially because, as a home winemaker, you can't sell them at all.

Late-harvest wines get their collective name from the fact that the grapes are allowed to stay on the vine longer than usual — sometimes months longer — developing enough sugar to allow for both an alcoholic fermentation and some residual sweetness.

Winemaking protocols

Ninety percent of late-harvest winemaking is indistinguishable from making white table wine:

- ✔ Destem and crush the grapes.
- ✔ Allow the juice to settle and clarify for a day or two.
- ✔ Make any necessary adjustments to acidity and pH at the start.
- ✔ Ferment the clarified juice cool and slow, aiming for 60°F (16°C) or slightly lower and for a daily Brix drop of between 0.5 and 1 degree.
- ✔ Prevent malolactic fermentation when the alcoholic fermentation is done with SO_2 and perhaps lysozyme. This keeps the acid level up, balances the sugar, and avoids potential flavor problems (geranium notes) from the interaction of lactic acid and sorbate.
- ✔ Keep the wine cool, clarify it over time, fine it with bentonite for protein stability, and filter it for clarity before bottling.

The only difference is the sugar thing — which is a little like saying the only difference between steak tartare and a nicely grilled T-bone is cooking. How you handle the sugar depends on the state of the grapes when they arrive.

Sticky tips from the pros

Canada's burgeoning wine industry has modest international visibility, especially when compared to its larger and louder neighbor to the south. But one exception is the worldwide reputation of the ice wines from Ontario's Niagara Peninsula, including a highly prized (and priced) bottling from Iniskillin Wines made from, of all things, Cabernet Franc.

Iniskillin winemaker Bruce Nicholson describes ice wine production as "extreme winemaking." The grapes may stay on the vines into January, even February, exposed to the elements, bears, deer, and birds. Wind can easily blow the crop off the vines. When all goes well, and the grapes spend a week or so at –8°F (–22°C), the volume of juice from the whole-cluster pressing (the frozen water stays behind) goes down to about 150 liters (40 gallons) per ton, less than a third of the yield of normal grapes. Fermentation at high Brix isn't easy, nor is filtration with so much sugar still in the wine. No wonder these wines aren't cheap.

California winemaker Jim Klein at Navarro Vineyards in Mendocino County's Anderson Valley — a former home winemaker, by the way — emphasizes the care that must be taken with botrytized grapes. (See the section "Botrytis: The noble rot" elsewhere in this chapter.) He says to break clusters open to make sure they aren't covered with black fungus; you should have purple berries (from formerly white grapes) with some grey tufts of botrytis spores on them. If you get a mixture of clusters with and without botrytis, separate them and make two batches of wine. Klein crushes his grapes and lets them sit for a few hours, perhaps overnight, so that the thick juices really start flowing. He suggests mixing rice hulls or grape stems in with the grapes to aid in pressing. Once the cake of grapes has gotten a hard press, take it apart, put it back, and press it some more.

Klein prefers neutral yeasts, so-called Champagne strains like EC-1118, and does cool, slow fermentation, with the Brix dropping around one degree a week. If the starting sugar was high enough, the fermentation will stop itself. Chilling and sulfur dioxide stop the malolactic. Because of the plentiful sugar, he notes, late-harvest wines routinely get SO_2 additions at rates slightly higher than normal, including a final insurance dose at bottling.

The best starting point for late-harvest winemaking is late-harvest grapes: sugar up around 35° Brix or higher, with at least a smattering of *Botrytis cinerea,* a fungal infection that can be a good thing for late-harvested grapes. The upcoming section, "Botrytis: The noble rot" talks about botrytis in more depth.

With true late-harvest grapes, sugar control means stopping the fermentation at a target point by chilling the wine, adding sulfur dioxide, and (for homies) adding potassium sorbate to stabilize the mix of alcohol and sugar.

The alternative strategy is to use standard-issue white grapes, ferment them dry, treat the wine with sorbate to kill the yeast, and then re-introduce the desired sugar — either by dissolving cane sugar or adding an unfermented portion of the original juice. The advantage of this retroactive late-harvest strategy is you have more precise control over the exact amount of sugar in the wine; the downside is that the wine will have more alcohol than classic late-harvest examples and, of course, no trace of botrytis.

True late-harvest technique

Late-harvest fermentations take some extra work to start and to stop. The extremely high sugar levels at the beginning — 35°, even 45° Brix — are a little much even for hungry yeast, so doubling the normal yeast addition rate is common to kick-start the alcoholic conversion.

Commercial wineries stop fermentations by chilling wine in tanks with refrigeration and simultaneously adding SO_2. At home, controlling temperature takes longer and so it is less precise. Putting the wine in a chest-style freezer is best for rapid cooling; if the carboy is sitting in a bath of cold water inside the freezer, so much the better. Using a refrigerator slows the fermentation rate somewhat, but not quickly. In either case, add SO_2 at a dosage appropriate to the wine's pH, along with a dose of potassium sorbate. You may end up with a little more alcohol and a little less sugar than you wanted, or vice versa, but because the sorbate stabilizes the wine, you can fine-tune the sugar and alcohol later.

Exact target numbers are impossible to specify; what works for a particular wine depends on the intensity of the fruit flavors and the level of acidity. The classic parameters are a set of tens: about 10 percent alcohol, 10 percent or more sugar, and close to 10 grams per liter of acid. But lighter, semi-sweet wines can also be a delight. A starting Brix of 26°, for example — which would represent very high ripeness for some varieties in some climates — could be stopped at 11 percent alcohol (consuming 20° of the 26° of Brix) and 6 percent sugar, making for a nifty summer sipping wine. So, no recipe. You learn what works through trial and error, plus a lot of tasting.

Don't be afraid to fiddle with the result of stopping the fermentation. Do some taste trials with samples that have small adjustments to the sugar level, the acidity, and the percentage of alcohol, which can affect the wine's body. Use the results of the tasting trials to tweak the entire batch of wine.

Retroactive late-harvest concoction

Working retroactively is not a method for making world-class dessert wine — but it can make mighty tasty dessert wine nonetheless. You, the winemaker, manipulate the chemistry, rather than relying on the grapes and yeast. But because finding true late-harvest grapes is tough, recreating the conditions after-the-fact has its advantages.

Starting with, for example, full-flavored white grapes at 22° or 23° Brix, ferment the juice dry for an alcohol around 12 percent. Rack the wine, treat with SO_2 and lysozyme to prevent malolactic action, and let it clarify for a few weeks. Treat with bentonite for heat and cold stability, and then with sorbate to prevent re-fermentation. Then do tasting trials and add different amounts of sugar and perhaps acid until you like what you're drinking.

The advantage of this approach is that you have more control over the exact amount of sugar in the wine; the downside is that, in general, the alcohol ends up higher than with the true late-harvest method.

Either way

Because late harvest-style dessert wines are prized for their heady, beguiling aromatics, picking a yeast strain that emphasizes floral and exotic fruit properties would seem logical. Most commercial winemakers who work in this style, however, do it differently. They argue that because the grape varieties typically made into this style — Riesling, Gewürztraminer, Chenin Blanc — are loaded with aromatic material anyway, and frequently bring some botrytis character as well, a better choice is a more neutral yeast strain that can handle lots of sugar and not produce anything stinky. You may also consider a yeast strain with low alcohol tolerance, which will start to run out of gas on its own before all the sugar is exhausted.

For increasing sweetness, the unfermented juice of the same batch of grapes — what the Germans call *Süssreserve* — is ideal. The grape juice reinforces the wine's fruit flavors and doesn't dilute the wine like adding sugar dissolved in water. If you're planning a late-harvest wine, set aside a portion of clarified juice — maybe 5 or 10 percent — after pressing, dose it with sulfur dioxide for stability according to the juice pH, and freeze the juice — refrigeration won't do the job — until you adjust the sweetness. How much juice to reserve depends on how sweet you want the final wine to be. If you use cane sugar, dissolve it in as little warm/hot water (or wine) as possible.

Doing the math to figure out the proportions for tasting-trial samples is more complicated for juice than for sugar. (The math for sugar is in Chapter 5.) Get out a pencil and paper or a calculator, start with the fact that each degree of Brix translates to 10 grams per liter of sugar, and you'll figure it out.

Besides managing the sugar level, tasting and testing acidity are the other key parameters in late-harvest wine — certainly more important than alcohol. Low acidity is what makes some off-dry (slightly sweet) wines — like low-end White Zinfandel — annoying and makes some syrupy dessert wines cloying. Bright acidity prevents mouth fatigue, so tasting trials and accurate testing are essential.

The frozen shortcut

One more home winemaker trick is to start with frozen juice. If you buy frozen juice, let it thaw most of the way, with a good-sized ice chunk still floating in the middle. Because sugar-water requires a lower freezing point than plain water, pulling out the ice cube reduces the total water content, raising the Brix of the remaining liquid. Presto: late-harvest juice.

Botrytis: The noble rot

Often, when the weather is right — that is, bad — grapes left on the vine develop a particular mold called *Botrytis cinerea*. This mold has enough miraculous effects that it is known as "the noble rot." When this same fungal infection attacks grapes early in the ripening cycle, it's known as *bunch rot*, and growers go to great trouble to prevent it from happening.

But on otherwise clean fruit, late in the season, accompanied by a high sugar buildup, botrytis adds magical, nutty, honeysuckle, and dried-fruit flavors with an appealing bitter note on the finish. By cracking the skins of the berries, it encourages dehydration and a further climb in the percentage of sugar, sometimes over 40 percent. Developing botrytis requires, first of all, that the fungus be around. Growers sometimes spray a cloud of the critters into a vineyard block hoping they will work their magic. Fastidious wineries use only the best bunches — that is, the most infected — or even just the best berries, picked off by hand one by one.

Botrytis also requires a certain amount of rain and humidity late in the season; too much rain, or a little hail mixed in with the rain, can destroy the entire crop. If the grapes get cold enough to freeze at just the right time, they may go into a variant called *ice wine*; the frozen berries end up with even more sugar, making for more intense wines. If they freeze at the wrong time, they're mulch. Consequently, leaving grapes on the vine well into November, maybe January, is a very risky business.

Finding the perfect late-harvest grapes is a chore. Any grower cultivating them intentionally probably won't share, because these precious, nicely infected babies make valuable wines. You might find a grower with a few rows of an appropriate variety that never got harvested and strike a deal to keep them hanging on, just in case lightning strikes. And if you can't find the perfect grapes, you can concoct something similar at home.

Be careful about the botrytis part; make sure your grower knows noble rot from riff-raff rot. You can easily smell the difference on the grapes. Botrytis gives off a heady, exotic, decadent odor, while other fungal infections smell like something long-abandoned at the back of your refrigerator.

Good grape choices

Someone, somewhere, has undoubtedly made late-harvest-style wine from every grape planted, red and white. Most late-harvest wine, however, comes from white grapes, both the aromatic and the fruity, even herbal varieties.

In the aromatic cohort, the natural volatile characteristics combine with botrytis, if it's present, for a seriously intense experience. Riesling is the star variety here, although late-harvest Gewürztraminer can be lovely, and honey-tinged late-harvest Chenin Blanc is another winner. Muscat works in this style, too, though it more often gets made in a fortified style (see the next section, "Fortifying Your Wine"); Muscat also grows best in warmer climates where the chances of botrytis are slim.

Other varieties have a place, too, such as Sémillon, Sauvignon Blanc, and Furmint, as well as several white hybrids. Late-harvest Chardonnay works surprisingly well. For these grapes, the presence of some botrytis character is a definite plus; without it, the wines can lack complexity.

Fortifying Your Wine

Adding extra alcohol to wine became popular in the 18th century. Because winemakers didn't have a clue about yeast or malolactic bacteria, but were shipping vast amounts of wine around the world, a lot of wine went bad in transit. By fortifying some of the wines, all that spoilage stuff mysteriously stopped; and as a bonus, the wines — Portuguese port and Spanish sherry in particular — were knockouts, almost literally.

The three main groupings of *fortified wines* — port, sherry, and amped-up aromatic grape wines — all involve adding alcohol and retaining sugar, in slightly different proportions, using slightly different methods. Of all the specialty wines in this chapter, fortified wines are the easiest to pull off at home, and can add a definite exclamation point to your next dinner party.

Port — Portuguese and otherwise

Port gets its name from the town of Porto (well, actually, Oporto) at the mouth of the Douro River in northern Portugal. The grapes, mainly indigenous Portuguese varieties, are grown further up-river, in an astonishing series of steep, river gorge hillsides covered with terraces and vines. Most of the grapes are made into wine and aged in Porto and its suburb across the river, Villa Nova de Gaia, before shipping out to the rest of the world.

Port comes in many styles, some (like Ruby Port) bottled young and fruity, some (like Tawny Port) spend years mellowing in barrels; some especially good years are declared as Vintage Ports. The Douro is the last major holdout of *foot-treading* — crushing and macerating grapes by walking on them, over and over — which is in fact a gentler process than machine crushing.

Elsewhere in the world, all manner of port-style wines are made out of every imaginable red grape, including a lot of Zinfandel and Petite Sirah in California. What makes them port-like is the combination of alcohol and sugar, not the flavor profile. Nothing is wrong with these wines — except when they're called "port."

Winemaking protocols

The basic target parameters for port are around 6 percent sugar and 19 or 20 percent alcohol. Acidity tends to be slightly on the high side compared to red table wines, because ports do not typically go through malolactic fermentation, which drops the acidity. The pH level is not a big concern, because the elevated alcohol puts a lid on possible microbial spoilage.

In traditional port winemaking, the grapes start off on a normal red fermentation, and when the sugar drops to around 6° Brix — meaning the alcohol might have gotten to around 10 percent — you add enough neutral spirits (distilled, unflavored grape alcohol) to get the alcohol up to around 20 percent and stop the fermentation quickly, within an hour or two.

Use the highest-proof spirits you can find. If you have a friend at a winery or distillery (I won't tell) who can provide 190-proof spirits, that's ideal. If not, Everclear, widely available and normally used to spike fraternity party punches, weighs in at 151 proof. Though it's made from grain, not grapes, Everclear is neutral in flavor and works fine. Do not use something like vodka, where the comparatively low alcohol percentage would dilute your precious port. Standard-proof grape brandy has the same problem; you might like the additional oak influence, but not the dilution.

The alcohol level prevents malolactic activity. You press, clarify, age, and blend the wine to suit your style, and bottle it after anywhere from several months to several years.

Naturally, you can find many variations on this theme. Port houses rely on different combinations of grape varieties — rarely fewer than three and often half a dozen or more. Some winemakers press the grapes before adding the fortifying alcohol, some press soon after adding. Most use entirely neutral spirits, some use brandy that brings the flavors of oak aging.

The magic moment for adding spirits might come at 3 a.m. Or, you might project from hydrometer readings that it should occur at 3 a.m., get up at 2:30, and discover the sugar is already down to 4° Brix.

Whenever you reach the right sugar level, decide whether to press before or after fortification. Adding alcohol while the grapes are still present can extract a little more from the skins, but adding to the wine after pressing makes mixing the alcohol and snuffing out the yeast much easier. Either way, the grapes get pressed before the wine goes completely dry, which means a little less tannin extraction than a standard red.

Do the math a couple of times before you dump in the spirits. Figure out how much you need based on the volume of wine and the alcohol percentage of the spirits you're adding — and remember that the addition increases the total volume of the wine. Five gallons (19 liters) of wine at 10 percent alcohol contains 0.5 gallons (1.9 liters) of alcohol. If you add 1 gallon (3.8 liters) of Everclear, which is 75 percent alcohol, the total alcohol will be 1.25 gallons (4.7 liters). But now the total liquid volume is 6 gallons (23 liters), which means the alcohol is just around 20 percent. Hey, that's pretty close!

Before starting the fermentation, get a good reading on the starting Brix (so you can calculate the fortification) and make sure the acidity is reasonably high, at least 6 or 7 grams per liter. The sugar will need that acidity for balance in the final wine.

When the fermentation stops and the wine is pressed, let the wine settle for a few days, then rack into vessels for storage. Port benefits from the slow oxidation and rounding of barrel aging, preferably in used or neutral wood. But you can make a fine beverage in carboys by adding a light dose of oak cubes. When the wine is largely clarified, taste it for balance and see if you need to increase the alcohol, sugar, or acidity. With all that sugar to counter any astringency, your port shouldn't need fining for excess tannins. Filtering the port will make it look that much better.

Plan B

The alternative home method, often practiced, is much like the retroactive late-harvest strategy discussed earlier in the chapter. Ferment the wine dry and do the math. Add sugar dissolved in as little water as possible, and enough spirits to get the numbers into port range. If you do this immediately after fermentation, the malolactic should never kick off. Most wine drinkers would have trouble telling the difference between ports made the traditional way and the reconstructed way (if the same grapes are involved).

And this way, you never have to get up at three in the morning.

When making addition in this reconstructed method, be conservative — err on the low side for additions of sugar and alcohol — so you have some wiggle room for fine-tuning as the wine matures.

Good grape choices

Making your own "port" from the traditional Portuguese varieties — Touriga Nacional, Touriga Franca, Tinta Roriz, Tinta Cão — is a great project, if you can locate the grapes. Acreage for these varieties is increasing in California, partly for dry red wines, partly for port, so be hopeful and alert.

Otherwise, you can make good port-style wine from almost any combination of full-bodied, deep-colored red varieties: Cabernet Sauvignon, Syrah, Zinfandel, Petite Sirah, or Norton, for example. Lighter-colored grapes that make medium-bodied wines — Pinot Noir, Grenache, Sangiovese — are not common choices, but might work as lighter, young-drinking wines. Red hybrids? No problem. If you're processing a large volume of almost any red, think about diverting a fraction to your port program.

Even though the wine ends up full of sugar and alcohol, the grapes themselves do not need to be super-ripe, approaching port qualities while still on the vine; normal ripeness is fine. After the wine is bottled, expect it to develop nicely for at least a few years.

High-octane beauties

Most California "ports" are made from grapes not seen in Portugal. But a handful of dedicated producers grow the traditional Douro Valley varieties, which flourish in parts of the unglamorous Central Valley where the climate, as in the Douro, can be hot as blazes. One of the pioneers is Quady in Madera County, an operation with the whimsy to call its port-style wine Starboard.

Quady winemaker Mike Blaylock says their grapes get picked at normal ripeness and get the standard treatment at the crusher. Fermentation temperature gets up to just under 90°F (32°C), with four punchdowns daily. "The biggest problem for every port winemaker," he says, "is forgetting to watch the fermentation adequately and continuously; it gets away from you. The yeast will make your life as hard as possible." He prefers to press the grapes before fortification, to make stirring easier — the alcohol won't incorporate voluntarily. Blaylock insists on neutral grape spirits for the fortification, but has come to appreciate "dirty" (unrefined, unfiltered) pot-still brandy for the final, fine-tuning additions. Ports are likely to taste slightly hot and alcoholic when they're bottled, he observes, but mellow over time.

In Cucamonga in Southern California, Galleano Winery owner/winemaker Don Galleano uses the traditional Palomino and Mission grapes for his sherries, but acknowledges that for drier styles, many white varieties can do the job. Galleano doesn't try to reproduce the elaborate Spanish system of aging, nor does he use the distinctive flor yeasts common in Spain — those idiosyncratic critters would put the rest of his winery at risk.

Galleano's sherry-making is a lot like making port, only with white grapes and more exposure to oxygen. Grapes are picked very ripe, relatively low in acid, crushed, and fermented on the skins (not normal white wine procedure) until the alcohol reaches about 8 percent. Since the grapes come in late in the season, the winery has enough free-floating yeast around that no inoculation is needed. The juice/wine is drained off the grapes and fortified to about 20 percent or slightly higher, and then the grapes are pressed, and that juice is fortified, providing blending options. For dry-style sherries, fortified to around 16 or 17 percent, he thinks grapes with higher acidity and lower Brix are appropriate.

Sherry

Sherry may be the most under-appreciated wine style on the planet. In drier Fino, Manzanilla, and Amontillado versions, it's a terrific food wine, and not just for Spanish tapas. In the heavier and headier Oloroso and dessert styles, it holds its own with the best ports from neighboring Portugal.

Winemaking protocols

Classic sherries from the area around Jerez de la Frontera on Spain's southwestern Atlantic coast combine two winemaking techniques you're not likely to duplicate at home. The most famous is the *solera* system of aging: Barrels of wine from each successive vintage slowly drain into each other by gravity. Wine is drawn off from the bottom barrel for bottling, giving each new release a small contribution from many layers of aging. You could build this in your garage, but you probably won't.

In addition, many sherries benefit from a special kind of yeast, called *flor*, which tolerates high alcohol and develops on the top surface of finished wine exposed to air. Flor adds a complex, nutty flavor found nowhere else. In a normal wine, flor oxidation would be a fatal fault; for sherry, it's the secret ingredient. You probably don't want this in your garage, either, because of the potential to infect other wines. But if you're feeling lucky, commercially packaged flor yeast is available.

You also have the option of making something sherry-like using port winemaking techniques — a strategy employed by many commercial sherry makers outside Spain (see the sidebar "High-octane beauties"). The basic steps for a sweet-style sherry might look like this:

1. **Start with very ripe, sugar-laden grapes.**

2. **Destem and crush the grapes, but don't press them; retain the skins for the fermentation.**

3. **Start a normal fermentation, as though these were red grapes.**

4. **Try to get the fermentation temperature somewhere between normal whites and reds, up to around 75°F (24°C) or slightly higher.**

5. **Press the grapes when the sugar level has dropped down to 6° or 8° Brix.**

6. **Fortify the wine with grape spirits (or grape brandy) to raise the alcohol to around 20 percent, stopping the fermentation.**

7. **Let the wine settle, and rack it into containers for aging.**

If the wine goes into barrel, fill it to only about 85 percent capacity, leaving room for air and oxidation. In a carboy, leave generous headspace, and don't fill the airlock with water — a small piece of cotton prevents bugs or dirt from getting inside and lets air through.

The alcohol should be sufficient to prevent microbial spoilage, eliminating or reducing the need for SO_2. Normal SO_2 additions would retard oxidation, but you want oxidization in this special case. Taste periodically to see how the wine is progressing — the flavors may take a year or more to develop.

For dry-style sherry, start with normally ripe white grapes. Ferment the grapes on the skins until dry, press, then add a small fortification to bring the alcohol up to 16 or 17 percent, and age similarly to sweeter styles. If you want to take the flor plunge, more common for dry styles, add the culture shortly after pressing and fortification. Dry-style sherry should be ready for bottling sooner than sweet styles.

Good grape choices

Finding the traditional Spanish sherry varieties, notably Palomino, is a long shot. Most white grapes are serviceable. I suggest that because you may not have the advantage of the distinctive flor character, you might up the ante by using an aromatic variety — Muscat or perhaps Chenin Blanc — for all or part of the fermentation.

Vin doux naturel

The final major category of fortified, sweet wines is what the French call *vin doux naturel* — "naturally sweet wine." The wine got its sugar honestly, from the grapes. Wines in this style are made around the world: fortified Muscat Beaume-de-Venise in the Southern Rhône, fortified Chenin Blanc in South Africa, fortified Muscat in Spain and Italy. Aromatic white grape varieties predominate; but then, the family includes *Banyuls,* fortified red Grenache from the south of France.

The basic logic for *vin doux* is the same as for port and sherry: start a fermentation, stop it partway through with an addition of alcohol, clean it up, and bottle it. The difference is that the *vins doux naturels* are a little lighter, a little fresher, and slightly lower in alcohol. They're vinified to retain and emphasize the fruit, not the power and heft that goes with port, and without the oxidation of sherry.

Winemaking protocols

For aromatic white varieties, grapes are picked at normal ripeness, crushed, then pressed, and only the juice gets fermented. Fermentation temperatures are kept low, under 60°F (16°C). Because these are aromatic grapes, the winemaking strives to hold on to all those floral goodies.

The parameters for these wines are about 6 percent sugar and 16 to 18 percent alcohol, so the shock of fortification happens when the fermenting wine gets down to its last 6 percent of sugar. The spirits added are always neutral, never flavored with oak or anything else. The wines are also chilled at this point, further retarding yeast activity and preserving fruit character. The fortified alcohol level, though lower than typical port, is normally high enough to prevent malolactic fermentation.

Commercial versions of *vins doux naturels* are almost always aged in stainless steel to preserve freshness. Carboys are perfect for homies. Because the elevated alcohol puts the brakes on the wine's evolution, the wine can be clarified, filtered, and bottled quickly. In the bottle, over time, some maturation can occur.

As with other fortified styles, you can reverse the order, fermenting the wine dry, then adding unfermented juice and spirits back in to achieve the desired chemistry. In a home setting, to ensure stability, treating the fermentation with potassium sorbate is a good idea, just in case some ultra-vigorous yeast strain happens to be present that can handle 17 percent alcohol.

Good grape choices

Muscat is the prime candidate for making fortified wine yourself. Another good choice would be Muscat. And for that matter, Muscat shouldn't be overlooked.

Barring that, Chenin Blanc does a very nice job, as does Gewürztraminer. If you have some Grenache around, turn a gallon of it into a mock-Banyuls; you'll have some nifty half-bottles for unusual presents.

Putting Bubbles in Your Bottles

Full disclosure: Making sparkling wine is above my pay grade. (Buying a lot of it is above my pay grade too, but that's a different matter.) Everything I know I got from a book or a conversation with someone who knows what they're doing (and you can find those books and people as easily as I can). However, I have tasted many homemade sparklers that were straight-up delicious, made by people who did not otherwise seem to have extra-human powers. So clearly, kids, you can do this at home.

Adopting the sparkling mindset

Sparkling winemakers aren't like the rest of us; they do everything differently.

Dessert wines violate most of the basic rules for making table wines; sparklers violate the rest of them. Grapes, whatever the variety used, need to be harvested short of normal ripeness, down around 18° to 20° Brix. Those really tart grapes get fermented into really tart, dry wines — called *base wines.* Base wines are high enough in acidity that tasting them takes an iron palate, and thinking ahead to how they will work as finished bubblies takes practice. The base wine gets a dose of sugar and a fresh dose of yeast, goes into a heavy Champagne-style bottle with a beer-style crown cap, and does another mini-fermentation, filling the bottle with carbon dioxide bubbles.

The bottle, stuck by the neck into a rack, gradually gets rotated from right-side-up to upside-down, little by little — a process called *riddling* — until all the dead yeast gunk is collected in the neck of the bottle, which is now pointing down. To close the deal, the neck is machine-frozen, gunk and all. The bottle gets set right-side-up again, the crown cap comes off, and the pressure blasts the plug of yeast out of the bottle.

Within a second or two, using your hands and various kinds of semi-automated equipment, the bottle gets refilled to replace the wine that spritzed out. A small dose of fresh sugar syrup is usually added to balance the acidity, and the final, Champagne-style cork gets inserted.

Piece of cake, once you get the hang of it.

Or, as always, you can try Plan B: Ferment the base wine, clean it up, kill any remaining yeast with potassium sorbate, and filter it. Put the wine into a beer keg and fill it with bubbles under gas pressure. Then move it from the keg into bottles, again under pressure. Alternatively, use a soda canister, the technology soda jerks used to carbonate fizzy drinks on the spot by pumping gas into syrup; you just use wine instead.

These aren't the methods Dom Perignon used in the monastery in the old days when the blind monk (my winemaking hero) allegedly "saw stars" and invented sparkling wine. Does it work? Why else would it be in this book?

Making good grape choices

The Champagne region in France built its reputation on three grapes: Chardonnay, Pinot Noir, and Pinot Meunier. The rest of the world tends to regard these as the "real" sparkling wine grapes. But lots of other varieties make delightful bubbly. Aromatic whites are good candidates — Riesling, Chenin Blanc, Muscat, Gewürztraminer. Several French-American hybrid grapes, especially Seyval, make great sparklers. And leave it to the Aussies to find a way to put bubbles into Shiraz: big, fat, fruity, dark, fizzy red wine.

Part VI
The Part of Tens

In this part . . .

In handy list format, this part shares warnings about things that can go wrong (and how to make them less likely), ideas about rendering your winemaking more economical without lowering quality, and my contributions to the eternal debate over home brewing versus home winemaking.

Chapter 21

Ten Mistakes Most Home Winemakers Make at Least Once

Good winemaking involves scrupulous attention to detail, even for the most experimental, free-spirited winemakers. Of course, nobody's perfect; ask any veteran commercial winemaker about notable cellar mishaps, and you'll be in for a long evening. This chapter can help you avoid some of the most common home winemaking mistakes, which makes it a good checklist to consult now and then to make sure you're paying attention.

Full disclosure: I have committed every mistake listed, except the last one.

The Old "Malolactic in the Bottle" Trick

You need to control malolactic fermentation by either preventing it from happening at all or making sure it finishes completely. Getting stuck in the middle is your basic winemaker's nightmare. When that happens, the nice, clear white wine you bottled three months ago suddenly has floating strands of crud in it, not to mention stale vegetable aromas and possibly enough carbon dioxide pressure to blow the corks out.

Take appropriate steps to squelch malolactic fermentation or complete it, and always run tests. Otherwise, an unpleasant surprise in one vintage or another is inevitable. (Chapter 7 is the place to turn for a full discussion.) Rest assured that malolactic malfunctions don't just happen to novice homies; prominent wineries have had to issue recalls.

Failure to Test

Testing for malolactic activity or completion is just the tip of the testing iceberg. Your taste buds may tell you how much you like your grapes or your wine, but they can't tell you everything. Without testing for sugar at harvest, how do you know if you need to add water or sugar to get the wine in balance? Without testing for residual sugar, how do you know it's really dry, and not likely to start re-fermenting? Without testing for pH, how do you know how much sulfur dioxide to add to keep the wine stable? Can you imagine a chef not knowing the oven temperature? I talk about testing issues in Chapter 7 and give advice on SO_2 quantities in Appendix D.

Doing Math in Your Head . . . Badly

Many winemaking operations require doing simple math: Dividing A by B and then multiplying by C to get the additions for water, sugar, acid, and sulfur dioxide right, or for figuring proportions when you're blending, or preparing samples — the list goes on.

You can do some calculations in your head. Others might trip you up, like those with pesky decimal points. If NASA scientists can still get metric and U.S. measurements mixed up on Mars rockets, you can mess up in your garage, too. With things like acid and SO_2, a math error can ruin your wine.

Do calculations on paper, so you can see the steps; do them twice; and don't do them in a hurry.

Sanitation "Good Enough for Home Winemaking"

Knowing that you can't easily match the sanitation levels of controlled commercial facilities in your laundry room or garage can tempt you to not bother trying. The cleaning required for winemaking soaks up time and takes a lot of work, so shortcuts can be quite attractive. The most common lapses in sanitation come from assuming that something that *looks* clean *is* clean — despite the fact that *microbes*, as the name suggests, are only visible through a *microscope* — and from assuming that something you cleaned two weeks ago is still clean today. I harp on the importance of sanitation in Chapter 4.

Letting Temperature Slide

Of all the environmental variables in home winemaking, temperature is the most often neglected. I've heard plenty of excuses. "I don't have a really cool place in my house, so my white wines ferment pretty warm — nothing I can do about it." Get some ice; get a fan. "I was fermenting such a small amount of red grapes, and it was winter, and the temperature never got very high." Get an electric blanket. Particularly during fermentation, do something — temperature matters. Chapter 4 addresses temperature in more detail.

Sloppy Topping

Minimizing headspace and keeping oxygen at bay with tight-fitting bungs and airlocks seems simple enough. But normal life can distract you from winemaking. It's easy to let a barrel go too long without checking on evaporation, thus promoting oxidation, or to let all the water in an airlock evaporate, allowing air inside a carboy. Making good wine means keeping close watch, even when you think nothing's happening. You would be amazed at how often bungs and airlocks simply fall off, or pop out because the wine warms up and increases in volume, or get toppled by the winery cat, or get knocked off their perches by the carbon dioxide from alcoholic or malolactic fermentation. Check early; check often.

Not Labeling Your Wine Jugs

As soon as you have two containers of wine — well, at least two containers of wine of the same color — the chances of getting them confused grow exponentially. Once you get to three or four reds or whites, it's a jungle. Commercial wineries have horror stories about accidentally pumping a tank of Merlot into a tank of Sauvignon Blanc and then having to sell their "rosé" on the bulk wine market.

Label everything, even when the jugs' contents seem obvious to you. And pay special attention after a racking session, when a former Zinfandel carboy may now contain Syrah. No, you can't just remember.

Drifting Attention during Routine Operations

Letting your mind wander is natural, but not useful in your winery. Watching wine gently flow from point A to point B is mesmerizing. Racking wine from a barrel into a series of carboys can take five minutes per container, and instead of standing around, you convince yourself you can run inside the house and grab a cup of coffee — and you get back ten seconds too late to find wine all over the floor. Running a filtration, you strike up a conversation with your assistant cellar master, only to discover you have been sucking air from the now-empty source for a good while, flooding your filtered wine with oxygen. As soon as you think a process can run itself, it won't: guaranteed.

Waiting (and Wishing) for Problems to Go Away

Winemakers often convince themselves that time alone will heal everything. Because some aspects of wine do indeed change with time, this illusion is even more attractive: Tutti-frutti fermentation aromas dissipate; in-your-face oak flavors recede; flavor profiles change during aging. But the stink of hydrogen sulfide doesn't go away; volatile acidity stays around; chemical imbalances like high pH or searing acidity don't right themselves (Chapter 8 gets into all this). Waiting to fix a problem only makes matters worse.

Underestimating Your Wine (making)

Cooks who present guests with homemade pies get oohs and aaahs and maybe a round of applause. Home winemakers deserve the same, but too often pour their efforts with an apology: "It's just homemade." *Just?* If you follow the most basic procedures in this book, you'll make commercial-grade wine; if you add a few simple wrinkles — the things discussed in Parts III and IV — you will make very good wine indeed.

Don't be defensive about being an amateur; you deserve bonus points for doing it without getting paid.

The attitude you project about your wine — not by boasting, but by things like putting real labels on it and serving it alongside wines from the pros — affects how your wine tastes to you and your growing circle of admirers.

Chapter 22

Ten Ways To Save Money (and Make Better Wine)

As I write this chapter, a major worldwide recession is taking the fun out of a lot of people's discretionary budgets, and putting a crimp in the wine business. But even in boomier times, home winemaking isn't cheap, and those of us without inherited wealth have to look for ways to save a buck (or a Euro, or whatever). This chapter offers tips on corralling costs without sacrificing wine quality.

Make More Wine

Increasing your production may seem like the last way to save money, but if you calculate costs by the bottle, the economies of scale are compelling. Buying grapes in larger quantities can get you a break on the price; using carboys and fermenters more than once in a season spreads the capital investment across more output; bottles, corks, chemicals, testing kits, and other supplies get cheaper when you buy them in higher volumes.

And if the total bill for the season appears daunting, spread the costs around. You can't legally peddle your homemade wine, but you can recruit another winemaking co-conspirator or two as winery partners, filling "their" carboys right alongside "your" carboys, and sharing the costs. Bonus feature: Your helpers love to do routine, boring chores around the winery.

Make Several Wines from One Grape

Instead of making more wine, try making more kinds of wine from the same raw material — which makes you feel as though you've made more wine. Just about any red grape, for example, can be trisected into a little rosé, a lot of red wine, and a teensy batch of a fortified, sweetened, port-like dessert wine. If whites are your thing, make some dry and some sweet, or half oaked and half unoaked. And if you work with two or three grapes, the blending options multiply like yeast cells in sugar syrup.

Instead of having more of one wine than you can drink, you end up with wines for multiple uses and occasions. As a bonus feature, you find out a lot more about different styles of winemaking.

Find Cheap Grapes . . . Carefully

After a couple harvests, you'll start to hear about good deals on grapes. You may hear about excess fruit some grower can't sell, so-called *second crop* grapes that ripen after the main harvest has been completed, or the fruit of start-up and backyard vineyards. They may be terrific grapes, but they may not: Be careful.

Free or discounted grapes can be a bonanza, but they still have to meet quality standards: Bargain grapes may be "bargains" for a reason. Just because the price is attractive doesn't mean the wines will be charmers. No matter what the price, always find out as much as you can about your potential grapes before you get them home. Grapes are the main part of your winemaking budget, and good grapes are the only way to fine wine.

Make More Whites

White grapes are frequently cheaper than red ones, and the costs of white wine production are generally lower, because you spend little-to-no money on oak. Whites also turn around faster, heading for bottle in a few months, long before most reds, so you get a quicker drinkable return on your investment.

I know some home winemakers insist that only Big Reds are worth the trouble, but I beg to differ: Whites are versatile food wines, winners in warm weather, more challenging for the home winemaker, better bets in competitions (because of fewer entries), and just the thing to give Aunt Martha as a present.

Get Glamour-Free Grapes

Unless you have some amazing personal connections, prime Cabernet Sauvignon grapes are likely to be quite expensive, and Pinot Noir prices can put Cabernet costs to shame. Chances are, however, you can find a deal on Barbera, or Carignane, or Seyval grapes. Plenty of great wine gets made from non-glamour grapes, and your reduced investment brings new taste experiences, new dinner table conversations, new winemaking knowledge, and relief for jaded palates — yours and your friends.

Make the Most of Barrels

Moving up to using barrels, even small ones, requires a good chunk of change, so the wise winemaker gets the most out of that investment. Barrels perform two tasks — adding oak flavors and making rounder wines — and both contributions can be stretched out in an economical fashion. Properly maintained barrels are useful for years and years; the gush of vanilla and spice flavors disappears, but the effects on evaporation, concentration, and integration continue. If you need a hit of oak, toss in some chips. On the other hand, new barrels — especially smaller ones, half- and quarter-sized — can easily impart more oak flavor than your wine wants, so cycle two or more wines through for a few months at a time. You save money by using the same barrel for many purposes over many years, and you get better-balanced wine because you can control oak more closely.

Use Oak Alternatives

Barrels have totem-like status in the wine world. That's why nearly every winery shows visitors its barrel room, even though most barrels start to look the same on the second visit. Oak alternatives, on the other hand — staves, chips, cubes — are vaguely disreputable. Some winemakers feel using oak alternatives is a form of cheating associated with soulless industrial winemaking. I say, "Hogwash."

Your goal as a home winemaker is to make the best wine you can on the budget you have, and oak adjuncts are lifesavers. Oak chips in a carboy fermentation mimic the wood in barrel fermentations; oak cubes enhance flavor, overtly or subtly, at a fraction of a fraction of the cost of barrels; a handful of oak morsels gives the winemaker more precision in flavor coloration than a full barrel does. In a perfect world, I suppose all wine would be made in barrels; and in that same world, no fermentation would ever stick and every wine would score 100 points.

Stretch Out Bottling

Most novice home winemakers, thrilled that their maiden efforts really do taste like wine, insist on bottling the wine far too early. In the commercial marketplace, high-quality whites usually take a year or two to show up, reds take two or three or four. Too often, homies want their whites by the February after harvest and their reds by June, if not sooner.

Slow down the pace; let your wines grow up before you (and your friends) drink them. That way, you cut your annual budget and improve your wine. Sure, some light whites and pinks are ready to roll by the dawn of the new year, and bless their hearts; but bigger whites take a while, and serious reds just get better in barrel — even a dinky barrel — for a year or more. Time is not only money; it's quality, too.

Do the Equipment Math

For small quantities of home wine, and likely for your first few home crushes, invest cautiously in major equipment. Sure, you need a few carboys and maybe a trash can fermenter, some testing supplies and a few yards of plastic tubing, but hold off on that (USD)$500 basket press or (USD)$400 filter rig until you know you're seriously hooked.

Of course, after a while, all those (USD)$25-a-pop rental fees and crush fees and whatever fees add up, making owning your own equipment a money-saver. I started off renting everything, then bought a motorized crusher and a basket press, both of which were bigger than I needed. After selling them at a steep loss, I went back to paying through the nose for services, and then finally found used equipment that paid for itself in a single harvest. It took me years to realize that spending (USD)$100 on a hand-held pH meter would eliminate all sorts of testing costs. Don't be as clueless as I was; do the math.

Corners Not to Cut

Watching your budget is fine, but beware cutbacks that can undermine the quality of your wine. Skimping on sanitation, temperature control, accurate testing, or good-quality topping wine — and most of all, on grapes — would be the very definition of "penny wise and pound foolish." Better to cut back on production, or downgrade packaging, or skip the competition entry fees. The better your wine is, the more you'll want to drink it, and the less you'll spend on the commercial competition — another net gain in cash flow.

Chapter 23

Ten Differences between Wine(makers) and Beer(brewers)

In This Chapter

▶ Divinity versus Doppelbock

▶ Snob appeal meets suds power

▶ Geeks, party animals, and adult beverages

*H*ome winemaking and home beer brewing are both excellent hobbies. Both are great ways to make first-class beverages, and both activities will amaze, impress, and increase your circle of friends. And in both cases, alcohol is involved, and unlike distilling hard liquor, both are legal. Beyond that, the wine culture and the beer culture are much farther apart than Mars and Venus.

Wine Gods Rule

Beer and wine were both common in the ancient world, but only the wine gods got top billing: Dionysus in Greece and Bacchus in Rome. Later on, Christianity featured Biblical accounts of Jesus turning water into wine, not into pilsner, and the sacrament of communion in Catholic and some Protestant services isn't celebrated with India Pale Ale. Over several millennia, wine has been associated with the ecstatic, the romantic, the transcendent, and the artistic, beer mainly with darts, bleacher seats, and bar fights.

Only Wine Requires Training Classes

Novice wine drinkers are often terrified about their lack of knowledge: Where can I learn the right vocabulary? How do you read a German wine label? What the heck does "cassis" mean? Answering these questions requires an enormous wine education industry, full of beginner and advanced classes, critics (pompous and otherwise), and thousands of books about how to enjoy wine properly, free of embarrassing error. Mastering beer involves familiarity with basic refrigerator operation; knowledge of bottle cap removal — by twisting and church key; ability to pour without (much) spilling; and a knack for locating your own mouth. Class dismissed.

Only Beer Has Drunken Frat Boy Ads

Beer advertising seems designed to tie the beverage as closely as possible to brain-dead, loutish, testosterone-driven behavior — an odd, if wildly successful, strategy. Wine advertising is close to non-existent — another peculiar strategy. Some of us remember the golden years of Orson Welles intoning a vow to "sell no wine before its time," which in the case of the Paul Masson wines of that era (the 1970s) probably meant the minute it was bottled, if at all. Welles was dumped for admitting he never touched the brand he pitched, and wine advertising never regained its stride. How about bright-eyed, well-coiffed sorority girls practicing their French by trying to pronounce *Muscadet de Sèvre de Maine*, while sipping some? Maybe returning veterans extolling the values of the flag, apple pie, and "big, fat, juicy, *&%##+^-ing Zinfandel!" Anything would be better than the beer ads.

Nobody Cares whether Beer Can Age

Fine wines develop interesting qualities with age, but the obsession with ageworthiness can go too far. A wine shop customer, selecting a bottle with a life expectancy of an hour and a half, will nonetheless often ask the staffer, "Will it age?" The staffer will make something up, and both will nod knowingly. This kind of exchange does not occur in the beer world. Now, if someone offers to share a rare Barolo from the 1970s with me, I will be most appreciative; but if the proposed treat is a 1985 Moosehead that has been saved for an occasion just like this, I will likely have other plans.

A corollary: When was the last time you saw a magazine article about a well-heeled beer collector with a 65,000-bottle cellar?

Sparklers, not Suds, Launch Ships

Wine — especially sparkling wine, the form most like beer — has a hammerlock on special occasions. Champagne is the commissioning beverage of choice in every seafaring nation, even beer-happy Germany. Perhaps it's the greater price that makes bubbly appropriate to the occasion; but somehow, hurling cases of beer against the prow of a new ocean liner wouldn't have the same cachet. More peculiar, given the endless association of beer and sports, the locker rooms of World Series winners are afoam with bubbly, some being consumed, some shaken up and sprayed at the cameras — behavior much more appropriate to beer. I'm sure some wedding receptions have toasted the happy couple with mugs of Guinness, but I've never been invited to one of those occasions. New Year's Eve: bubbly. But note: Beer rules at beach volleyball competitions.

Pairing — Simple and Complex

Wine drinkers obsess about the "right" wine to go with particular foods — much more than chefs worry about the "right" vegetable to accompany catfish or the "right" dessert after a meal of pasta primavera. Many wine writers and publishers of newspapers, magazines, and books think the pairing ritual constitutes a pressing social problem, worthy of endless ink and bandwidth. Frequently, the recommended matches feature a fancy dish that uses obscure ingredients and a wine with an unpronounceable name made from a minor grape variety from a fly-away part of the former Yugoslavia — available in only one wine shop west of the Mississippi. Good luck reproducing that magic moment.

The way out of this house of mirrors is to drink wine you like with food you like, which is how the beer-drinking public does it. If you're an ale fan, you'll probably like it just fine with a rib eye steak, filet of sole, or celery sticks and onion-soup dip. And if you're in a lager mood, you won't lose much sleep about whether it goes with fried chicken or Thai curry.

Nobody Makes Fraudulent Beer

Imitation, we are told, is the sincerest form of flattery. On that premise, a brisk business in counterfeit wine has thrived for centuries, sometimes just putting fancy labels on pure plonk, sometimes going to extravagant lengths to make junk wine seem old and authentic. The famous "Thomas Jefferson wines" that surfaced in the 1980s — ostensibly vintages from the best Bordeaux houses in the 1780s, allegedly belonging to the wine-savvy third president of the United States — were elaborate forgeries, meriting a delightful book, *The Billionaire's Vinegar*. Cutting-edge research chemists hold international conferences devoted to newer and better analytical methods for detecting wine fraud: Did you know, for example, that wines from the second half of the 20th century can be vintage-dated by measuring the amount of Carbon-14 they contain, residue from the era of atmospheric nuclear testing in the 1950s?

Wine is well worth faking; beer, not so much. Why invest thousands of dollars in a scheme to manufacture and market ersatz Molson Export Ale or Dos Equis Amber? Why not just brew some beer, give it a goofy name, and sell it? American patriot Sam Adams's name graces a beer brand, but no one claims it came from his estate.

Restaurant Respect

Wine drinkers get considerably more attention at restaurants than beer drinkers, and the snazzier the eatery, the greater the disparity. Leather-bound wine lists go on forever; beer lists run half a page, if that. Sommeliers may drink a lot of beer in their free time, but they get paid to offer guidance about wine. Opening wine at the table is an elaborate ritual; when was the last time a waiter offered you the chance to sniff a crown cap? Good restaurants, believing that the customer is always right, let people return wines with or without reason; can you imagine the look on your waitperson's face if you said, "I think this pitcher of Heineken is corked"?

The Best of Both Worlds

For all its elevated status, snob value, and air of superiority, the wine world has an open secret that levels the adult beverage playing field: Commercial winemakers and homies drink a lot of beer in the course of their winemaking. No evidence exists for a corresponding stampede of brewers to pop the cork on a good Bordeaux while drying their hops.

Mixing Patience with Fun

The staff at my local beer and winemaking shop has observed thousands of customers over nearly 30 years in the business, and they offered me one simple generalization about the two camps of producers: Home winemakers have more patience, but home brewers have more fun. If you've read this far, you know why wine needs patience; but on the fun part, join me in turning that demeaning comparison around. *Santé!*

Part VII
Appendixes

The 5th Wave   By Rich Tennant

"The wine is supposed to breathe, Martin,
not hyperventilate."

In this part . . .

For reference, this final section includes details on topics that come up throughout the book (or may have crossed your mind) again and again:

- ✔ A glossary of winemaking terms

- ✔ Conversions for United States measures to metric, grapes to wine, and so on

- ✔ Resources for information, equipment, and grapes

- ✔ Calculations for determining sulfur dioxide additions and their relationship to pH levels

Appendix A

Glossary

acid, acidity: Element in grapes and wine that produces sensations of tartness in the mouth; wine grapes primarily contain *tartaric acid*, but also likely *malic acid* and some other trace acids.

airlock: A plastic fixture filled with water and inserted into a rubber stopper that keeps air out of carboys.

bung: A solid stopper, generally made from silicone, for closing off barrels.

cap: The floating mass of grape skins and seeds that rises to the top during red wine fermentation.

carbon dioxide (CO_2): A gas produced during fermentation, and the basis of carbonation of sparkling wines. CO_2 is also used in home winemaking as an inert protection against oxidation.

carboy: A narrow-mouthed glass or plastic jug used for fermenting white and pink wines and storing white, pink, and red wines for aging.

crush: Using pressure to crack grape skins and release juices, the first step in winemaking; also shorthand for the whole annual period of harvest and fermentation.

crusher-destemmer: Machinery, either hand-crank or motorized, that separates grape berries from the stems and cracks the skins, letting juice run.

dry or **dryness:** The condition in which all the available and fermentable sugar has been transformed into ethanol.

enology: The systematic, scientific study of winemaking.

fermentation: Also known as *primary* or *alcoholic fermentation*, the process by which yeast activity transforms sugar into ethyl alcohol.

filtration: Removing particulate matter from wine by forcing it through a filter medium under pressure; the *tighter* the filtration, the smaller the trapped particles.

fining: The use of various chemical or biological agents to remove one or more compounds from a wine to improve clarity, stability, or balance.

free run: The wine that drains out of a wine press operation without the application of pressure, as opposed to press wine.

fruit: Grapes grow in clusters of individual berries, all of which frequently just gets called fruit.

headspace: The empty area at the top of any wine container, filled with air or inert gas.

hydrogen sulfide (H_2S): The most common and prominent of a group of sulfur-containing compounds produced by yeast that is exposed to too much stress (from temperature or nutrient deficiency, for example); aromas range from rotten eggs to rancid garlic.

lees: Dead, spent yeast after the conclusion of a fermentation.

lees contact or **lees stirring** or **bâtonnage:** Keeping wine in contact with spent yeast during aging, and sometimes stirring it around, to continue extraction of desirable compounds.

malolactic fermentation (malo, ML, or MLF): The process by which bacterial cultures transform malic acid from grapes into lactic acid.

must: Juice that is ready for fermentation, either by itself for white wines or mixed with grape skins, pulp, and seeds for red wine fermentation

off-dry: Refers to slightly sweet wines, with 1 or 2 percent residual sugar, as opposed to very sweet dessert wines.

pH: The measure of the balance of positively and negatively charged ions (or the balance of acidic and base properties) in a substance. The neutral, even balance of water is defined as a pH of 7.0; wine runs in the range of 3.0 to 4.0. For many winemaking decisions, knowing the pH is extremely important.

phenolics: Important compounds in wine grape skins, including pigments (anthocyanins) and tannins.

press: Manual or motorized machinery that squeezes juice from grapes before or after fermentation.

punchdown: Pushing the cap of skins and seeds that floats to the top of a red wine fermentation back into the liquid to aid extraction.

racking: Transferring wine as it settles and ages from one container to another, leaving dead yeast and other solids behind. Racking is accomplished either with a pump or by gravity siphon through a racking tube.

residual sugar (rs): Unfermented sugar left, intentionally or unintentionally, in a fermented wine.

sulfur dioxide (SO$_2$): Chemical compounds widely used in wineries for protecting wine from spoilage and sanitizing equipment. This substance is behind the phrase "contains sulfites" on wine labels.

stuck fermentation: A problem arising when yeast ceases or greatly slows down its activity during fermentation, leaving unfermented sugar and producing off odors — not a good thing.

terroir: French term for the concept that the natural character of the place grapes are grown — soil, climate, and so on — is reflected in the distinctive taste of the wines made from those grapes.

thief: Metal, glass, or plastic tube used for drawing small samples of wine from larger containers.

topping off: Adding wine to a carboy or barrel to minimize the air inside.

vinifera: Species of grape most familiar to North American winemakers. It includes Chardonnay, Cabernet, and so on. Good wine also gets made from indigenous North American grape species and from French-American hybrids such as Chambourcin and Seyval.

vintner: Someone who makes wine, or who owns a winery, whether amateur or professional.

viticulture: Techniques and practices for wine grape growing; counterpart to enology.

volatile acidity (VA): Vinegary or nail-polish-remover aromas produced by acetic acid and other compounds, often the result of unwanted bacterial activity. A little is inevitable, too much is dreadful.

whole cluster press: An operation that skips destemming and crushing and gets right to the squeezing of juice. Often used by commercial white wine makers, this technique is difficult to pull off at home.

Appendix B

Conversions

∙ ∙

This appendix offers general guides to useful winemaking conversions of various sorts.

Volume, Weight, and Temperature

Throughout the book, I give you temperatures and volumes in both U.S. measures and their rough metric equivalents. But when you need to do your own math, turn to the commonly used conversions used in winemaking:

- **Liquid volume:**
  - 1 gallon = 3.79 liters
  - 1 liter = 0.26 gallons
- **Weight:**
  - 1 pound = 0.45 kilograms
  - 1 kilogram = 2.29 pounds
- **Temperature:**
  - Fahrenheit = $(C \times 9/5) + 32$
  - Celsius = $(F - 32) \times 5/9$

Land to Grapes to Bottles

Chances are you're curious about the conversions unique to grape growing and winemaking — such as how many pounds of grapes go into a bottle of wine, or how many liters of wine in a case, or how many cases get made from an acre of vines. Well, the following table satisfies your curiosity:

Volume to Measure	U.S. Measure	Metric Measure
Vineyard unit	1 acre = .40 hectare	1 hectare = 2.47 acres
Yield units	1 U.S. ton = .91 metric ton 1 pound = .45 kilograms	1 metric ton = 1.10 U.S. tons 1 kilogram = 2.20 pounds
Vineyard yield (premium grapes)	3 U.S. tons/acre	6.74 metric tonne/hectare
Liquid volume unit	1 gallon = 3.79 liters	1 liter = .26 gallon
Yield of grapes to wine (commercial)	1 ton = 175 gallons red; 1 ton = 160 gallons white	1 metric ton = 730 liters red; 1 metric ton = 667 liters white
Yield of grapes to wine (home)	100 pounds = 7 gallons red, 6 gallons white 1 U.S. ton = 140 gallons red, 120 gallons white	100 kilograms = 58 liters red, 50 liters white 1 metric ton = 583 liters red, 500 liters white
Liquid to bottles (750 ml bottles)	1 gallon = 5.1 bottles	1 liter = 1.33 bottles
Cases to liquid	1 case = 2.38 gallons	1 case = 9 liters
Cases per ton (commercial)	1 U.S. ton = 75 cases red, 68 cases white	1 metric ton = 83 cases red, 72 cases white
Grapes per bottle (home)	2.8 pounds of red grapes per 750-milliliter bottle, 3.25 pounds of white	1.27 kilograms of red grapes per 750-milliliter bottle, 1.47 kilograms of white

Appendix C

Resources

· ·

*H*ome winemaking resources are everywhere — all over the Web, as near as your local wine or beer-making shop, and quite possibly available through the commercial wineries you visit anyway. A quick Internet search for the phrase "home winemaking" yields more Web sites than you want to visit. Join a winemaking club or visit a shop, and your cup — er, wineglass — of information will runneth over.

This appendix contains a short list of useful winemaking resources. You can likely find many more on your own, but the resources I name here are those I've found valuable and that will probably be around for a while.

Print Publications

Although the Internet holds vast quantities of information, sometimes a solid, print publication is just the ticket.

Magazines

My one big plug in this department is for *WineMaker* magazine (http://winemakermag.com) — a magazine for which, fortuitously enough, I have written for several years. As hobby magazines go, this one is serious. It covers everything from kit wines to home vineyards and contains technically solid articles that get reviewed before they get published. Tell 'em I sent you, and they'll charge you exactly the same as anyone else.

For more hardcore homies, commercial wine trade magazines (and their Web sites) can be full of interesting information. I suggest checking out *Wines & Vines* (www.winesandvines.com), *Vineyard & Winery Management* (www.vwm-online.com), and *Practical Winery & Vineyard* (www.practicalwinery.com).

And for those hopelessly beyond hardcore, the *American Journal of Enology and Viticulture* (www.ajevonline.org) publishes cutting-edge winemaking and grapegrowing research from around the world. Be prepared to deal with lots of chemistry chicken wire diagrams and Latin species names.

Books

Neither I nor the good folks at John Wiley & Sons want to spend much time promoting other home winemaking books in this space. However, you can find excellent titles on specialized subjects that don't get much attention in this book — fruit wines, mead, and so on. And because winemaking is hardly an exact science, someone else's spin on things can be useful, too.

I do suggest one publication that is in no way competition — because it's free. The 44-page booklet, *Making Table Wine at Home*, by George M. Cooke and James T. Lapsley of the University of California at Davis, is available in hardcopy or as a set of downloadable PDFs from `wineserver.ucdavis.edu/content.php?category=Winemaking`.

For the truly technically minded, two standard references are *Principles and Practices of Winemaking*, by Roger B. Boulton, Vernon L. Singleton, Linda F. Bisson, and Ralph E. Kunkee (Aspen Publishers, 1999) and the *Handbook of Enology,* by P. Ribéreau-Gayon, D. Dubourdieu, B. Donèche, and A. Lonvaud (John Wiley & Sons, 2006, two volumes). These books aren't cheap, but they are full of scientific winemaking information.

Online Information

Home winemaking Web sites abound, and the following are worth visiting:

- ✔ **The British Columbia Amateur Winemakers Association** (`www.bcawa.ca`) offers a wealth of solid technical information.

- ✔ **The Sacramento** (California) **Home Winemakers** Web site (`www.sachomewine.org`) offers useful section about winemaking chemistry and provides links for purchasing grapes.

- ✔ **Wine Press.US** (`www.winepress.us`) has an eclectic mix of winemaking info, discussion forums, home winemaking photos, and more, including discussions of kit and fruit wines.

- ✔ *WineMaker* magazine's Web site includes a Resource Guide page (`www.winemakermag.com/guide`) which includes a sulfur dioxide dosage calculator, a blending spreadsheet, and a locator for home winemaking clubs in your area.

Nearly every state and province has some form of agricultural extension service, normally connected to local universities, and many of them have some focus on grapegrowing and winemaking. One of the best is the collection of Enology Notes publications from Virginia Tech (`www.fst.vt.edu/extension/enology/enologynotes.html`), but check out your own region, too.

Grapes and Juice

Keeping track of all the grape sources for home winemakers in North America is a fruitless — pardon that one — task. You'll have better luck asking around and hitting the Web than reading whatever list I could compile, which would be out of date faster than you can say "Tempranillo."

One longstanding, highly reputable source of grapes for both the United States and Canada does merit a mention: Brehm Vineyards (`www.brehm vineyards.com`). Peter Brehm did a lot to point home winemakers toward fresh grapes in the 1970s, and he still distributes a wide variety of premium fruit, fresh and frozen, from prime vineyards in California, Oregon, and Washington.

Equipment and Supplies

The winemaking shops and online suppliers on this list should be able to supply anything mentioned in this book, with the exception of the final two specialized purveyors.

- ✔ **E.C. Kraus** (`www.eckraus.com/index.htm`) offers a range of wine kits and all manner of equipment.

- ✔ **Fall Bright, the Winemakers Shoppe** (`www.fallbright.com`) in upstate New York offers grapes, juice, winemaking supplies, and endless links for information.

- ✔ **Home Brew Heaven** (`http://store.homebrewheaven.com`) sells winemaking equipment, supplies, kits, fruit wine bases, testing equipment, and more.

- ✔ **More Wine!** (`http://morewinemaking.com`) sells anything and everything in winemaking equipment and supplies, from the humblest gizmo to multiple yeast products to professional-grade machinery.

- ✔ **Oak Barrel Winecraft** (`www.oakbarrel.com/`) in Berkeley, California (my local shop) has been a Bay Area institution for three decades, offering the full range of supplies, equipment, and grapes.

- ✔ **Presque Isle Wine Cellars** (`www.piwine.com`) in Pennsylvania offers winemaking equipment, discussion boards, and information for finding grapes in the Lake Erie area.

- ✔ **StaVin** (`www.stavin.com/homewines/products.htm`), one of California's leading providers of oak products for the commercial wine industry, also caters to home winemakers.

- **The Wine Smith** (www.thewinesmith.biz) in Mobile, Alabama, sells a full range of home wine and beer-making supplies and equipment, in a state whose policies are not exactly pro-alcohol.

- **Wine Aromas** (www.winearomas.com) sells one very specialized but extremely useful line of products: kits of small sample vials of aroma samples, everything from red wine and white wine aromas to smelly wine faults, under the name Le Nez du Vin. A great way to train your snitter.

- **Winemaking Superstore** (www.winemakingsuperstore.com) has a name that says it all — it has everything from chemicals to testing equipment to machinery to labeling supplies.

People

No room here for all the names and addresses of helpful folks who could give you good advice on winemaking. But your part of the world probably has its own stockpile of knowledgeable people — you just have to look for them.

Start with other home winemakers. Get to know your fellow vinifiers through winemaking shops or online bulletin boards or local winemaking clubs. A few homies may be too full of themselves to chat with mere novices, but 99 percent are happy to talk, share stories, offer advice, and pour their wines as examples. You can even learn a good deal from tasting someone else's badly made, not-that-tasty wine; it might be full of clues about approaches to avoid.

Commercial winemakers are also much more willing to help a homie out than you might think. I don't recommend calling a winery halfway across the country at two in the morning to ask for help with your stuck fermentation, but if you haunt the tasting room of a particular winery, or if you're signed up for its wine club, or you met the winemaker at a wine dinner, chances are you can get information, moral support, and may even a line on some good grapes. Commercial winemakers spend their lives helping each other out — and as a homie, you aren't even part of the competition.

Appendix D

Sulfur Dioxide (SO$_2$) and pH

Wineries use *sulfur dioxide* — otherwise known as SO$_2$ — for two distinct purposes: cleaning equipment and preserving wine against microbial and oxidative spoilage. To do both jobs, you add SO$_2$ in different doses, preparation types, and with different levels of precision. Also, to properly use sulfur dioxide as a wine additive, you need a basic understanding of the underlying chemistry, which includes understanding that pH is part of the equation.

Forms of SO$_2$

Sulfur dioxide is available as a liquid, powder, tablet, and gas. Winemakers, both commercial and home, have all manner of systems for making up different solutions to suit their purposes.

Most often, home winemakers (and many commercial wineries) use powdered *potassium metabisulfite* — sometimes referred to as PMBS, or KMB/KMBS (K is the chemical symbol for potassium) — as their source of SO$_2$. PMBS isn't identical to SO$_2$, and doesn't even contain pure SO$_2$. But when PMBS is dissolved in water or wine, chemical reactions produce pure molecules of SO$_2$, which is the active agent that does the work. PMBS is also available in convenient, pre-measured tablets (Campden tablets). But because winemakers need to have an accurate scale for measuring all kinds of additives and ingredients, you might as well measure your own PMBS, too, because you need it for various purposes.

Sanitizing with SO$_2$

Sulfur dioxide dissolved in water is a winery sanitation mainstay. SO$_2$ isn't a great cleaner — sodium percarbonate and elbow grease are my candidates for that job — but it does kill off stray microbes. Using SO$_2$ as part of the cleaning/sanitizing regimen for carboys, tanks, barrels, equipment, hoses, tools, bottles, and surfaces should be an integral part of your winery routine.

My suggestion is to make up a 10 percent solution of PMBS. Dissolve 1½ cups of PMBS in a gallon of cool water (or 100 grams per liter of water) and stir it thoroughly. Keep the solution in a closed container. When you want to use some of the solution, dilute it by half by adding water; at the full 10 percent strength, the SO_2 solution can literally take your breath away.

Use the diluted solution for rinsing equipment and storage vessels after cleaning them, and for dipping small tools — a thief for drawing wine samples, a stirring rod, a hydrometer for measuring Brix — before each use, so as not to carry stray microbes from one barrel or sample to the next. Keep the solution in a covered, clearly marked container, and make up a fresh batch in whatever quantity you need every two or three months. The strength of the SO_2 will dissipate with evaporation, but because you are using this solution for cleaning, the precise strength isn't important.

Do **not** use warm or hot water for making up your SO_2 solution. Heat will cause the sulfur aromas to become airborne immediately, causing burning sensations in your nose and throat. A small sniff won't hurt most people, though breathing SO_2 can be dangerous for people with asthma. SO_2 in all its forms is a toxic substance — remember, you're using it to kill things — so handle it with caution.

Adding SO₂ Based on pH

Beyond winery sanitation, SO_2 keeps the wine itself clean and stops troublesome microbial invaders and the ravages of oxidation. The philosophical debate about sulfur dioxide additions gets covered in Chapter 4; this appendix covers the how-to part.

You typically add sulfur dioxide (in the form of potassium metabisulfite, or PMBS) at three points in the winemaking process:

- ✔ Right at or after crushing, to knock down initial microbial counts
- ✔ Right after fermentation is complete (including a malolactic fermentation, if that's in the cards), to stabilize the wine during aging
- ✔ At bottling, to provide some insurance for the wine's continued cleanliness

In addition to these three points in your wine's lifetime, extended aging for several months (reds or whites) means you should periodically monitor the SO_2 levels, which fall over time, and probably give them a booster shot or two along the way.

The timing is easy to grasp; but calculating the amounts takes some careful work. Determining the amount of PMBS to add to your wine depends on a combination of the following:

- The **purpose** of the addition
- The **pH** of the wine
- The **existing level of SO$_2$** in the wine
- The **volume** of wine or juice to be treated
- The results of your **calculations**

Rather than making the math even more complicated by using a solution of PMBS in water, I suggest simply calculating the SO$_2$ required for a particular addition, measuring out the appropriate amount of PMBS (see the upcoming tables) on a scale, dissolving it in a little cool water or a bit of juice or wine — three or four times the volume of the PMBS — and stirring it into the wine.

I have two pieces of advice about SO$_2$ additions:

- One large dose of SO$_2$ generally has a bigger impact — more shock for the microbes — than a series of small ones; adding 30 parts per million (ppm) once is more effective than adding 10 ppm three times.

- If you aren't exactly sure about how to approach a particular SO$_2$ addition, err on the low side, not the high side. You can always retest the level and add more; you can't take it out.

The best way to understand how pH, SO$_2$ levels, wine volume, and the math all work together is to go through the different occasions when you may need to add SO$_2$. The final sections of this appendix walk you through the scenarios.

At the crusher

This one's easy. The purpose of adding SO$_2$ at the crusher is to get bad microbes out of the way of the good ones — clearing the path for the yeast you are about to add. In this case, the pH of the juice doesn't matter, and the existing level of SO$_2$ is bound to be zero. Standard practice, therefore, is simply to add 25 to 50 ppm of SO$_2$ (in the form of PMBS) to the crushed grapes or pressed juice.

For 1 gallon of crushed grapes or pressed juice, the initial addition would be between 0.20 and 0.33 grams of PMBS; multiply by the number of gallons of pressed white juice or the potential volume of red wine (7 gallons per 100 pounds). Per liter or crushed grapes or pressed juice, the addition would be between .05 and .08 grams. See Table Appendix D-1.

Weigh out the proper amount of PMBS, dissolve it in a small amount of cool water, and be sure to stir and mix the addition thoroughly into the juice.

After fermentation

This is the most important time for getting the SO_2 right. After the yeast and (if you choose) the malolactic bacteria have done their jobs, your wine has no need of further microbial activity. Layer upon layer of chemical reactions may work their magic, but the microbial phase is over. At this point, a relatively large SO_2 addition, determined by the wine's pH, seals the transition from fermentation to aging.

The SO_2 added at the crusher has now disappeared, bound up with other compounds or fallen out of the wine, so the starting level is for all practical purposes zero. Three variables affect the math. I strongly advise you to read through the next few paragraphs at least once to grasp the logic; from then on, you can just use the tables in this appendix.

The most important variable is the wine's pH, which will likely not be the same as it was at harvest. So you need to take a fresh, accurate measurement.

The pH of the wine controls how a given addition of PMBS sorts itself out in chemical reactions; in technical chemistry terms, what matters is the amount of SO_2 in the *molecular* form. What you need to know is that the lower the pH, the greater the portion of an addition that arrives in the molecular form; the higher the pH, the smaller the proportion. Furthermore, the variation isn't simple and linear; it's a logarithmic connection, meaning a higher pH needs a much bigger addition to achieve the same effect. (One of the many reasons high pH winemaking is troublesome.)

Fortunately, Tables Appendix D-1 and Appendix D-2 help you figure this out.

Whether you're putting this wine through a malolactic fermentation plays a role in how much SO_2 you add. (Chapter 7 discusses the pros and cons of malolactic fermentation.) If you want to use sulfur dioxide to prevent malolactic and kill off the stray bacteria that might try to do the job, your wine needs a bigger addition of SO_2. If the wine has already gone through malolactic — as nearly all reds do — you can provide protection with a lower dosage. Those higher and lower levels are referred to respectively as *0.8 ppm molecular* and *0.5 ppm molecular*. You don't need to know all the chemistry behind those numbers, you just need to know what they signify in a table.

Finally, some of the molecular SO$_2$ you add to the wine soon gets bound up with other compounds and effectively neutralized as a fighting force; only part of it remains on duty. The combination of *free* and *bound* SO$_2$ is called *total* SO$_2$. You can measure free and total SO$_2$ and figure the bound portion by subtracting free from total. The implication is that to achieve the level of free SO$_2$ required at your wine's pH, you will need to add more than the target amount, because some SO$_2$ will end up bound.

The first step in calculating a post-fermentation sulfur addition is to look up the SO$_2$ level that corresponds to your wine's pH. Table Appendix D-1 includes that information for both the 0.5 and the 0.8 molecular targets.

Table Appendix D-1   Target SO$_2$ Levels for Different Wine pH

pH	0.5 ppm molecular	0.8 ppm molecular	pH	0.5 ppm molecular	0.8 ppm molecular
2.90	7 ppm	11 ppm	3.50	25 ppm	40 ppm
2.95	7 ppm	12 ppm	3.55	29 ppm	46 ppm
3.00	8 ppm	13 ppm	3.60	31 ppm	50 ppm
3.05	9 ppm	15 ppm	3.65	36 ppm	57 ppm
3.10	10 ppm	16 ppm	3.70	39 ppm	63 ppm
3.15	12 ppm	19 ppm	3.75	45 ppm	72 ppm
3.20	13 ppm	21 ppm	3.80	49 ppm	79 ppm
3.25	15 ppm	23 ppm	3.85	57 ppm	91 ppm
3.30	16 ppm	26 ppm	3.90	62 ppm	99 ppm
3.35	18 ppm	29 ppm	3.95	71 ppm	114 ppm
3.40	20 ppm	32 ppm	4.00	78 ppm	125 ppm
3.45	23 ppm	37 ppm			

The next step is to determine the quantity of PMBS needed to hit that target molecular SO$_2$ level for a given volume of wine. The numbers in Table Appendix D-2 include two "fudge factors" — that is, they account for the fact that not all of the PBMS turns into SO$_2$, and that some of the SO$_2$ will quickly become bound and ineffective. For the parts-per-million target in the left-hand column, add the number of grams of PBMS in the cell under the appropriate volume in the top row — and calculate anything in between.

Table Appendix D-2   Grams of PMBS for Different Volumes and Levels

Target Amount of SO_2	1 gal	5 gal	30 gal	1 liter	10 liters	100 liters
10 ppm	0.07	0.33	1.97	0.02	0.18	1.85
20 ppm	0.13	0.66	3.94	0.03	0.34	3.43
30 ppm	0.20	0.99	5.91	0.05	0.53	5.28
40 ppm	0.26	1.31	7.88	0.07	0.69	6.86
50 ppm	0.33	1.64	9.86	0.09	0.87	8.71
60 ppm	0.39	1.97	11.83	0.10	1.03	10.29
70 ppm	0.46	2.30	13.80	0.12	1.21	12.14
80 ppm	0.53	2.63	15.77	0.14	1.56	15.57
90 ppm	0.59	2.06	17.74	0.16	1.56	15.57
100 ppm	0.66	3.29	19.71	0.17	1.74	17.41

The reason Table Appendix D-2 doesn't cover every ppm addition and every volume is that — trust me — it will do you good to do some of the math yourself. The minute you get casual about SO_2 additions — settling for a quick glance at a dog-eared chart and carelessly dumping in chemicals — the chances of screwing up your wine increase dramatically.

You use a generic formula to make this calculation. For those still mired in U.S. measures, this will do the trick:

(gallons of wine) × (ppm of addition) × (0.0066) = grams of PMBS

(The 0.0066 factor converts the results to grams, a metric unit, and accounts for the fact that only a part of the PMBS turns into SO_2.)

If you're working in liters, the equivalent formula is:

$$\frac{\text{liters of wine} \times \text{ppm of addition}}{576}$$

After you have double-checked your math, weigh out the appropriate number of grams of PMBS, dissolve the PMBS in a small amount of water or wine — just enough to put it into solution — and add it to the wine. Give a good stir to spread it around.

At bottling

Like additions at the crusher, the final addition before bottling doesn't require advanced math. The purpose is just a final send-off, giving the wine protection against oxidation in the bottle. The 25 to 30 ppm range is normal practice for most reds and whites. A few minor variations are as follows:

- ✔ For **sweet wines,** a slightly higher addition — perhaps 50 ppm — is common, because the presence of sugar degrades the strength of the addition.

- ✔ For **low pH wines** — 3.3 and below — you may reduce the addition by one-third. A high level of SO_2 (high for the low pH) can yield volatile, burnt-match aromas soon after bottling (although they will go away over time in the bottle).

- ✔ For **high pH wines** — 3.8 and above — bumping the final SO_2 addition up to 50 ppm is reasonable, assuming you expect to keep the wine in the bottle for any significant time.

As the discussion of testing for free and total SO_2 in Chapter 3 describes, the testing techniques available for most home winemakers are quite inexact. If there's one time that it's worth splurging to have a professional lab test your wine's SO_2, bottling is it. The only sure way to know how much, if any, SO_2 your wine needs for its new life in the bottle is to know how much is there already — discussed more in the next section.

During aging

As your wine sits and stews in its own yummy juices, the free SO_2 gradually loses strength — more of it gets bound, and some of it volatilizes into the atmosphere. Periodically, you need to measure the free SO_2 level and probably refresh it with a new addition. Typically, you do this when you rack the wine for clarification, which you do two or three times in the course of aging.

The procedure during aging is basically the same as the post-fermentation addition, except that your wine already has at least some free SO_2 on board. That requires one more process:

1. **Measure the pH.**

   It may have changed over time, either by itself, or through blending, or through increasing or decreasing acidity.

2. **Look up (and calculate as needed) the appropriate SO_2 level for that pH.**

   Consult Table Appendix D-1.

3. **Test the wine to see how much free SO_2 is currently there.**

   Chapter 3 talks about testing.

4. **Subtract the existing SO_2 from the target.**

5. **Find the appropriate quantity of PMBS to close the gap for the volume of your wine.**

   Table Appendix D-2 can help.

For example, if you have a Zinfandel in barrel with a pH of 3.6, you would like to have (according to Table Appendix D-1) 31 ppm of free SO_2 to keep everything copasetic. When you run the SO_2 test, you discover the free SO_2 is down to 19 ppm. That means you need to bump it up by 12 ppm, which translates, according to Table Appendix D-2, into a shade over 0.07 grams per gallon. Measure out the PMBS, dissolve in a little water, add it to your wine, and sleep better at night.

Index

• C •

• Z •